BEYOND
BLACK AND WHITE

SUNY Series, Power, Social Identity, and Education
Lois Weis, editor

BEYOND
BLACK AND WHITE

*New Faces and Voices in
U.S. Schools*

edited by
Maxine Seller
Lois Weis

State University of New York Press

Published by
State University of New York Press, Albany

©1997 State University of New York

Printed in the United States of America

For information, address the State University of New York Press,
State University Plaza, Albany, NY 12246

Production by David Ford and Christine Lynch
Marketing by Dana Yanulavich

Library of Congress Cataloging-in-Publication Data
Beyond black and white : new faces and voices in U.S. schools / edited
    by Maxine Seller and Lois Weis.
        p.   cm. -- (SUNY series, power, social identity, and
    education)
    Includes bibliographical references and index.
    ISBN 0-7914-3367-6 (hc : alk. paper). -- ISBN 0-7914-3368-4 (pb : alk.
paper)
    1. Minorities—Education—United States.   2. Multicultural
education—United States.   I. Seller, Maxine, 1935–   .   II. Weis, Lois.
III. Series.
LC3731.B487   1997
371.97'00973—dc20   96–31147
                                                                CIP

10 9 8 7 6 5 4

ACKNOWLEDGMENTS

This volume has benefited enormously from the editorial suggestions of Priscilla Ross. We extend our thanks to Priscilla as well as to the secretarial assistance of Sally Claydon and Pat Glinski at SUNY Buffalo. Rukiyaa Morton, graduate student, was also enormously helpful in putting the volume together and we greatly appreciate her help. We also thank the authors who have shared their expertise with use and all the families who struggle daily to educate their children in our schools.

Three chapters in this book were originally published elsewhere:

" 'Those Loud Black Girls': (Black Women), Silence, and Gender 'Passing' in the Academy," by Signithia Fordham, is reprinted by permission of the American Anthropological Association from *Anthropology & Education Quarterly* 24:1, 1994. Not for further reproduction.

" 'Becoming Somebody': Central American Immigrants in U.S. Inner-City Schools," by Marcelo M. Suarez-Orozco, is reprinted by permission of the American Anthropological Association from *Anthropology & Education Quarterly* 18:4, December 1987. Not for further reproduction.

"Gayness, Multicultural Education, and Community," by Dennis Carlson, is reprinted by permission of Caddo Gap Press from *Educational Foundations* 8:4, 1994. Not for further reproduction.

We acknowledge the editors' kind permission to reprint.

CONTENTS

III. HEARING SILENCED VOICES:
OTHER "MINORITIES"

PREFACE

There has been much research within the past fifteen years on race, social class, and gender as related to schooling (see, e.g., McLaughlin and Tierney 1993; Weis 1993; Grant 1992; Schofield 1989). Numerous studies focus on the ways in which schools privilege some groups of children and marginalize others. This takes place through teacher-student interaction patterns as well as through notions of what constitutes legitimate knowledge (see Young 1971). While this work has been powerful in many respects, it tends to construe difference along a narrowly constructed black-white dichotomy. In other words, most contemporary work on education, when it takes into account differences among students in schools, focuses on African American and white students, rather than recognizing the complexity of the current American landscape. We do not mean to suggest that work on the racial dimensions of inequality in schooling is irrelevant or ought not be done. On the contrary, we value this work greatly. What we do mean to argue is that the discussion of schooling be expanded to recognize the growing heterogeneity within the "black" and "white" communities and the wide range of additional communities, many of them Latino or Asian whose children are in American schools today. Despite a growing body of relevant research, there is too little understanding of the fact that schools now serve children from numerous ethnic, racial, and cultural groupings, well beyond what is represented by a simple black-white dichotomy. Again, despite a growing body of research, there is also too little understanding of the impact of gender and social class on the schooling and home experiences of students from varying racial, ethnic, and cultural backgrounds.

This volume takes up the challenge by prying open a discussion of diversity in American schools that goes well beyond the notion of black and white, and well beyond the idea that whites or blacks can be looked at as any kind of homogeneous grouping. White communities are fractured by ethnic, religious, and social class lines, as well as lines of sexual preference, and communities of color are fractured as well. In prying open this discussion, we hope to introduce readers to the lived complexities of life in American schools and encourage the centering of voices often not heard, even in volumes that aim to center historically silenced voices. While previous work has taken us a long way toward hearing the voices of marginalized groups in our society, the complexity of race, ethnicity, and gender demands continued exploration of these issues. *Beyond Black and White*, then, stands as vivid testimony to the myriad of voices in today's schools, and the wide range of cultures which are now represented in our classrooms.

NEW FACES: NEW RESEARCH

The purpose of this book, then, is to call attention to the unprecedented diversity of children in American schools today. Since there is not enough space to provide material on every group whose children are in American classrooms, we have selected twelve articles representative of the wide range of these groups. The first part of the book, "Rethinking Familiar 'Minorities,'" includes articles about African Americans, Mexican Americans, and American Indians, groups whose children American schools have dealt with, though not successfully, for many years. The second part of the book, "Newcomers: School and Community," focuses on children who are relatively new to American schools. This part includes articles on children from immigrant communities who have come to the United States in significant numbers only in the past few decades, such as Haitians, Dominicans, Vietnamese, Salvadorians, as well as children from older immigrant communities whose numbers have increased dramatically in recent years, such as Chinese and South Asians. The concluding part, "Hearing Silenced Voices: Other 'Minorities,'" deals with social and cultural groups struggling for recognition, or voice, *as groups*, including gays and lesbians, Appalachians, and white working-class males.

This book seeks not only to highlight the presence of diverse groups in the schools, but also to introduce the reader to some of the new research dealing with this diversity. The study of diverse communities is, by its very nature, multidisciplinary. Therefore we have drawn on the expertise of scholars from sociology, history, anthropology, African American studies, and other disciplines, scholars who, not surprisingly, address their topics with varied methodologies. The topics covered in the various chapters suggest the range of questions scholars are exploring today about children, communities, and schools. The first part of the book explores new questions or offers new perspectives on familiar racial and ethnic communities. For example, the chapter on Native Americans focuses on urban Indians rather than on the more frequently studied reservation, or rural, Indians. While much research focuses on the educational problems of African American males, we have chosen to include a chapter that focuses on African American women, exploring school experience at a unique intersection of race, gender, and social class. And while much research on Mexican American education deals with working-class families and the difficulties of teaching their children English, we include a chapter about the struggle of middle-class Mexican American families to teach their children Spanish. The chapters in part two, "Newcomers," provide important information about traditional topics such as the immigration, settlement, and acculturation patterns, but they also explore new issues about how ethnic identity, family life, and community institutions affect school achievement. Chapters in the third part, "Hearing Silenced Voices," do more than provide information about gays and lesbians, Appalachians, and white working-class males in the schools. They challenge the traditional definitions of "minorities" and raise new issues about inclusion and exclusion in a changing American society.

The chapters in all three parts of this book deal with common themes—"minority" status, empowerment, "marginality," and resistance in American schools and in diverse American communities. Although these themes have taken on new urgency at the close of the twentieth century, they are not new. Indeed, diverse communities have struggled with educational issues since the beginnings of American colonial and national history. Our introductory chapter, therefore, briefly examines the history of group life in the United States and its relationship to education.

REFERENCES

Grant, Carl, ed. 1992. *Research and Multicultural Education: From the Margins to the Mainstream.* Washington, D.C.: Falmer Press.

McLaughlin, Daniel, and William Tierney. 1993. *Naming Silenced Lives.* New York: Routledge.

Schofield, Janet Ward. 1989. *Black and White in School.* New York: Teachers College Press.

Weis, Lois, ed. 1993. *Class, Race, and Gender in U.S. Schools.* Albany: State University of New York Press.

Young, Michael F. D. 1971. "An Approach to the Study of Curriculums Socially Organized Knowledge." In M. Young, ed., *Knowledge and Control.* London: Collier Macmillan.

Introduction

Diversity in the United States did not begin in the late twentieth century. As this historical survey will show, American children have always come from a variety of racial ethnic, religious, and other communities and this fact has had an impact, albeit a changing impact, on their school experience. The impact of group identity on children's schooling has been shaped by at least four factors:

1. The degree of difference between the cultures of children's home communities and the cultures of their schools;

2. The meaning and value both communities assign to their differences;

3. The political and social relations between the two communities, including the degree to which one has the power to impose its will on the other;

4. The agency of the home community, that is, the active efforts of community leaders, parents, and sometimes children to resist, change, supplement, or replace what is offered by the school.

DIVERSITY AND SCHOOLING TO THE MID-NINETEENTH CENTURY: AN AGE OF CONGRUENCE

Diverse from its beginnings, the land that would become the United States was home to dozens of indigenous cultures and colonized by Spanish, French, Swedish, Dutch, Russian, and English speaking Europeans. At the close of the American Revolution, the new republic was populated not only by the English, but also by Native Americans of many tribes or nations, African Americans both free and enslaved, Welsh, Scots, Irish, Scotch Irish, French, Spanish, Germans, Poles, Italians, Scandinavians, and other ethnic groups as well as by Anglicans, Presbyterians, Methodists, Catholics, Jews, Quakers, Moravians, and a wide variety of other religious sects and denominations.[1] Despite the racial, ethnic, and religious diversity of the United States in its colonial and early national periods, there was little conflict between the communities from which

1

children came and the schools to which they went. Indeed, at no time has there been greater congruence between community and school. This was true for two reasons: First, many children did not go to school at all, but were educated at home or apprenticed to a trusted neighbor. Second, children who did go to school attended institutions chosen, perhaps even created, by their parents, as public schools did not exist until well into the nineteenth century.

Before the coming of the public school, wealthy parents hired tutors for their children or, after the mid-eighteenth century, sent them to private academies. Other parents joined with relatives or neighbors to hire a teacher or sent their children to a nearby dame school, to a school sponsored by their church or synagogue, or, if the children were boys, to a New England town or Latin grammar school.[2] Whether children were taught in a neighbor's kitchen, an African American church, or a private academy, the curriculum, language of instruction, teaching methods, discipline, religious training, differential (and usually inferior) treatment of girls—indeed, the entire culture of the school was compatible, if not identical, with the culture of the home. It was also compatible with the social, ethnic, and religious community in which the home was embedded.

The congruence between family, community, and school gave children the advantage of an easy transition from home to school and an education free of cultural conflict. However, there were also significant disadvantages. In an environment in which home, school, and community were so close as to be almost indistinguishable, children had little chance to learn about diverse lifestyles or different values. Moreover, in an era in which all schooling was private and voluntary, girls suffered serious gender discrimination in education and many children, including a disproportionate number of the poor and virtually all of the enslaved African Americans, had no schooling at all.

The congruence between school and community experienced by most children before the coming of the public school was not, however, experienced by all. The relatively small number of native American children who were educated in Christian missions found their schools not only different from but hostile to their traditional community life and, indeed, deliberately destructive of that life. In what would later become the southwestern states, Spanish speaking Jesuit and Franciscan missionaries, assisted by Spanish soldiers, established fortified border settlements that served as church, home, workplace and school for Christianized Indians of all ages. Here, under strict discipline and military guard, children were forced to adopt the dress, work habits and sex roles as well as the religion of Spanish colonial authorities (Weber 1982; Webb 1982). In the English colonies Protestant clergymen undertook similar educational activities, although on a smaller scale and without overt military support (Axtell 1984, 54–57; Salisbury 1972; Szasz 1988). Congregationalist minister Eleazar Wheelock, better known as the founder of Dartmouth College, established a boarding school in Lebanon, Connecticut in 1754 to train Native American boys to become ministers and missionaries and native American girls to become their wives and assistants. The young people were separated from their homes and communities so that a new lifestyle featuring male agriculture, female domesticity, and Protestant individualism could be substituted for traditional "uncivilized" hunting and gathering communal lifestyles (Wheelock 1767; Szasz 1980).

These early educational experiments reflected not only the great differences between Native American and European colonial cultures but, more importantly, the negative evaluation of the former by the latter. They also reflect the imbalance in political and military power that enabled Europeans to impose their will on at least some elements of the indigenous population. Despite the imbalance in power, there was resistance. In the Spanish Empire resistance took the form of armed uprisings. In both the Spanish and the English colonies, students protested by running away (despite harsh punishments if they were caught) and by reverting to native beliefs and lifestyles at the earliest opportunity (Wheelock 1767; Szasz 1980; Ronda 1977, 66–84). Despite questionable results, missionaries and, later, the United States government continued to isolate and acculturate Native American children in boarding schools throughout the nineteenth and well into the twentieth centuries (Prucha 1976, 265–91; Szasz 1977, 60–80).

THE DOMINANCE OF THE PUBLIC SCHOOL: CONFLICT REPLACES CONGRUENCE

Beginning in New England and the Midwest and spreading after the Civil War to the South and the farthest frontiers, state-supported public schools gradually replaced families and private or religious schools as the educators of most children in the United States. By the early twentieth century, ninety percent of all children who were in school were in public schools. Moreover, by the early twentieth century the percentage of school aged children actually attending school had increased enormously, as most states passed and enforced compulsory attendance laws. Often marginal before 1850, schooling now became increasingly important in the lives of American children.[3] The relationship between home and school communities also became increasingly important, as did issues of inclusion, exclusion, and acculturation.

Most public schools were controlled by English-speaking, native-born, middle-class, white Protestant men, men who felt duty bound to inculcate all students with the behavior and values of their own community. Students who looked, spoke, and behaved like the "schoolmen" continued to experience congruence between home and school. However, many students experienced conflict rather than congruence. These students included African Americans in the South and, increasingly, in the North as well; Mexican Americans and Puerto Ricans incorporated after the Mexican and Spanish-American Wars; voluntary immigrants from Asia, the Caribbean, and, in much greater numbers, Europe; and working-class children and girls of all social classes, the last two groups previously underrepresented but now visible in the classroom in unprecedented numbers. Clearly, the ethnic, class, and gender communities from which these children came were different from the schools to which they went.

The relationship between children's home and school communities was affected, as already noted, not only by the degree of difference between the two, but also by the meaning each assigned to that difference. African American children in the late nineteenth and early twentieth centuries did not differ significantly in language or behavior from white children of similar social class. However, the white community saw darker skin color as such an important and stigmatizing difference that they barred African American children from the new public education altogether or relegated them to separate and grossly inferior schools. White immigrant children were admitted into public schools. However, their native languages and traditions were interpreted as dangerously un-American and were therefore vigorously suppressed.[4]

Even "minority" children whose families wanted them to assimilate into "mainstream" American often found their encounters with the public school painful. Teachers and textbooks ignored or denigrated their heritage and, by implication, their families and themselves. Catholics, Jews, and children of other religious minorities were marginalized by Protestant worship in the schools. Some problems were caused by prejudice on the part of teachers or stereotyping on the part of the school, as when African Americans, immigrants, working-class children, and girls of all social groupings were assigned to vocational and other nonacademic tracks, regardless of their abilities or preferences. Other problems were caused by cultural conflicts: for example, some ethnic and religious communities found coeducation, physical education, and other common school practices culturally unacceptable. Less tangible but equally troubling were conflicts over values; public schools stressed competition and individual achievements, while some ethnic communities stressed cooperation and valued the welfare of the family or the group more than individual achievement.

Communities whose children experienced these and other difficulties reacted in a variety of ways. Recognizing the political component in educational decisions, immigrant communities marshalled what political resources they could to make the changes they saw as desirable. Baltimore, Cincinnati, St. Louis, Buffalo, and other cities with large German-speaking populations organized successful political campaigns—including rallies, petitions, and parades—to get the German language into the public school curriculum as a "foreign" language, a language of instruction, or both (Kloss 1977; Troen 1975, 55–62). The German community could do so because they controlled a significant number of votes in these cities, because they had a well-developed institutional structure, and because their educational, economic, and social status was, for an immigrant community, relatively high. The low status but large and politically sophisticated working-class community of East European Jews in New York City was also successful in at least one attempt to influence their children's education. Allied with Tammany Hall politicians, thousands of children and adults engaged in school boycotts and street violence as well as more traditional electoral politics to block a school reform program (the Gary Plan) they feared would consign their children to vocational rather than academic education (Cohen and Mohl 1979, 35–66).

No community fought longer or harder to influence their children's education in the public schools in the late nineteenth and early twentieth centuries than the African American community. Led by ministers, business men, and a cadre of strong women, African Americans fought first for access to public education even if it was segregated, then for the improvement of segregated facilities (including qualified black rather than unqualified white teachers), and finally for integrated education. As early as the 1850s African Americans in Buffalo, New York, conducted a campaign for integrated education that included a "sit-in" by two young teenaged girls in a hostile white school. In the South, where political action could result, literally, in death, African American teachers in segregated schools substituted academic for "industrial" education and introduced African and African American history when they could (Webber 1978; Anderson 1988; White 1969).

Communities worked to supplement as well as to change the education offered their children by the public schools. Settlement houses, churches, women's clubs, and other community institutions set up programs to prepare young children for entry into the schools and to support their continuing progress there. African American women's clubs made the establishment of nursery schools and kindergartens a priority. In settlements such as New York's Educational Alliance, Jewish communities taught English to preschoolers and to newly arrived school-age immigrants. Mexican American communities established "little schools" to give their Spanish-speaking children a basic English vocabulary before entering the public schools (Giddings 1988; Brumberg 1986; Ratterway 1984, 32–33). Communities established supplementary programs not only to prepare children for public school but also to give them knowledge they would not find in the public schools. Scandinavians, Jews, the Russian and Greek Orthodox churches, and East European nationalist societies set up after-school and weekend programs to teach traditional language, religion, and culture. Socialists in both immigrant and native-born communities set up socialist Sunday schools to present their children with an alternative to the capitalistic orientation of the public school (Fishman 1980; Fishman and Nahirny 1966/1978; Teitelbaum and Reese 1983, 429–49).

Some communities organized not only to change or supplement public schooling, but also to provide substitutes or alternatives. Wealthy and socially privileged communities maintained many private, usually single-sex, schools that taught not only academic subjects, but also the speech patterns, sports, and social graces essential to the community's lifestyle. In the African American community, private academies like the Institute for Colored Youth in Philadelphia (active in the latter half of the nineteenth century), trained teachers and served as showcases to convince doubting whites that African Americans could profit from higher education. Roman Catholics established extensive networks of parochial schools that educated thousands throughout the nation, especially in industrial cities with large immigrant populations (Perkins 1983, 18–33; Buetow 1970).

SCHOOLS AND COMMUNITIES AFTER 1950: INCREASING COMPLEXITY

After 1950 the relationship between children's diverse home communities and the public schools became increasingly complex. This was true because "minority" communities became more varied and more vocal and because educational ideologies became more controversial and more overtly political. It was also true because education became more important. With the decline of well-paid industrial jobs and the rise of the new "information economy," young people needed education through high school and beyond, not only for social mobility, but for economic survival.

The number of children from recognizable "minority" communities rose rapidly after 1950, as did the variety of communities from which they came. Many children still came from the older racial and ethnic communities with which schools were familiar (though by no means comfortable). However, others now came from newly self-conscious and politically organized communities of feminists, lesbians and gays, and persons with disabilities. A massive wave of Asian and Latino (as opposed to earlier, predominantly European) immigration and a growing militant Christian fundamentalist community added further to the already wide range of group life in the United States and in American public schools.

Further complexities stemmed from the fact that neither the older communities nor the newer ones were static or homogeneous. Class, gender, and political conflicts within communities followed their children into the classroom. So did conflicts among "minority" communities themselves and between these communities and the changing, self-defined "mainstream" of American life. The relationship between racial, ethnic, and religious groupings and the schools was further complicated by the progressive blurring of boundaries. As mixed marriages increased, increasing numbers of children entered the schools with multiple or changing group identities.

By the early 1990s a quarter of all school age children were racial minorities, a proportion experts expected to rise to thirty percent by the year 2000, and over a hundred different languages were spoken in the schools (Bennett 1990, 15). Old certainties were no longer certain: a "black" child might be African American—or he might be a member of a family recently arrived from Haiti, Cuba, Nigeria, Ethiopia, or the Dominican Republic. A teenager might identify herself as a young woman, a lesbian, a Latino, a Catholic, or a member of the middle class, or as any combination of these sometimes conflicting identities at different times and under different circumstances. Clearly, the educator who hoped to understand the students of the late twentieth century, whatever his or her own community affiliations, faced a challenging task.

Parents, students, and community leaders, too, faced a challenging task, since, like their predecessors, they had to cope with schools that were culturally different from and politically more powerful than themselves. Some accepted American schooling as they found it, despite cultural conflicts and unequal treatment, either because they lacked the language skills, time, and other resources to attempt change or, especially if they were voluntary immigrants, because they believed that the schools would, in fact, prepare their children for success in the new environment. As in the past, others sought to change public schools, to supplement them, or, less frequently, to create substitutes for them.

The relationship between "minority" communities and schools was more complex than in the past not only because diversity was greater, but also because community activism was more intense. In the 1960s and 1970s African Americans, followed by Mexican Americans, Native Americans, women, gays and lesbians, and the disabled formed national movements to promote pride in their group identities, to critique their treatment in "mainstream" society, and to win social, political, economic, and educational equality. These groups made educational demands—including the study of their history and present status in the school curricula, equal access to all educational programs, and respectful and effective instruction for their children—and these demands became integral parts of broad national movements for social and political rights. These demands also became part of national as well as local debates about allocation of resources, educational priorities, group as opposed to individual rights (affirmative action), and changing definitions of national identity.[5]

In the twentieth century, as in the nineteenth, self-conscious and organized communities used numbers, votes, demonstrations, and other political resources to change the education offered their children in the public schools. Community pressure, combined with a relatively liberal political atmosphere, resulted in significant improvements in the 1960s and 1970s. In the decades that followed, improvements were also facilitated by changing educational personnel and ideologies. Although still badly underrepresented, especially in leadership positions, women and members of minority racial and ethnic communities were becoming visible as scholars and as teachers and administrators in public schools, where some became agents of change. Perhaps more important, the long dominant ideology of the public school as enforcer of the melting pot was challenged. Many educators ("mainstream" and "minority") now advocated one of the many variants of cultural pluralism instead, suggesting that schools should recognize, even support, multiple lifestyles and belief systems.

The relationship between communities and schools in the late twentieth century became more complex also because the federal government, for the first time, became heavily involved. The problems of children from educationally disadvantaged communities were addressed in the 1960s and 1970s by a series of federal court decisions, laws, and policies, beginning with the school desegregation decision of 1954 and continuing with *Lau v. Nichols* (1974), which required schools to provide equal educational opportunity for children who spoke languages other than English; Title I (1972), which provided additional resources for poor children; Title IX (1972), which guaranteed women equal access to most educational programs; and PL 94-142 (1975), which specified educational rights for children with disabilities. The politically conservative 1980s saw funding and enforcement for many of these and other federal educational initiatives cut. However, the role of the federal government in mediating many aspects of the relationship between diverse communities and the schools seemed likely to continue.

Some communities continued their efforts not only to change public education, but also to create substitutes for it. Angry and frustrated at the public school's continuing failure to educate many of their children, African American parents and educators created independent, often African-centered, "alternative schools" (Lomotey and Brooks 1988, 163–78). The fastest growing alternative schools, however, were the Christian schools founded by Protestant fundamentalists who opposed the secularism and what they considered the loose discipline and morals of the public schools. Ironically, as new culturally specific alternatives to the public schools opened, older alternative schools found their existence threatened by changing neighborhoods and rising costs. As their original immigrant clientele moved away, Catholic schools in inner-city parishes closed their doors, or opened them to children of different ethnic, even different religious backgrounds. Elite single-sex private schools responded to economic and social pressures by becoming coeducational and by admitting racial, religious, and ethnic minorities formerly excluded (Wagner 1990; Kraushaar 1972). In the 1990s, however, as in the 1890s, most American children were in public schools. Therefore it was—and is—mainly in the public schools that the complex relationships between communities, schools, and children must be addressed. By calling attention to the variety of old and new communities represented in American schools and to the emerging educational research about those communities, this book contributes to the ongoing conversation about diversity and schooling in the United States.

We are committed to a thriving public sphere in which the voices of many can be heard. Our goal here is to let these voices move through debates about/with public education. This text contributes to this centering. We ask teachers, scholars, and students to join us in infusing diverse voices into a thriving democratic public sphere. With this we invite you into our text.

NOTES

1. For figures on immigrant and racial minority populations over time, see Roger Daniels, *Coming to America: A History of Immigration and Ethnicity in American Life* (New York: HarperCollins, 1990).

2. For a summary view of colonial education, see Lawrence A. Cremin, *American Education: The Colonial Experience, 1607–1783* (New York: Harper & Row, 1970).

3. On the origins and growth of public schooling, see Carl Kaestle, *Pillars of the Republic: Common Schools and American Society 1789–1860* (New York: Hill and Wang, 1983); David Tyack, *The One Best System: A History of American Urban Education* (Cambridge: Harvard University Press, 1974); and H. Warren Button and Eugene F.

Provenzo, Jr., *History of Education and Culture in America,* 2nd ed. (Englewood Cliffs, N.J.: Prentice Hall, 1989).

4. Educational deprivation of African Americans and other racial minorities is documented in Meyer Weinberg, *A Chance to Learn: A History of Race and Education in the United States,* Cambridge: Harvard University Press, 1977). For the impact of schooling on various European immigrant communities, see Bernard J. Weiss, ed., *American Schooling and the European Immigrant, 1840–1940* (Urbana: University of Illinois Press, 1982) and Robert Carlson, *The Quest for Conformity: Americanization through Education* (New York: Wiley, 1975).

5. A useful history of some of the social movements of the late twentieth century and the issues they raised is Lawrence H. Fuchs, *The American Kaleidoscope: Race, Ethnicity, and the Civic Culture* (Middletown, Conn.: Wesleyan Press, 1990).

References

Anderson, James D. 1988. *The Education of Blacks in the South 1860–1935.* Chapel Hill: University of North Carolina Press.

Axtell, James. 1984. *The Europeans and the Indians: Essays in the Ethnohistory of Colonial North America.* New York: Oxford University Press.

Bennett, Christine I. 1990. *Comprehensive Multicultural Education: Theory and Practice,* 2nd ed. Boston: Allyn and Bacon.

Brumberg, Stephen. 1986. *Going to America, Going to School: The Jewish Immigrant Public School Encounter in Turn of the Century New York City.* New York: Praeger.

Buetow, Harold A. 1970. *Of Singular Benefit: The Story of U. S. Catholic Education.* New York: Macmillan.

Cohen, Ronald D., and Raymond A. Mohl. 1979. *The Paradox of Progressive Education: The Gary Plan and Urban Schooling.* Port Washington, N.Y.: Kennikat Press.

Fishman, Joshua. 1980. "Ethnic Community Mother Tongue Schools in the U.S.A." *International Migration Review* 14.2 (Summer): 306–35.

Fishman, Joshua, and Vladimir Nahirny. 1966/1978. *Language Loyalty in the United States.* New York: Arno Press.

Giddings, Paula. 1988. *When and Where I Enter: The Impact of Black Women on Race and Sex in America.* New York: Bantam Books.

Kloss, Heinz. 1977. *The American Bilingual Tradition.* Rowley, Mass.: Newberry.

Kraushaar, Otto F. 1972. *American Nonpublic Schools: Patterns of Diversity.* Baltimore: Johns Hopkins University Press.

Lomotey, Kofi, and Craig Brooks. 1988. "Independent Black Institutions." In Diane T. Slaughter and Deborah J. Johnson, *Visible Now: Blacks in Private Schools.* New York: Greenwood Press.

Perkins, Linda M. 1983. "The Institute for Colored Youth in Philadelphia: An Argument for the Race." In *Blacks in Pennsylvania History: Research and Educational Perspectives*. Harrisburg: Pennsylvania History and Museum Commission.

Prucha, Francis Paul. 1976. *American Indian Policy in Crisis: Christian Reformers and the Indian 1865–1900*. Norman: University of Oklahoma Press.

Ratteray, J. 1984. "Hispanics Pursue Alternatives to Unresponsive Public Schools." *Caminos* 5.10: 32–33.

Ronda, James P. 1977. "'We Are Well as We Are': An Indian Critique of Seventeenth Century Christian Missions." *William and Mary Quarterly*, 3rd series, 34: 66–82.

Salisbury, Neal. 1972. "Conquest of the 'Savage': Puritans, Missionaries, and Indians 1620–1680." Ph.D. dissertation, University of California, Los Angeles.

Szasz, Margaret Connell. 1977. *Education and the American Indian: The Road to Self-Determination since 1928*. Albuquerque: University of New Mexico Press.

———. 1980. "'Poor Richard' Meets the Native American: Schooling for Young Indian Women in Eighteenth-Century Connecticut." *Pacific Historical Review* 49.2 (May): 215–36.

———. 1988. *Indian Education in the American Colonies 1607–1783*. Albuquerque: University of New Mexico Press.

Teitelbaum, Kenneth, and William Reese. 1983. "American Socialist Pedagogy and Experimentation in the Progressive Era." *History of Education Quarterly* 23:4 (Winter): 429–49.

Troen, S. K. 1975. *The Public and the Schools: Shaping the St. Louis School System 1838–1925*. Columbus: University of Missouri Press.

Wagner, Melinda Bollar. 1990. *God's Schools: Choice and Compromise in American Society*. New Brunswick, N.J.: Rutgers University Press.

Webb, Elizabeth Buckland. 1982. *Indian Life at the Old Missions*. Lincoln: University of Nebraska Press.

Webber, Thomas L. 1978. *Deep Like the Rivers: Education in the Slave Quarter Community, 1831–1865*. New York: W. W. Norton.

Weber, Daniel J., ed. 1982. *New Spain's Far Northern Frontier: Essays on Spain in the American West 1540–1821*. Albuquerque: University of New Mexico Press.

Wheelock, Eleazar. 1767. *A Brief Narrative of the Original Indian Charity-School at Lebanon in Connecticut, New England*. London: n.p.

White, Arthur O. 1969. "The Black Movement against Jim Crow Education in Buffalo, New York, 1800–1900." *Phylon*, 30:4 (Winter).

PART
I

Rethinking Familiar
"Minorities"

1

ANN LOCKE DAVIDSON _____

Marbella Sanchez

On Marginalization and Silencing

MARBELLA: Well, a Mexican is someone who knows how to depend on himself. And he has to have a different character from other people.

INTERVIEWER: How is that?

MARBELLA: Well, it's a . . . it's a strong character. It doesn't let itself get vanquished very easily. For example, if someone says "I am going to be a doctor," and if another person, or other people say to him "No, don't do that because it's a very long path, very complicated" or something, well, he mustn't let himself be discouraged by what they said. If he wants to study that, he has to do that. And not give up because other people told him "No, don't do that."

The sizzle and smell of garlic fill the air. It is "Lab day" in foods class at Explorer High School. I lean against the hard steel corner of a stove, listening to Marbella Sanchez, a sophomore Mexican immigrant, as she stirs her darkening garlic.

Marbella's teacher approaches. "How are you doing Marbella?" "Muy bien maestra. Me gusta la comida italiana." (Very well, teacher. I like Italian food.) The teacher glances at me, laughs slightly, and tries again. "It looks like that's about ready. What else are you going to put in there?" "Cebollas, tomates, salsa de tomates . . . qué más?" (Onions, tomatoes, tomato sauce . . . what else?) The look and laughter come again: "I don't understand a thing she's saying."

I am puzzled. While English is Marbella's second language, I know from personal experience that her English comprehension is excellent; I usually spoke to her in English, as my Spanish oral proficiency is low.[1] Moreover, though Marbella spoke to me in Spanish, I have heard her speak English to her teachers and listened to her argue that learning English is the key to success in America. While certainly more comfortable speaking Spanish, Marbella is quite capable of responding to her teacher's queries.

With cleanup approaching, Marbella approaches her teacher, asking for the worksheet that each cooking group is required to complete: "Maestra? Tiene mi papel?" (Teacher, do you have my paper?) Mrs. Everett looks at Marbella blankly. Marbella gestures to a pile of worksheets and Everett, reading Marbella's movement, hands her a paper. Now, I can't contain my curiosity. "Marbella," I laugh, "Why don't you ask her in English?" Marbella smiles and laughs back. "Tenemos una regla. Los martes y jueves, hablamos puro Español." (We have a rule. On Tuesdays and Thursdays, we speak only Spanish.)

Over the time that I came to know Marbella, I discovered that she and her small group of friends have many rules. Some, such as that above, serve to support the group as they struggle to assert their identity in a country where they feel pressure to conform. Others help them as they work to achieve academically as part of proving that being Mexican gives one the "strong character" that facilitates resilience in a new society. Marbella's conformity to these rules is reflected not only in scenes like that described above, but in high academic achievement. During her first three semesters at Explorer High School, Marbella earned all As and Bs, with one 3.67 and two 3.5 GPAs. During the second semester of her sophomore year, Marbella's mother was diagnosed with a tumor. As a result, Marbella missed twenty-three days of school, as she and her sister took turns staying home to provide basic health care. Still, Marbella maintained a 2.67 GPA. In short, Marbella demonstrated that, for her, part of being Mexican is having a strong, oppositional character that enables academic success. Further, Marbella manifests aspects of the ideology others have described as typical of immigrant minorities (Gibson 1987; Ogbu 1987). Voicing faith in the American opportunity structure, Marbella believes academic achievement will result in future economic success: "It's to learn English, that's what's necessary to triumph here. To know English. And to succeed in school" (ES50STEN: 795–808).

Yet oppositional character and manifestations of immigrant identity were not all I saw during the months I knew Marbella. Over time, Marbella revealed a fearful, sometimes resigned and frequently silent self equally connected both to her sense of ethnicity and immigrant status, a self that has emerged as Marbella has realized her marginalized position and encountered disciplinary technologies (Foucault 1979) at her high school. This, Marbella's separatist self, shrinks from asserting its rights and fears interaction with American-born peers. Emerging in relation to the structure of the high school, this aspect of Marbella's persona reveals links between institutional practices and the construction of school-based identities.

Drawing on the notion that the selves youth create are embedded in disciplinary relationships laced with power and meaning (Kondo 1990; Foucault 1983), this chapter considers Marbella's ideology and shifting manifestations of identity in relation to guiding social and institutional relationships at the school level. I will argue that Marbella's behavior must be located and interpreted not only in relation to her historical status as an immigrant youth, but in relation to institutional mechanisms and power dynamics that work to nurture and sustain public "silencing" (Fine 1991; Weis and Fine 1993) at the school. The data presented emerged from interviews with Marbella, field observations at her high school, and interviews with adults at Explorer, collected as part of a larger study focussed on the social construction of ethnic identity among diverse youth (Davidson 1992, 1996).[2]

STEPPING BACK:
MARBELLA'S VOICE CONTEXTUALIZED

Before moving forward with the specifics of Marbella's case, I step back briefly to locate her voice in a long-running and developing theoretical discussion that cuts across the fields of anthropology and sociology. This chapter can be read as one of several recent efforts (Davidson 1996; Raissiguier 1994; Weis 1990) to encourage movement beyond purely "culturalist" perspectives on schooling. My purpose, therefore, is not only to detail the particular story of a particular youth, but to move beyond predicting and explaining student ideology and behavior in terms of social class or minority status characteristics. Here, I first outline the poststructural approach to power and identity construction taken in this chapter, and then situate this approach in relation to a culturalist perspective.

A concept central to the forthcoming analysis is the poststructural notion of power as an "action upon an action" (Foucault 1983, 221). Power does not determine others but rather structures the possible field of action, "guiding the course of conduct and putting in order the possible outcome" (Foucault 1983, 220). Power is conceptualized as being embodied and enacted in both personal and institutional relationships. At the same time, individuals are not inert objects; rather, individuals can and do resist the meanings they encounter even as others seek to push them towards comprehensible categories.

At the institutional level, disciplinary technology (isolating, ordering, systematizing practices) and serious speech acts (truth claims asserted by an expert in an area) are factors that work to enact power relations, primarily through contributing to a definition of what is "normal" in advance. Both can therefore be viewed as practices that teach, or "discipline" participants to the meaning of institutional (and social) categories such as prisoner, soldier, teacher, ESL student. In schools, for example, the taken-for-granted, "objective" division of students into academic tracks can be viewed as a disciplinary technology that highlights differences and disciplines students and teachers to particular conceptions about the meaning of high and low achievement in students. Likewise, because youth may view certain adults (e.g., guidance counselors or teachers) as privileged authorities with specific knowledge about higher education, life chances, and so on, their assertions may be viewed as serious speech acts: knowledge to be studied, repeated, and passed on to friends. A network of serious speech acts may come to constitute a system that works to control both the production of discourse and the conceptualization of persons.

Previous ethnographies have documented relationships between student identity and academic engagement (cf. Fordham and Ogbu 1986; Suarez-Orozco 1989; Willis 1977). With a few notable exceptions, however (cf. Weis 1990; Raissiguier 1994), such studies have focused principally on links between large-scale economic, political, and historical factors and the identities that youth construct. Reflecting a culturalist perspective, such work places primary emphasis on the ideology students *bring* to school; links between school-based factors (such as disciplinary technologies) and student identity are not discussed. For example, educational anthropologists (Fordham and Ogbu 1986; Matute-Bianchi 1986; Ogbu 1987; Suarez-Orozco 1989) have identified differences between "involuntary" and immigrant minority ideology, accounting for these differences in terms of historical factors. "Involuntary minorities," defined as peoples originally brought to the United States through slavery, conquest, or colonization (African Americans, Native Americans, some Mexican Americans and Native Hawaiians are examples), are said to have a skeptical attitude toward opportunities for gainful employment and social mobility due to historical experiences with economic and political oppression and racism. This skepticism is manifested in the form of oppositional ethnic identities: cultural differences are presented as markers of identity to be maintained in opposition to the dominant culture. Groups may also develop secondary cultural differences, claiming and exaggerating certain behaviors, symbols, events, and meanings as appropriate for the group because they are not characteristic of members of another population (Ogbu 1987). Among these may be anti-academic behaviors that demonstrate resistance to schooling; thus oppositional identities can enter negatively into the academic process, affecting engagement and motivation.

In contrast, "immigrant" or "voluntary minorities," peoples who moved more or less voluntarily to the United States, are said to be more optimistic about the American opportunity structure, both because they have less experience with its realities and because economic and political conditions in the United States are sometimes better than in the home country. Immigrants may manifest a "dual frame of reference," in which opportunities in the United States are constantly compared and assessed in light of the situation in the country of origin (Gibson 1987; Suarez-Orozco and Suarez-Orozco 1993). Immigrant minorities therefore are said to be more likely to believe that the effort they devote to school work will pay off, and they strive accordingly.

Such work is useful not only for advancing the dialogue concerning differences in ethnic minority group achievement, but also for considering the role that broader historical and economic circumstances play in day-to-day classroom activities. Taken to an extreme, however, a culturalist perspective implies that the meanings, behaviors, and perceptions associated with a specific background are relatively fixed, exerting a constant influence on students' academic work. In telling Marbella's story, this chapter reveals how an immigrant orientation can be weakened and distorted in an environment that offers little to its immigrant youth. I demonstrate how the school works actively to discourage and silence Marbella's pro-academic oppositional persona, disciplining her toward more silent and separatist manifestations of identity. I return now to Marbella's story, beginning with background information that provides insight into the development of her strong oppositional character.

MEMORIES OF MEXICO:
FOUNDATIONS FOR "STRONG CHARACTER"

Marbella, along with her younger brother and older sister, crossed the U.S.-Mexico border in the summer of 1989 to join her mother. The transition was radical. Marbella left behind not only a familiar language and culture, but the rural lifestyle she'd grown accustomed to in Tecuala, a small agricultural town approximately 800 miles south of San Diego, near the Pacific coast:

> Almost everybody in the town was friendly . . . There were about 600 people. That was as many as could be there. Almost everybody knew each other. . . . where I am from, life is calm, it is like the country. (ES50STAB: 506–28)

It was during her childhood that Marbella learned that being Mexican requires strength of character. Born in 1975, Marbella is one of thousands of Mexican children who grew up during a period of economic crisis ("La Crisis"), a period in which Mexico's stagnant economy, price inflation, drastic currency devaluation, and growing national debt affected countless rural families (Macias 1990). Marbella's autobiographical interview reflects her place in history, as she recounts her mother's struggle to support her three young children after her husband abandoned his family (Marbella was three years old). Marbella recalls how her mother, faced with limited and low-paying opportunities for work, moved the family first to her own mother's home and then to a rented room. For four additional years, Marbella's mother struggled to make ends meet by working at night, but eventually left in search of more lucrative work in Hermosillo, a larger city 570 miles to the north. Eight-year-old Marbella and her siblings remained behind. From third to sixth grade, Marbella saw her mother only once per month.

According to Marbella, her early history is by no means unique. When asked what she and her friends talked about in elementary school, for example, she replied: ". . . we would talk about our parents. Most of us just had one parent; none of us had both a father and a mother. We often talked about that. My grandma always told us that we were too young to talk about those things" (ES50STAB: 327–32).

As Marbella began sixth grade in 1985, her mother's sisters joined the wave of Mexican emigrants leaving for the United States in search of work. Marbella's mother returned to Tecuala to live with her mother and children. Three years later, still unsatisfied with the level of support she could provide, Marbella's mother followed her sisters to the United States. Marbella dropped out of school to help her grandmother, working thirteen-hour days packing mangos during the harvest season. Marbella's mother worked to save the money necessary to bring Marbella and her two siblings to the United States; they joined her one year later.

Despite the difficult economic circumstances Marbella associates with her youth, she retains a positive orientation toward characteristics she perceives as representative of her culture. She emphasizes interpersonal relationships and mutual aid in her stories and descriptions:

> I don't act like many people here who are American; they act differently than we do . . . for example, like at dances. Our dances and theirs are different. We like to celebrate and I know they do too. But I've gone to some American dances, and they don't dance. When a man goes and asks an American girl to dance and she says no, then it's because he is ugly or something. Well, no [we don't do that], we like to get along together at dances and at parties.
>
> Or if we go out for a day of fresh air, we go as Mexicans. We go out for the day and we like to get along together. Everybody pulls his weight, no? Well, nobody says things like "You didn't work." If somebody doesn't have money and he can't bring anything, well, it doesn't matter that he doesn't bring anything. But he still has to be there, because he's our friend (ES50STEN:153–81).

Enacting these behaviors and norms, Marbella's mother, out of work herself, took two youth (Marbella's close friends) into her home when their mother left for work in another U.S. city during the 1990 recession. Marbella's descriptions and her mother's behavior are in accord with the heavy emphasis on mutual aid and support among kin found in Mexican agrarian communities (Uribe, Levine, and Levine 1994).

Besides bringing memories of economic hardship, Marbella recollects successful, happy days in elementary school:

> Everything was easy in school. The teacher helped us. If we didn't understand, she would explain slowly. . . . I had her for three years, so I thought everything was easy. I liked school a lot. If I couldn't go to school I would stay home very sad. I really liked going to school because I had fun. . . .
>
> Another thing I remember is when I was seven. We were going to go on parade and I was going to carry the school's banner. It was very nice because all the people were there seeing us and I was at the front of the parade. . . . It feels very nice to carry the flag because they choose the most intelligent student. It's a very pretty feeling because when they choose you everyone says "So, you're smart!" (ES50STAB: 30–46, 454–74)

Marbella's descriptions also suggest that her mother (who graduated from high school) and grandmother place high priority on Marbella's education. For example, because of Marbella's exceptional performance during her elementary years, the family pooled its resources in order to enroll her in a secondary private school usually restricted to the elite. The family believed this would provide Marbella with a better education. Marbella recalls the decision:

There were only two schools there [in Tecuala]. I wanted to go to the federal [public] one, and my grandmother didn't want me to. She put me in the school that I didn't like. That school was only for rich people. It was a school you had to pay for, only for those who had money. . . . Because she had some land, she was going to sell it so I could go to that school. . . . My aunts who were working here [in the U.S.] sent money so I could go.

Marbella also describes her mother's continued efforts to support her children's transition to their United States high school, despite her long days doing janitorial work:

Sometimes when we have bad grades she says to us "What happened?" and "What went wrong?" and we tell her and she helps us with that. And she talks to the teacher, and she tells him that we need him to give us the work again to see if we can do it well.

My mom really likes to be informed about how we're doing. Sometimes, well, if we are doing poorly in school, perhaps she can help us with something . . . she studied, she studied a lot in Mexico. Sometimes neither I nor my sister understand algebra and well she—very rarely—but she helps us. Sometimes she can't help us because like she's working. She works from six in the morning to four or five in the afternoon; she arrives at five, takes a bath and she's gone at seven at night and she goes out [to work] until two or three in the morning and she doesn't have time. (ES50STC: 1189–1247)

Like her daughter, Marbella's mother believes that learning English and graduating from high school are essential first steps to "become someone."

Marbella's memories of economic struggle, her successful elementary and middle school history, and her mother's support are relevant to understanding Marbella's drive to succeed and readiness to challenge those who doubt her intelligence. At the same time, her positive memories of Mexico and positive orientation toward norms and values she associates with Mexican culture are relevant to her desire to resist pressures to assimilate. I turn now to consider these aspects of Marbella's persona.

MARBELLA'S GAMBLE:
AN OPPOSITIONAL SELF

It's like a bet to be here. It's like a bet that we ought to win because we need to demonstrate to other people that we indeed can make it. That it's not because we are Hispanic we can't make it. At times they [Americans] are

> treating you badly, right? Then you say to yourself "I am
> going to demonstrate to those people that I indeed can be
> something, and that I have the capability to be some-
> thing. It's not because I'm Hispanic that I can't make it."
> At these times, they give you desire to study more and
> become someone more quickly, so as to demonstrate to
> all the world that it is not because you are Mexican you
> are going to stop below.   (ES50STEN: 441–63)

Gambling on academic success, Marbella manifests a public ethnic identity
that is both pro-academic and oppositional. In a one hour interview focusing
on the meaning of her ethnicity, Marbella speaks of becoming someone ("lle-
gar hacer alguien") three times, "being something" twice, and succeeding four
times. Marbella's drive appears to stem as much from her desire to make a
public political statement about her Mexican origin ("to demonstrate to those
people") as to advance her self-interests. Further, while willing to work hard to
succeed in school, Marbella resists pressures to conform, asserting the linguistic aspects of her ethnic identity.

The pro-academic aspect of Marbella's public identity reveals itself in the
strategies she has adopted to achieve, in her readiness to assist fellow immigrants with academic work, and in her stubborn attacks on institutional road-
blocks that impede her educational progress. It was reflected, for example, in
the rules Marbella and her peers created to maintain high standards for the
group: holding parties at six-week grading periods and allowing only those
with As and Bs to attend, going to the library at lunch to study as a group when
a test is approaching.

It showed in physical science class, when Marbella yanked a desk from
under the feet of two male immigrant peers, ignoring their yells of protest and
chastising them for their boisterous classroom behavior: "Quiet! I can't hear
anything."

It was revealed during Marbella's freshman year, as she resisted her school's
efforts to channel her into low-level mathematics. Approaching her school's
vice-principal of guidance, Marbella argued for recognition of her academic
abilities: "She wanted to leave me in basic math, but I talked a lot with her
until she let me go to pre-algebra. The only thing you do in basic math is what
little kids do: addition, division, and multiplication" (ES50STD: 458–66).

The premium that Marbella places on her education can also be seen in
the severe critiques she reserves for teachers that she perceives as failing to respect the intelligence of her and her peers:

Now we have not advanced in the book. We haven't done very much, the teacher uses up all the time explaining and we don't do anything. Sometimes he spends one whole week on one page. We don't feel comfortable because he treats us like if we were kindergarten kids. We feel bad, the teacher feels that we don't understand even the simpler concepts. I don't like the teacher treating us like little kids. We understand, the problem is that he is not consistent in his explanations. (ES50STD: 831–50)

Among her teachers, Marbella is recognized for her academic efforts and friendly, almost radiant persona:

SOCIAL STUDIES TEACHER: If I were to have an image of what I thought a nun [was like]. . . . Goodness just comes out of her. And she would be like, she would be an excellent teacher. She would be an excellent teacher for children. . . .

In my social studies class, she did *well*. She didn't do barely passing. She *did* well. . . . The writings that she submitted to me, the sentence structures were well written. In Spanish, of course. The structures were good. Her thoughts were good. When we had to construct thought to go beyond, [like answer] OK, why. The why question was answered, completely. Some kids might do one sentence, she would do a full paragraph on the why questions.

SCIENCE TEACHER: Sparkly Marbella . . . real concerned about her grades, starting off the beginning of the year. And wanted to be sure she had everything done right, that all the points were there.

COMPUTER LITERACY TEACHER: She's an excellent student. She knew her keyboard when she came in and she always does her work. Sometimes when she finishes her assignments she will go back and do some more practice work.

Marbella is perceived as both cooperative and hard-working, "excellent," "concerned," and thoughtful.

While clearly conforming to academic behavioral norms, Marbella simultaneously resists pressures to assimilate. It is clear, for example, that the majority of her teachers want and expect Marbella to speak English. Yet, as previously mentioned, Marbella resists by choosing to speak Spanish on particular days of the week. Marbella and her friends have also worked together to engage in more public forms of protest against such pressures:

INTERVIEWER: You said that the woman who drives the bus now is very nice. Was there another person before?

MARBELLA: Yes, before there was a woman who spoke Spanish. It seemed like she didn't like us speaking Spanish. She said that we were not civilized, and all kinds of things. She said that we should speak English, since we were in this country we shouldn't speak Spanish. We came to talk to the office to say that we didn't like her anymore. (ES50STD: 218–40)

Marbella also demonstrates resistance to assimilationist pressures by insisting that her American-born acquaintances make some effort to cross into her social world. When, for example, Marbella spied an advertisement for study in Mexico during a visit to a university, she ripped it from the wall and urged me to enroll so I could improve my Spanish.

Marbella describes herself as having carefully selected friends who support both the pro-academic and oppositional aspects of her identity: "Well, you know, I don't have a lot of friends because I am selective. Because I won't hang out with a person who doesn't like to study" (ES50STA: 507–11). Like her, Marbella believes that her peers are oriented toward "becoming someone" and behaving in a serious, rather formal, manner:

My friends, they think that a Mexican is someone who goes forward, someone who becomes someone, who has a career and who can triumph in a country that is not his own. And also, they think that speaking—or perhaps character—that speaking correctly is one of the most important things. Because if you speak like, I don't know, like a "cholo" [a person linked to a local gang structure] or something like that, well, that is not good. If you speak correctly you can get a better job than someone who does not speak correctly. (ES50STEN: 578–95)

Marbella compares her orientation and behavior to that of her fellow immigrants, whom she describes as oriented toward socializing rather than academic achievement:

Well, I only have a few friends, only a few true friends, five only. We are always together because we share the same ideas. For example, we don't use bad words when we talk like the other girls here. Also, they [other Latina immigrants] invite us to leave school early [cut class] with them. That is why we don't have many friends. We come to school to study, not to go out. Also, they don't like us because our grades are better than theirs [are]. . . . We usually fight. They said I am crazy. And not too many talk to me anymore. (ES50STB: 270–84, 300–302)

Confirming Marbella's description, the school's English as a Second Language (ESL) resource teacher describes a general trend toward academic disengagement among Explorer's immigrant students. He points out that while many youth enter with a desire to succeed, their desire dampens over time:

> The students that come here tend to be just arriving from Mexico, and they still have a lot of high expectations that you can build on. When students have been here a few years, that rubs off. And they kind of lose their enthusiasm, and their spirit, and their hope. . . . Some of them had unrealistic dreams, and so when you first come here you think you can do it, and then you realize "Well, maybe I can't." (ES090ST1: 438–61, 744–61)

In the context of the description above, Marbella appears both resilient and somewhat unusual, resisting a more general trend toward disengagement from the educational process.

In sum, Marbella presents herself as highly motivated, eager to attain bilingual skills, and determined to maintain and assert her ethnic identity. For Marbella, being Mexican means having the strength of character to succeed academically. Marbella believes that such success, through enabling her to "become somebody," will enable her to mount an effective challenge to negative stereotypes.

A SECOND LOOK:
MARBELLA'S SILENT, SEPARATIST SELF

> INTERVIEWER: Is there tension between the Hispanics and Americans?
>
> MARBELLA: No, the groups don't mix.
>
> INTERVIEWER: The groups don't mix?
>
> MARBELLA: No, because they try to humiliate us . . . to many of us, including me, they call us things.
>
>   (ES50STA: 407–14)

> MARBELLA: I avoid fighting in the school, because I know I am the Mexican, and in a fight between a Mexican girl and a white girl, the Mexican cannot win.
>
>   (ES50STA: 444–49)

Ironically, Marbella is at once determined to challenge and infiltrate, yet resigned to her marginalization and segregation, hopeful about her future chances yet pessimistic about near-term prospects. These seeming contradictions are manifested most clearly in Marbella's interview transcripts, as her optimistic statements are paralleled by an emphasis on the importance of remaining silent in the face of discriminatory actions, an affinity for some segregationist practices that shield and protect, and expressions of skepticism about whether her immigrant voice is being heard. Thus, coexisting with Marbella's opposition is a passive, silent and separatist self far different than the persona described in the preceding section.

This is the self who, having been hit by a group of American peers, fell silent and turned away: "I have a P.E. class, and there are some Americans with me, and so, it was my turn, it was my turn to play basketball. Then—well because in Mexico they gave us some basketball classes so I know a lot and I always beat them—they got mad. . . . Later they stopped me, and one of them hit me. . . . I paid no attention to them. . . . My classmates asked me, 'Why are you afraid of them?' . . . 'Why bother? [I said]. It is not worth the trouble'" (ES50STA:434–49).

This is the self who rationalized her isolation in P.E. during her sophomore year (90 percent of the youth in Marbella's class are Latino, most of them immigrants). "It's probably better that way. Because they [Americans] treat us badly."

This is the self whose English voice falls silent because of a European American peer: "I want to talk to her [my teacher] in English, but there is always a gringo named John there, and he is very mean. . . . That's why I don't speak in English with Mrs. Bryant anymore. Since she understands Spanish, I talk to her in Spanish" (ES50STD: 991–1006).

This is the self who expresses futility about bringing actions she perceives as discriminatory or disrespectful to the attention of powerful adults in her environment:

> We go to Mr. Acevedo [the principal]. Then, because none of us can communicate well with him, and they [European American peers] can, they tell him what they want to. And so it sounds like we are the ones who don't respect them. "How can that be?" I ask. "If they don't respect us, how are we going to respect them?" (ES50STA: 490–98)

Marbella believes that the silent, separatist aspects of her persona are the product of her location in a social system in which she and her peers are viewed and treated as inferior. Concluding that European American youth do not respect her, Marbella shrinks from social interaction:

> They think that they are better than us. They think that because we are in their country, we are underneath them. That makes us afraid to talk to them in

English because we think they will laugh at us. . . . If we are talking in English, they look at us like they disapprove of our speaking English. They look at us funny and giggle. (ES50STD: 939–71)

These meanings structure Marbella's behavior in ways that are somewhat antithetical to the goals and beliefs she expresses. For example, Marbella emphasized her conviction that English mastery was essential to her future: "It's to learn English, that's what's necessary to triumph here. To know English. And to succeed in school" (ES50STEN: 795–808). Yet Marbella often falls silent in integrated settings, not speaking unless spoken to. During the days I spent with Marbella at school she spoke to just two culturally different peers: the first a Filipina immigrant, the second a Spanish-speaking European American who volunteers as a tutor in Explorer's ESL classrooms. Marbella explains:

In the [one] class where I have contact with Americans well, I simply don't speak to them. The only one where I'm around them is Link Period [homeroom] and [there] I apply myself to my homework and don't pay attention to them. But, if they speak to me politely, I speak to them. But if not, well, I just ignore them and do my homework. (ES50STEN: 866–75)

Marbella describes herself as profoundly hesitant to engage in the casual, everyday conversation necessary to achieve English mastery, to engage in linguistic activity that would enable her to begin to "demonstrate to other people that we indeed can make it" (ES50STEN: 442–43).

For Marbella, being Mexican necessitates a certain resignation to actions and procedures meant to silence or degrade, a certain degree of distancing behavior in order to protect herself from psychological harm. In the quote which opens this chapter, she speaks of the importance of struggling against efforts to vanquish. Yet, at a basic level, Marbella expresses a feeling of powerlessness relative to her European American peers and succumbs to their efforts to silence her.

I turn now to Marbella's school experiences, focusing on identifying and naming practices that enable the "structuring of silence" (Weis and Fine 1993). I first consider school-based factors that discipline Marbella and those around her to a set of beliefs about what it means to be Mexican, marginalizing immigrant Latino youth and removing much of the force from their achievements and voice. To understand Marbella's hesitancy to demonstrate her bilingual and academic competencies, one must consider the value placed on such competencies by those around her. Second, I consider disciplinary policies and relationships that act upon and constrain Marbella's ability to critique and resist.

The latter provide additional insight into Marbella's tendency to remain silent in the face of insult or acts of discrimination.

SORTING MECHANISMS:
THE MARGINALIZATION OF MARBELLA

MARBELLA: Later we will be in the medium classes, but since we don't speak English, we are in the lowest classes.   (ES50STA: 149–52)

HUBERTO, ESL AIDE: Most of the things Explorer is doing, they never think, you know, they never talk to [immigrant] students, "Hey, Explorer is doing a tutoring program, an awards program." We're the last to know. They never call us, they never tell us about what the school is doing for the students, you know. . . . They seem—they don't care about us. That's why they—most of the students—want to quit school. Because they feel discriminated [against] or isolated. And it's really sad when someone doesn't care for you.

(ES105ST1: 196–224)

The first set of practices that work effectively to silence Marbella can be located in disciplinary mechanisms that marginalize youth based on linguistic status and delegitimate immigrants' academic accomplishments. Marbella, like her fellow 355 Latino students in need of language assistance (25.3 percent of the student body), was placed in the ESL track as soon as she arrived at Explorer. Here, Marbella was effectively segregated from the remainder of the school population for the academic day. During her sophomore year, for example, Marbella attended English/reading ESL, algebra, P.E., physical science, computer literacy, and foods. Of these six classes, five (foods being the exception) were composed almost entirely of immigrant youth (almost all of them Latino). Thus, Marbella's only consistent opportunity for contact with language-proficient youth occurred during five-minute passing periods, the lunch hour, and a thirty-minute "link" period (homeroom) following lunch.

Segregation ostensibly enables students to receive academic content in their native language. However, Marbella had only one teacher during her first two years of high school that spoke Spanish. In reality, for many second-language learners, segregation has at best allowed for reduced class size (25–30 youth versus 35), bilingual aides, and slowed speech on the part of European American teachers with little or no training in second-language instruction.

At times, it was difficult for me to find justification for Marbella's segregation. For example, in Marbella's computer literacy course, thirty immigrant students learned word processing and typing skills. When asked what made this an ESL class, the teacher explained that in reality, the only difference was that she did not test the students for speed. Though initially planning to integrate ESL vocabulary into student work, the teacher said she had received little cooperation from teachers in the form of vocabulary lists.

Likewise, though P.E. is officially integrated, Marbella had just two European American classmates out of a group of approximately thirty youth in her class. This goes against school policy. However, according to the vice-principal of curriculum, grouping policies at the departmental level (along with "scheduling difficulties") permit resegregation to occur: "It's not purposeful. . . . Now what may have happened, they may have regrouped the kids out there. You get a hundred kids, and half of them may be Hispanic. They may regroup those kids. . . . And they are supposed to be regrouping by skill level" (ESO72ST2: 688–701). In Marbella's case, "skill level" correlated with linguistic and ethnic status, a relationship that went unquestioned by those around her.

Policies both amplify and attach status to Explorer's academic differentiation. Most importantly, high-achieving ESL students are shut out of the honor society because they cannot take the classes that qualify them for admission. Though students like Marbella were recognized at a year-end awards banquet, the banquet was held in the evening and only ESL students and their parents attended. The achievements of immigrant youth were thus not made part of the public school discourse, keeping evidence of their existence hidden from European American and English-speaking Latino peers.

Academic segregation is augmented by policies that distance and separate youth, fostering social segregation by socioeconomic (and thus linguistic) status. For example, students such as Marbella who qualify for free or reduced-price lunch must line up inside the school cafeteria for hot meals. Lunch lines for youth who buy hamburgers, pizza, and other popular fare are located in the outside courtyard. As a result, youth of color dominate the dimly lit cafeteria, while groups of European American youth dominate the area outside. (During the ten days I ate lunch in the cafeteria, I and a group of special education students were the only European Americans present.) Because of the strong relationship between immigrant status and income, a great many of the youth hidden from public view are second-language speakers. Marbella feels that academic and social segregation combine to contribute to her isolation: "Most of the students I've met are Chicanos, not Americans, because there are no Americans in my classes. Only Chicanos. . . . Since last year almost all the Mexicans get together in the cafeteria and the gringos meet outside . . . since the very beginning" (ES50STD: 1058–76).

The necessity of English comprehension for social participation is also communicated in a daily speech event: the posting (and occasional reading) of the school bulletin. The bulletin advertises school activities and scholarship opportunities. It is read and posted in English, despite the complaints of the school registrar:

> REGISTRAR: I fight like crazy to get a lot of things in Spanish. It's very hard to make sure that a lot of these fliers that go out, for instance for the kids—I feel that the kids are being left out of student activities. The Hispanic kids. Because like all of the announcements are always in English . . . aren't they? Every day, have you ever heard them? Yeah, they're in English. The daily bulletin is in English. How are they going to hear anything? And I don't know, maybe in their classrooms the teachers are translating them but I seriously doubt that. You know, telling them about information.
>
> INTERVIEWER: What is it that makes it hard to do that [get things translated]?
>
> REGISTRAR: I don't know. We've got the personnel here who speak Spanish. There shouldn't be any reason why the daily bulletin should not be translated into Spanish, every single day. . . . I've asked. I've said, "Why don't we tell them in Spanish? I think it's a good idea." I don't know, maybe they are trying to encourage the kids to learn English. (ES117ST1: 164–97)

The regular posting of the daily bulletin becomes a speech act that structures access to information by linguistic status.

In the context of this social system, Marbella has become increasingly aware of her marginalization. The quote which opens this section indicates that she knows that ESL classes are not looked upon in the same way as other classes at her high school. Marbella's perception of her marginalization is also reflected in her assessment of her academic experiences, summarized below:

> I think my teachers should learn another method of teaching, because the one they use is not very effective. I also would like them to realize we are intelligent, that we can do things, would like them to not discriminate against us, to treat us like civilized persons, not like some sort of objects. (ES50STC: written protocol)

Consistent with the meanings the broader institutional environment transmits concerning the marginalized status of immigrant youth, Marbella feels that many teachers also misjudge their students' abilities: "I have seen some who, because they see that you are Mexican, they don't give you something that . . . something difficult that really you can do. They make it very easy for you. And for the Americans they make it a little bit more difficult. Because they think that, I don't know, that you can't do it . . . that you are not intelligent, or maybe, I don't know" (ES50STEN: 1040–70). At the same time, Marbella feels relatively powerless to challenge the school's efforts to channel her into courses characterized by low expectations: "I guess the only area in which I have control is in my understanding of the subjects. But not in the manner of choosing them" (ES50STD: 606–10).

According to Marbella, no one interviewed her about her prior school history upon her arrival at Explorer. Rather, she was given a schedule and told what she would take after being tested for English and Spanish language comprehension. Though she successfully resisted her placement in basic math, Marbella found herself in a clothing course during her freshman year, and was placed in foods rather than continuing computer literacy as a second-semester sophomore: "I liked computers better, but I had to take cooking. . . . I wrote down two choices, first computers and then cooking. But in computers there wasn't room for anybody else, so they had to put me in cooking" (ES50STD: 285–93).

DISCIPLINARY POLICIES AND TECHNOLOGIZED RELATIONS: THE PACIFICATION OF MARBELLA

> DAVE SANTOS, ESL AIDE: To me, the biggest problem that I see at this school, [is] that the kids aren't listened to. I mean, they're crying for help, and no one is out there.   (ES106ST1: 125–30)

In the preceding section, I described practices that both marginalize Marbella and diminish her accomplishments. Here, I describe disciplinary relationships that control and pacify Explorer's student body, thereby working directly to structure and ensure Marbella's silence.

As a ninth grader, Marbella moved into an environment caught up in significant social change. Prior to court-ordered desegregation in the mid-1980s, Explorer's student body was 81.8 percent European American, with the majority of these students middle and upper-middle class. By 1990, when Marbella was a sophomore, the enrollment of youth of color had jumped from 18.2 to 58 percent; of these, 30.6 percent qualified for free or reduced-price lunch. The majority of Explorer's new students were of Mexican descent; in all, Latino students made up 40.6 percent of Explorer's student body in 1990.

Increasing concern and anxiety about these new students have paralleled this diversification. According to the principal, fear, doubt, and outright skepticism about the feasibility of working productively with these youth have been clearly expressed:

> The faculty feel "We had a perfectly good school, look what they've done to us.". . . The faculty frustration level has risen by leaps and bounds. . . . Teachers who've been here for years and now have different kids . . . a lot are old and have no capacity to change. Teachers have been used to lecturing and leading the lesson. They aren't getting satisfaction from kids' achievement now, because they aren't achieving. (ES06801: 257–61, 164–75)

Teacher worries reached their height soon after Marbella's arrival at Explorer, when a stabbing incident confirmed teachers' general impressions that the school was out-of-control. Worries about low skills, student hostility, parental investment, and immaturity are themes that run through the interviews carried out with thirty faculty members at Explorer, and nearly 60 percent of the faculty listed disrespect for authority as their primary concern in a survey carried out by the administration in the months following this incident.

In the context of this situation, adults at Explorer have invested new and concentrated efforts in controlling and pacifying the student body. The current disciplinary system emphasizes reconnaissance, surveillance, and adult control, enabled by the monitoring of student activity during passing periods and lunch time and an identification of students operating as "key players" in the environment. Students' movements are closely monitored and strictly controlled by the discipline principal and two campus assistants. The campus is patrolled by assistants, who communicate by walkie-talkie. Adults in these roles generally do not communicate with youth during the lunch hour and passing period, but rather watch and monitor student movements. Youth seen on campus during classroom hours are subject to immediate referral to Saturday school. Describing the atmosphere, one high-achieving European American youth observed, "It's like a police state really sometimes. All these guys buzzing around with walkie-talkies. . . . This year I tried to walk from the library to the locker room in middle of eighth period to change [for track]. Two people tried to give me Saturday school."

Though these tactics affect all students, certain policies make clear that the administration is particularly concerned about the activities of Latino youth. Soon after the stabbing incident, certain colors associated with Latino gangs were banned from campus. Students wearing two or more pieces of red or blue—the colors associated with rival Latino gangs—were called into the discipline office and given one warning. According to the disciplinary principal, this "colors campaign" was integral to an effort to identify "major players" on campus. Based on the students who visited his office, the discipline principal compiled a list of names. Defiant youth were quickly expelled, and the remainder were watched carefully. Statistics lend insight into the impact of such policies. The absolute number of youth suspended after such policies were instituted at Explorer increased by 50 percent. Almost all of this increase came about due to increases in the number of youth of color suspended. In 1990–91, 54 percent of the youth suspended were Latino, though they made up just 40 percent of the total school population.

Explorer's system of school-level surveillance has been complemented by classroom disciplinary mechanisms that insure quick removal of youth perceived as disobedient from the classroom. First, teachers have been given the perogative to remove any student from the classroom at any time, sending them to "in-school suspension." Second, youth sent to the discipline principal's office due to classroom conflict face likely reprisal, typically "Saturday school" or in severe instances suspension. This principal (Mr. Joyce) describes himself as a "traditionalist"; this, he explains, means that he is likely to support a teacher before a student and does not believe in giving second chances. Explaining further, Joyce adds:

> I'll sit here, and I'll listen, and I'll point out what I think the school's position is on their particular behavior, what I think their parent's position is, and then I'll drop the bomb on 'em. And a lot of kids think, well he's listening, he's explaining, I'm going to get off. And then boom! I'll put them on the hook. It's a surprise but they've accepted it. I guess that's a sort of a traditionalist approach. (ES100ST1: 127–84)

Six of the fifteen Explorer youth interviewed compared Joyce unfavorably to the previous vice-principal of discipline. Most often, students complained that Joyce refused to trust or listen to youth: "Mr. Joyce, whatever the teacher said, that must be right, 'cause teachers don't lie, so . . ." (African-American male); "He must fancy himself like a Stalin figure because he'll see you and come up to you and 'Where are you going?' He is so much more disciplinary than the guy last year and as a result I think people are more rebellious. He won't trust you with anything. It's like a police state" (European American male).

Consistent with the descriptions above, references to fears about going unheard and the futility of protest run through much of Marbella's discourse. In three of our five interviews, Marbella describes incidents in which she felt immigrant youth were first mistreated, and then their protests ignored or discounted. Typically, as in the incident below, Marbella perceives linguistic and ethnic differences as relevant to the eventual outcome of these conflicts:

> I don't like that class because the teacher is very racist. We have Hispanics, or actually Mexicans [immigrants], and there are some Americans there. Sometimes he chides us a lot and he doesn't say anything to them. Like sometimes we have to wear a blue and white shirt. If you wear a sweater, you have to wear the sweater underneath and the shirt on top.
>
> Yesterday this—I have a friend named Bernardino. He was wearing his white shirt underneath a black sweater. And there were two Americans who were also dressed like that. Then the teacher said a lot of things to the Mexican, Bernardino. And he made him take it off and put it on top of the sweater. And he didn't say anything to the two Americans. Because of that, we all got mad because he didn't say anything to them. And he has to be equal with everyone.
>
> He told him that he was going to throw him out of that class, because he didn't like stupid people who don't follow the rules in his class. Like he [Bernardino] knows English well, so he [the teacher] asked him "Why is it like that with you?"
>
> [Bernardino asked] "Why didn't you say anything to the rest of the students? . . . Because the rest of them are American?" And he [the teacher] told him "That has nothing to do with it. Here it has nothing to do with Mexican or American. Here, it has to do with how we come dressed. You are nobody to tell me anything. I am the teacher and you are the student." (ES50STC: 406–49)

Logically, the school disciplinarian would assist in the resolution of these and other conflicts. However, based on her observations, Marbella doubts whether Joyce would intercede on behalf of herself or peers such as Bernardino. Further, she believes that Joyce is not impartial when weighing the testimony from members of different ethnic groups:

INTERVIEWER: Can you talk a little bit about Mr. Joyce's discipline?

MARBELLA: Well, I remember mentioning [before] that sometimes he is not so good. He can be a little bit racist with us, the Mexican students. For instance, about a week ago we had a pep rally here in the gym. . . . A gringo and the Mexican had a fight outside the gym. Mr. Joyce didn't tell him anything, he didn't say anything to the gringo or the Mexican. Later on, inside, the

Mexican was making noise over where the seniors were. The gringo was where the juniors were and shouted "Fuck your mother" at him. Of course the Mexican got mad and went over to where the gringo was. Mr. Joyce grabbed him, took him outside and threw him out of school for three days, but he said nothing to the gringo. All the Mexicans there were very upset, so we started shouting and he got mad. Most of us went outside the gym. . . . I think most of the Mexicans now purposely don't behave because they don't like Mr. Joyce. (ES50STD: 750–91)

In sum, Marbella does not view the disciplinarian as a likely ally in her struggle.

Though situated in a disciplinary system focused on efficiency and control, Marbella could speak to other adults in the environment. However, Marbella's descriptions suggest that she does not have the types of relationships that facilitate the voicing of concerns and it appears that the responsibility for reaching out has been placed on her shoulders. For example, Marbella's homeroom teacher is responsible for monitoring her students' academic progress and conferring with students about course selection. (There are no counselors at Marbella's high school due to budget cuts.) This teacher speaks Spanish and Marbella describes their relationship as good. However, though she attended this class daily, Marbella did not have a serious conversation with her teacher about her courses. As Marbella sees it, "She is always busy, she doesn't seem to have time" (ES50STD: 481–83). Likewise, Marbella knows that the vice-principal of guidance has information about colleges and careers. She, too, appears busy: "I went once and she was busy that day. She is always busy giving tests" (ES50STD: 553–54). When Marbella's pattern of attendance changed substantially during the second semester of her sophomore year due to her mother's illness, those charged with monitoring attendance did not ask Marbella where she had been. Finally, despite her "sparkly" personality and model behavior, Marbella does not draw attention; neither the vice-principal of discipline nor the vice-principal of guidance recognized her name.[3] The latter spoke fluent Spanish and monitored the cafeteria where Marbella ate everyday during the lunch hour.

In sum, there is no one in the environment that appears to be inviting Marbella or other immigrant youth to voice their concerns. Further, because the school's emphasis is on managing and controlling conflict, it could be risky for Marbella to confront a teacher or peer. At some level, Marbella appears to recognize and act upon this. ("I avoid fighting in the school, because I know I am the Mexican, and in a fight between a Mexican girl and a white girl, the Mexican cannot win.")

Support for Oppositional Identity:
Freshman Social Studies

Thus far, I have focused on Marbella's awareness and sensitivity to practices that marginalize and silence. In this section, I change course, describing a classroom that Marbella praised throughout her freshman and sophomore years. Marbella frequently referred to the empowering messages, worthwhile content, and valuable information she encountered in social studies— all factors relevant to the construction to her oppositional identity. In this class, an examination of cultural diversity, Mexican culture and history, and aspects of the American opportunity structure were explicit parts of the curriculum.

Marbella's teacher, Mr. Vargas, is a fluent Spanish speaker and bilingual specialist who chose to return to the classroom after spending seven years in the district office. There, he worked as an ESL resource person, training teachers "how to deal with a tough subject like biology without watering it down . . . and being able to one, have that kid succeed, two, not be frustrated when you're doing it, and number three, make that kid a part of the school" (ES04401X: 177–85). Vargas believes that low expectations for language minority students, reflected in an unchallenging curriculum, are a major impediment to their advancement. Based on this belief, Vargas has created a curriculum that asks students to go beyond memorizing names and places to analyzing how and why historical events occurred. In addition, students are given major assignments that require research outside of the classroom. For example, as a freshman Marbella worked in a group to prepare a five-minute oral report on an ancient culture of her choice. Students were required to prepare visual aides, and to offer both information and their opinion about their chosen culture.

Many of Vargas's assignments parallel those found in Explorer's other English-language freshman social studies classrooms. However, Vargas's students also consider American cultural processes and their implications. Vargas explains:

> I tell them "You can not make it if you don't understand something." They need to understand where they are. And where they are has different values, and different norms, and different situations. And, to do this, then we have to look inside ourselves. And we do this, I have them look inside of themselves. Who am I? And where are we going?
>
> And we looked at rules and regulations, and where did they come from? And can we make a difference in our lives if we had rules and regulations that guided us, ourselves? (ES044ST1: 487–516, 543–51)

Vargas also discusses the existence of racism, not only in America as a whole but also within their high school: "I talk to them about racism, and how it exists, and how it affects everybody, and the black experience. . . . And I told them, you know, to expect it. They [the faculty] will tolerate skin color, they will tolerate everything except the language. I tell them, you've got to learn English" (ES044ST1: 561–68).

According to Marbella, this is the only class where she has been given the opportunity to explore her own as well as others' heritages. When asked how teachers speak of her heritage, Marbella replied:

> It's not spoken about very well—the Mexican heritage—here in the United States. . . . Mr. Vargas is the only one that talks of the Mexican heritage, or that has us look up things in libraries, about Mexican culture and other things. . . .
>
> Last year I was in his class. He asked us to discover how Mexico really was. He asked us to examine Mexican culture; he gave us books bought in Mexico. And he told us that our culture was very grand, and that we mustn't lose it, our culture . . . and that it is marvelous, that culture, no? And also we examined the Chinese culture. And he also asked us to examine the Indians of the past, to explore how they were living and all that. And how they arrived in Mexico, and all that. (ES50STEN: 692–716, 774–87)

Marbella also says that Vargas is the only adult who has helped make the norms and values in her new environment more explicit:

> INTERVIEWER: Has there been someone or something that has helped you in your transition after moving to the United States?
>
> MARBELLA: Yes. Mr. Vargas talked to us about the American culture and the Mexican culture. . . . I learned a little bit. For instance, about some presidents, about the natives who first got here. . . . We also talked about how Americans are, the way they behaved. Mr. Vargas asked a Mexican and an American to stand in front of the class and behave the way they really were, that way we could see.
>
> INTERVIEWER: For example?
>
> MARBELLA: Mr. Vargas had the same conversation with the Mexican and with the American, but the answers [to the questions he asked] were different. (ES50STD: 1300–1343)

As part of his effort to educate his students about the new social system in which they find themselves, Vargas also provides youth with basic information about the ways and means to varied colleges and careers. For example, Vargas organizes Saturday trips to local universities so that students can learn about higher-education opportunities. According to Marbella, Vargas is also adamant in encouraging his students to take courses with academic content. For example, after lobbying for an ESL science class, Mr. Vargas "told us a lot about that class, he told us that we needed that class. Maybe not exactly as a prerequisite for graduation, but to understand many things about life" (ES50STD: 271–75). Further, Vargas urges his students to avoid classes like clothing and foods because electives such as computers better their chances of college acceptance. Marbella also indicated that Vargas was the only person in her environment who has provided her with information about various career options:

> INTERVIEWER: You mentioned receiving information about careers in Mexico but not here. Have they given you information about different classes here?
>
> MARBELLA: Mr. Vargas is the one who has given us some information about careers. He talked to us about salaries, about the requirements to enter that field, and about what college we have to go to for that major.
>
> INTERVIEWER: When did he told you that? Was it during class time?
>
> MARBELLA: It was in class. He gave us all a book, and he spent about three days talking about careers and colleges. That was last year. (ES50STD: 393–406)

As Marbella sees it, Mr. Vargas "talks to us about life, about what we should do, that we should succeed, and he helps us a lot in our subjects so that we can move forward" (ES50STA: 145–48).

At the institutional level, Vargas has made some moves to counter the disabling messages emanating from Explorer's disciplinary technologies. For example, as a group his students formed a ballet folklórico dance group in order to assert their cultural presence in the school. This later became an elective:

> [In class we brainstormed] What is one way we can have an impact on this school? So we made up a club, the folkloric [dance] class, that's what came from [the discussion] last year. From them! And now, you know, it's taught as a class. But it came from them. (ES044ST1: 516–36)

Vargas also intervened in an incident involving Marbella's best friend, Concha, helping her to resist a disciplinary action that she and he viewed as inappropriate:

He [Concha's teacher] gave a rule, or he said something, that "If you don't bring your book to class tomorrow, you will be sent to SIS [in-school suspension]." Which, in this case, if you had two SISs, you would go to Saturday school. And Concha, accidentally, or by design by someone else, her book was lost in the locker room. The girl's locker room. Didn't have the book the next day. So that *edict* [Vargas's voice is edged with anger] which Mr., which that gentleman said, you know, "This is an edict and you follow it." She comes in, no book, he knew it, she knew it, boom! SIS. Saturday school. You're dead, right where you are. She came to the only person that I guess she could find, you know, I just happened to be there. Actually no, she did look for me. (Laughs) That's right. She found me, and she said "I'm going to in-school suspension. For no fault." In Spanish. "Can you help me?" And then she explained what happened.

So I took that explanation to the gentlemen, and I asked him "Would you *not* do this? Would you *believe* her? Because I believe her, and I believe what she's saying is true." And he said, you know he said that because, sure. . . . But I'm not sure that he did [believe her]. *I* believed her. When a kid tells me that, when a kid sensitive like Concha would tell me or anyone "This is what happened," you know, I *do*, because I've been in those shoes before. I've been in those shoes before. I've looked at people and I've said "Please believe me, I really did the work," you know. But he didn't believe her. He didn't believe her. (ES044ST1: 295–349)

Because Vargas provides a curriculum in which students have the opportunity to explore cultural diversity, social systems, and racism, because he helps his students gain a better understanding of the ways and means to attend college and to pursue various careers, and because he serves as a resource to assist in fights against attempts to discipline, Marbella views Vargas as a significant and meaningful source of support.

REFLECTIONS

Marbella is a youth buoyed and strengthened by her ethnic self-conceptions, while at the same time aware and fearful of forces that constrain her movement. While Marbella's ethnicity serves as a source of force and power, it also becomes an eddy she retreats to for protection. Marbella's ability to maintain her particular brand of opposition is impressive, given the array of constraining disciplinary technologies aligned against her. In many ways, she manifests an ability to resist constraints on her academic development—an ability described as characteristic of immigrant minorities (Suarez-Orozco 1989). A culturalist perspective would focus principally on the pro-academic aspects of Marbella's ideology, linking them to her immigrant status. Yet the silent, separatist aspects of Marbella's persona also exist. These aspects of her behavior not only slow Marbella's acquisition of the cultural and linguistic skills necessary to assert her rights, but also suggest a certain resignation to disciplinary practices and procedures.

While Marbella believes that educational achievement will result in improved economic opportunities, she is also quite aware that her chances are structured and limited by inequitable academic opportunities. I have linked the silent and resigned aspects of Marbella's persona to her growing recognition of structured inequality, a recognition that has been enabled only with two years of experience in an American high school. In particular, Marbella is aware of and responsive to practices in the environment that work to marginalize immigrant minorities and to pacify youth. With regard to marginalization, academic and social segregation—buttressed by policies and practices that both support its existence and esteem the achievements of English-speaking youth—works effectively to delegitimate Marbella's accomplishments. Importantly, in failing to find ways to incorporate the language and culture of 40 percent of the student body into the official school discourse, and in failing to provide public recognition to its high-achieving ESL students, Explorer misses a prime opportunity to challenge conceptions of Latino students' academic abilities. Further, Explorer conveys the message that the knowledge and skills from students' ESL world are less highly valued and somehow different than those from the world of their European American classmates.

Disciplinary practices and technologized relations work to control and pacify Explorer students, thereby structuring the silent, separatist aspects of Marbella's persona. Easy to overlook, these features of the environment are extremely circumscribing. Without a place for voice, and with an efficient disciplinarian who is quick to assess and dispose, Explorer's immigrant students are effectively silenced. One ESL aide believes that the level of frustration among the youth is reflected in their self-defeating screams of frustration: "You hear a lot of *La Raza* always shouting and screaming, and you try to talk to them and they're real defensive. And I think that's part of the—you get here, you sit down, everyone's talking, no one's really paying attention to you, you don't understand" (ES106ST3: 284–91).

Resource constraints, limiting the ability of so many public schools to respond to diversity, are also relevant to Marbella's situation. With one exception, Marbella has had no bilingual teachers and few teachers with ESL training, despite the fact that she attends the district school designated as the primary receiving ground for newly arrived immigrants. On the whole, according to one bilingual teacher, the situation for immigrant youth has improved markedly: "They [the faculty] have accepted the growth of ESL from the way it was when I first walked in, where there was ten students and no materials. Nothing, nothing, nothing. To now, where ESL is a big department, big budget by the books. And then people have acknowledged that ESL is not bogus. That was a key operating word four years ago. Bogus" (ES044ST1: 605–14). Yet Marbella's teachers describe themselves as underprepared, inexperienced, and uncertain about how to handle their classroom situation. There were villains in Marbella's descriptions—a clothing teacher who pulled hair to gain the attention of Spanish-speaking youth, the P.E. teacher who would not let Bernardino wear his sweater over his T-shirt. Nevertheless, the majority of Marbella's teachers appeared to be well-meaning yet frightened to take pedagogical risks, patient, yet not sure how to be of assistance. As Marbella put it, "They understand that we are Mexican, and we cannot exactly do everything. They help us as much as they can, the teachers do" (ES50STEN: 957–61). The problem, as Marbella points out, is that adults so often underestimate, so often downscale their expectations, rather than providing scaffolding appropriate to high-level cognitive engagement. Marbella is left marginalized, fighting harder to prevent others from structuring her into a category that she knows is a simple and false social construction.

NOTES

An earlier version of this chapter appeared in Davidson, A. L., *Making and Molding Identity in Schools: Student Narratives on Race, Gender, and Academic Engagement* (Albany: State University of New York Press, 1996).

In the text of this chapter, quotations are identified by file code. The file code of the epigraph, an excerpt from an interview, is ES50STEN: 652–72. The interviews are part of a public-use file that will eventually be made available to interested researchers through Stanford's Center for Research on the Context of Secondary School Teaching.

1. All interviews were conducted in Spanish by a male European American interviewer. I was generally present as well.

2. The research reported in this chapter reflects one component of a year-and-a-half-long ethnographic study carried out at three high schools. Funded by a Spencer Dissertation Year Fellowhip and the Center for Research on the Context of Secondary School Teaching, the research was designed to explore how youth conceptualize their ethnicity and assert their ethnic identity across varied curricular settings, with the purpose of illuminating school-based factors and practices that work to mold students as they go about making ethnic and academic identities. This investigation, focusing in-depth on twelve diverse youth, was situated within the Students' Multiple Worlds Study

(Phelan, Davidson, and Yu 1993), a broad investigation of fifty-five high school youths that considered factors that impact students' academic and social engagement with the school community. Both investigations relied on ethnographic methods: intensive interviews, carried out over a two-year period; observations of youth in and out of the classroom; and analyses of school (e.g., statistical data on tracking, suspension rates) and individual (e.g., attendance patterns, grades) record data. Faculty, staff, and administrators at each of the high schools were also interviewed. For a detailed account of this study, see A. L. Davidson, *Making and Molding Identity in Schools: Student Narratives on Race, Gender, and Academic Engagement* (Albany: State University of New York Press, 1996). For more information on the Students' Multiple Worlds Study, see P. Phelan, A. Davidson, and H. Yu, "Students' Multiple Worlds: Navigating the Borders of Family, School and Peer Cultures," in P. Phelan and A. Davidson, *Renegotiating Cultural Diversity in American Schools* (New York: Teachers College Press 1993).

3. Ironically, it appears that model behavior may be partially responsible for Marbella's invisibility. She describes her younger brother, who does poorly and causes problems in school, as relatively well known: "My mother has to call every week, because they told my brother that if he doesn't act better that he was going to have to return to Mexico. And because of that she has to call each week to ask about my brother's education" (ES50STC:1173–87).

References

Davidson, A. L. 1992. "The Politics and Aesthetics of Ethnicity: Making and Molding Identity in Varied Curricular Settings." Unpublished Ph.D. dissertation, Stanford University, Stanford, Calif.

Davidson, A. L., *Making and Molding Identity in Schools: Student Narratives on Race, Gender, and Academic Engagement* (Albany: State University of New York Press, 1996).

Fine, M. 1991. *Framing Dropouts: Notes on the Politics of an Urban Public High School.* Albany: State University of New York Press.

Fordham, S., and J. U. Ogbu. 1986. "Black Students' School Success: Coping with the 'Burden of Acting White.'" *Urban Review* 18.3: 176–206.

Foucault, M. 1979. *Discipline and Punish.* New York: Pantheon.

———. 1983. "The Subject and Power." In H. L. Dreyfus and P. Rabinow. *Michel Foucault: Beyond Structuralism and Hermeneutics,* 208–26. Chicago: University of Chicago Press.

Gibson, M. A. 1987. "Punjabi Immigrants in an American High School." In G. Spindler and L. Spindler, eds. *Interpretive Ethnography of Education: At Home and Abroad,* 274–81. Prospect Heights, Ill.: Waveland Press.

Kondo, D. 1990. *Crafting Selves: Power, Gender and Discourses on Identity in a Japanese Workplace.* Chicago: University of Chicago Press.

Macias, J. 1990. "Scholastic Antecedents of Immigrant Students: Schooling in a Mexican Immigrant Sending Community." *Anthropology and Education Quarterly* 21.4: 291–318.

Matute-Bianchi, M. E. 1986. "Ethnic Identities and Patterns of School Success and Failure among Mexican-Descent and Japanese-American Students in a California High School: An Ethnographic Analysis." *American Journal of Education* 95.1: 233–55.

Ogbu, J. 1987. "Variability in Minority School Performance: A Problem in Search of an Explanation." *Anthropology and Education Quarterly* 18.4: 313–34.

Phelan, P., A. L. Davidson, and H. C. Yu. 1993. "Students' Multiple Worlds: Navigating the Borders of Family, Peer and School Cultures." In P. Phelan and A. L. Davidson, eds., *Renegotiating Cultural Diversity in American Schools,* 52–88. New York: Teachers College Press.

Raissiguier, C. 1994. *Becoming Women, Becoming Workers: Identity Formation in a French Vocational School.* Albany: State University of New York Press.

Rodriguez, L. J. 1993. *Always Running: La Vida Loca: Gang Days in L.A.* New York: Simon & Schuster.

Suarez-Orozco, M. 1989. *Central American Refugees and U.S. High Schools: A Psychosocial Study of Motivation and Achievement.* Stanford, Calif.: Stanford University Press.

Suarez-Orozco, M. M., and C. M. Suarez-Orozco. 1993. "The Cultural Psychology of Hispanic Immigrants: Implications for Educational Research." In P. Phelan and A. L. Davidson, eds., *Renegotiating Cultural Diversity in American Schools,* 108–38. New York: Teachers College Press.

Uribe, F., R. Levine, and S. Levine. 1994. "Maternal Behavior in a Mexican Community: The Changing Environments of Children." In P. Greenfield and R. Cocking, eds., *Cross-Cultural Roots of Minority Child Development,* 41–54. Hillsdale, N.J.: Lawrence Erlbaum Associates.

Weis, L. 1990. *Working Class without Work: High School Students in a De-industrializing Economy.* New York: Routledge.

Weis, L. and M. Fine. 1993. *Beyond Silence Voices: Class, Race and Gender in United States Schools.* Albany: State University of New York Press.

Willis, P. 1977. *Learning to Labour.* Westmead, England: Saxon House.

2

DAVID R. M. BECK

The Chicago
American Indian Community
An "Invisible" Minority

You tell all white men "America First." We
believe in that. We are the first Americans.
We are the only ones, truly, that are 100
percent. We, therefore, ask you while you
are teaching school children about America first, teach them truth about the first
Americans.

—Memorial of Grand Council Fire of
American Indians to Mayor William Hale
Thompson of Chicago, December 1, 1927

Today, according to census figures, there are approximately seven thousand
American Indians in Chicago, with an additional seven thousand in the surrounding areas.[1] With some seven million people living in the Chicago metropolitan area, American Indians are a small minority. In fact, for cultural,
economic, and political reasons beyond their small numbers, American Indians are one of the least visible minority groups in Chicago. Even many life-
long area residents do not realize that American Indians live in the city. The
city of Chicago recently demonstrated its official ignorance of the Indian population and its problems when it excluded Indians from the list of minorities
whose businesses are eligible to apply for minority set-aside contracts.[2]

Yet American Indians have lived in and passed through the Chicago region far longer than anyone else has, and have maintained a continuous presence for centuries. That presence has been marked by three key features which

have come to define both the Indian community's development and its problems: diversity, marginality to the larger society, and maintenance of a separate cultural identity by both individuals and community-based organizations.

The community's diversity has a long history, but it stems largely from (1) Chicago's unique position as an industrial center, and (2) the Bureau of Indian Affairs (BIA)–sponsored program of relocation, which from the 1950s to the 1970s helped cause the resettlement of Indian people moving from the reservations to cities looking for work. Chicago, designated as a national relocation center, is in a state without Indian reservations, so all relocatees were from elsewhere. Even before this program began, Chicago's Indian population had been growing rapidly and broadly in the post–World War II years because of booming factory work. Current estimates show that Indian people of over a hundred different tribal backgrounds live in Chicago.

The community's marginality is imposed from the outside and in some ways supported from within the community. America has not yet come to terms with the notion or the legal reality of nations within a nation, and has attempted in various ways to force American Indians to give up their cultural identity and hegemony in exchange for white ways. Though these American attempts have been destructive, they have been unsuccessful. American Indians have stubbornly fought to maintain their cultural traditions, tribal sovereignty, and separate identities even against great odds. This is complicated today by the fact that approximately three fourths of the 2 million American Indians in the United States live off of federally recognized reservations, in rural areas, in tribal groups unrecognized by the federal government, and in urban areas.[3] American Indians living off of reservations, significantly less than one percent of the nation's population, are nearly invisible in the United States. Yet they are also one of America's most at-risk populations.

Scholarly and media misrepresentation of urban Indian communities like Chicago's have added to their marginality to the larger society. The conditions, problems, and needs of Indian people in Chicago have been shaped by numerous separate but interrelated histories: the tribal and community histories of those Indian people who have made the city their home, either permanently or temporarily, and the distinct history of this urban Indian community. Because of these complexities, urban Indian communities have rarely been studied by scholars, and even less frequently understood. Most studies of urban American Indians focus on the rapid urbanization of the American Indian population in the post–World War II era and dwell on the disruptive forces of the federal relocation program and migration, or on urban living, using those as a basis to analyze Indian responses and adaptations. As a consequence, these studies emphasize problems, most often of alcoholism and adjustment to city life, instead of either community cultural tradition or development.

Urban American Indians have also sought to remain outside of the mainstream, in part because of this misunderstanding of them by the larger society, but for other significant reasons as well. Historic treatment by federal, state and local governments, churches and schools, which has been so destructive to many Indian communities and individuals, is one factor. There are few if any Indian people whose families have not been affected negatively by one or more of these influences. These personalized experiences have made individuals understandably reluctant to involve themselves in activities sponsored by these groups.[4]

Urban Indian communities like Chicago are fluid, with individuals and families travelling back and forth between city and reservation on a regular basis. Younger people do this in search of a better-quality environment or education for themselves and their children, while many older community members retire to the reservations to which they or family members have ties. This precludes an integration into the life of the larger community, since for many the city is viewed as a temporary rather than a permanent home.

Community members who remain in the city participate in but to a large extent do not become part of mainstream culture. Even those who do attempt to become part of mainstream culture are marginalized by that culture. One American Indian suburban grade school student recently reported that her teacher in school taught the class that Indians were part of American history, but not part of the current American scene. She was told that there are no Indians alive any more. In addition, for children and even adults the burden of being American Indian is often made more difficult by peers, teachers, coworkers, and others who assume that because the person is American Indian, he or she can answer any questions about any tribe's history or literature or culture.[5] The inability to answer such questions, many of which border on the ridiculous, while understandable, is also demoralizing.

The third feature shaping Chicago's Indian community is its maintenance of cultural identity. This has been done by individual families, by people working in leadership positions within the community, and by community organizations. In fact, this is the primary force defining community development. Beginning with Carlos Montezuma, who moved to Chicago in the late nineteenth century and remained almost until his death in 1923, and continuing with others such as Mrs. Charles Fitzgerald and Scott Henry Peters in the twenties and thirties, and Willard LaMere from the forties through eighties, the community has had forceful leaders working actively to improve conditions for Indian people and to develop community institutions.

Early leaders focused more strongly on pursuing rights for Indian people on reservations back home and on redefining for themselves and the American public the views of Indians as a race, while later leaders focused more exclusively on problems within Chicago as the Indian population grew rapidly, but all concentrated their energies on bettering Indian people's lives in ways that were remarkably consistent with their cultural backgrounds. The founding of the Indian Council Fire in 1923, and the American Indian Center in 1953, which was followed by the subsequent proliferation of community organizations in the 1970s, all reflect desires within the community to serve by helping individuals within the context of Indian cultural values, for example.

Indian people have maintained a cultural identity because they have been able to adapt traditional tribal values to their new circumstances. Despite broadly different cultural and historical situations among tribes, several fundamental values permeate many Indian cultures including urban communities. Among those values identified have been maintenance and development of family relationships, responsibility to the community, and reciprocity and generosity, or sharing.[6] Ironically these same values often prevent Indian people from pursuing or even desiring to pursue the "American dream," which is based largely on individualism, consumerism, and material possessions.

To understand how this came to be and what all of this means in relation to today's Chicago American Indian community we need to first understand that community's history.

After Black Hawk's defeat at the hands of the United States Army in 1832, the final treaties ceding Indian lands in Illinois to the United States were negotiated.[7] This effectively removed all Indian tribes, though not all Indian individuals, from the state.[8] Indian traders continued to travel to the city during the nineteenth century bringing fish and berries to sell, and later in the nineteenth century travelling Wild West shows brought Indian people into the city. The Great Lakes shipping industry also employed Indian people who stopped in Chicago when their ships did.

Through the end of the nineteenth and into the twentieth century American Indian groups continued to stop in Chicago when passing through, not only traders and working people, but travellers as well. Because Chicago was a rail hub for the Midwest, and because the nation lacked a unified rail system, transcontinental travellers switched trains in the city. Indian delegations from the Midwest and Great Plains often passed through or spent the night in

Chicago while on their way to lobby Congress or to meet with the President of the United States or the Commissioner of Indian Affairs.[9] Beginning in 1893 and lasting into the 1940s, American Indians came to Chicago to set up camp for local celebrations. Individual people from all of these groups sometimes stayed in Chicago, for short or longer periods of time. All of this was an early basis of both the community's diversity and its fluidity.

At the encampments, visitors were invited to come see what federal officials, scholars, and the general public all viewed as the last vestiges of a dying race, or a reminder of America's past. The Indian Village at the 1893 World's Columbian Exposition, for instance, was a carefully planned part of the ethnology exhibit, which was meant to be an object lesson in the progress of mankind. This display contained both artifacts of past civilizations and living peoples from throughout the world. Following the ideology of Social Darwinism, this combination was intended to illustrate the steps of civilization mankind had undergone. The Indian exhibit was placed at the start of the evolutionary scale.[10] Events like this and their treatment by the press and by organizing officials helped cement the marginal treatment and view of American Indians by the larger society.

The best-known early-twentieth-century Indian resident of Chicago was Dr. Carlos Montezuma, the Yavapai stomach surgeon. He was a nationally acclaimed physician and a national Indian leader, but he also served as a one-man social service agency for Indians in Chicago. When Indian delegations passed through the city, en route to Washington, D.C., he graciously met them and made their stay in Chicago pleasant; when Indians became stranded in the city, he interceded with their reservation agencies to help provide the opportunity for them to return home; when Indians came to the city in need of work, he helped them find it. In fact, he informally worked together with the BIA warehouse in Chicago in this latter capacity. In 1904 when a train wrecked in Maywood, Illinois, several Indian members of a travelling Wild West show were injured, some critically. Dr. Montezuma not only treated the Indians as patients, but fought (albeit unsuccessfully) through the BIA system for better compensation on their behalf. These local roles of acting as family and helper for Indian people of all backgrounds in the city, place Montezuma firmly within a tribal cultural tradition in which those tasks were a natural part of leaders' daily activities.[11]

While Dr. Montezuma lived in Chicago the Indian population was so low that it can be considered negligible. The 1910 federal census counted only 188 American Indians in the city, not enough to form much basis of community. Were it not for Montezuma's fame and the occasional encampments held in the city, for which representatives from various local and sometimes distant tribes travelled to Chicago but which were also attended by local tribal members, there would be virtually no documentary record of Indians in Chicago previous to the 1920s.

Nonetheless, in 1919 the Illinois State legislature deemed the Indian presence significant enough to warrant a special holiday. Following the lead of other state legislative bodies, it passed a law proclaiming the fourth Friday in September as American Indian Day, a holiday still celebrated in Chicago's Indian community.

The early celebrations of Indian Day, held from 1920 to 1923, featured encampments at Forest Preserves which tens of thousands of visitors attended in order to catch a glimpse of a way of life considered to be part of the past. These were sponsored by a newly created organization, the Indian Fellowship League (IFL), which consisted of both Indian and white members. These two groups of people unfortunately had conflicting agendas. The white members wanted the Indians to aid in the conservation movement and enjoyed attending pageants which featured Indian cultural events. The Indian members on the other hand, Chicago residents who themselves were of thirty-five different tribal backgrounds, wanted to use the organization to work actively on behalf of Indian tribal rights which were being denied by the federal government.[12] The IFL soon disbanded in disarray, but its conflict represents the marginality of Chicago's Indian population even among non-Indians who wanted to work with them. It also demonstrates the strength of the Indian desires to work on behalf of Indian people in order to protect political and cultural rights which were guaranteed in nineteenth-century treaties.

The death of Carlos Montezuma in 1923, a blow to both Indians in Chicago and to the national Indian leadership, occurred just as a new permanent organization, again of mixed Indian and white membership, came into existence. The Grand Council Fire of American Indians, later known as the Indian Council Fire, exhibited many of the same theoretical conflicts among its leadership as had the IFL. Despite this, for many of its early years it provided both a social and social service outlet to the local Indian population.

The Council Fire's makeup of Indian membership was also diverse, and the Indian leadership among its members represented a new group of Indian people moving to cities: those educated in off-reservation boarding schools. These schools, run both by churches and the BIA, supported with federal money, were notorious for their attempts to obliterate Indian cultures and cultural ways. Like other federal programs aimed at destroying Indian cultures, this too, though destructive in many ways, failed. The leaders who came to

Chicago from the boarding schools continued the tradition of leadership brought to the city by Montezuma, by battling for Indian tribal rights and for recognition of the value of Indian culture within the context of American culture, and by acting as family and support to Indian people in need. This happened until the Indian membership lost control of the Council Fire to the white leadership in the late 1930s.[13]

The Indian population in the city of Chicago remained relatively low, officially numbering less than a thousand, until the 1950s. During and after World War II, however, the population grew dramatically. Indians were among the workers who moved to cities for factory jobs during the war. After the war Indian veterans moved to cities like Chicago. As economic conditions on most reservations remained in states of crisis and even worsened, Indian people left to find employment in Chicago and other cities.

At the same time, a federal Indian policy shift, one prong of a broader federal attempt to downscale government, aimed on several fronts to dissolve federal responsibilities to Indians. This shift brought with it one of the most destructive policies ever applied to tribes, termination, and also brought the relocation program, established in 1952 to sponsor Indian migration to cities.

Six cities including Chicago were designated as relocation centers, with offices established to aid newcomers in finding housing and employment. The BIA also hired relocation officers who worked on reservations to encourage and aid Indian people in moving to the city, providing transportation funds, moral support, and directions to the urban relocation offices. Of the 122,000 Indians who moved to cities between 1940 and 1960, over 31,000, approximately 25 percent, came under the auspices of the relocation program.[14] The BIA conducted the relocation program until 1972. In that time 13,377 Indian people ("units" in BIA terminology) were relocated to Chicago.[15] Nationally as many as 75 percent of Indians moving to cities did *not* come as part of the relocation program during this time. In Chicago the estimate stands at 50 percent. In fact, even before relocation, Indian people chose to move to Chicago because they knew other Indians already lived there.[16]

Chicago was a bewildering place to many of these new residents, for whom the BIA provided little support after the initial contact. The size of the city and its buildings, the crowding of its people, the noise, the streets, and an almost alien way of life were all new to many rural Indian people used to reservation life. Many migrants suffered from loneliness and alienation when they first arrived.[17]

Also alien was the way they were expected to live. Contrary to federal promises, the BIA housed relocatees in temporary housing often near or on skid row. Many were not used to living in the unsanitary conditions in which they found themselves in Chicago. Also, the BIA often housed Indian people far from their places of work or job training. Some returned home immediately, others waited until they had enough money to return, and still others remained. In the later years, some relocatees came through the program a second time, hoping again to find a better life in the city.[18]

The Indian Council Fire, though still in existence, no longer served either social or social service functions for most Indian people in Chicago. Some individuals of course continued to serve these functions through the 1940s and 1950s. One was Willard LaMere, whose family had lived in Chicago since at least the 1920s; another was Anna P. Harris, renowned for her generosity and hospitality toward Indian people of all backgrounds passing through Chicago.[19] Aside from several bars, however, there were few places where Indian people could go to meet each other.

Then in 1953 an initiative from among Indian people in Chicago, with the support of the BIA and local welfare organizations, led to the founding of the All Tribes American Indian Center, the first urban center in the nation. Later "All Tribes" was dropped from the title, but it served as a signal that all Indian people were welcome, that the incipient community's diversity was being recognized in a positive manner.

That diversity expanded rapidly in the 1950s and 1960s. In one typical year, 1957, the BIA placed people of forty-eight different tribal designations in Chicago, including people from the Southwest, California, the Northwest, the Northern Plains, the Southern Plains, the Southeast, and the Midwest. BIA officials sometimes relocated people far from their homes to make it more difficult for them to return. As a result, people of dramatically different cultural backgrounds, sometimes people who were of tribes which were traditional enemies, now lived together. The BIA found jobs for relocatees throughout the city, but found most of the housing in Uptown, a North Side port of entry neighborhood for a wide variety of urban migrants.[20]

Uptown formed the core of the Chicago Indian community for two decades. When the Indian Center purchased a building in the late 1960s, it did so in the heart of Uptown. The center provided both social services and a social outlet for Indian people in Chicago. Numerous cultural clubs founded throughout the years met at the center, including language clubs at which members met to converse in their native languages, recreational clubs including a canoe club and athletic clubs, and programs for youth and community elders. Social services included educational, daily living assistance, counseling, and food programs. In 1954 the center sponsored its first powwow, an annual event which still draws thousands of Indian participants and visitors to Chicago each November.

Although all of these activities helped Indian people adjust to city life and to maintain not only cultural ties but cultural traditions, several factors made this much more difficult. Physical disconnection from home communities made it hard to maintain the language, and to take part in ceremonies and community events. Although traditional ceremonies, for instance, occurred in the city, they often did so sporadically or in modified ways.

Another major problem was the disruption of the family system. While not true in every case, generally parts of families, whether individuals or parents and children, migrated to Chicago together. The support system provided by extended families in which grandparents, aunts, uncles, and cousins often played roles as significant as parents and siblings, was left behind. As much as anything, this loss has proven destructive for families in poverty in the city.

By the end of the relocation era in the early 1970s a host of community-based organizations were established, most in Uptown, to meet the increasing needs of the community. These helped in various ways to maintain traditional tribal cultural values in Chicago. People created new "families" in their organizational affiliations, while the organizations took the collective responsibility to work for the betterment of the community, especially its neediest members. These organizations have created a web of support for community members in the areas of health, education, and employment, and have provided spiritual, cultural, and social outlets as well.[21]

The values, though, conflict with those of the larger society, and maintaining them is difficult in a diverse and marginalized community. That difficulty became heightened, ironically, as people's working conditions stabilized and they moved closer to their jobs. The Indian population has now dispersed widely throughout the city and suburbs.[22] People still maintain connections with each other through the organizations and the events they sponsor, such as powwows, but doing so is an increasing hardship.

Despite the positive aspects of community development which have occurred over the past four decades, Indian people still face severe problems in Chicago, due to both their marginality in the larger society and their diversity. Education levels remain low, while unemployment levels remain high, and the poorest segment of the community consists of female-headed single-parent households with children. Underemployment and lack of skill levels for better jobs, both directly related to the education problem, are also significant.

In Chicago less than 15 percent of Indian adults have college degrees, a number higher than the national average for Indian adults of 10.1 percent, and much improved since the early 1970s when only four Indian adults with college degrees could be identified in Chicago. By comparison, however, over 33 percent of white adults in Chicago have college degrees. Over a quarter of Indian adults in Chicago have never graduated from high school.[23]

Two recent surveys of Indian education in the Chicago public schools found conditions in a state of crisis, and indicate that things are not improving. Native Americans have a higher dropout rate than any other racial or ethnic group within the Chicago Public Schools. In 1986 the dropout rate of American Indians in Chicago Public High Schools stood at 70.8 percent. For white students that number was 41.4 percent; for African American students, 40.5. And of American Indian students entering high school in 1990, 51.4 percent dropped out by their sophomore year, while 65.8 percent had dropped out by the junior year, which indicates that the statistics of the mid-1980s, rather than improving, may actually be worsening. Nationally, the Indian dropout rate is figured at approximately 35 percent, but that number is considered low because it is calculated beginning with the sophomore year, while many students drop out in the freshman year when they reach the legal age of 16.[24]

"It is clear," in the words of a 1992 report, "that *American Indian children in Chicago have all the risk factors associated with poor school achievement.*" These risk factors include a high incidence of single-parent households, sub-poverty-level incomes, parents lacking high school diplomas and not often being home when the child is, and siblings who have dropped out of school. Of American Indian students who dropped out, 100 percent had already failed two or more courses.[25] The high school dropout rate is high, but many Indian students do not even make it out of junior high. Without support from families, and without extended family to help provide that foundation which children seek to find, many children join street gangs, become delinquent, or move to society's fringes in other ways. Intervention needs to begin therefore at the grade school level or earlier.

A follow-up report, reflecting on the dire situation described in the first report, warned,

> Beyond that, "poor school achievement" is, in and of itself, a "risk factor" for future success. In other words, those dropout statistics we're seeing are apt to be seen as unemployment statistics in the near future, and as today's dropouts begin to raise families, they become "risk factors" in *their* children's future. As Chicago's Native American population is disproportionately young, the social ramifications are potentially disastrous for a community already under siege. . . . 30% of Chicago's Native American population is under age 18, as compared with 18% under 18 of Chicago's white population.[26]

The diversity and marginality of Chicago's Indian community are often unnoticed by educators, and the community's stubborn insistence on maintaining not only cultural ties but cultural values and tradition often baffles educators.

As an example, the diversity of Chicago's Indian community extends also within the family. Continuing a phenomenon that grew with the mixing of Indian children at boarding schools in the early twentieth century, American Indian men and women from various tribal backgrounds are today raising children in cities like Chicago, and throughout Indian country. The children and even the parents and sometimes grandparents in these families are of mixed tribal backgrounds.

This makes understanding of family and tribal history even more critical in children's understanding of their place in society. A person may be enrolled in one tribe, but identify more strongly with another since he or she may have grown up more in relation to that community. A person may have a family background with two or more tribal affiliations in which the tribes are traditional enemies. This can be a difficult and confusing addition to the other identity crises faced by children entering adolescence, many of whom have to contend as well with additional outside pressures from street gangs, poverty, a weak and uncomfortable educational system, weakened family structures, and a society which virtually ignores them.

Educators therefore need to be aware both of the differences between American Indian students, and sometimes of the differences within those students' own families. One educator recently said of a thirteen-year-old Chicago Indian boy, "He doesn't know anything about his own history; he doesn't even know about the Trail of Tears."[27] The boy was a Wisconsin Ho-Chunk; his tribe's history has had more than its share of tragic upheaval, including forced relocations, but the "Trail of Tears" was experienced by the Cherokees who left the southeast for Oklahoma, not the Ho-Chunk who stayed in Wisconsin. Little wonder that he finds his education irrelevant!

Ultimately, as Indian people have learned time and again through painful historical experience, Indian problems must be resolved by Indian people in order for resolution to be effective. That way solutions can be made within a relevant cultural context and within the context of community development within which Indian people are decision makers. In Chicago these educational problems, for example, are now being attacked head-on by community organizations and members, from parent committees to a grade school magnet program to a local Indian-established- and -run college, NAES (Native American Educational Services) College, in a multigenerational context that includes employment and education as part of the solution.

Moneys from Title IV, Part A (now Title V) of the Indian Education Act supported elementary and high school programs for Indian students in Chicago beginning in the 1970s. Those programs closed in the late seventies and in the eighties, however. In 1988, as the result of a program proposed by the Chicago Board of Education, the Audubon Elementary School in the Uptown community began a program in which sixty Indian students were "clustered" in the school, similarly to a magnet school. The curriculum in the school has been reshaped to include teaching of Indian history and culture, both to Indian students alone for a part of the day, and to the entire school. The idea is to affirm the value of Indian culture and history to Indian students and to make non-Indian students aware of the continuing presence of this small minority in American society.

In the meantime, in the mid-1970s, Indian people in the Chicago community founded NAES College to address the problem that even of those American Indians attending college in the United States, fully 90 percent never earned a degree. (The number has not much improved by the mid-1990s, unfortunately.) This was due largely to two factors: the irrelevance of higher education to Indian community needs, and the failure of conventional systems of higher education to account for the cultural problems Indian students encounter in higher education systems. In 1984 NAES earned accreditation from the North Central Association of Colleges and Schools to confer a Bachelor of Arts degree in Community Studies.[28]

NAES College's Chicago campus has been actively involved in the Audubon School program since its inception, helping design it, and then with support from the State of Illinois, running first a role-model component within the program, and later becoming more actively involved. In the fall of 1994 the college began to develop a Family Education Model at the school which intends to involve youth, parents, community, and teachers in actively working to help the program meet its potential. NAES students are involved at all levels, from active participation in the parent committee, which serves as a program watchdog, to the tutoring program, to teacher training. The Indian teachers who run the program are NAES graduates. No formal assessment of the Audubon Program has yet been made, so its success is undefined. But it does provide a much-needed source of stable development within the community.

Individuals outside of the Indian community must be able to recognize the problems Indian students face if they are to be helpful in the process of problem resolution and community development. They must also be able to both accept and understand the community's diversity, to help eliminate its marginality in those areas in which the community does not desire to remain outside of the larger culture, and to respect the community's maintenance of cultural tradition and values, even when that conflicts with such American values as individualism, material possession, consumerism, and coercive leadership. Educators must take on the responsibilities of learning the historical and cultural conditions of the Indian people they serve, of making non-Indian people aware of those cultures and histories, and of making the educational system relevant to Native American students. Perhaps with such recognition and help Indian communities like Chicago's will be able to move toward a more positive future.

NOTES

The author presented some of these ideas and text in a paper "How Chicago American Indian Organizations Display Traditional Leadership Characteristics" presented at the American Society for Ethnohistory Conference in Bloomington, Indiana, November 5, 1993. A 1993 National Endowment for the Humanities Summer Seminar under the direction of Roger L. Nichols at the University of Arizona provided an opportunity for some of the background research for this piece, as did work partially supported by the Illinois Humanities Council, NAES (Native American Educational Services), and the University of Illinois at Chicago History Department from 1986 to 1988 which resulted in *The Chicago American Indian Community, 1893–1988: Annotated Bibliography and Guide to Sources in Chicago* (Chicago: NAES College Press, 1988).

1. *1990 Census of Population and Housing Block Statistics, East North Central Division*, CD90-1B-4, September 1992.

2. This followed in the wake of the United States Supreme Court's 1989 *Richmond v. Croson* decision, which requires cities to prove that minority preference contracts go only to minority groups that have been historically discriminated against. City representatives said they were unable to locate any Indian-owned businesses, which means they failed to look in the city phone book under either American Indian or Native American. The American Indian Economic Development Association, an Indian-run organization in Chicago which works to support Indian-owned businesses, is fighting the city on this issue. The situation was still unremedied in 1994.

3. The 1990 census counted the population of American Indians, Eskimos, and Aleuts at 1,959,234. Of these 437,358 live in American Indian or trust lands, and 1,100,534 are classified as urban. *1990 Census of Population General Population Characteristics, United States* 1990 CP1-1, table 9, p. 13, and *1990 Census of Population General Population Characteristics, American Indian and Native Alaska Areas* 1990-CP-1-1A, table 1, p. 1.

4. Several of these factors in relation to Chicago's American Indian community are discussed in Bryan Marozas, *Demographic Profile of Chicago's American Indian Community* (Chicago: NAES College Press, 1984) in relation to undercounting of Indians by federal census takers in the 1980 census.

5. A group of twenty urban, rural, and suburban American Indian children in a Summer Cultural Program at the University of Illinois at Chicago in July 1994, for example, created a long list of stereotypes and racially based problems they face in their everyday lives. One of the things which makes them most angry is being considered "experts" on Indians simply because they are Indian.

6. For discussion of this, see LaDonna Harris in collaboration with Dr. Jacqueline Wasilewski, *This Is What We Want to Share: Core Cultural Values* (Americans for Indian Opportunity, 1992).

7. The final Illinois treaties reprinted in Charles J. Kappler, ed., *Indian Treaties, 1778–1883* (New York: Interland, 1972 [orig. 1904]) include: Treaty with the Winnebago, 1832, pp. 345–48; Treaty with the Sauk and Foxes, pp. 349–51; Treaty with the Potawatomi, 1832 (October 20), 353–56; Treaty with the Potawatomi, 1832 (October 26), 367–70; Treaty with the Potawatomi, 1832 (October 27), 372–75; Treaty with the Piankeshaw and Wea, 1832, 382–83; Treaty with the Chippewa, Etc., 1833, 402–15. For a discussion of the relation of the war against Black Hawk to the treaties, see Helen Hornbeck Tanner, *Atlas of Great Lakes Indian History* (Norman: University of Oklahoma Press, 1987), 159.

8. Some individual Potawatomi people, for example, received land that is now in Chicago in the treaties they helped negotiate. The Treaty with the Chippewa, Etc., 1829, for example, granted land to Billy Caldwell (Sauganash) and Alexander Robinson (Kappler, 298). See also "Last Pottawatomies Win a 20-Year Fight," *Chicago Times*, September 19, 1941, and a map by Virgil J. Vogel, "Former Indian Reservations" in Cook County Forest Preserves in "Indians, Treaties and Claims" folder, Chicago Historical Society clip-files.

9. These trips are remembered through oral histories and can also be traced through newspapers and other printed sources.

10. Robert W. Rydell, *All the World's a Fair: Visions of Empire at American International Expositions, 1876–1916* (Chicago: University of Chicago Press, 1985), 45; Letter from Brigadier General R. H. Pratt to Franklin K. Lane, Secretary of the Interior, May 21, 1913, in John William Larner, Jr., ed., *The Papers of Carlos Montezuma, M.D., including the Papers of Maria Keller Montezuma Moore and the Papers of Joseph W. Latimer* (Wilmington, Del.: Scholarly Resources, 1983) microfilm reel 3, and *The Historical World's Columbian Exposition and Chicago Guide . . .* , Illustrated from Official Drawings by Horace H. Morgan, LL.D. (St. Louis: James H. Mason & Co., Publishers), 269–70, 294. The latter referred to "the aborigines of this country" as an "almost extinct civilization, if civilization it is to be called." The book urged visitors to see the Indian exhibit, warning that "it is more than probable that the World's Columbian exposition will furnish the last opportunity for an acquaintance with the 'noble red-man' before he achieves annihilation, or at least loss of identity."

The Indian presence at the 1903 Chicago centennial celebration is described in a variety of sources. See David Beck, *The Chicago American Indian Community,* 47–48, and Chicago newspapers. For example, the *Chicago Daily Tribune* ran at least fourteen articles and cartoons between September 25 and October 1, 1903, relating to the Indian participation in that event.

11. For a biography of Montezuma, see Peter Iverson, *Carlos Montezuma and the Changing World of American Indians* (Albuquerque: University of New Mexico Press, 1982). The three collections of papers on Carlos Montezuma are *Carlos Montezuma Papers, 1892–1937* at the State Historical Society of Wisconsin, also on microfilm; John William Larner, Jr., ed., *The Papers of Carlos Montezuma, M.D.*, microfilm (Wilmington, Del.: Scholarly Resources, 1983); and Montezuma Papers, Ayer Modern Manuscripts (Chicago: Newberry Library). See also David Beck, "American Indians in Chicago Since 1893: Selected Sources," in Terry Straus, ed., *Indians of the Chicago Area*, 2d ed. (Chicago: NAES College Press, 1990), 170–71; David Beck, "The 1904 Train Wreck," *NAES RULE* 35 (September 1987); and Beck, "How Chicago American Indian Organizations," 4–5.

12. Minutes of Indian Fellowship League meeting, October 15, 1920, handwritten, 20 pages, Indian Fellowship League Folder, Welfare Council of Metropolitan Chicago Box 246, Chicago Historical Society Manuscript Collections; Rosalyn R. LaPier, "'Pipe of Peace Nearly Out at Paleface Feast': Indian Interest Groups in Chicago and the End of Assimilationist Policy in America," master's thesis, DePaul University, draft, pp. 11–28.

13. Reports of Work of the Indian Council Fire, May 1932–February 1933, and May 1933–February 1934, Century of Progress, Indian Council Fire Papers, University of Illinois at Chicago Special Collections; Lapier, "Pipe of Peace Nearly Out," 29–49, 68. For brief biographies of two Indian people who attended Indian boarding schools and then moved to Chicago where they assumed leadership roles in the community, see Rosalyn LaPier, "'We are not savages, but a civilized race': Scott Henry Peters and His Attempts to Change the Image of Indians," paper presented at the Great Lakes History Conference, October 1992; and Rosalyn LaPier, "Francis M. Cayou: Athlete at Carlisle Indian School," presented at the 1993 Annual Meeting of the American Society of Ethnohistory, at Indiana University, November 4–6, 1993.

14. Kenneth R. Philp, "Stride toward Freedom: The Relocation of Indians to Cities, 1952–1960," *Western Historical Quarterly* 16:2 (April 1985): 179. On federal policy in this period, see Donald L. Fixico, *Termination and Relocation: Federal Indian Policy, 1945–1960* (Albuquerque: University of New Mexico Press, 1986) and Larry W. Burt, *Tribalism in Crisis: Federal Indian Policy, 1953–1961* (Albuquerque: University of New Mexico Press, 1982).

15. Robert V. Dumont, Jr., "Chicago 1973—Notes from a Visit," typed manuscript, NAES College Library, pp. 2–3.

16. Chauncina White Horse, "The Indians of Chicago: A Perspective," typed manuscript, NAES College Library, p. 86; Donald L. Fixico with the assistance of Lucille St. Germaine, ed., "Native Voices in the City: The Chicago American Indian Oral History Project," unpublished manuscript, Community Archives of NAES College, pp. 17–19.

17. Fixico with St. Germaine, pp. 8–21.

18. Others relocated a second time to other cities which they found more to their liking.

19. See Willard LaMere, "History of Indians in Chicago," audiocassette tape of lecture for course of same title, 10–9–79 in NAES College Library, partially transcribed; Chicago Oral History Project Transcript 009, interview of Willard LaMere by Claire Young, January 16, 1983; and Chicago Oral History Project Transcript 016, interview of Susan Power by David R. Miller, September 26, 1983, pp. 5–6. Chicago Oral History Project transcripts are held by both the Newberry Library and the NAES College Library.

20. Dumont, p. 3; David Beck, "Relocation in Chicago," *NAES RULE* 42 (Summer 1993), 5–7; Fixico, *Termination and Relocation*, p. 134. See also Elaine M. Neils, *Reservation to City, Indian Migration and Federal Relocation* (Chicago: University of Chicago Department of Geography Research Paper No. 131, 1971).

21. See Dumont's discussion of the role of the Native American Committee in the early 1970s, for example.

22. Rosalyn R. LaPier, "Chicago's American Indian Community: A Demographic Report Based on the 1990 Census," unpublished manuscript, 1994, NAES College Library.

23. Calculations made from numbers in 1990 Census Equal Employment Opportunity CD ROM File; 1970s information from Dumont, p. 4.

24. George Cornell, ED349148, *American Indian Education in the Chicago Public Schools: A Review and Analysis of Relevant Data and Issues* (Chicago: NAES College Press, 1992), 36–38; Branda Carl, RC019369, *American Indian Education in the Chicago Public Schools: Another Look* (Chicago: NAES College Student Field Project, May 1993), 13–14. Document available through ERIC. Both studies warn that the small population of Native Americans in the Chicago Public Schools can cause a higher probability of statistical error: Cornell, p. 40; Carl, p. 16.

25. Cornell, pp. 41, 46–47. Emphasis in original. Document available in ERIC.

26. Carl, p. 1.

27. Personal observation.

28. Previous to this NAES granted a bachelor's degree through Antioch College in Yellow Springs, Ohio, which had an outreach program that helped a variety of communities in the United States to develop higher education institutions relevant to their needs. NAES is currently the only remaining private, Indian-operated B.A. college in the United States.

3

Irene Villanueva_____

The Voices of Chicano Families
Life Stories, Maintaining Bilingualism, and Cultural Awareness

Much research has been conducted on language attrition, the diminution of bilingualism across time, and the fact that within three generations of migrating to the United States the native language is eliminated (see Fishman et al. 1966; Gal 1979; Grosjean 1982; Hakuta 1982: Hernández-Chávez 1978; Lieberson et al. 1975: Pease-Alvarez 1993: Sánchez 1983: Veltman 1979; Wong-Fillmore 1992). While this observation may be accurate, it neglects an important issue, the parents' dilemma of maintaining competence in Spanish and English. Parents often struggle to maintain first language competence for themselves and their children. In this chapter, I will describe these dilemmas and the strategies that parents employ to maintain bilingualism and the forces which impinge upon them, making it difficult to do so. Also, the voices of the parents provide their perspectives on cultural and linguistic border crossing (Hicks 1988; Giroux 1992; McLaren 1993).

A conflicting view of this reality is often cited by English Only advocates who are concerned about cultural assimilation. US English, an offshoot of the Federation for American Immigration Reform (FAIR), promotes tighter restrictions on immigration, organized around the supposed need to establish English as the official language in the United States. Their efforts are based on the misconception that recent immigrants are indifferent toward learning English and that the use of English is threatened by the sheer numbers of speakers of other languages. In fact, nothing could be farther from the truth. Spanish-speaking immigrants, for instance, are known to convert to English after residing for a number of years in the United States, with each successive generation shifting more and more in that direction (Veltman 1988; Sánchez 1983). In this monolingual context, institutionalized efforts toward maintaining a dual language facility among youth are often actually nothing more than programs which help to make the transition to English (Hakuta 1982).

Given the emphasis on English and the tendency toward monolingualism in the United States, I will focus on a small group of highly educated Chicano parents and their attempts to secure bilingualism for their children. I will explore their goals for their children regarding the maintenance and development of two languages. I will also present the dilemmas they have encountered related to their objective of developing bilingualism and biliteracy in their children.

FAMILY PROFILES

Seven Chicano families in Southern California participated in this study, including 17 children, 13 parents, and 18 grandparents. Interviews were conducted and videotapes of family interaction were gathered over a period of two years. Although some of the grandparents were deceased or not living in the household, background information was obtained on all. Only six of the grandparents were born in the United States. Out of the parents, eight were first generation born in Mexico, and six were second and third generation in the United States. The majority of the parents and grandparents lived in an urban environment. Two of the U.S.-born parents lived in a rural community until they graduated from high school, upon which they then moved to the city. Two of the Mexican-born parents also had rural experiences before moving to urban settings in Mexico and then immigrating to the United States as adolescents.

Formal education was also a significant role in the lives of all family members. While two of the first generation parents entered the United States young enough to begin their formal education in this country, five others received their elementary education in Mexico, varying from two to seven years. All of these first-generation parents either began or continued their formal education in the United States. Parents who participated in this study all graduated from high school. Of the thirteen high school graduates, five had some community college experience, while eight graduated from the university. In addition, six of the eight college graduates, most of them women, continued their formal education, receiving either a credential or a graduate degree. For the most part, the parents held skilled and professional positions.

While this sample may represent highly educated professional Chicano families, we must also acknowledge their uniqueness. All but one of the parents in this study who had college experience was also the first generation in their family to have graduated from high school and attended college. They were also often either the only one or the first of their siblings to have gone to college. This group of Chicano families is even more unusual when compared to the educational experience of the grandparents' generation. Of the grandparents, the majority had limited formal education. Many, for example, had an eighth-grade education or less, while only some graduated from high school. A very small portion of the grandparents received any post-secondary education, and those who did—one male and one female—pursued college as adults. For the most part, the grandparents worked in unskilled and skilled occupations, such as that of farmworker, cook, housekeeper, printer, firefighter, and so on. Only two of the grandparents held professional occupations.

This group of families is not representative of the Chicano or Mexican community. They are exceptions, representing the few educated and professional Chicanos in the United States. However, their family experiences and interactions with their own children are important practices, and when we compare them to family practices from other ethnic and social class groups, they may not be so unusual after all. The fact that these parents learned skills from their parents which they were able to apply to their school experience as well as transfer to their own children is important. Also, the fact that they may have applied those skills in different ways than their siblings is something which many of them acknowledge and something which they also have passed on to their younger siblings. As grandfather Talamantes said, *"Cada familia es un mundo"* (Each family is a world in itself). This idea reinforces the notion of acknowledging the differences as well as the similarities in the individual and not assuming that all children will follow the same course because they come from the same family or culture. In these seven families of urban and rural experiences, of Mexican- and U.S.-born parents and grandparents, individual siblings have followed very different paths.

GOALS AND DILEMMAS IN MAINTAINING LANGUAGE AND DEVELOPING BILINGUALISM

Six of the seven families indicated that Spanish was the native language of the children. These bilingual parents acknowledged that they made a conscious decision to establish Spanish as their children's native language. They stated cultural as well as functional reasons for maintaining Spanish. Most of them agreed with Jeanne's rationale:

> Para apreciar la cultura, y también. . . . pa' que pueda hablar con sus abuelos.
> [In order to appreciate the culture, and also, . . . to be able to speak with her grandparents.]

These parents made a conscious effort to create a bilingual environment during their children's early childhood years. For example, if the mother worked outside the home, the parents provided either a Spanish-speaking nanny, grandmother, or another member of the extended family to care for the children during the day. Thus, thirteen of the seventeen children were native Spanish speakers and all of them had contact with grandparents and extended family. These children also had exposure to English through formal preschool experience as well as informal experiences and interaction with bilingual members of the extended family, friends, in the neighborhood, television, and so on.

The children's bilingualism appeared to be important to these parents. In addition to a stated goal of native language maintenance, the parents expressed concern about their children's development of Spanish. For example, the parents of three-year-old Analisa acknowledged that they made a conscious effort to speak only Spanish with her and to provide opportunities for her to interact with her monolingual Spanish-speaking grandparents, with a great grandmother, and other bilingual relatives.

> J: Pues, empezamos hablando puro español con ella en la casa o fuera de la casa. Compramos libros, discos y la llevamos con sus abuelos para, pa' que habla más con ellos.
>
>   [Well, we began speaking only Spanish with her at home or outside of the house. We buy (Spanish) books, records, and we take her with her grandparents in order to, in order for her to speak more with them.]

In addition to these experiences with Spanish, all of the children also had interaction in English. For example, Analisa had learned English through her interaction with older English-speaking cousins, as well as a high-school-age babysitter, people in the neighborhood, and from watching television:

> Q: Y ¿dónde aprendió el inglés?
>   [And where did she learn English?]

> J: Primero pienso, con, pues, con sus primos que no hablan español. Y luego, con la primera muchacha que la cuidaba, Christine. Y después, pues con, como ella anda con nosotros todo el tiempo, fuera de la casa, . . . habla con todos, en el banco, en el restaurante, en la oficina. . . . Y también, pienso con, también con *Sesame Street*, y *Mr. Rogers.*
>
>   [First, I think with her cousins who don't speak Spanish. And then, with the first girl who took care of her, Christine. And, later, well, with, since she's always with us, outside of the house, . . . she talks with everyone, in the bank, in the restaurant, at the office. . . . And also, I think with, also with *Sesame Street* and *Mr. Rogers.*]

The Sánchez family also acknowledged that none of the children's cousins spoke Spanish. Thus, the children's interaction at family functions were limited to Spanish with grandparents and other adults, and English with their peers.

Q: ¿Con quién hablan inglés?
     [With whom do they speak English?]

T: Con los amigos de la escuela.
     [With their friends from school.]

F: En la escuela, con nosotros, con sus primos.
     [In school, with us, with their cousins.]

T: Sí con sus primos, puro inglés.
     [Yes, with their cousins, only in English.]

F: Mis sobrinos no hablan español.
     [My nieces and nephews do not speak Spanish.]

As the children began to acquire the second language, it became apparent that the forces outside of the home were strong. Even for three-year-old Analisa, who had no formal preschool experience or English instruction, both parents had become aware of her preference for English and were consciously striving to maintain Spanish as a means of communication in the home.

Q: Y la niña, ¿siempre habla español o inglés?
     [And the child, does she always speak Spanish or English?]

J: Ahora, el inglés es el idioma preferido de ella. Sí puede hablar español.
     Sí entiende todo, pero . . .
     [Now, English is her preferred language. She can speak Spanish. She understands everything, but . . .]

In fact, her father made a more concentrated effort to not only provide Spanish input for Analisa, but he also expected her to speak only Spanish to him.

H: Ese es muy difícil. Porque, 'horita, le gusta hablar en inglés. Y cuando habla conmigo, yo todo el tiempo le pregunto, que me debe de hablar en español. Y cada vez que empieza a hablar en inglés, umm, . . . yo le pregunto a ella que me debe de hablar en español. A primero, le pregunto, y si empieza hablar en inglés otra vez, le pregunto otra vez. A veces, antes se ponía un poco enfadada, porque le estaba preguntando cada, cada vez que me decía algo en inglés, yo le decía a ella—pos dígame en español. Pero como los últimos tres o cuatro meses, ya no se enoja. Ya no se enfada conmigo, porque ya sabe. Empieza algo en inglés, se olvida, le digo—pues dígame en español. Y luego, ella lo dice en español.
     [That's very difficult. Because, now, she likes to speak in English. And

when she speaks with me, I always ask her to speak with me in Spanish. And each time that she begins to speak in English, umm, . . . I ask her to speak to me in Spanish. At first, I ask her, and if she begins to speak in English again, I ask her again. Sometimes, before she would become a little angry, because I was asking her each, each time that she would tell me something in English, I would tell her "Well, tell me in Spanish." But about the last three or four months, she doesn't get angry anymore. She doesn't get angry with me, because now she knows. She begins something in English, she forgets, I tell her, "Tell me in Spanish." And then, she says it in Spanish.]

As the children got older the tendency to speak English was stronger. Yet the Sánchez family also agreed that their children, Maya and Jojo, spoke only Spanish to the baby, but that they had to remind the children to respond in Spanish when they spoke to them.

Q: Los niños hablan español o inglés?
      [Do the children speak Spanish or English?]

F: Entre ellos mismos, inglés.
      [Between themselves, English.]

A: Y con Uds?
      [And with your parents?]

F: Si los acordamos que tiene que ser español, hablan español, si no, hablan. . . . Pero al niño, al bebe le hablan español, los dos.
      [If we remind them that it has to be Spanish, they speak Spanish, if not, they speak. . . . But to the baby, to the baby, they speak to him in Spanish, both of them.]

Thus, while Spanish was spoken in the home and appeared to be the native language of the children, it was used through the children's infancy and early childhood years by all members of the family.

According to six of the seven sets of parents, the intrusion of English began at the preschool age. As the children began their formal schooling, the emphasis on English presented a dilemma for these parents who were struggling to provide a bilingual atmosphere and maintain Spanish in the home. Delia discussed the difficulties of sustaining bilingualism among her three children, their language development and societal emphasis on one language over another, as well as the children's awareness of and concern about the dominance of one language over another and their conscious effort to retain Spanish.

Q: ¿Con quién hablas inglés?
      [With whom do you speak English?]

D: Okay, hablo en inglés con mis compañeros del trabajo, con mis amigos, a veces en inglés y español mezclado, umm, con mis niños, la mayoría del tiempo, ahora que ya requieren en su trabajo de escuela que les hable más en inglés para explicarles. Ummm, ellos también están dejando un tantito el español, ya me han dicho algo. Me dicen,—Oyen, se nos está olvidando, vale más que hablamos más español en la casa.

[Okay, I speak English with my friends from work, with my friends, sometimes it's English and Spanish mixed, umm, with my children, most of the time, now that they're required in their school work that I speak with them more in English in order to explain to them. Ummm, they're also starting to lose a little bit of Spanish, they've already told me. They say, "Listen, we're forgetting it, we better speak more Spanish at home."]

D: Pero, ya, porque en la escuela les exigen mucho el inglés, empezaron más hablar inglés, y practicarlo para, pos, sobresalir en escuela y dejaron poco a poquito de hablar español y ahora se están dando cuenta que no han hablado mucho en español, ni practicado, ni comunicado con mucha gente en la misma cantidad que hacían antes. Hmhmm.

[But, now, because in the school English is emphasized, they began to speak more English, and to practice it in order to, well, succeed in school and they little by little they stopped speaking Spanish and now, they're starting to realize that they haven't spoken much in Spanish, nor practiced, nor communicated with very many people, in the same amount as they used to before. Hmm.]

Two other parents spoke of their children's inclination to speak more English and less Spanish. Bertha and Francisca said their children were native Spanish speakers until they began school. However, by the time they reached ages eight and ten, English had become their dominant language. This shift was attributed to the fact that Spanish has predominantly informal and oral functions while English has formal and academic functions.

Q: [Los niños] ¿Pueden leer y escribir en español?
[Can the children read and write in Spanish?]

B: No, no pueden leer y escribir [en español]. Pueden leer poquito. Pero, escribirlo, no. Hay muchos factores aquí en los Estados Unidos que, realmente dificulta lo que, la razón los niños no escriban y lean el español, a menos de que sean mandados a una escuela donde se les enseña el espanõl pero realmente en todo lo que está alrededor es en inglés para ellos. Entonces tienden ellos a dominar más el inglés. Es común.

[No, they can't read and write (in Spanish). They can read it a little. But, not write it. There are many factors here in the United States that really make it difficult, the reason that the children don't write and read Spanish, unless they were to be sent to a school where Spanish is taught, but really, everything that surrounds them is in English. So, they tend to use English more. It's common.]

The shift to English dominance also corresponds to the fact that in the Southwest, bilingualism is primarily dynamic and Spanish proficiency is primarily oral rather than literate (Sánchez 1983, 46).

REPLACING THE NATIVE LANGUAGE WITH A SECOND LANGUAGE

Early in this study, two families (Reyes/Fuentes and Sánchez) with preschool age children stated that they were seeking bilingual preschools, while the Carrera family decided to move to a more "bilingual" neighborhood in order for the children to hear Spanish in their environment. However, these families acknowledged that they were researching the availability of bilingual preschool programs and found that the emphasis was on teaching English as a second language rather than development of the native language in a bilingual environment.

> H: Esas, estamos buscando uno. Pero todavía no hallamos un lugar que podemos decir que va ir allí. Sí queremos un programa que enseña inglés y español.
> [Those, we're looking for one. But we still haven't found a place that we can say that she's going to. We do want a program that teaches English and Spanish.]
> J: No hay programa bilingüe aquí, programas bilingües aquí. Sí hay, pues no, no son. Como Head Start, esos no son bilingües. Son para que ellos aprenden inglés.
> [There isn't a bilingual program here. There are, but no, they're not. Like Head Start, they're not bilingual. They're for them to learn English.]

Although they continued to search for a bilingual program until Analisa was four years old, they didn't consider those available to be true bilingual programs since program goals were not to develop or maintain bilingualism, rather they were to transition to English.

DEVELOPING LITERACY SKILLS IN SPANISH

While the Reyes/Fuentes family contemplated the possibility of living in a Spanish-speaking country in order for Analisa to develop her bilingualism and become biliterate, and the Sánchez family considered enrolling the children in a Mexican school in order to develop literacy skills in Spanish, the Carrera family had in fact lived in Mexico for two years. As Carla was beginning kindergarten, Jorge was entering second grade, and Tino was approaching junior high school, the family decided to enroll the children in Mexican schools in order for the three children to receive native language instruction and learn to read in Spanish before returning to the United States and continuing their education. Delia described the children's educational experience in the United States and Mexico.

> Q: . . . cuando empezó la escuela, no estaba en un programa bilingüe Jorge, o Carla, o sí?
> [When they started school, were Jorge or Carla in a bilingual program?]
> D: Jorge, estaba en un programa bilingüe porque yo lo llevaba a la escuela. Entonces él fue al kinder, y a primero en español casi todo aquí. Lo querían poner en inglés, porque en realidad ya hablaba bastante inglés, más que los otros niños, verdad? Pero, yo les decía que no, porque yo quería que estuviera en ese programa. Carla, empezó pues la preprimaria en Guadalajara e hizo kinder, pues es el kinder, la preprimaria, y primero en Guadalajara. Entonces, cuando regresamos estaba a como mitad del año, pero de primer año. Entonces, la pusimos en inglés, porque no teníamos otra a ese tiempo. Y luego la cambié cuando empecé a trabajar otra vez, como yo tenía un permiso del trabajo, cuando empecé a trabajar otra vez, entonces, la llevaba conmigo y la puse en un programa bilingüe. Y otra vez, me decían—habla bastante inglés. Y les decía—a mi no me importa, aquí la quiero. Y ella puede ir a otros cursos y hacer el inglés, si quiere—, verdad? Y le puede hacer en diferente nivel, porque en realidad no necesita el inglés que están enseñando a los otros niños que estaban en su salón, verdad? Estaba más avanzada. Entonces, no más me veían media rara, pero yo les dije que eso es lo que quería, y pues, sí, así la hicieron. Pero, luego, tuvimos que cambiar de allí también, verdad. Entonces, ahora, está solamente en inglés.
> [Jorge was in a bilingual program because I used to take him to school. So he went to kindergarten, and to first in Spanish, almost all here. They wanted to put him in English, because in reality, he already was speaking a lot of English, more than the other children. But, I told them no, because I wanted him to be in that (bilingual) program. Carla, began prefirst in Guadalajara and she did kindergarten, well, it's kindergarten, prefirst, and first grade in Guadalajara. Then, when we returned she was at about mid year, but of first grade. Then we put her in English, because we didn't have another (bilingual class) at the time. And then I changed her when I began to work again, since, I had a leave of absence, when I began to work again, then I used take her with me and I put her in the bilingual program. And again, they used to tell me, "She speaks enough, she speaks enough English." And I would tell them, "It doesn't matter to me, I want her here (in the bilingual

program). And she can go to other classes to do her English lessons if she wants to, right? And she can do it at a different level, because in reality she doesn't need the English (ESL) that's being taught to the other children who were in her class, right?" She was more advanced. Then they would just look at me rather strangely. But, I told them that that was what I wanted, and well, yes, that's the way they did it. But then, we had to move from there also, right? So, now, she's in English only.]

As Delia explained, when they returned to the United States at mid-year Carla was placed in an "English-only" first-grade class because there was no bilingual program in the neighborhood school. In second and third grade, however, she was placed in a bilingual program and transitioned to English in fourth grade. Jorge had been in bilingual kindergarten and first grade in the United States, continued his Spanish instruction in Mexico for grades two and three, and was placed in an "English only" fourth grade on his return. Although Tino had also been enrolled in the Mexican schools, he had never been in a bilingual program in the United States and continued his high school education in the regular English program. Thus, both Carla and Jorge were transferred to all English classes by fourth grade. This placement corresponds to the transitional type of bilingual programs in the United States which emphasizes transition to English rather than the development of true bilingualism.

The importance of bilingualism and biliteracy is a dilemma for parents who seek to maintain and develop the native language of their children with little support from society and educational institutions. Thus, the learning and development of Spanish as well as English, and becoming biliterate, are considered important goals of these families. Javier spoke of the children learning to read in Spanish and credited Delia's efforts in teaching them.

Q: ¿Quién les enseñó a los niños a leer el español?
      [Who taught your children to read in Spanish?]

J: El español yo creo que Delia tuvo mucho que ver con enseñarles eso, a leer español. No nada más eso, pero estudieron en la escuela en México tres an, no, dos años, en escuela en México y allí pues aprendieron también bastante, a leer español.

      [Spanish (reading), I think that Delia had much to do with teaching them that, to read in Spanish. Not just that, but they studied in school in Mexico three, no, two years, in school in Mexico, and there, well, they learned a lot also, to read Spanish.]

None of the parents stated that they believe that their children must reject their native language and culture in order to succeed. On the contrary, they emphasized the belief that their children need to become bilingual, biliterate, and bicultural in order to succeed in the United States. All of the parents declared their rationale for maintaining bilingualism as instrumental and utilitarian, in that it is necessary in order to converse with the grandparents and other monolingual Spanish-speaking relatives. As Javier put it,

> J: . . . por la razón de que vivimos en una area predominantemente bilingüe y a parte de eso también por la cuestión de que muchos de nuestros familiares todavía hablan español primeramente.
> [because we live in a predominantly bilingual area and besides that also because many of our relatives are still native Spanish speakers.]

Although they use Spanish in the home and in their work, these parents found that it is difficult to maintain bilingualism in their children. Those who sought bilingual preschools for their children were unsuccessful. In fact, the parents discovered that rather than working to develop and strengthen the children's native language, most of the preschools, like the elementary schools, emphasize ESL instruction and treat the bilingual child as requiring remedial education. Thus, these parents found it necessary to prepare their children for preschool by either keeping their children at home in a predominantly Spanish environment until about age four, while gradually increasing the use of English at home and providing a familiar bilingual environment until the child could accommodate to an all-English setting. Those parents who sent their first child to preschool or Head Start were discouraged by the emphasis on English. In retrospect, they consider problems the children had in school a result of not having fully developed their linguistic and academic foundation in the native language. Other parents provided what they felt was a strong foundation in Spanish, preparing their children with "readiness" concepts and an awareness that instruction would be conducted in English. In addition, five of the seven families had researched the preschool and elementary schools before enrolling their children, so that while they may not have been able to fulfill a bilingual need, they also sought schools which would provide a positive, creative, affective, and nurturing learning environment. Thus, was the introduction and intrusion of English in the children's life.

While the schools emphasize transition to English, these parents have sought other means of encouraging and developing their children's bilingualism. In addition to encouraging academic success which is necessarily in English, the parents have also provided interaction in Spanish at home, as well as with grandparents and other Spanish-speaking adults. These parents and their associates also serve as models of educated and bilingual professionals. They work in occupations in which knowledge of Spanish is regarded as an asset, for example, the legal profession, education, and in community or social service agencies. Thus, the children are in contact with positive role models who acknowledge their bilingualism and culture as resources and qualities of which they are proud.

EXTRACURRICULAR ACTIVITIES IN A BILINGUAL BICULTURAL ENVIRONMENT

In addition to the home environment and extended family, the parents also provided extracurricular activities for the children which promote and encourage the use of Spanish for cultural activities—music, dance, arts, and sports. These organized activities provide opportunities for the children to participate and interact in Spanish with other bilingual children and families.

All parents and children are involved in the teaching and learning of culture. These children, because of their interaction with their parents, extended families, friends, and classmates, were also becoming bicultural. Their parents consciously selected various cultural experiences, some of which may be more mainstream, others more Chicano or Mexican, and all of which the parents believe are important for the child. For example, in addition to organized activities such as soccer and the San Diego/Tijuana children's choir, Claudia and José also took piano lessons, and were involved in Brownies and Boy Scouts.

Another example of the cultural experiences some of these parents provided for their children occurred in the Carrera family. They chose to live in Mexico when their children were in primary school in order to provide cultural experiences, as well as educational instruction in Spanish, and a sense of identity for the children. While they lived there, Tino participated in folkloric dance while Carla was involved in gymnastics. Since they returned to the United States Tino and Jorge participated in wrestling and karate and Carla also took part in karate. Rather than assume that the wrestling and karate activities were strictly mainstream, however, a look at the neighborhood and other children in the groups revealed that many Mexican children also participated. The activities also took on a more Mexican flavor when the families came together for team competitions, tournaments, picnics, and so forth. Because of the families involved, the conversations were in Spanish, and Mexican food was served at the picnics. The use of Spanish at these events was culturally important for several reasons. First, language denotes culture. In addition, the fact that the families chose to speak Spanish at these functions is a sign of solidarity and group membership. The parents demonstrated their involvement and interest in their children's activities, while at the same time representing the Chicano and Mexican community.

In addition to the organized activities—soccer, children's choir, folkloric dance, and so on—all of the families also participated in social functions and cultural traditions such as weddings, baptisms, birthday parties, and family gatherings which provided much of their children's social and cultural experiences. Thus, the parents were striving to provide positive experiences with Mexican cultural traditions as well as organized mainstream activities in order for the children to be able to function, and indeed, succeed in both cultures.

Every one of these families also strived to retain their unique culture and transmit it to the next generation. Their efforts at providing Chicano and Mexican cultural experiences for their children were varied, and included use of the Spanish language, association with other Latinos, and participation in Chicano and Mexican cultural events in the community. Efforts were made to include the children in the extended family and gatherings with older Spanish-speaking family members. The children participating in this study were also involved in numerous cultural and social activities in the Chicano community, such as Hispanic Future Leaders workshops and summer programs for teens; community cultural celebrations of Mexican holidays; extracurricular activities such as soccer; children's choir in which children from Tijuana and San Diego participated together; music appreciation and familiarity of Mexican music; as well as daily preparation of traditional foods.

These families consider their goal of maintaining bilingualism an important one. Having attended school in the United States, the parents realize the pressures of society to conform to an English-speaking world. Recognizing the realities of schooling in the United States to succeed in school, their children have become English-dominant in order to succeed in school. Yet they have also been able to maintain and use Spanish in a variety of situations outside of school.

CULTURAL IDENTITY VERSUS ACCULTURATION AND ASSIMILATION

English may be the dominant language of the children because of the emphasis on English in the schools and society. The children nevertheless are developing a cultural awareness and identity as Mexican or Chicano. In contrast to some members of their extended families who not only lose Spanish language skills, but also desire to assimilate into the mainstream society, these parents worked at maintaining their language as well as their culture. They identified themselves as Mexican or Chicano and consider themselves bicultural in that they were able to function both in the mainstream society as well as in the Chicano community.

During the children's early years, their cultural awareness may be regarded as the parents' teachings. However, those children beyond ten years of age, especially junior high and high school age, voiced their awareness and sense of cultural identity. Because of the children's participation in family and community cultural activities and events, for instance, ethnic and cultural celebrations, as well as their participation in family discussions regarding social and political issues, the children identified themselves with the Chicano community.

For example, fifteen-year-old Florencia described a relative as one who "doesn't have the culture," intimating that this cousin does not identity herself as Chicana. On another occasion, Florencia related a story about an incident with a high school counselor in which she and another cousin were counseled to take an "easy class" rather than a college preparatory course. Florencia decided for herself which course she needed in order to later be able to satisfy college admissions requirements and proceeded to counsel her cousin. However, the academic counselor directed her to leave the office and her cousin was made to stay alone with the advisor. Florencia interpreted the interview and "guidance" of the counselor as discriminatory based on their surnames rather than academic achievement or potential.

In the same family, the following year, upon Florencia's return from Europe as an exchange student, thirteen-year-old Daniela proposed that she might follow in her sister's footsteps and become a foreign exchange student in another three years. When asked where she would like to study, she stated, "It has to be a Spanish-speaking country 'cause that's the language." Thus, Spanish was both the language that she identified with and the one that she recognized she needed to develop.

Another example of the children's awareness of cultural identity was that of José Antonio. When he was twelve years old, a number of children at his school were interviewed to participate in the filming of an educational program on early California history. José related that he correctly determined that the interviewer was looking for someone to play the part of the child/narrator. Thus, he offered information about his family, his knowledge of Spanish and English, and demonstrated pride in his Mexican heritage. He was selected as the narrator of the program.

Most of these children had experienced situations in which they were required to identify themselves with an ethnic group and they identified themselves as Mexican. Also, as many other children, they had experienced discrimination and prejudice, and they were able to identify social injustice as institutional and not only affecting themselves as individuals but all others with whom they identified. For example, in seventh grade, Jorge wrote an autobiography in which he discussed his personal struggle to maintain a high academic standing as it conflicted with peer pressure and his personal need for group membership.

These children have been provided with cultural and academic experiences and resources which strengthens their cultural identity. Their bilingualism is still developing and while it has not been supported in the schools, they have a resource which they know will later be recognized and beneficial to them. Because they have a linguistic foundation in Spanish, it will easily be developed as they continue their academic careers.

Their parents are contributing to their education and preparation in ways which the schools are not aware of, as I discovered through interviews with the teachers. The parents serve as mediators for their children and the children are approaching an age at which they themselves are beginning to recognize and acknowledge their parents' influence. A postcard from Florencia, while an exchange student in Europe, acknowledged her parents' efforts to provide her with greater opportunities as well as a sense of responsibility toward her community and society. The parents serve as models for their children and the Chicano community by their involvement in their occupations and community, as well as by their awareness of and involvement in social and political issues. Thus, the children's social and cultural awareness will allow them to identify with the Chicano community, to continue as their parents, to work to create a better society for the community as a whole.

CONCLUSION

The parents in this study have been able to develop a degree of bilingualism for their children. The majority of the parents were conscious of their efforts to provide a Spanish-speaking environment for the early childhood years in order for the children to be able to communicate with the grandparents and other Spanish-speaking adults. The children became aware of their bilingual abilities and used them in appropriate situations, distinguishing when to speak Spanish and when to use English. However, by about age three, or contact with a preschool experience, the parents were aware of a conflict between their personal goals of bilingualism, the societal goal of English dominance, and the educational goal of transition to English. The children soon became dominant in English, acknowledging its academic functions in school and using Spanish for informal and social functions. According to Fishman (1971), the diglossic situation which these families foster contributes to bilingualism, that is, English use for formal and academic domains, and Spanish use for informal and intimate domains. Without diglossia, "bilingualism is unstable and usually results in a shift to monolingualism in the more prestigious language" (Hakuta 1982, 188).

These parents are clearly extraordinary in their goals of maintaining bilingualism and cultural identity. In a society where one language, English, has more prestige than another, and where "success" is judged in terms of attaining proficiency in that language as a means of assimilating to the mainstream culture, these parents have taken extreme steps in their efforts to maintain their language and culture. They spoke Spanish in the home almost exclusively during the early childhood years of their children. They provided a Spanish-speaking grandmother or nanny as the surrogate mother when the mother worked outside of the home. They work in positions as role models, that is, lawyers, teachers, and in community and social service, and use their bilingual skills in their occupations. They sought bilingual preschool experiences for their children. They provide trips to Spanish-speaking countries for their children and enrolled their children in Spanish-speaking schools. And they live in a geographical area which is close to their extended family for reinforcement and experience in a bilingual environment.

When one considers the fact that, in general, the native language is eliminated within three generations of migrating to the United States, these second- and third-generation parents are working against all odds to provide a bilingual environment for their children. In fact, even within their own families, these particular parents are unusual in their efforts to maintain Spanish and their cultural identity. As one grandparent (Sánchez) acknowledged the loss of Spanish in his family,

> The only thing that we were lax, was we didn't push the Spanish. See, I regret that today because well, it wasn't pushed on me. . . . I admire Tony when he insisted the kids speak Spanish at home.

Tony is the only one of his children, and Maya, Jojo, and Michael, the only ones of his grandchildren who were fluent in Spanish and able to communicate in Spanish with their grandparents and great-grandparents. Thus, even within their extended families, these parents acknowledged that their goals and efforts for language maintenance are unusual in that the cousins of their children are predominantly monolingual English speakers.

In spite of these efforts to make Spanish the native language of the children, and creating an environment in which the children would be encouraged to become bilingual, all of these children were sensitive to the outside forces which emphasize the dominance of English in the society. Thus, once they became enrolled in school and participated in an academic environment which emphasized English, they quickly became English-dominant. Although most of the children have not developed Spanish academically, that is, literacy in Spanish, they have maintained oral proficiency in Spanish.

In addition to the bilingual experiences provided for the children to maintain Spanish, the parents provided a variety of cultural experiences for their children. The children's early exposure to Mexican and Chicano practices and activities provided positive experiences in the Chicano community and enabled the children to identify themselves as members of the community. Thus, as the children grew, they began to voice their cultural awareness and identify with the community in a positive way. The children had a positive attitude about their cultural identity. In fact, their cultural pride and self-esteem was evident by the way in which they identified others as lacking "the culture," the way in which they volunteered to demonstrate their knowledge of their heritage to strangers, and their awareness of social issues, such as discrimination and inequality which effect the community as a whole as well as themselves as students.

It is not simply their maintenance of Spanish and cultural awareness which makes these children extraordinary. As Gardner and Lambert found (1972), language and cultural maintenance may actually contribute to pride and self-esteem, which in turn contribute to success in the second language. In addition, Cummins (1982) maintains that the development of competence in the native language is essential for success in cognitive development (see also Cummins 1980; 1978; and Krashen 1981). Thus, the linguistic and cultural maintenance together with the academic success of the children and their involvement in extracurricular activities provided them with cultural capital which they had already begun to utilize in their interaction with the mainstream society. Because these children have been able to maintain Spanish, develop a cultural awareness and identity, while at the same time developing an awareness of larger social issues, they have also set goals for themselves. Their parents, as the first generation to attend college, did not consider themselves prepared for college. However, these children have been prepared by their parents to expect to attend college, to carry on the legacy of a committed and concerned Chicano with a goal to create social change.

The voices of these Chicano families present their narratives and oral histories as presentations of self and a critical consciousness of their sociohistorical experience (see Saldívar 1990). Tierney (1993) spoke of the importance of collecting life histories in order to "document how we live now so that we might change how we live now" (p. 4). These families are doing both, relating their life histories and making changes in their daily lives. Their goals and efforts toward maintaining bilingualism illustrate a consciousness of identity, one that is successful in two languages and two cultural environments.

NOTE

I wish to acknowledge the University of California President's Dissertation Fellowship, and the University of California, San Diego, Chancellor's Office for their support. A version of this paper was presented for a symposium on Minority Narrative Voices of Interpretation and Critique, at the American Educational Research Association, San Francisco, April 1995.

REFERENCES

Cummins, James. 1978. "Educational Implications of Mother Tongue Maintenance in Minority Language Groups." *The Canadian Modern Language Review* 34: 395–416.

———. 1980. "The Cross-Lingual Dimensions of Language Proficiency: Implications for Bilingual Education and the Optimal Age Issue," *TESOL Quarterly* 14, 2 (June): 175–87.

———. 1981. "The Role of Primary Language Development in Promoting Educational Success for Language Minority Students." In *Schooling and Language Minority Students: A Theoretical Framework,* Los Angeles: California State Department of Education, Evaluation Dissemination and Assessment Center.

Fishman, J. A., V. C. Nahirny, J. E. Hofman, and R. G. Hayden. 1966. *Language Loyalty in the United States.* The Hague: Mouton and Company.

Gal, Susan. 1979. *Language Shift: Social Determinants of Linguistic Change in Bilingual Austria.* New York: Academic Press.

Gardner, Robert C., and Wallace E. Lambert. 1972. *Attitudes and Motivation in Second Language Learning.* Rowley, Mass.: Newbury House.

Giroux, Henry. 1992. *Border Crossings.* New York: Routledge.

Grosjean, F. 1982. *Life with Two Languages.* Cambridge: Harvard University Press.

Hakuta, Kenji. 1982. *Mirror of Language: The Debate on Bilingualism.* New York: Basic Books, Inc.

Hernández-Chávez, Eduardo. 1978. "Language Maintenance, Bilingual Education and Philosophies of Bilingualism in the United States." In James E. Alatis, ed., *Inter-*

national Dimensions of Bilingual Education. Washington, D.C.: Georgetown University Press.

Hicks, Emily D. 1988. "Deterritorialization and Border Writing." In Robert Merrill, ed., *Ethics/Aesthetics: Post-Modern Positions*, 47–58. Washington, D.C.: Maisonnueve Press.

Krashen, Stephen D. 1981. "Bilingual Education and Second Language Acquisition Theory." In *Schooling and Language Minority Students: A Theoretical Framework.* Los Angeles: California State Department of Education Evaluation Dissemination and Assessment Center.

Lieberson, S., G. Dalto, and M. E. Johnston. 1975. "The course of mother-tongue diversity in nations." *American Journal of Sociology* 81: 34–61.

McLaren, Peter. 1993. "Border Disputes: Multicultural Narrative, Identity Formation, and Critical Pedagogy in Postmodern America." In Daniel McLaughlin and William G. Tierney, eds., *Naming Silenced Lives: Personal Narratives and Processes of Educational Change,* 201–35. New York: Routledge.

Pease-Alvarez, Lucinda. 1993. "Moving In and Out of Bilingualism: Investigating Native Language Maintenance and Shift in Mexican-Descent Children." Santa Cruz, Calif.: National Center for Research on Cultural Diversity and Second Language Learning.

Sánchez, Rosaura. 1983. *Chicano Discourse: Socio-historic Perspectives.* Rowley, Mass.: Newbury House.

Saldívar, Ramon. 1990. *Chicano Narrative: The Dialectics of Difference.* Madison: University of Wisconsin Press.

Tierney, William G. 1993. "Introduction: Developing Archives of Resistance: Speak, Memory." In Daniel McLaughlin and William G. Tierney, eds., *Naming Silenced Lives: Personal Narratives and Processes of Educational Change,* 1–5. New York: Routledge.

Vasquez, O. A., L. Pease-Alvarez, and S. M. Shannon. 1994. *Pushing Boundaries: Language Socialization in a Mexican-Immigrant Community.* New York: Cambridge University Press.

Veltman, C. 1988. *The Future of the Spanish Language in the United States.* Washington, D.C.: Hispanic Policy Development Project.

———. 1979. *The Assimilation of American Language Minorities: Structure, Pace and Extent.* Washington, D.C.: National Center for Education Statistics.

Villanueva, Irene P. 1990. "Cultural Practices and Language Use: Three Generations of Change." Ph.D. dissertation, University of California, San Diego.

Wong-Fillmore, L. 1991. "When Learning a Second Language Means Losing the First." *Early Childhood Research Quarterly* 6: 323–46.

4

SIGNITHIA FORDHAM ⎯⎯⎯⎯⎯⎯⎯⎯⎯⎯⎯⎯⎯⎯⎯⎯⎯⎯⎯

"Those Loud Black Girls"
(Black) Women, Silence, and
Gender "Passing" in the Academy

In the academy[1] women are compelled to "pass"[2] as the male dominant "other" if they desire to achieve a modicum of academic success (Pagano 1990, 13; K. Scott 1991, 150; White 1985, 36). "Passing" implies impersonation, acting as if one is someone or something one is not. Hence, gender "passing," or impersonation—the coexistence of a prescription and proscription to imitate white American males and females—suggests masquerading or presenting a persona or some personae that contradict the literal image of the marginalized or doubly refracted "other." For example, Patricia Williams (1988), an African American who is also a Harvard Law School graduate, describes the seemingly contradictory strategies her mother encouraged her to use to succeed in the academy. These strategies were intended to negate her identification with her mother—a dubious role model for success in the academy and the larger society. These same strategies were also supposed to motivate her to reclaim the disinherited white components of her identity.[3]

> My mother was [constantly] asking me not to look to her as a role model. She was devaluing that part of herself that was not Harvard and refocusing my vision to that part of herself that was hard-edged, proficient, and Western. She hid the lonely, black, defiled-female part of herself and pushed me forward as the projection of a competent self, a cool rather than despairing self, *a masculine rather than a feminine self.* (P. Williams 1988, 20, emphasis added)

Likewise, Pagano describes how the academy compels female teachers to hide their femaleness to obtain the desired academic approval of their male peers and superiors. She notes that female teachers often

> present [themselves] as the genderless "author," "artist," or "scientist" . . . [in order] to quell any doubts [they] may have about [their] right to so present

81

[themselves], to speak in the voice of authority—the tradition—and to compete with [their] male colleagues for scarce academic resources . . . hunch [their] bodies in shameful secrecy as [they] walked the corridors of [their] departments for fear that someone would notice [they] were in drag. (Pagano 199, 13)

Gender "passing" is thus a reality for both African American women and white women. Indeed, it could be debated that the first— and some would argue the only—commandment for women in the academy is "Thou must be taken seriously." "Thou must be taken seriously" is a euphemism for "Thou must not appear as woman." Therefore, for women to be taken seriously in the academy, they must not only receive a form of schooling the contents of which prepares them to survive and prosper in a world organized by and for men (not women) (Rich 1979, 238), but in addition they must transform their identity in such a way that the resulting persona makes the female appear not to be female. This evolving persona reflects and highlights socially defined maleness. "Being taken seriously," then, implies discarding or at least minimizing a female identity in a self-conscious effort to consume, or at least present the appearance of being, the male dominant "other." It also suggests avoiding the traditional dichotomous definition of womanhood: good girl– bad girl, virgin–seductress, angel–whore. The problem, however, is much larger than a common or universal definition of womanhood; it is also the larger society's "acceptance of and complicity in a hierarchy of female goodness that imputes moral superiority to some women's lives and immorality to others" (Palmer 1989, 151).

In America, white womanhood is often defined as a cultural universal.[4] Yet the moral superiority of white womanhood is rarely explicitly verbalized in the academy. Indeed, it is most often labeled "femaleness" minus the white referent. Nonetheless, *white* and middle class are the "hidden transcript[s]" (J. Scott 1990) of femaleness, the womanhood invariably and historically celebrated in academe. In striking contrast, black womanhood is often presented as the antithesis of white women's lives, the slur or "the nothingness" (see Christian 1990; Walker 1982) that men and other women use to perpetuate and control the image of the "good girl" and by extension the good woman. Hence, the academy's penchant for universalizing and normalizing white middle-class women's lives compels black women and other women of color to seek to appropriate the image and attempt to consume the lives of the female "other."

Ironically, gender "passing" is rarely identified as a factor in the differentiated academic performance of African American and white American students. It is also seldom identified as a factor producing asymmetrical outcomes in African American males' and African American females' school performance. This response persists despite widespread acknowledgment that (1) African American students' school performance is gender-differentiated at all levels of the academy (Fleming 1978, 1982, 1983, 1984; Fordham 1988, 1990; Fordham and Ogbu 1986; Garret-Vital 1989; Gurin and Epps 1975; Lewis 1988; Meisenheimer 1990; Sexton 1969; Smith 1982); (2) America's patriarchal system is stratified, with some males having more power and privileges than other males in the patriarchy; and (3) African American females are doubly victimized by the existence of a two-tiered patriarchy.

A central goal of the analysis presented in this article is to identify and describe how the existence of a subversive, diverse womanhood among African American women, juxtaposed with a two-tiered dominating patriarchy, influences and often adversely affects academic achievement. An ancillary goal is to document how the absence of "official" recognition of gender diversity in a predominantly African American high school in Washington, D.C., mutilates the academic achievement of large numbers of female African American students. I begin the analysis by briefly describing the research site: Capital High and Capital Community. In the next section of the analysis I present the conceptual context, offering both a narrative of how gender is repeatedly constructed and negated in culturally and racially stratified social systems and a discussion of the repetitious construction of an egalitarian ideal within the African American community. My goal here is to delineate a culturally distinct route to womanhood among African American women. Specifically, I discuss issues involving the symbolic transformation of African American women's gendered "self."[6] Included in this section is a somewhat detailed discussion of the theoretical frame, highlighting anthropological discussions of egalitarianism and how the existence of this process within the African American community creates pockets of "safe cultural space" for the promotion of African American women's self-definition (see Collins 1991). I end this section by fusing these arguments to claims regarding the black fictive kinship system,[7] highlighting improvisation or the ad hoc[8] construction of the African American gendered "self." In the fourth section of the article I present a somewhat general discussion of how the desire for academic success combined with the negation or suppression of gender diversity among African American females at Capital High compels them to silence and/or emulate the male dominant "other." I also include in this section documentation of African American females' resistance to this silence and imitation mandate. Although acknowledging the common features of the high-achieving female students—they work hard, they are silent; when they vocalize, they speak "in a different voice" (Gilligan 1982)—I focus my analysis on Rita, a high-achieving female who symbolizes this composite image. Rita, I argue, epitomizes black women's struggle to commingle or fuse two divergent lives concurrently. I postulate that she is both unwilling and unable to be silent. She is also irrevocably committed to the retention of her female, African American gendered "self." Moreover, I argue, her speech is masked and disguised in ways that nullify and negate the perception of her femaleness. I try to show how her speech, thinking, voice, and writing styles emulate the dominant male "other" while embracing her largely unconscious perceptions of African American womanhood. I also cite several examples of how the child-rearing practices of the parents and teachers of the high-achieving females unwittingly cremate these young African American women's efforts to flee the African American community and, in the process, paradoxically enhance their affiliation with the larger American society. The concluding section of the article focuses on some of the possible implications of constructing an African American female for success in the academy and the excessive price she pays for transforming her gendered "self."

The Social Context of the School

Capital High School (a pseudonym) is located in a predominantly African American section of the city of Washington, D.C. Essentially, it is a school within a school. As a school within a school, Capital attracts students from all socioeconomic segments of the city of Washington. Indeed, its recruitment efforts are very successful. More than a fourth of the students are noncommunity residents who travel from various parts of the city to participate in the school's advanced placement and humanities programs.[9] Hence, Capital High is not a school that can be accurately labeled low-income or inner-city, euphemisms for slums and the "underclass." The school's complex student body and diverse, rudimentary class structure[10] do not lend themselves readily to such uncomplicated labeling. It is far more accurate to label Capital a "magnet school," because through its multilevel, multirigorous curriculum it accurately reflects the diverse population of the entire city.

The first two years of the study were the most intense. During the first year, thirty-three eleventh-grade students whose parents had consented to their participation in the study served as key informants. As key informants, these students were self-consciously interrogated. They were interviewed, observed, and analyzed for more than a year. These students formed a varied group, representing both high-achieving and underachieving students—male and female—and the diverse population described above. My interactions with these students included classroom observations, home visitations, observations of before- and after-school activities, and formal and informal interviews. I also observed and interviewed their parents, teachers, and other school officials.

Following a year of interrogating the key informants, the second year of the study included administering an in situ survey to 600 students in grades nine through twelve. For the analysis presented here, data from twelve of the high-achieving students—six males and six females—and twelve of the under-achieving students—six males and six females—were examined and interpreted.

In the tradition of sociocultural anthropology, I spent virtually every school day from September to June—and most weekends—in the field, collecting data and trying to understand why, how, and at what cost African American adolescents achieve school success. To protect the identity of the community and its residents, I gave the school the fictitious name Capital High; the community in which it is located was labeled Capital Community. A large number of the students come from one-parent homes; some of them live in public or low-income housing. Of the nearly 2,000 students, almost 500, about one-fourth of the student body, are eligible for the reduced lunch program.

The school's population (students and teachers) is predominantly black. However, virtually every department has at least one white teacher, with the English Department having the largest number— four females. In addition, the teachers who teach the more advanced or "difficult" classes (i.e., Advanced Placement English, Advanced Placement Physics, Chemistry, Advanced Placement Mathematics, Government, et cetera) are white. They are also the teachers who serve as sponsors for the JETS Club, It's Academic, the Chess Club, and so on. Hence, there is virtually no relationship between the white teachers' power and influence in the academic learning, achievement, and emerging perceptions of the students and their numbers at the school. Further, there is in place at the school a four-tier curriculum: two special programs (Advanced Placement and Humanities); the regular curriculum, where most of the nearly 2,000 students are centered; and a program for those students in need of special education. In addition, where there are areas of overlap in the regular curriculum and the two special academic programs, students are grouped according to their performance on standardized examination. And, based on test results, they are permitted and/or required to take the appropriate courses for their skill levels.

THE CONCEPTUAL CONTEXT

Constructing and Nullifying Cultural-Specific Femaleness

In a socially, culturally, and racially stratified society like the United States, cultural-specific routes to womanhood are inevitable. Indeed, the stratified nature of state systems suggests the following: (1) gender construction is not universal and (2) status inequity vis-à-vis gender is a *sine qua non* in such contexts. Hence, femaleness in such contexts is not the same for all women, just as maleness is not the same for all men. Gender diversity (i.e., what it means to be male or female in different social classes and social groups) is rarely officially acknowledged in the academies of contemporary nation-states. Therefore, like most other women of color, African American women are compelled to consume the universalized images of white American women, including body image, linguistic patterns, styles of interacting, and so forth. Because womanhood or femaleness is norm referenced to one group—white middle-class Americans—women from social groups who do not share this racial, ethnic, or cultural legacy are compelled to silence or gender "passing." Although all women born and reared in America are "educated in romance," in Holland and Eisenhart's (1990) term, and victimized by sexism, not all American women take the same train to a common sexist station. Therefore, as Evans suggests:

> [Anthropologists] need to examine the ways by which the Women's Movement has perpetrated a type of cultural imperialism that takes the oppression of white women as its norm and develops its theory from the experience of a small minority of women in global terms. (1988, 189)

"Those loud Black girls"[11] is an example of both the diversity of gender construction in Euro-American contexts and the efforts to suppress that diversity. It is also a quintessential example of African American women's commitment to being visible as culturally specific women. Curiously, these young women appear to be motivated to highlight the practices of gender-specific constructions in contexts that compel male impersonation or, at the very least, the adoption of a male voice.[12] "Those loud Black girls" is also an example of how a people's history is reflected in their daily lives. As Davis (1971) argues so convincingly, African American women bring to the academy—broadly defined—a history of womanhood that differs from that of white or any other American women. African American women's history stands in striking contrast to that generally associated with white womanhood and includes (1) more than 200 years in which their status as women was annulled, compelling them to function in ways that were virtually indistinguishable from their male slave counterparts; (2) systemic absence of protection by African American and all other American men; (3) construction of a new definition of what it means to be female out of the stigma associated with the black experience and the virtue and purity affiliated with white womanhood; and (4) hard work[13] (including slave and domestic labor), perseverance, assertiveness, and self-reliance. In other words, the history of African American males and females includes an extended period when gender differences were minimized, resulting in a kind of "deformed equality" (Davis 1971) or, as Cary (1991) describes it, a period when African American females were "officially" classified as the "neutered 'Other.'"

These images flooded my psyche the day I discovered Grace Evans's (1980) article entitled "Those Loud Black Girls." At long last, I thought, someone has accurately captured what I learned about black womanhood at Capital High and what I personally experienced growing up African and American. Since the word *anecdotal* is almost always preceded by the word *merely,* prior to reading Evans's essay, I never quite trusted the validity of my personal experiences. Growing up female and African American in American society, I learned early on to discount the validity of my experiences. Evans, an African American social studies teacher in the public school system in several inner-city schools in London, locates "those loud Black girls" in the following setting:

> In staffrooms [of the schools] a common cry to be heard from white teach-ers—usually women, for male teachers seldom revealed that everything for them was not firmly under control—was, "Oh, those loud Black girls!" This exclamation was usually followed by the slamming of a pile of folders on to a table and the speaker collapsing into a chair or storming off to get a cup of coffee. The words were usually uttered in response to a confrontation in which the teacher's sense of authority had been threatened by an attitude of defiance on the part of a group of Black girls in a classroom or corridor. The girls' use of patois and their stubborn refusal to conform to standards of "good behavior," without actually entering the realm of "bad behavior" by breaking any school rules, was exasperating for many teachers. The behavior of the girls could be located in the outer limits of tolerable behavior, and they patrolled this territory with much skill, sending a distinct message of being in and for themselves. (Evans 1988, 183)

Evans goes on to admit that, as an African American student in a pre-dominantly white high school in the northeastern United States, she was *not* one of "those loud Black girls." Indeed, she acknowledges that it was her in-visibility, her silence, as well as her link to a successful male, her brother, that enabled her to become the "successful" student she was in high school. She asserts:

> I was not a loud Black girl myself; I was one of the quiet, almost to the point of silent, Black or "coloured" girls who did her homework, worked

hard, seldom spoke unless spoken to and was usually to be found standing on the margin of activities. I demanded no attention and got none. In the early years of my schooling I was considered by most of my teachers to be at best an average or just above average student, certainly not a particularly promising one. If it had not been for an elder brother whose academic excellence was noted at an early age, I probably would have remained ignored by teachers, but word got around in the schools I attended that I was his sister, and teachers began to expect more from me. Looking back, I believe that my silence stemmed from two things: a perception on my part of minority status and a very deliberate priming for the professions that my parents began when I was very young. (Evans 1988, 184)

Elsewhere I described the black girls who were academically successful at Capital High as "phantoms in the opera" (Fordham 1990). 1 made this assertion because the academically successful black girls achieved academic success in the following ways: (1) becoming and remaining voiceless or silent or, alternatively, (2) impersonating a male image—symbolically—in self-presentation, including voice, thinking, speech pattern, and writing style, in the formal school context when formally interacting with their teachers in classrooms, assemblies, club meetings, and so forth. At the same time, however, I noted that silence for the African American female is not to be interpreted as acquiescence. Rather, I argued that silence among the high-achieving females at the school is an act of defiance, a refusal on the part of the high-achieving females to consume the image of "nothingness" (see Christian 1990) so essential to the conception of African American women. This intentional silence is also critical to the rejection and deflection of the attendant downward expectations so pervasive among school officials.

Pagano acknowledges and describes women's forced emigration toward silence and maleness in the academy. She declares: "The more successful [women] have been as students, scholars, and teachers, the greater has been [their] active participation in [their] own exclusion (Pagano 1990, 12). She goes on to document how women pawn their collective voice in exchange for success in the existing patriarchic structure. By engaging in such practices, she argues, women ensure the continued existence of authority in the male image and their (women's) complicity in the lie that asserts that they are naturally silent. She concludes by asserting that women who either remain or become silent are instrumental in maintaining female dependency and invisibility in the academy. Hence, "those loud Black girls" are doomed not necessarily because they cannot handle the academy's subject matter, but because they resist "active participation in [their] own exclusion" (Pagano 1990, 12).

In analyzing a small portion of the Capital High ethnographic data, Pagano's claim is verified in a predominantly African American context. The following general patterns emerge among the high-achieving females: (1) resistance as a tenuous, ghostlike existence and status at the school; (2) the coexistence of excellent grades and the appearance of an erasable persona; (3) parenting, teaching, and child-rearing practices that reward their silence and obedience with good grades, as well as the assertive suppression and denial of physicality and sexuality; (4) alienation and isolation from the black fictive kinship system's ad hoc orientation; and (5) the assiduous commingling and maintaining of an academically successful persona *and* a "nice girl" persona with very little external reward or remuneration from parents or guardians, especially mothers. Such parental child-rearing practices suggest that nurturing a black female for success—as defined by the larger society—is far more disruptive of indigenous cultural conventions and practices than previously thought. Evans acknowledges some of the costs involved:

> The prize of a good education [is often] attained at the cost of great sacrifice on the part of one's parents, sometimes the entire family. Aside from this cost, another price is paid by the recipient of an education, and this is the personal cost of the process of deculturalization, or de-Africanisation, whereby all personal expressions of one's original African culture are eliminated and [Euro-American] codes established instead. The mastery of standard English to replace West Indian patois is only one aspect of this transformation. It includes training the body to adopt European body language and gesture, and the voice to adopt European tones of speech and non-verbal expression. . . . The price of a good education, a [Euro-American] education, in short, was, and still is, the denial of one's Black cultural identity. This is the price of entry to the middle-class. It is this legacy of education as a double-edged sword that creates a similar suspicion towards Black teachers on the part of Black students as exists on the part of the Black community towards Black members of the police force. The presence of Black faces does not change the essential nature of an institution, nor does it alter its ethos. (Evans 1988, 185)

In stark contrast, the following salient patterns are common among the underachieving females in the study: (1) striking visibility and presence—(these young women were known by everyone at the school and did not try to minimize the disruption that their visibility implied); (2) lack of congruency between grades and standardized test scores, with standardized test scores frequently dwarfing grade point average (GPA); (3) parenting and child-rearing practices that suggest unconditional support for their daughters' self-defined academic plans and other espoused goals; (4) encapsulation and immersion in the black egalitarian (i.e., fictive kinship) system (see Fordham 1987, 1988, 1991a, 1991b; Fordham and Ogbu 1986); and (5) obtaining and maintaining support and nurturing from peers and the significant adults in their lives. In the next section I discuss how anthropologists have traditionally framed egalitarianism and how it appears to operate in the contemporary African American community. I end this discussion by fusing these arguments to the black fictive kinship system, including its improvisation or ad hoc orientation.

Ad-Hocing and Evoking an Egalitarian Ideal

The existence of an egalitarian ideal within the African American community does not imply the absence of hierarchy. Hierarchy and hierarchies exist in contemporary African American communities. Individuals are categorized and ranked. Age, sex, and individual characteristics are the usual distinguishing elements. However, as Flanagan (1989, 248) points out, anthropologists' historical claims regarding the existence of egalitarian societies do not eliminate the hierarchy between individuals. Like all anthropologically described egalitarian societies, universally employed criteria are visible: "age, sex, and personal characteristics." Like other groups that anthropologists have identified as practicing an egalitarian ideology, members of the African American community negotiate areas of dominance and status and the contexts in which they will mark these characteristics.

Anthropologists have consistently attributed to societies labeled egalitarian principles of reciprocity—including the sharing of food and power—an undifferentiated economy, and, in some instances, the control of productive as well as reproductive resources (Flanagan 1989, 247). Egalitarianism in the African American community embraces all of these elements. In fact, this approach to life appears to have emerged in response to their American enslavement. To survive, enslaved Africans learned to "live with" the lack of differentiation externally imposed upon them as slaves and, ironically, to make use of the lack of differentiation in ways that not only assured their survival (as individuals), but also promoted the growth and well-being of the entire group.

The idealization of an egalitarian ethos within the African American community also does not imply the absence of "historical tensions . . . and the interpersonal power struggles that form a part of daily existence" (Flanagan 1989, 247). There are tensions and power struggles within African American communities. Indeed, some people would argue that these features are everywhere, even more rampant than they are in the dominant society. The presence of these tensions and power struggles does not, however, negate the centrality of the claim I am making in this analysis: In African American communities, an egalitarian ideal or ethos influences the behaviors and responses of African American peoples. Self-actualization is thus fully realized only in so far as the individual becomes validated through other people. Achieving human status means perceiving oneself as being intimately connected to other people. Consequently, the most highly valued group strategies are those that enable the individual to be seen as embodying those qualities and characteristics that will enhance the status of the group. In this way, he or she is seen as personifying the egalitarian ideal.

In the African American community, ad hocing or improvising one's life is what comes to mind when I attempt to capture the torturous relationship between the individual and the group.[14] Ad hocing or improvising one's life suggests constructing an identity that, on the one hand, does not violate one's sense of "self," while, on the other hand, enhancing one's sense of fit within a given context. *Improvisation* is the term used most frequently in describing African Americans' constructions of music, especially jazz (see Keil 1966) and, more recently, rap (see Powell 1991; Rose 1991). It also captures the patterns found in other aspects of the material and nonmaterial culture of African Americans, including dance, quilting (Wahlman and Scully 1983), speech practices (Baugh 1983), and so forth. In each of these very different areas, symmetry is obtained not through uniformity, but through diversity.

At Capital High, the effects of the idealization of the egalitarian ethos are manifestly obvious. They are most visible in the kind of orientation that makes it unnecessary for everyone to possess the same level of expertise in the same subject areas. They are also evident in the various ways the students respond to this process. Leveling behaviors are not difficult to detect. They are manifested in many aspects of the actors' interactions. This egalitarian approach to life coexists with a static, individually competitive, nonleveling curriculum and course of study in the high school context. Further, because the curriculum is what really matters, it is juxtaposed with the widespread lack of individual competition and individual improvisations among the students at the school. The egalitarian ethos is also evident in Capital High students' tendency to seek unity in race and group solidarity rather than individualism and socioeconomic class.

Coexisting with this egalitarian ethos, however, is a not too subtle African American gender hierarchy embedded in both the African origins of the group and the dominant Euro-American patriarchy. This gender hierarchy is less conspicuous and in some ways barely visible to the unskilled observer. Nevertheless, it exerts an extremely powerful influence on the behavior and expectations of the students—male and female—at the school.

Because African Americans' gender hierarchy both parallels and diverges from the organizational structure in place in the dominant segment of American society—that is, because it is a synthesis of that which is both African and American—black males are in the power (or is it more accurate to say, the most visible?) positions at Capital High. It is they who manipulate the formal school rules. For example, class schedules at the school are planned and prepared by these men with the tacit support of the women. Also, although rules regarding when school will begin and end, what holidays will be celebrated, when football games and other athletic events will be scheduled, are made by several bureaucrats downtown in the administrative offices, Capital's principal often takes it upon himself to modify these official rules to meet the academic needs of Capital students, as he perceives them.

The gender hierarchy at Capital is also pregnant with tensions, conflicts, traditions, and subtle internal meanings. Black females are conversant with black patriarchy, with its refracted African American origin as well as its subordinate status vis-à-vis the dominant society's patriarchy. They also are familiar with how that authority is expressed and how they are expected to respond to it. It is, however, the splicing and grafting of the dominant Euro-American patriarchal system onto the preexisting black patriarchy, with its vastly different authority base, that is implicated in how black females learn to seek and, in some instances, achieve school success. Regrettably, space limitations do not permit a discussion here of how men of African ancestry in America fuse and seek to replicate the dominant male role.

As I have already indicated, the distinctively constructed gender roles of African peoples in American society are frequently ignored, disparaged, or ridiculed in the larger American society. For example, Elsa Barkley Brown insists that, more than virtually any other people, "African American women have indeed created their own lives, shaped their own meanings, and are the voices of authority on their own experience" (1988, 15). This is their reality, she argues, because, as noted above, for more than 200 years women of African ancestry were not allowed to construct their identity as they had done in the various African countries from which they had come. Nor were they permitted to impersonate womanhood as constructed and practiced by Euro-American women. Hence, womanhood as remembered, and femaleness as observed, were not available to them; they had no choice but to improvise a new definition of femaleness that would be a synthesis of the bicultural worlds they remembered and inherited.

Against this background, African American women are not seen as the archetypal symbol of womanhood, as is the case for white American women.

Indeed, role ambiguity has always haunted the life of the African American woman. Sojourner Truth is said to have lamented "Ar'n't I a Woman?" (White 1985); Zora Neale Hurston (1969) described black women as "mules," suggesting the existence of strength and endurance. Hurston's image conflicts with that of the white American female for whom idleness—until the feminist movement of the seventies—was the quintessential symbol (Sacks 1976). Indeed, according to Palmer, for the white American woman to transform the unconscious link of women with "sex, dirt, housework, and badness," she [the white woman] "needed another woman to do the hard and dirty physical labor. She needed a woman different from herself, one whose work and very identity confirmed [her] daintiness and perfection" (1989, 138). In other words, she needed a black woman.

LEARNING SILENCE AND GENDER "PASSING"

Gender "Passing": The Female High Achievers

As Rich (1979) and Pagano (1990) suggest, gender "passing" in the academy is unavoidable. Also, as I have already indicated, during the schooling process women receive a form of schooling the contents of which prepare them to survive and prosper in a world organized by and for men, not women (Rich 1979, 238). Consequently, "being taken seriously," that is, becoming a good student, implies certifying male knowledge, conferring the names of the father and contradicting (women's) own biology (Pagano 1990, 37–38).

The high-achieving female students at Capital High are living by the first academic commandment for women: "thou must be taken seriously." At the same time, each of them is guilty of seeking a "safe cultural space"[15] to retain their varied perceptions of the gendered African American "self." Virtually all of them—Alice, Sia, Lisa, Katrina, and Maggie—are thought of as serious young women, headed for the fast track and a life away from the ghetto. Each of these women is somehow able to walk the tightrope that living two divergent lives mandates. In striking contrast, Rita presents a less balanced persona. Like the other high-achieving female members of the sample, she is compelled to commingle two divergent lives. The important distinction, however, is that she is far less willing than her high-achieving female counterparts to camouflage, in the school context, her perceptions of the gendered African American female "self."

Rita is acknowledged to be a brilliant student, but all her teachers and many of her peers worry about her because she presents a "polyrhythmic, nonsymmetrical, nonlinear" persona. She is bold and sassy, creative, complex, and indeflatable. She frequently challenges the values and rules of the school with conviction, vacillating between demanding total adherence to the dominant ideology of the larger society on the part of her teachers and other school administrators and discounting and disparaging these same values and rules in her personal life. Her actions suggest a "contradictory unity"—an attempt to suture that which is socially defined as incompatible, both in terms of her perceptions of what it means to be black and female and in masking the mastering aspects of the school curriculum. For example, Rita identifies math as her weakest subject in the core curriculum. At the same time, however, she is quite knowledgeable of how computers function and is able to decipher and manipulate computer hardware and a bevy of software quite well.

It was the possession of these computer skills that inspired her math teacher, Ms. Costen, to pay her $40 to develop a program for one of her friends who was failing a computer course. Partly as a sick joke and partly because Rita is convinced that Ms. Costen was acting inappropriately when she asked her to perform what she perceived to be an intellectually dishonest task, she deliberately sabotaged the computer program. She also did not return the $40. Her reasoning was that Ms. Costen is a teacher and teachers are supposed to be paragons of virtue, modeling behaviors and attitudes sanctioned by the larger society. In general, although Rita expects teachers to rigorously adhere to the norms, values, and rules of the educational establishment, she feels that it is acceptable and even admirable for her and her peers to blatantly flaunt these same ideals by resisting and outsmarting the teachers at their own game. As she perceives it, her efforts and those of her peers are to be labeled subtle, ongoing resistance to the celebration of the dominant "other" endemic at Capital High. As students, she and her peers are free to subvert the existing dominating system. On the other hand, as a teacher, Ms. Costen—despite her blackness—does not have the same options available to her. As Rita perceives it, Ms. Costen's role as teacher takes precedence over her connectedness to the black community. Also, according to Rita's perception, her teacher's desire to create a "safe cultural space" is a contested concept.

Hence, like those "loud Black girls" discussed in Evans's essay (1988), Rita refuses to "conform to standards of 'good behavior' . . . without actually entering the realm of 'bad behavior' by breaking any school rules." Rather, she lives on the edge, self-consciously stretching legitimate school rules to help her retrieve a safe cultural space. She is a master craftsperson, baffling her teachers, decertifying the sanity of her mother and most other family members, and ultimately assuring officials at St. Elizabeth's[16] that their beds will be occupied. The following description of Rita's behavior resonates in this analysis.

As I have already indicated, all thirty-three key informants were eleventh graders. During the spring of the academic year, those students who had performed well on the PSAT were strongly encouraged by their teachers and other school officials to apply for admission to the colleges that they were interested in or that had indicated an interest in them. Since Rita had the highest score on the verbal component of the exam, she had received letters from numerous colleges inviting her to apply. Responding to these letters was no problem. Her dilemma emerged when her English teacher, Ms. Apropos, asked all the students in her English class to share their essays so that she could help them make a good impression on the various admissions committees. She advised them to write strong, upbeat essays that reflected a positive outlook on life. The other students followed her advice unequivocally. They created positive, upbeat essays.

Rita was the only exception. She decided not to write an essay in this genre. She chose, instead, to write about the value of death and dying. Ms. Apropos was speechless. She could not believe that a teenager whose life is on the uptake would even be capable of thinking such morbid, melancholy thoughts. Ms. Apropos had secretly harbored doubts about Rita's sanity for a long time.[17] These fears grew by leaps and bounds when she assigned the class *The Crucible* and Rita refused to read it, claiming that it violated her religious beliefs.[18] When she later asserted that she was going to write about death and dying in her college admission essay, all doubts regarding her mental stability were removed. Ms. Apropos was absolutely sure that "girlfriend" was crazy. This initial impression was reinforced when she tried and failed to get Rita to change her mind.

Rita's willingness to display these dialectic characteristics at school appear to make her an unfeeling and thoughtless person. She is not. Admittedly, she has learned the ideology of the society well. And, at some level, she believes that American society is truly democratic and that the individual makes it or fails based solely on ability. In the school context she is committed to the meritocratic ideals promulgated there and does not want to have any information around her that might suggest that what she has learned, and perhaps is learning, in school is misleading or even untrue. She is definitely a child of the post–civil rights era, in that, like many nonblack persons, she wants to believe that African Americans have achieved socioeconomic parity with the dominating group: white Americans.

> Some—a lot of times I have people ask me "Do you think you are a white person?" But I don't know, maybe it's me. Maybe I don't carry myself like a black person. I don't know. But I'm black. And I can't go painting myself white or some other color, it's something that I have to live with. So it's the

way it is, and it's not like having herpes or something—it's not bad. It's—I
think it's just the same as being white, as far as I'm concerned—everybody's
equal. (Interview with author, May 4, 1983)

At the same time, Rita's consistent practice of breaching the cultural assumptions so valued in the school context often leads her teachers to erase
their perception of her as a bright, intelligent person. Also the "slam dunking"
part of her persona that propels her to the margins of good behavior, without
actually forcing her into the realm of "bad behavior," makes "shrinking lilies"
out of most adults who interact with her or, alternatively, motivates them to
avoid contact with her, if that is an option. Needless to say, Rita submitted
her essay on the value of death and dying. She was also accepted at her chosen
institution.

As noted above, the most salient characteristic of the academically successful females at Capital High is a deliberate silence, a controlled response to
their evolving, ambiguous status as academically successful students. Consequently, silence as a strategy for academic success at Capital is largely unconscious. Developing and using this strategy at the high school level enables
high-achieving African American females to deflect the latent and not too latent hostility and anger that might be directed at them were they to be both
highly visible and academically successful. Invisibility is a highly valued prerequisite for academic success. This is particularly true for these young
teenage girls whose evolving sexuality and reproductive capabilities actually
undermine their chances of success in the public domain. Learning silence,
then, is an obligatory component of Capital's high-achieving females' academic success. They are taught to be silent by their parents, teachers and other
school officials, and male peers—both explicitly and implicitly—in order to
allay the perception that they are just women, that is, that they will behave in
ways typically associated with women and femaleness. Gilligan (1982) has described women as being preoccupied with "relationships." Further, she asserts
that this "way of knowing" (relating) is not loudly applauded in the academy.
With only a couple of exceptions, the high-achieving females at Capital High
are invisible in the highly visible arenas at the school (e.g., classrooms, assemblies in the auditorium, and so forth). Females are encouraged to be "seen
rather than heard," to be passive rather than assertive.

Like Evans (1988), prior to her teachers' realization that she was geneti-
cally connected to an academically successful male, the high-achieving females at Capital High are not central; they are more liminal and marginal than
their high-achieving male cohorts. These women's voices are heard primarily

through what they write and their pithy responses to questions asked in the classroom and other formal school contexts. They rarely speak extemporaneously in the classroom context. When called upon by their teachers, they are able to answer correctly and politely, but they generally do not announce or celebrate their presence by speaking or in some way making themselves visible. Curiously, the female exceptions—principally Rita—use the voice of a comedian or clown to convey their visibility, a persona used almost exclusively by the high-achieving male students. Rita's high-achieving female cohorts refuse to join her in her impersonation of the "other." The high-achieving females appear to be afraid to speak because speech will bring attention to their female "selves." It also may be that, intuitively, as Lewis and Simon point out, these "women know that being allowed to speak can be a form of tyranny" (Lewis and Simon 1986, 461). As young African American women, the high-achieving females at Capital High are intimately conversant with feelings surrounding dissonance and place.

Most of the academically successful girls acknowledge that this newfound silence represents a change from the way they once behaved in school. Each of them can recall when her female voice was not a deterrent to academic success. Some of them attribute their growing, evolving silence to parental controls that are increasingly directed toward limiting both their extrafamilial activities and the fulfillment of their female sexuality. Others are unable to articulate why they have come to be silent. They only know that, for some reason, they are learning or have learned not to speak, not to be visible.

At Capital High, most parentally supported limitations are intended to minimize their daughters' femaleness, especially their emerging sexuality. Paradoxically, the female high achievers interpret their parents' seeming lack of support as having the unintended consequence of unmasking their evolving invisibility. For example, Rita's mother made her quit the track team because she feared that Rita would get involved in some undesired activities, including a sexual relationship with some "little boy." Rita indicated that her mother's demand had the unintended consequence of putting a spotlight on her, making her more visible and subjecting her to ridicule.

It is important to acknowledge that a common, relentless theme in the child-rearing practices of virtually all of the mothers of the high-achieving females is an absolute insistence that their daughters be "taken seriously." In addition, these mothers demand control of their daughters' lives and even the options they seriously consider for their futures. The mothers' conditional support for their daughters' voiced academic aspirations confuses them, making their enormous efforts in school appear less valuable. For example, Rita's mother was ambivalent about her daughter's desire to go to college. Indeed, it is probably more accurate to say that she was fearful of Rita's school achievement and what it meant in terms of options for her.

> I'm going to tell you like this, Ms. Fordham: I am really happy that Rita's doing what she's doing [in school], and I'm not going to be hypocritical about it. But if Rita didn't go to college, it would not make me a bit of difference. . . . No, it would not. Because, like I said, you know, education is good. And I think that Rita—she says that she wants to go into neurology, or something to that effect. And from studying the Bible and looking at the events the way that they are today, the Bible shows that this system is not going to be here that long. Whenever it is that it's going to come to an end—well, not the system, it is not going to end, but the end of wickedness, we don't know. See, the Bible says there's going to be people that's going to survive the destruction of the system of things. But from looking at the way that things are going on the world scene, and looking at your colleges and things today, I mean, they have—the individual, when they're going to college and things, they go there for the right purpose—because there's a lot of kids that go there and—for the right purpose, but a lot of things happen in college. See? And . . . I mean kids that get hung up with drugs, and these sororities and things now, the things that they—r [I] was reading some article in the paper about these sororities [fraternities] initiating these young guys, and they died from drinking all this—over-drinking and stuff like that, the things they make them do. And, basically, I just—you know, I'm just not that enthused. (Interview with author, May 5, 1983)

The intensity of this mother's ambivalence about her daughter's desire to go to college, as well as Rita's prior assertions regarding her mother's lack of support for her academic efforts, led me to ask her if she would be happier if Rita did not go to college.

> I think I would. . . . Yeah. Because I'm not looking forward to a future, you see, because the system is crumbling, basically. I know education and every—I'm not against learning, now, don't misunderstand me, I'm not against learning. I'm happy that Rita has the qualifications and things to go to college. I mean, were things different and we were living at a different period of time, I mean, it would be all right. Now her father's all for it, you know, and I'm not totally against it, but I'm saying—looking at—for people now to plan a career—and I mean, I've seen people with college degrees and everything, they [black people] cannot even get a job. (Interview with author, May 5, 1983)

The sources of this mother's ambivalence were quite varied. There was the religious principle mandating that unmarried women remain in their parents' home until marriage. There was also the verbalized fear of crime and drugs and other unacceptable social problems. Still further, there was the non-verbalized fear of her daughter's emerging sexuality and femaleness. There was also a fear of how success would change and perhaps further alienate her daughter from the family and the African American community.

> I believe that if Rita put her mind to it—I mean, if she wasn't into the specific field that she wanted to, she could learn about—you know, just taking, maybe taking some courses or something. But I'm not pushing the college [idea]. Truthfully, I'm not pushing it. But like I said, it's up to her father. (Interview with author, May 5, 1983)

At this point in their young lives, the high-achieving females read their parents' insistence on silence and invisibility in the school context and strict extrafamilial limitations—no dating, no after-school activities, and so forth—as well as uncertainty and/or ambivalence about their academic goals, as a lack of support for what they dream of doing: going to college immediately after high school and living their lives in ways that parallel their white American peers.

The silence attendant to female academic excellence is exacerbated in the school context where, again, the high-achieving females are given episodic, rather than continuous, unlimited support for their academic achievement and their voiced future dreams. This is the reality, despite the fact that the teaching staff and other adult members of the school are primarily African American and female.[19] The following example of a counselor's response to Katrina's—another high achiever—excellent performance on a required District of Columbia public school system exam is illuminating.

Ms. Yanmon is Katrina's counselor. In fact, she is the counselor of all the students who participate in the advanced placement program at the school. They are virtually her only counselees, even though they make up less than a fourth of the school's student population.

Like every other student at the school, Katrina took the LSE (Life Skills Examination). This is a District of Columbia Public School requirement. Every student must pass it before he or she is eligible for graduation. When I went to Ms. Yanmon's office to ask her if I might look at the scores of her other counselees who were participating in my study, she readily agreed. As I sat in her office looking at the test results, I mentioned that I had an extremely interesting interview with Katrina the day before. This is how I recorded our interaction in my field notes (February 4–8, 1983):

[Ms. Yanmon] does not talk about Katrina unless I [allude to] her [[first]. When I mentioned . . . that Katrina made a perfect score on the LSE, her response startled me. She [lamented the fact] that although Paul want[s] to be the valedictorian [of their class], her guess is that Katrina will be the valedictorian . . . , and Paul will be the salutatorian. . . . "Capital has not had a male [valedictorian] in about 10 years," [she mourned] . . . . "The girls do better." . . . She then asked to see the copy of [Katrina's] performance on the Life Skills Examination. I told her that [Katrina's] perfect score was the only one I had seen so far. . . . I was flabbergasted! This counselor had not talked with [Katrina] about her outstanding performance. [Ms. Yanmon acknowledged that she had not talked with Katrina about her exam results] and said, after looking at her performance sheet, . . . "I must talk with her about [this]."

Silence around female achievement was not unusual. In some ways, this silence suggested that school officials took their ability and willingness to do the work for granted; in other ways, the silence could be—and was—perceived by the students as discounting and/or disparaging their academic effort and achievement. At the same time, however, these girls were learning an important lesson for survival in the academy: the most efficient way to intersect the patriarchic system at the school is to perform all assigned tasks while remaining silent, to respond as if absent rather than present. In my field notes I recorded my response to Ms. Yanmon's seeming lack of interest in Katrina's LSE scores (February 4–8, 1983):

I could not help but wonder if [Ms. Yanmon] would have been so nonchalant about [Katrina's] perfect [exam] score if it had been made by either Paul or Norris.[20] I don't think so. All of the minute details began to return, [including] her reluctance to allow me to talk with Katrina as I was contemplating whom to include in the study.

Katrina admits that her higher grades in school have had all kinds of undesired, and sometimes unexpected, consequences in her life. For example, she has never had a lot of friends, so it would be a mistake to label her popular. She was quick to point out, however, that she did not mean to suggest that she is without friends. That was and still is not the case. It simply means that she has always been able to count on one hand the number of persons she could label "friend." She attributes some of this to her ability to perform well in school. Ironically, her higher academic performance has cost her a sense of voice.

Lisa, another high-achieving member of the sample, has a similar tale to tell. When her classmates teased her or pulled her hair, for example, she managed always to ignore them. As did Katrina, she refused to let them bait her into physical or verbal confrontations. Both Katrina and Lisa ignored their detractors, remaining silent when they were expected to (1) cry, (2) report their detractors to the principal or their classroom teachers, or (3) take some action that suggested a violation of their person or space. Regardless of the nature or source of the abuse they received, these high-achieving females' general reaction was to not respond; they refused to retaliate or show pain. Curiously, their silence promoted, and is implicated in, their subsequent academic success.

There is also the problem of the male high achievers who acknowledge fear of female academic success. For example, Paul, who would ultimately graduate salutatorian of the class, was extremely concerned about Katrina's higher grade point average. He and Norris, the student who would graduate third in the class, constantly joked about how to get rid of Katrina prior to graduation, with throwing her from the subway train being the most frequently mentioned method. Most of their conversations about Katrina's higher GPA were ensconced in the "ritualized insult" pattern characteristic of "Black street speech" (see Baugh 1983), but the fear and anxiety they experienced, especially Paul, because of Katrina's higher grade point average were unmistakable. These responses are most often seen as problematic. Let me now turn to a brief discussion of the cultural meaning and some possible social implications of these findings.

CONCLUSIONS AND IMPLICATIONS

I began this analysis by asserting that gender "passing" is a *sine qua non* for women in the academy if they desire to achieve a modicum of academic success (Pagano 1990, 13). I followed this observation by emphasizing that the first commandment for women in the academy is "Thou must be taken seriously." Further, I argued, for women to be seen as being serious about the work of the academy, they must receive (as opposed to claim) a form of schooling the contents of which prepares them to survive and prosper in a world organized by and for men, not women (Rich 1979, 238). I went on to point out that, for African American women in the academy, being taken seriously also means dissociating oneself from the image of "those loud Black girls," whose "refusal to conform to standards of 'good behavior,' without actually entering the realm of 'bad behavior' by breaking . . . school rules," severely undermines their limited possibilities for academic success. Moreover, I documented, with data from the Capital High research site, how "those loud Black girls" are doomed, how their reluctance to engage in "active participation in [their] own exclusion" (Pagano 1990, 12) from the academy strips them of a sense of power. J. Scott (1985) has described responses of this nature on the part of those who have been historically excluded as the "weapons of the weak." Audre Lorde asserts that responses in this genre on the part of African Americans and other peoples of color indicate that they know they cannot use "the master's tools . . . to dismantle the master's house" (1990, 287).

The distinctive history of people of African ancestry and their current social conditions, I argue, are implicated in the structure and configuration of their gender roles. African Americans' continuous, ongoing lack of dominance and power in the Euro-American patriarchic structure has had, and continues to have, severe implications for African American women (and men). Still further, I indicate that, in the case of the academically successful females at Capital High, silence and invisibility are the strategies they feel compelled to use to gain entry into the dominating patriarchy.

The findings presented here certify that at Capital High black females are the more successful students. Ironically, they are also the least visible. They are the people "passing" for someone they are not: the white American female and, ultimately, the white American male. Silence is implicated in their greater school success because it conceals their female voice and the resulting gender expectations.

For African American women, socialization to silence and invisibility is not without pain. It is painful because, as I documented in the above analysis, black females pay an inordinate price for academic success: it leads to an "ignorance of connections," an uncertain "fork in the road." Although I have talked about black girls' school achievement in one particular context (Capital High), it is important to acknowledge that parental ambivalence about the value of academic learning is not limited to the parents of the students at Capital High. The disheartening, unintended consequences associated with the uncertainty of academic excellence are frequently recorded in the research literature. For example, in her book *Talking Black* (1989), bell hooks describes how her parents' ambivalence about her preoccupation with school-related learning robbed her of her confidence, threatening her pursuit of academic excellence. At the same time, she acknowledges that it was her parents' ambivalence about the value of school and schooling that forever welded her to the African American community.

> My parents' ambivalence about my love for reading led to intense conflict. They (especially my mother) would work to ensure that I had access to books, but would threaten to burn the books or throw them away if I did not conform to her other expectations. Or they would insist that reading too much would drive me insane. Their ambivalence nurtured in me a like

certainty about the value and significance of intellectual endeavor which took years for me to unlearn. While this aspect of our [race] reality was one that wounded and diminished, their vigilant insistence that being smart did not make me a "better" or "superior" person (which often got on my nerves because I think I wanted to have that sense that it did indeed set me apart, make me better) made a profound impression. From them I learned to value and respect various skills and talents folk might have, not just to value people who read books and talk about ideas. They and my grandparents might say about somebody, "Now he don't read nor write a lick, but he can tell a story," or as my grandmother would say, [he can] "call out the hell in words." (hooks 1989, 79)

Socialization to silence and invisibility is also distressing because it isolates and alienates black girls from their more communal and popular underachieving female cohorts. Still further, learning to be silent can be so distressful that it sometimes results in a decision to abandon the effort to succeed in school because, in part at least, it evokes "ignorance of connections." This occurs because many of the high-achieving girls do not understand why their parents—particularly their mothers—and many of their female teachers do not appear to be supportive of their academic achievements.

However, lack of adult female support is a misperception. As hooks's analysis suggests, the seeming lack of support solders the African American female to the black community forever. It is also a misperception to see parental support as universally constructed. As this analysis suggests, parental support is not a universal construction. Indeed, this analysis documents that the existence of gender diversity and what it means to nurture are pervasive. Hence, for the African American female to achieve school success, all of the usual symbols of nurturing are turned upside down and/or inside out. These data clearly suggest that what can be labeled nurturing is cultural-specific. The academically successful females at Capital High are using a Euro-American definition of power and nurture in concluding that the significant adults in their lives are not supportive of their academic goals. They come to this enormous conclusion because they view their underachieving friends' parents' drastically different interactional patterns as the more appropriate model. The academically successful girls also study the Euro-American model via television and other media sources, including their textbooks. These sources strongly influence what they come to value and define as nurturing and supportive.

Regrettably, the high-achieving females at Capital High do not discern that their mothers and their seemingly unsupportive teachers are often unconsciously preparing them for a life away from the black community, a life in which they are the "doubly-refracted 'Other.'"[21] As the "doubly-refracted 'Other,'" the African American female's survival "out there" is largely dependent upon her ability to live a life saturated with conflict, confusion, estrangement, isolation, and a plethora of unmarked beginnings and endings, jump starts, and failures. It is also likely to be a life in which a family of procreation[22] and connections takes a back seat to "makin' it."

Therefore, the central questions haunting this entire analysis and smoldering in the lives of all African American females are the following: Is gender diversity something to celebrate? Should we seek its fragmentation? If so, how? Should our goal be to transform "those loud Black girls"? Should success for African American women be so expensive? Finally, should the African American female seek to reconstruct her life to become successful, pawning her identity as a "loud Black girl" for an identity in which she is the "doubly-refracted [African American] Other"?

NOTES

The research on which this analysis is based was funded initially by grants from the National Institutes of Education (NIE-G-82-0037), the Spencer Foundation, and a dissertation fellowship from the American University in Washington, D.C. More recently, a National Science Foundation training grant has afforded me time away from the classroom and the opportunity to consider and develop the analysis presented here. An earlier version of this article was presented at the Anthropology Bag Lunch Symposium in the Department of Anthropology, Rutgers University, New Brunswick, New Jersey, February 20, 1991. I wish to thank my colleagues in the Department of Anthropology at Rutgers for helpful comments and suggestions. I would especially like to thank the faculty, staff, and students at Capital High, their parents, and all other adults in Capital Community for allowing me to intrude in their lives. In addition, I wish to express a special note of thanks to Linda Chalfant and Professors Gerald Davis and Brett Williams for helpful comments and suggestions on successive drafts of this manuscript. I am solely responsible for this final version.

1. Loudness, as I am using it here, is not meant to convey the usual meanings, including noisiness, shrillness, flashiness, ostentatiousness, and so on. Rather, it is meant as one of the ways by which African American women seek to deny the society's efforts to assign them to a stigmatized status that Christian (1990) has described as "nothingness." Therefore, "those loud Black girls" is here used as a metaphor proclaiming African American women's existence, their collective denial of, and resistance to, their socially proclaimed powerlessness, or "nothingness."

As I am using the term, the academy includes all levels of schooling, but especially that aspect of schooling that begins at the secondary level, that is junior high or middle school and beyond. I am including precollegiate schooling in my definition of the academy because this is where notions of adult gender-differentiated behaviors—including possible mate selection—are initially nurtured and practiced.

2. Historically, in the African American community, "passing" meant appropriating the body of the "other" (i.e., the mulatto would pretend to be white and essentially assume a gender-appropriate white body) (see Brown, 1972; C. Green 1967; Ione 1991; Montgomery 1907; Washington 1987, What It Means to Be Colored in the Capital of the United States 1907 [author and publisher not listed]). Today, while blackness or Africanness is still a stigma, it is no longer the stigma it was. Therefore, in post–civil rights America, not very many people of African ancestry feel the need to assume a white persona to escape a stigmatized identity. Nonetheless, despite the wholesale acceptance of blackness by contemporary African Americans, blackness as a cultural symbol is still loaded with many social and cultural stigmata. Because it continues to be a stigma in many contexts, for example, "Dressed as Death in a black, hooded shroud" (Grove 1991, B1), some people of African ancestry resort to "passing" in a figurative rather than a literal sense. Hence, although the African American values his or her African ancestry and is secure with his or her identity as a person of African ancestry, he or she is compelled to this figurative "passing" because he or she cannot represent black and blackness and also appropriate the white [whiteness] of the "other" while retaining an idealized perception of an uncontaminated, nonhybridized "other." Against this backdrop, I am postulating that in the contemporary context some physically identifiable African Americans often feel obliged to engage in a kind of identity plagiarism (see Fordham 1993a) in which the racially identifiable African American body takes on the cognitive map of the racially and culturally dominant "other." In their construction of an idealized "otherness," these contemporary African Americans unwittingly lose that which invokes and fuels their creativity, that which gives voice to their African American humanness. Unable to speak or even think in their native voice, these individuals become a "sort of surrogate and even [subversive] [S]elf" (Said 1989, 3). Meanwhile, because they are compelled to assume the identity of the "other"—in exchange for academic success—they cannot represent themselves; they are forced to masquerade as the authentic, idealized "other."

3. P. Williams's (1988) maternal grandfather is racially identified as white.

4. I am sensitive to the possibility that I will be accused of making essentialist claims (Fuss 1989) regarding race as well as white and black womanhood. It is currently fashionable to argue that much of what is written related to these issues can be dismissed because the writer is likely to be accused of making claims regarding some "true essence—that which is most irreducible, unchanging, and therefore constitutive of a given person or thing" (Fuss 1989, 2). This is not my intention. What I hope to show in this analysis is how African American women are compelled to construct an ad hoc identity in a context where, for much of their history in this country, they have not only been barred from its "hallowed halls," but have also, at the same fume, been defined and represented by those who repeatedly defined them as "nothingness." I am not positing that there is some "pure or original [race or] femininity, a [race or] female essence, outside the boundaries of the social and thereby untainted . . . by a [racist or]

patriarchal order" (Fuss 1989, 2). Indeed, I realize that there is more than one of each of these, including white womanhood within the dominant community. Nevertheless, I am positing that when the issue is black and white womanhood, white womanhood in all its various forms is usually elevated.

5. It is important to point out that both black and white women "are objectified, albeit in different ways, . . . [in order to] dehumanize and control both groups" (Collins 1991:106).

6. See Fordham (1993c) for a detailed discussion of some of the implications affiliated with the transformation of the gendered "self."

7. See Fordham (1987, 1988) and Fordham and Ogbu (1986) for a detailed discussion of the emergence and development of the fictive kinship system in the African American community.

8. Elsewhere (Fordham 1993b) I offer a detailed discussion of how female students at Capital High create an African American female identity in a context that does not sanction gender diversity.

9. This is the fictitious name I gave the flagship academic program at Capital High.

10. As many researchers have suggested (see, for example, Cox 1948; Dollard 1957; Frazier 1969; Landry 1987; Ogbu 1978), race undercuts class in the African American community. Hence, class phenomena do not have the same meaning in the black and white communities. For example, Obgu (1978) argues quite convincingly that there is a lack of congruency among the various classes in the African American and white communities. As he describes it, middle class in the white community is not analogous to middle class in the black community. The same is true of the designations: working class, lower class, upper-middle class, and so forth. Furthermore, as I am beginning to analyze the quantitative data collected during the Capital High study, I am overwhelmed by the unanimity of the response to the following question: "Would you say that socially your family belongs to the upper class? middle class? the lower class?" Would you describe your neighborhood as mainly upper class? middle class? lower class? Almost invariably, the students chose "middle class" was the appropriate response.

11. I am indebted to Grace Evans (1988) for this characterization of African American females.

12. Payne (1988) supports Evans's (1988) analysis of gender diversity by noting that the school context is impregnated with male norms and values. These features are so pervasive, she argues, that for some women existence is tantamount to "suffocat[ing] in comfort" (see Emerson, cited in Hendrickson 1991). Payne highlights resistance as a primary female response to this construction of the academic context, even postulating that for some young women in the academy pregnancy is an attempt to validate and affirm their female "self" in this male-dominated institution.

13. Hard work is probably best described as work outside the home (i.e., paid labor). It is also accurate to describe hard work as laborious and intense. As enslaved females, African American women received no, or virtually no, remuneration for their labor outside the home. Once manumission occurred, they were further victimized in that they were not adequately compensated for their labor.

14. It may appear that I am making some essentialist or timeless claims about the African American community. That is not my intention. Indeed, I want to emphasize that I am not claiming that there exists out there some "true essence" (see Fuss 1989). Obviously, each African American constructs the world differently. The point I am making here is that, in spite of their differential understanding and perception, African Americans also share "socially acquired knowledge." In some contexts this is known as culture (see Bohannan 1992; Spradley and McCurdy 1989).

15. Following Collins (1991), I am defining a "safe cultural space" as a site where African American women are able to celebrate and applaud their varied sense of "self." Elsewhere (Fordham 1993b) I have indicated that the academy neither encourages nor promotes gender diversity. Further, I argue, because the African American female "self" is seen primarily as an illegitimate form, these women's quest for a safe cultural space is often pursued surreptitiously. Hence, finding a "safe cultural space" is a challenge for all African American females at Capital, regardless of level of achievement or academic effort.

16. A federally funded hospital for the mentally ill in Washington, D.C.

17. I am able to make this assertion because I was at the school for more than two years. During that time, I had numerous conversations with Ms. Apropos about Rita (she was only one of several students in the sample that Ms. Apropos taught) and many other students. I was able to observe many of these students in Ms. Apropos's English classes. She was one of several teachers who was willing to share with me information that went beyond the rudimentary, about the students, their parents, and the administrators. Ms. Apropos was frequently baffled and buoyed by Rita's contradictory behaviors, her concurrent acceptance and rejection of school norms and values.

18. For a more detailed discussion of Rita's ambivalent religious beliefs, see chapter 6 of my forthcoming book, tentatively titled: *Acting White and Book-Black Blacks: An Ethnography of the Dilemma of School Success at Capital High* (1993a).

19. I am not suggesting that this fact is unimportant. It is. However, as Lorde notes, "the master's tools will never dismantle the master's house" (1990, 287). Her argument indicates a need for an African American education that is not at the same time a "miseducation" (Woodson 1933).

20. Paul and Norris would graduate numbers second and third, respectively, in the shadow of Katrina, who would graduate first.

21. See Fordham 1993b.

22. A family of procreation suggests the active involvement of ego in producing a family.

References

Baugh, John. 1983. *Black Street Speech: Its History, Structure and Survival.* Austin: University of Texas Press.

Bohannan, Paul. 1992. *We, The Alien: An Introduction to Cultural Anthropology.* Prospect Heights, Ill.: Waveland Press.

Brown, Elsa Barkley. 1988. "African-American Women's Quilting: A Framework for Conceptualizing and Teaching African-American Women's History." In Micheline R. Malson, Elizabeth Mudimbe-Boyi, Jean F. O'Barr, and Mary Wyer, eds., *Black Women in America: Social Science Perspectives,* 9–18. Chicago: University of Chicago Press.

Brown, Lenha Woods. 1972. *Free Negroes in the District of Columbia, 1790–1846.* New York: Oxford University Press.

Cary, Lorene. 1991. *Black Ice.* New York: Knopf.

Christian, Barbara. 1990. "What Celie Knows That You Should Know." In David T. Goldberg, ed., *Anatomy of Racism.* Minneapolis: University of Minnesota Press.

Collins, Patricia Hill. 1991. *Black Feminist Thought: Knowledge, Consciousness, and the Politics of Empowerment.* New York: Routledge.

Cox, Oliver C. 1948. *Caste, Class and Race: A Study in Social Dynamics.* New York: Modern Reader.

Davis Angela. 1971. "Reflections on the Black Woman's Role in the Community of Slaves." *The Black Scholar* 3.4: 2–16.

Dollard, John. 1957 [1937]. *Caste and Class in a Southern Town.* Garden City, N.Y.: Doubleday.

Evans, Grace. 1988. "Those Loud Black Girls." In *Learning to Lose: Sexism and Education.* London: The Women's Press.

Flanagan, James G. 1989. "Hierarchy in Simple 'Egalitarian' Societies." *Annual Review of Anthropology* 18: 245–66.

Fleming, Jacqueline. 1978. "Fear of Success, Achievement Related Motives and Behavior in Black College Women." *Journal of Personality* 46: 694–716.

———. 1982. "Sex Differences in the Impact of Colleges on Black Students." In P. J. Perun, ed., *The Undergraduate Woman: Issues in Educational Equity.* Lexington, Mass.: Lexington Books.

———. 1983. "Sex Differences in the Educational and Occupational Goals of Black College Students: Continued Inquiry into the Black Matriarchy Theory." In M. S. Homer, C. Nadelson, and M. Notman, eds., *The Challenge of Change.* New York: Plenum.

———. 1984. *Blacks in College: A Comparative Study of Students' Success in Black and in White Institutions.* San Francisco: Jossey-Bass.

Fordham, Signithia. 1987. *Black Students' School Success as Related to Fictive Kinship: An Ethnographic Study in the District of Columbia Public School System,* 2 vols. Washington, D.C.: American University Press.

———. 1988. "Racelessness as a Factor in Black Students' School Success: Pragmatic Strategy or Pyrrhic Victory?" *Harvard Educational Review* 58.1: 54–84.

———. 1990. "Phantoms in the Opera: Black Girls' Academic Achievement at Capital High." Paper presented at the Annual Meeting of the American Anthropological Association, November, New Orleans.

————. 1991a. "Peer-Proofing Academic Competition Among Black Adolescents: 'Acting White' Black American Style." In Christine Sleeter, ed., *Empowerment Through Multicultural Education,* 69–90. Albany: State University of New York Press.

————. 1991b. "Racelessness in Private Schools: Should We Deconstruct the Racial and Cultural Identity of African American Adolescents?" *Teachers College Record* 92.3: 470–84.

————. 1993a. "Acting White and Book-Black Blacks: An Ethnography of Academic Success at Capital High." Chicago: University of Chicago Press.

————. 1993b. *Spawning the "Doubly-Refracted Other": African-American Women's School Success at Capital High* (in press).

————. 1993c. *Transforming the Gendered Self: The Construction of a Plagiaristic Identity and Academic Success* (in press).

Fordham, Signithia, and John U. Oghu. 1986. "Black Students' School Success: Coping with the 'Burden of "Acting White."'" *The Urban Review* 18.3: 176–206.

Frazier, E. Franklin. 1969 [1957]. *The Black Bourgeoisie.* New York: The Free Press.

Fuss, Diane. 1989. *Essentially Speaking: Feminism, Nature and Difference.* New York: Routledge.

Garret-Vital, Michelle R. 1989. "African-American Women in Higher Education: Struggling to Gain Identity." *Journal of Black Studies* 20.2: 180–91.

Gilligan, Carol. 1982. *In a Different Voice: Psychological Theory and Women's Development.* Cambridge, Mass.: Harvard University Press.

Green, Constance M. 1967. *The Secret City: A History of Race Relations in the Nation's Capital.* Princeton: Princeton University Press.

Grove, Lloyd. 1991. "Marching in a Different Parade: For Desert Storm Protesters, The Trail of Victory." *Washington Post,* August 2, p. B1.

Gurin, Patricia, and Edgar Epps. 1975. *Black Consciousness, Identity and Achievement.* New York: John Wiley & Sons.

Hendrickson, Paul. 1991. "Reporter Out of No Woman's Land: Gloria Emerson, Taking Sides From Vietnam to Gaza." *Washington Post,* June 5, pp. B1, B8, B9.

Hochschild, Arlie Russell. 1975. "Inside the Clockwork of Male Careers." In Florence Howe, ed., *Women and the Power to Change.* New York: McGraw-Hill.

Holland, Dorothy C., and Margaret A. Eisenhart. 1990. *Educated in Romance: Women, Achievement, and College Culture.* Chicago: University of Chicago Press.

hooks, bell. 1989. *Talking Black.* Boston: South End Press.

Hurston, Zora Neale. 1969. *Mules and Men.* New York: Negro Universities Press.

Ione, Carole. 1991. *Pride of Family: Four Generations of American Women of Color.* New York: Summit.

Keil, Charles. 1966. *Urban Blues.* Chicago: University of Chicago Press.

Landry, Bart. 1987. *The New Black Middle Class.* Berkeley: University of California Press.

Lewis, Diane. 1988. "A Response to Inequality: Black Women, Racism and Sexism." In Micheline R. Malson, Elizabeth Mudimbe-Boyi, Jean F. O'Barr, and Mary Wyer, eds., *Black Women in America: Social Science Perspectives,* 41–63. Chicago: University of Chicago Press.

Lewis, Magda, and Roger I. Simon. 1986. "A Discourse Not Intended for Her: Learning and Teaching Within Patriarchy." *Harvard Educational Review* 56.4: 457–72.

Lorde, Audre. 1990. "Age, Race, Class, and Sex: Women Redefining Difference." In Russell Ferguson, Martha Gever, Trinh T. Minh-Ha, and Cornel West, eds., *Out There: Marginalization and Contemporary Cultures,* 281–88. Cambridge, Mass.: MIT Press.

Montgomery, Winfield S. 1907. *Historical Sketch of Education for the Colored Race in the District of Columbia, 1807–1905.* Washington, D.C.: Smith Brothers.

Ogbu, John U. 1978. *Minority Education and Caste: The American System in Cross-Cultural Perspective.* New York: Academic Press.

Pagano, Jo Anne. 1990. *Exiles and Communities: Teaching in the Patriarchal Wilderness.* Albany: State University of New York Press.

Palmer, Phyllis. 1989. *Domesticity and Dirt: Housewives and Domestic Servants in the United States, 1920–1945.* Philadelphia: Temple University Press.

Payne, Irene. 1988. "A Working-Class Girl in a Grammar School." In *Learning to Lose: Sexism and Education.* London: The Women's Press.

Powell, Catherine Tabb. 1991. "Rap Music: An Education with a Beat From the Street." *Journal of Negro Education* 60.3: 245–59.

Rich, Adrienne. 1979. *On Lies, Secrets, and Silence: Selected Prose 1966–1978.* New York: W. W. Norton.

Rose, Patricia. 1991. "'Fear of a Black Planet': Rap Music and Black Cultural Politics in the 1990s." *The Journal of Negro Education* 60.3: 276–90.

Sacks, Karen. 1976. "The Rockefeller Gang Created Ladies." Unpublished ms.

Said, Edward W. 1989. "Representing the Colonized: Anthropology's Interlocutors." *Critical Inquiry* 15: 205–25.

Scott, James. 1985. *Weapons of the Weak: Everyday Forms of Peasant Resistance.* New Haven, Conn.: Yale University Press.

———. 1990. *Domination and the Arts of Resistance.* New Haven, Conn.: Yale University Press.

Scott, Kesho Y. 1991. *The Habit of Surviving: Black Women's Strategies for Life.* New Brunswick, N.J.: Rutgers University Press.

Sexton, Patricia Cayo. 1969. *The Feminized Male: Classrooms, White Collars and the Decline of Manliness.* New York: Random House.

Smith, Elsie. 1982. "Black Female Adolescent: A Review of the Educational, Career, and Psychological Literature." *Psychology of Women Quarterly* 6 (Spring).

Spradley, James P., and David W. McCurdy. 1989. *Anthropology: The Cultural Perspective,* 2nd ed. Prospect Heights, Ill.: Waveland Press.

Wahlman, Maude Southwell, and John Scully. 1983. "Aesthetic Principles of Afro-American Quilts." In William Ferris, ed., *Afro-American Folk Art and Crafts,* 79–97. Boston: G. K. Hall.

Walker, Alice. 1982. *The Color Purple.* New York: Harcourt Brace Jovanovich.

Washington, Mary Louise. 1987. *Invented Lives: Narratives of Black Women 1860–1960.* Garden City N.Y.: Anchor Press/Doubleday.

White, Deborah Gray. 1985. *"Ar'n't I a Woman?" Female Slaves in the Plantation South.* New York: W. W. Norton.

Williams, Patricia J. 1988. "On Being the Object of Property." In Micheline R. Malson, Elizabeth Mudimbe-Boyi, Jean F. O'Barr, and Mary Wyer, eds., *Black Women in America: Social Science Perspectives.* Chicago: University of Chicago Press.

Woodson, Carter G. 1933. *The Miseducation of the Negro.* Washington, D.C.: Associated Publishers.

PART
II

Newcomers
School and Community

5

Marcelo M. Suarez-Orozco _____

"Becoming Somebody"
Central American Immigrants
in U.S. Inner-City Schools

The problems facing Hispanic Americans in schools have gained increasing scholarly attention in the past two decades (Brown, Rosen, Hill, and Olivas 1980; Carter and Segura 1979; Hispanic Policy Development Project [HPDP] 1984; Lefkowitz 1985; Suarez-Orozco 1987a; Walker 1987). Although much research has been done to further our understanding of the issues facing Hispanic Americans in schools, many areas of the problem remain virtually unexplored. One such area that demands proper systematic treatment is related to the differences emerging from a consideration of the educational adaptation of the various Hispanic American groups.

Mexican Americans, mainland Puerto Ricans, Americans of Cuban descent, Americans of South American origin, as well as the recent immigrants from troubled Central American nations are distinct populations. They differ in demography and history, face different issues in schools, and should, therefore, be understood as such (Davis, Haub, and Willette 1983; Suarez-Orozco 1987b). For example, research suggests that Hispanics of Central and South American origin tend to do better in U.S. schools than their Mexican American and mainland Puerto Rican peers (Brown, Rosen, Hill, and Olivas 1980, 101; HPDP 1984, 2:57). According to some measurements, the differences in school functioning among the various Hispanic American subgroups are extraordinary. For example, HPDP reports that whereas 21.15 percent of the Mexican American sophomores dropped out of school in 1982, only 11.4 percent of the Hispanics of Central and South American origin dropped out of school that same year (HPDP 1984, 2:57). Davis, Haub, and Willette similarly conclude that Cuban Americans and more recent immigrants from Central and South America tend to be better educated than Mexican Americans and mainland Puerto Ricans (1983, 29). Likewise, Brown, Rosen, Hill and Olivas report that "Puerto Rican and Mexican Americans had much higher

non-completion rates [in high school] than the other Hispanic subgroups"
(1980, 101). I must underscore the fact that further research is needed to explore the different experiences among the various Hispanic American subgroups.

Yet the data already available tend to support Ogbu's contention (Ogbu,
1983, volume 18; Ogbu and Matute-Bianchi 1986) that overall *immigrant* minorities, such as Hispanics of Central and South American origin in the United
States, generally perform better in schools and certainly experience different
kinds of problems than *castelike* minorities, such as blacks, Mexican Americans, and Native Americans.

This chapter explores the specific issues facing recent arrivals from Central America as well as their unique motivational patterns in the context of re-
settling in the new land. The experiences of these immigrants will be framed
in reference to Ogbu's cultural ecological approach to the study of education
and minority status in plural societies (Ogbu 1974, 1978b, 1981). I must emphasize that due to a number of critical reasons, the Central American case
considered here is far from an ideal paradigm of immigrant adaptation to
schooling.

We have witnessed in the last seven years an impressive and continuous
flow of immigrants from war-torn Central America to the United States
(LaFeber 1984; Mohn 1983; Suarez-Orozco 1987b). It is difficult to find reliable estimates on the numbers of Central Americans now residing in the
United States. Some researchers estimate that between 300,000 and 400,000
Salvadoreans currently reside in the United States (Diskin 1983, 43). The Central American Refugee Committee [CRECEN] estimates that over 500,000
Salvadoreans now make the United States their place of residence (CRECEN
1985). CRECEN estimates that as many as 220,000 Guatemalans may be residing in the United States (CRECEN 1985). This is not counting the Nicara-
guans who came to the United States in one of several waves.

MIGRATION AND RESETTLEMENT:
THE IMMIGRANT ETHIC AND SCHOOLING

The research reported in this and other writings (Suarez-Orozco 1985, 1987a,
1987b) was conducted in two inner-city high schools containing over 600 recent arrivals from Central America. The study consisted of participant observations plus systematic ethnographic interviews with some fifty core informants from El Salvador, Guatemala, and Nicaragua. All immigrants had
entered the United States within five years prior to the research. Of the fifty,
thirty were males aged 14 to 19, and twenty were females aged 14 to 19. Thirty-

three of my informants came from El Salvador, nine from Guatemala, and eight from Nicaragua. All remained enrolled in school during the period of fieldwork.

In addition to work in the classrooms and counseling office, my formal position in one of the school sites as "Bilingual Parent/Community Liaison" put me in regular contact with parents, relatives, and guardians of most immigrant students. Toward the end of the ethnography, I collected, scored, and analyzed over 400 Thematic Apperception stories from the new arrivals.

In these sites teachers reported that, considering the very special problems that immigrant Central Americans face as a legacy of the war they had escaped and the pressures to work in the inner city to help the family (Arroyo and Eth 1985), the new arrivals in my sample were "desirable students," as one informant put it. For example, two bilingual teachers with ample experience in the field confided that they could never go back to teaching "American students" [read U.S. minority], because their immigrant students (mostly Central American and Asian) were so eager to learn, so appreciative, and, above all, so polite that they could not face regular unruly classes in the rough inner-city high school.

A number of my teacher-informants reported early on that these Central American students were well motivated to learn (particularly English). The teachers noted that immigrant students exerted greater effort, studied harder, and often received better grades than other minority students. The teachers reported that my informants were more respectful and "nicer to have around" than either Anglo or other minority students. More objective measures seem to confirm these impressions. For example, in both school sites the Central American students were statistically underrepresented in numbers of school suspensions (Suarez-Orozco 1987b). Five of the graduating recent arrivals from Central America in my sample (10 percent of the total sample) were accepted into prestigious American universities.

Many Central American students were learning English at a rapid pace. In fact, so many were learning English fast that in both school sites, teachers privately reported that the counselors systematically kept the immigrants in English as a Second Language [ESL] classes and lower-level bilingual classes longer than required. This was done because of lack of space in the regular English classroom.

A systematic pattern of subtle discrimination was evident as I became more intimate with the teachers, counselors, and staff. The powerless immigrant students were not a priority: they were thus assigned to lower-level classes, classes that in some cases they had successfully completed in their country of origin.

Recent arrivals from Central America were routed to overcrowded, under-staffed classes in overcrowded, understaffed, poor inner-city schools. Students found themselves trying to learn a new culture in a new language in the rather poisonous environment that has made the American inner-city school infa-mous. Drugs were on display for sale all around the schools. In both sites gang and ethnic violence was a common occurrence. Teachers were very much afraid of their students. They systematically complained that they had to oper-ate with far more students than they had been trained to teach.

Despite a school atmosphere of drugs, violence, low expectations, the cal-culated tracking of minority students to nonacademic subjects (in already nonacademic schools), bitter teachers, the seductive offers by more accultur-ated peers to join the street culture, and the need to work to help the family, my informants remained in schools trying to learn English. I was naturally at-tracted to these students. Indeed, considering the legacy of economic scarcity and political terror in Central America (Arroyo and Eth 1985; Durham 1979; Suarez-Orozco 1987b), it is most remarkable that *any* of these youngsters should stay in the inner-city schools, trying "to become somebody," seemingly against all odds. Although 10 percent of my informants did go on to enroll at major universities, it would be erroneous to imply that all Central American students became model students. Elsewhere (Suarez-Orozco 1987b) I explore in great detail why some younger new arrivals develop specific schooling problems in the inner city. Yet, I maintain, the intellectually challenging ques-tion is not to explain why some recent arrivals would leave school to join the labor market, or have learning problems, but why, given their current realities and immediate history, so many should stay in school at all.

A possible way to begin to approach this question is by exploring parental expectations among the new arrivals. Central American parents articulated the notion that a primary factor in the decision to escape to freedom was the wel-fare of the children. As one mother from Nicaragua put it, "We came here for them," referring to her five children. She added, "so that they may become somebody tomorrow. . . . I am too old, at my age it is too late for me . . . if any-thing, it is harder for me here than there [Nicaragua]." She had decided to leave her small town in rural Nicaragua over a year before our interviews because she was afraid that her oldest son, a sixteen-year-old, would be drafted to fight the *contras* on the Honduran border.

A dual frame of reference comparing present opportunities in the United States and past realities in the land of fear and economic scarcity emerged among the immigrants to face and interpret current conditions in the inner city. Because in most cases they had escaped their country in search of a better tomorrow and because their parents sacrificed a great deal for the journey north, recent immigrant students thought the advantages in the new land were self-evident and required little elaboration. For them it was very clear: despite ongoing difficulties there were more opportunities to study, more help to do so, better training facilities, and more and better future job opportunities in the United States than back home.

Once this theme was identified, I turned to isolate the emergence of a specific folk system of status mobility. Given that there was a collectively held perception among immigrants that more opportunities for advancement existed in the United States than in El Salvador, Guatemala, or Nicaragua, the next issue was to document specific shared beliefs on the nature of how one "makes it" in the new land.

Universally, informants reported that schooling was the single most significant avenue for status mobility. It is important to note that the majority of my parent-informants had been pushed out of school in their native lands (Suarez-Orozco 1987b). Some could not afford the luxury of schooling in remote rural areas of Central America. Others had to face hard physical labor at an early age to contribute to the family's income. The parents were mostly laborers and semiskilled laborers. The current opportunities open to their children in the new land were seen by many parents in contrast to their own experiences in Central America.

The belief in education as a key mode of status mobility in the host country was often constructed in opposition to the conceived system of status mobility in the country of origin. As one Salvadorean informant succinctly put it, "Here [US] is *what* you know, there [El Salvador] is *who* you know."

According to these immigrants, in the United States, schooling, knowledge, and individual effort emerged as the primary avenue for status mobility. On the other hand, in the country of origin, one made it through networks and friends of friends, or through nepotism or *"por apellido"* (because of one's last name) and not because of individual efforts, knowledge, or achievements.

To summarize, the fact that my informants left their land for a better tomorrow is of importance for understanding subsequent school adaptation. A dual frame of reference, comparing present and prior (often brutal) realities, emerged as a matrix in which they evaluate and face experiences. In thinking about the meaning of schooling and the future, immigrants often paused and made comparative evaluations between the "here" and the "there." And "here" schooling offered many opportunities for advancement. Next I explore how advancement became the idiom to repay parents and those left behind for their sacrifices.

The Psychosocial Context of Motivation

Most of the Central American students I came to know well were keenly aware of the degree of parental sacrifice involved in getting out of the country of origin (Suarez-Orozco 1985, 1987b). Parents often framed sacrifices in reference to the future of the children. Perceptions of parental sacrifice emerged as a key interpersonal concern among the immigrants as captured in their responses to the Thematic Apperception Test (Suarez-Orozco 1995).

Although they were greatly appreciative of their new lot in the United States, the immigrants continued to live through the hardships that must be endured in order to survive in a foreign land. Students saw their parents become janitors, maids, busboys, and, in some cases, take two jobs so they could go to school to receive the education the parents themselves never had.

The majority of my informants (64%) had one or more members of their nuclear family still residing in a war-torn Central American nation. Most of my informants (68%) worked about four hours a day, commonly after school, to help their relatives and those left behind with remittances. Some have reported that the recent arrivals from El Salvador alone send between 350 million to 600 million dollars annually in remittances (Pear 1987, 8).

Others, particularly young men, had left their entire nuclear family in Central America and were living in the United States with distant relatives or friends. In some of these cases parents had used vital resources to send a youth to the safety of the United States. Among these immigrants, I found a severe sense of responsibility to those left behind. Schooling efforts in the new land were framed in reference to a wish to "rescue" those relatives still in Central America (Suarez-Orozco 1985, 1987b).

Such interpersonal issues put a particular psychological burden to achieve on many of my informants. An intense sense of duty to less fortunate relatives gains center stage in the psychosocial profile of many immigrants. Guilt about one's survival and present opportunities in the new land not shared by those left behind fueled the immigrant's project for a better tomorrow, for themselves, and, most importantly, for their families.

Among many informants, and most particularly among those with close relatives remaining behind, something akin to "survivor guilt" has appeared (Bettelheim 1980, 274–314). The syndrome experienced by many of the recent arrivals from Central America is similar in some respects to the guilt described by Bettelheim occurring among some survivors of the Nazi death machine. Bettelheim described how survivors in the death camps often shared a belief that one's life was spared because someone else has suffered or died (Bettelheim 1980, 274–314).

Many immigrant youths live with the conscious knowledge that they were sent out of Central America, whereas others, including siblings and parents, had to remain. Among many informants, concern over those left behind becomes the focus in a plan to "rescue" others and to alleviate the ongoing hardships of those responsible for sending them to freedom.

PSYCHOCULTURAL CONSIDERATIONS
AND ACHIEVEMENT MOTIVATION

Psychological tests, ethnographic interviews, and participant observations allowed a careful consideration of the psychosocial profile of these immigrants. Most informants showed a remarkable sense of duty to the parents and family members for their suffering. This accentuated a wish to achieve, to do well in school, in order to repay parents and relatives, to make their endurance worthwhile by *"llegando a ser alguien"* (becoming somebody). The following case study in some ways provides a paradigm of a successful immigrant's psychocultural motivational dynamics. (For more extensive psychocultural analysis of fifty case studies, see Suarez-Orozco 1988.)

Antonio was a seventeen-year-old young man from El Salvador. He came to the United States with his mother, a maid, and older sister in 1981. None spoke any English then. His father, a postal worker in San Salvador, stayed behind.

Antonio completed the 9th, 10th, 11th, and 12th grade in the United States. During his senior year he had a cumulative grade point average of 3.75 (out of 4.0 possible points). During his senior year, Antonio was accepted into a very prestigious U.S. university. His father completed the 6th grade and his mother the 7th grade before they both had to work full time to help their respective families. Antonio's sister graduated from high school in El Salvador. In the United States, Juana, his mother, worked as a maid, often six days a week. Juana normally left at about 6 A.M. and usually came back after sundown. The work schedule was particularly hard on her during the winter months. Because she did not have access to a car, she had to take public transportation to the different homes she cleaned. And because the homes were usually in upper middle-class neighborhoods (and she lived in the inner city), she often had to take two, at times even three buses, to reach work.

Juana did not allow Antonio to work during the academic year. She noted that they came to the United States "so that he can study in peace and make a better tomorrow." Juana made it clear that they came to the United States so that the children could "become somebody" here. War and a wrecked economy in her native El Salvador had pushed away any fantasies that her children could escape out of the very modest existence she herself had endured. But in the United States things changed. As she concluded, "Antonio now has to dedicate himself to school."

In fact, Juana wanted Antonio to go to the university. She was full of pride when he was accepted: "He'll be the first *universitario* (professional) in the family," she observed with effervescent joy. As many other informants, Antonio was fully aware of why his mother wanted him to study: "She does not want me to lead a life such as the one they had to live when they were young. They had to work hard, sacrifice themselves," he said.

Antonio's plan was to become a professional. "I believe the most important thing I can do for my parents is to become a doctor, that would make them happy. l would be the first professional in my family." Like many other informants, Antonio said that he wanted to become a professional in order "to work with my community, to help the Hispanic community as a doctor."

In order to achieve this, Antonio studied hard four or five hours after school every day. He took his schooling very seriously, spending each one of his summers in the United States going to special summer programs at a local private university to learn more English and science.

Antonio was given the Thematic Apperception Test (TAT) in his native Spanish language in late 1984. The TAT consists of a series of vague drawings that are presented sequentially to the informant. The informant is simply asked to "make up a story" based on what he/she sees on the drawings. The narrative should have a past, a present, and a future. The TAT rests on the logic that presented with vague stimuli, informants will "talk about themselves." They will articulate their latent wishes, fears, dreams, and worries. The TAT has been widely used as an anthropological tool complementing ethnographic participant observations to capture systematically patterned interpersonal concerns in given populations (e.g., Lindzey 1961; Scheper-Hughes 1979; Wagatsuma and De Vos 1984). Representative parts of Antonio's TAT follow.

Card 1 [A boy contemplating a violin]:
[Takes a long look, over 30 seconds] May I begin? This is about a family that lives in a small town outside San Francisco. The family is composed of two brothers, the father and the mother. The family has financial problems, economic problems. They are thinking how to solve these problems. Up to now the children do not know anything about this. But the father and the mother are worried about it. They cannot hide their worry over this problem. During one of the conversations between the mother and the father, one of the boys realizes the nature of the problem. At that point, the child that found out

about the problem went to tell his brother. They begin to talk about the problem and about what they will [do] to help.

That same evening one of the brothers is doing his schoolwork. He can not concentrate on his schoolwork because he is thinking about the economic troubles facing his family.

The two brothers then organize a campaign. They read the want-ads in the paper and they find that there is a job for two kids to deliver newspapers after school. They begin to work after school so that the mother and father do not realize. That way they get together enough money between the two of them to pay their parents' debt.

Analysis: This story captures the interpersonal context of achievement motivation among many Central American informants. The motivation to achieve is most often directly related to a wish to help relieve parental suffering (Suarez-Orozco 1987b). Also note how in the story economic problems emerge as interfering with academic tasks. This was a common issue among my informants, who often noted that the need to work often prevented them from studying as much as they would like to.

Card 2 [A farm scene, a young woman is in the foreground with books in her hands, in the background a man is working the land. A woman leans on a tree]:

This is about a girl named Maria. She was a country girl, a very beautiful farmer that lived with her mother and her brother. Maria's family was a hard working farm family. They cultivated the land. Maria's brother was a hard working man, he worked very hard next to his mother. They had a hard life.

Maria was a studious woman. She looked at her family's future and her own future. One day Maria went to the city. In the city she realized how different life there was from life on her farm. She said, "One day I shall have the commodities city families have." Seeing the difference between the city and her farm, Maria began studying and studying. She studied more and harder than ever. She went to the most prestigious universities of her country, with scholarships and working part-time.

Finally Maria was able to move her family, her mother and brother from the farm to the city. They lived for a long time with Maria. But the family did not really like city life, they went back to the country. Maria was very sad, so she went back to her farm to help them there, to work with them there, to teach there.

Analysis: The hard-working family lived off their work on the land. Maria, a studious character, was concerned about "her family's future." One day she goes to the city and sees how life in the city can be different, *significantly not only for herself but for her sacrificing mother and brother.* There she was witness to the commodities of city life. She saw a difference. As is the case with many immigrant informants, a comparative perception of opportunity leads the *dramatis persona* to further hard work, through study. Studying becomes the way out of a hard existence. The perception of opportunity juxtaposed with a realization of familial sacrifice is the framework in which motivation flourishes. Here is a chance to help change the hard life of one's relatives. Studying prepares Maria to attend "the most prestigious universities" and with the help of available scholarships and part-time work she makes it.

"Finally she was able to move her family" from the farm to the city. Her objective was not mere self-advancement and independence but rather, to help the family out of hard farm work. This is the meaning of success. But there is a conflict between the young professional and her farm relatives. The mother and brother do not really like life in the city. Maria is saddened by their choice to go back. Yet, rather than breaking off with her family and staying in the city, she chooses to go back with them to further help them, "to teach there."

Upon close scrutiny, the structure of the motivational pattern in Antonio's story about Maria and Antonio's own life are, perhaps not surprisingly, isomorphic. Both are witness to the hard work the family must endure to survive. Both are further motivated by a perception of opportunity in a new land. In neither case is the achieving motive rooted in an individualistic wish for self-betterment, or in a wish for becoming independent. Rather, the aim is to help end, through studying, the family's hardships.

> *Card 6BM* [A man in the foreground looks down; a somewhat older looking woman in the background looks out a window]:
>
> Luis was an attorney in the city. He had many offices and was very rich. He lived with his children and spouse in a mansion north of the city. Luis worked well with his coworkers and was a family man. He always took interest in his children and spouse. Nobody knew about Luis's past.
>
> His past was a sad past. Ever since he was a little boy he had to work in the streets: shining shoes, or selling tickets in buses. But he was interested in his studies. Through studying he achieved his law career.
>
> Once Luis became an attorney he forgot his family. He forgot where he came from. He forgot that he had a mother that struggled for him when he was a little boy. One day Luis's mother went to visit him in his office. His mother was very sick, she had a few months to live. She told Luis this because she wanted him to inherit her house. When Luis heard this he became very sad because now he could not do anything for his mother: she would have needed medical attention two years before, and he was not there next to her then, so she was not treated.

Luis could not find the words to beg her to forgive him. But his mother knew that Luis was sorry for what he did. She forgave him.

When Luis's mother died, he went back to the place he once lived with her. Being a very rich man, he founded three schools to help the needy classes in his community.

Analysis: Luis, the high achieving wealthy attorney, had a dark past. His sad past is not that he had to work shining shoes to become a rich attorney. Rather, it was that he had committed a serious transgression. Luis violated a law so fundamental it need not be in the books: "He forgot his family. He forgot where he came from. He forgot that he had a mother."

The consequences of this callous disregard for his mother, who so "struggled" on his behalf when he was a boy, are devastating. The mother will die and there is nothing the powerful attorney can do to prevent this. It is too late; he should have been next to his mother two years earlier when she needed medical attention.

Luis was overcome by sadness. He was so paralyzed that he could not even bring himself to beg her forgiveness. Yet the all-understanding, sacrificing mother forgave him anyway. She "knew that Luis was sorry."

It is psychosocially significant that the story should not end with her death and his sorrow. In fact, his mother's death brings Luis back to his people.

At the end, her death was not in vain. It brings him back to his people *so he can share with them,* as he should have done before the tragedy occurred. It is of symbolic significance that he should choose to honor his mother by donating three *schools* to needy people. School was his way out of poverty, and the schools he donated should do the same for his people. He learned his lesson the hard way: one can not achieve and forget.

Dynamically the story is an exceptional capsule of basic interpersonal themes among many immigrants. The hero makes it with the help of a sacrificing mother who struggles so he can get ahead. Rather than turning to her, he chooses to leave her and his people behind. This is a severe violation that is certain to bring devastating consequences.

Let us underline the emergence of a pattern in which achievements are neither individualistic nor for the sole purpose of independence or self-advancement. Rather, achievements are embedded in a pattern of cooperation and mutual nurturance. One "makes it" with the precious help of significant others, and must turn to them to complete the cycle.

Card 13B [A barefoot boy, sitting down in front of a door]:
This is about a boy, Rodolfo. He lives in a hamlet outside the city. He is

a poor boy, from a very poor family. So he had to work hard from a young age. At five years of age he has to go to work and live a street life.

His mother is sick. His father left her when he was born. Rodolfo has to work shining shoes and selling candies in the buses. Sometimes he even works at night to earn enough to have a tortilla to eat.

One day Rodolfo began thinking about the future. Will he be a good man? Or, will he be a bad man? He also thinks about school and the streets and the differences that exist between the two. After thinking about all this he discovered that there was a great difference between the street and school: that difference is knowledge. Knowing what is good and what is bad.

After meditating about this, Rodolfo told his mother that he was going to do his best to continue in school. He told his sick mother not to worry about anything because he would also work. . . . He would work for both . . . and study, no matter how hard it was to do both or how much he would suffer. This is what Rodolfo did. Years passed and he was a model student in his school. After finishing high school he went to the university to study law. He chose law because he thought that it would be the best way to help as many poor children, as he once was, as possible.

Analysis: Little Rodolfo had to work since the age of five to buy food. His poor mother was sick, his father left them. Rodolfo paused to meditate about his future and concluded that there was a fundamental difference between the street and school: knowledge. Knowledge represents a capacity to tell good from bad. Rodolfo thus chooses to go to school over street life. He tells his poor, sick mother not to worry because he will take care of both: he will study and work.

He becomes a model student and chooses a career to help as many poor kids as possible.

The pattern emerging is isomorphic to previous stories: the boy from a poor home has the insight that education is the route out of misery. Through hard work and study he becomes an attorney. Rather than turning away from his people, he both studies and works so his poor sick mother would not "worry." At the end, his achievement is translated into helping "as many" poor kids as possible. The culmination is not some sort of narcissistic self-indulgence, but rather the conversion of success into concrete help for his people.

In summary, among the recent immigrants the emergence of perceptions of opportunity in the new land became intertwined with a severe sense of duty to relatives and other folk (Suarez-Orozco 1987b). Achievement motivation in this case does not follow the pattern found among more individualistic Anglo-Americans described by McClelland and associates (McClelland 1961, 1984). In McClelland's Anglo-American samples, high achievement need was often correlated with high independence need, a pattern contrary to the Central American case. In fact, the Central American case shows high achievement motivation related to a wish for affiliation and mutual nurturance. For example, in a sample of fifty responses to TAT card 1, 36 percent of the Central American stories were about achievement and nurturance (where the boy achieves to help others or with the help of others). And in fifty responses to card 2 of the TAT, fully 56 percent of the Central American stories were about achievement coupled with nurturant themes. (For a full analysis of other TAT themes among fifty new arrivals, see Suarez-Orozco 1988.)

CONCLUSION

Almost all of the Central American informants stated that in the United States, schooling was the key to a better future for themselves and their families. I must emphasize that, as stated earlier, some recent arrivals, particularly younger ones (14- to 16-year-olds in my sample), do become vulnerable to systematic school hostilities and the psychosocial factors derivative of having escaped the culture of terror in Central America. I note it would be an error to think that all Central Americans became model students. Many developed specific problems, which I consider elsewhere (Suarez-Orozco 1988). Having said this, I repeat that the intellectually challenging question remains why, given their history and ongoing reality in the inner city, do so many of the Central American youth stay in school at all?

To conclude, a key implication emerging from this ethnographic research is that, obvious as it may seem, not all Hispanic American students share the same problems. As Ogbu (1973, 1983; Ogbu and Matute-Bianchi 1986) has advocated, we need more comprehensive comparative studies exploring the different *kinds* of school problems facing different kinds of minority populations. As my research suggests, immigrants from Central America do not face the same problems in schools as their U.S.-born Hispanic peers.

The Central American students escaped a situation of war and misery. *That* reality overshadowed many of the subsequent hardships and marginality encountered in the new land. For many informants the sacrificing life of family members and the folks "back home" remained a significant point of reference against which to check more current developments. In their eyes, the relative advantages of life in the United States were self-evident. In this context many developed notions in which schooling emerged as the most important avenue to make it in the new land, and, in turn, to help their less-fortunate relatives.

REFERENCES

Arroyo, William, and Spencer Eth. 1985. "Children Traumatized by Central American Warfare." In Spencer Eth and Robert S. Pynoos, eds., *Post-Traumatic Stress Disorder in Children,* 103–20. New York: American Psychiatric Press.

Bettelheim, Bruno. 1980. *Surviving and Other Essays.* New York: Vintage Books.

Brown, George H., Nan L. Rosen, Susan T. Hill, and Olivas Estabon. 1980. *The Condition of Education for Hispanic Americans.* Washington, D.C.: United States Department of Education, National Center for Education Statistics.

Carter, Thomas P. and Roberto D. Segura. 1979. *Mexican-Americans in School: A Decade of Change.* New York: College Entrance Examination Board.

Central American Refugee Committee (CRECEN). 1985. *CRECEN National Bulletin,* 1.2: 1–8.

Davis, C., Carol Haub, and JoAnne Willette. 1983. *Trouble in Our Backyard: Central America and the United States in the Eighties.* New York: Pantheon Books.

DeVos, George. 1984. "Ethnic Persistence and Role Degradation: An Illustration from Japan." Paper presented at the American-Soviet Symposium on Contemporary Ethnic Processes in the USA and the USSR, New Orleans.

Diskin, Martin, ed. 1983. *Trouble in Our Backyard: Central America and the United States in the Eighties.* New York: Pantheon Books.

Durham, William. 1979. *Scarcity and Survival in Central America: Ecological Origins of the Soccer War.* Stanford: Stanford University Press.

Hispanic Policy Development Project (HPDP). 1984. *Making Something Happen: Hispanics and Urban High School.* 2 vols. New York: Hispanic Policy Development.

LaFeber, Walter. 1984. *Inevitable Revolutions: The United States and Central America.* New York: W. W. Norton.

Lefkowitz, Bernard. 1985. "Renegotiating Society's Contract with Public Schools: The National Commission on Secondary Education for Hispanics and the National Board of Inquiry into Schools." *Carnegie Quarterly* 29.4: 2–11.

Lindzey, Gardner. 1961. *Projective Techniques and Cross-Cultural Research.* New York: Appleton-Century-Crofts.

McClelland, David C. 1961. *The Achieving Society.* Princeton: D. Van Nostrand.

———. 1984. *Motives, Personality and Society: Selected Papers.* New York: Praeger.

Matute-Bianchi, Maria E. 1986. "Ethnic Identities and Patterns of School Success and Failure Among Mexican Descent and Japanese-American Students in a California High School: An Ethnography Analysis." *American Journal of Education* 95.1: 233–55.

Mohn, Sid L. 1983. "Central American Refugees: The Search for Appropriate Responses." *World Refugee Survey,* 25th Anniversary Issue, 42–47.

Ogbu, John U. 1974. *The Next Generation: An Ethnography of Education in an Urban Neighborhood.* New York: Academic Press.

———. 1978. *Minority Education and Caste: The American System in Cross-Cultural Perspective.* New York: Academic Press.

———. 1981. "School Ethnography: A Multilevel Approach." *Anthropology and Education Quarterly* 12.1: 3–10.

———. 1983a. "Indigenous and Immigrant Minority Education: A Comparative Perspective." Paper read at 82nd Annual Meeting of the American Anthropological Association, Chicago, November 16–20.

———. 1983b. "Minority Status and Schooling in Plural Societies." *Comparative Education Review*, 27.2: 168–90.

Pear, Robert. 1987. "Salvadoreans Cite Fears on Return." *New York Times*, Sunday, April 26, pp. 1, 8.

Scheper-Hughes, Nancy. 1979. *Saints, Scholars and Schizophrenics: Mental Illness in Rural Ireland.* Berkeley: University of California Press.

Suarez-Orozco, Marcelo M. 1985. "Opportunity, Family Dynamics and School Achievement: The Sociocultural Context of Motivation among Recent Immigrants from Central America." Paper read at the University of California Symposium on Linguistics, Minorities and Education, Tahoe City, May 30–June 1.

———. 1986. "In Pursuit of a Dream: New Hispanic Immigrants in American Inner City Schools." Ph.D. dissertation, Department of Anthropology, University of California, Berkeley.

———. 1987a. "Towards a Psycho-Social Understanding of Hispanic Adaptation to United States Schooling." In Henry T. Trueba, ed., *Success or Failure? Learning and the Language Minority Student*, 156–68. Cambridge: Newberry House.

———. 1987b. "Spaanse Amerikanen: Vergelijkende Beschouwingen en Onderwijsproblemen. Tweede Generatie Immigrantejongeren." *Cultuur en Migratie.* 2: 21–49.

———. 1988. *In Pursuit of a Dream: The Experience of Central Americans Recently Arrived in the U.S.* Stanford: Stanford University Press.

Suarez-Orozco, Carola and Marcelo. 1995. *Transformations: Immigration, Family Life, Achievement Motivation Among Latino Adolescents.* Stanford: Stanford University Press.

Walker, Constance L. 1987. "Hispanic Achievement: Old Views and New Perspectives." In Henry T. Trueba, ed., *Success or Failure? Learning and the Language Minority Student*, 15–32. Cambridge: Newberry House.

6

Patricia Pessar

Dominicans

*Forging an Ethnic Community
in New York*

Whether Dominicans speak among themselves or with others about their migration experiences certain phrases are likely to recur. *"No había futuro"* ("There was no future"), they state, to explain why they have left a much revered homeland. Not surprisingly, they go on to say that they have come to the United States to *"progresar"* ("to advance economically"). Because, *"aquí hay trabajo"* ("here there is work") for those who are willing to "trabajar duro" ("work hard"). A final point in Dominicans' discourse on immigration may surprise native-born Americans accustomed to the notion that immigrants come to settle. I refer to the fact that many intend to return home in order to best enjoy their hard-fought gains in social and economic standing. In their words, in New York *"hay trabajo pero no hay vida"* ("there is work, but there is no life").

Over the years, some have returned home as true success stories with enough wealth to support an upper-middle-class lifestyle.[1] Still others have managed to fashion binational lives which combine social relationships and economic investments in both the Dominican Republic and the United States. For most, though, social and economic advancement has been far harder to attain. Rather than looking to the Dominican Republic for their immediate, or even more distant futures, increasing numbers have come to forge individual lives and ethnic institutions in the United States. As we shall see, for many of these people, both the "Dominican dream" of a rapid and successful return back home and the "American dream" of going from rags to riches remain elusive. They struggle, instead, with a deteriorating New York economy, overcrowding, limited education and skills, high incidences of female-headed households, and racial and ethnic discrimination (see Hendricks 1974; Georges 1990; Grasmuck and Pessar 1991; Pessar 1996).

131

"Aquí No Hay Futuro"

Si de aquí saliera petroleo
pero que hubiera luz y esperanza
. . . sin visa para soñar.

If petroleum left from here
There would be light and hope
Without the need to dream about a visa.[2]

The "need to dream about a visa" in the lyrics from a popular Dominican *merenge* points to the enormous importance of migration to the United States. As the song makes clear, the Dominican Republic has no oil to trade on the international market. Revenues from the major export, sugar, cannot support the economic and social demands of this developing nation. Rather than striving to forge a development plan that could employ its population at home more productively, Dominican politicians and policymakers have seemed content to export people. And people have proved to be a "bumper crop." Indeed, some 520,151 persons identified themselves in the 1990 United States census as having Dominican ancestry, with 347,858 of these having been born in the Dominican Republic (U.S. Dept. of Commerce 1991). During the 1980s the Dominican Republic ranked third in the world with regard to the proportion of its overall population that emigrated to the United States. While large-scale emigration dates back to the mid-1960s, over half (52 percent) of all Dominican immigrants entered the United States between 1980 and 1990 (Grasmuck and Pessar 1996, 290).

A "middle-class bottleneck" is how one researcher has accounted for this massive outmigration (Bray 1984). Captured in this phrase is the type of unequal development that has characterized the Dominican Republic for many decades. On the one hand, Dominican politicians and policymakers have introduced economic and social programs that have stimulated growth in the middle and upper working classes. On the other hand, true economic and political power have remained in the hands of a small elite. This group has resisted reforms which would diversify the economy and permit a more equitable distribution of wealth. In the absence of these reforms, the expanding middle sectors have been deprived of an adequate internal market to demand their labor, services, and goods (Grasmuck and Pessar 1991).With economic opportunities constrained at home, members of the middle strata have sought economic advancement in the United States. They leave behind a group of unemployed and underemployed who, while eager to emigrate, do not have the social and financial resources needed to reach the United States. Some among this latter group enter the ranks of the Dominican "boat people"—individuals who cross the shark-infested Mona Passage in search of employment in Puerto Rico (Duany 1990).

While economic factors predominate in the decision to emigrate, political events have motivated some to depart, and have even, on occasion, facilitated outmigration. In the early 1960s, after several years of political turmoil following the assassination of the dictator, Rafael Trujillo, the United States government greatly increased the supply of visas available for Dominicans. Still smarting at the establishment of a Communist regime in Cuba, the United States feared that the Dominican Republic, too, might embrace Communism. The then–U.S. ambassador to the Dominican Republic advocated the granting of wider access to visas as a safety valve against further political unrest and as a way to improve relations between the two countries (Martin 1966; Mitchell 1992). Politically motivated migration continued well into the 1970s, when there was increased repression and the violation of human rights in the Dominican Republic.[3] Some of the political exiles and dissidents who left the Dominican Republic in the sixties and seventies have emerged as political activists in New York. They have organized both for political change back home and for greater participation for Dominicans in U.S. politics (Georges 1987).

CHAIN MIGRATION

While it is true that most Dominican immigrants originate from the middle and upper working classes, social networks are critical in determining who among them is able to relocate abroad. When Dominicans describe emigration to the United States, they speak about the *cadena*: the chain that links one immigrant to another. Would-be immigrants must either strike out as pioneers and form their own migration chain or, more commonly, seek to link themselves with an established one.

For the most part, it is kinship that links the members of a *cadena*. Although U.S. immigration law favors "family reunification," the definition of the "family" in immigration legislation does not reflect the extended network of cooperating kin who constitute the practical and moral "family" for most Dominicans.[4] According to U.S. immigration law, the spouses and unmarried children of temporary resident aliens are the only family members accorded preference for visas within the quota system. For most Dominicans, however, the "true family" extends far beyond these boundaries to include married children, parents, and siblings. The result is that extralegal and illegal migration practices are often used, frequently in highly creative ways, to reunite the socially and culturally meaningful Dominican family.

The Ramírez family's experiences highlight how chain migration operates in all its complexity. All *cadenas* begin with a pioneer. In the Ramírez family it was Willy, the owner of a furniture store in the city of Santiago. In 1975, at the age of 45, he was experiencing problems meeting both the demands of his creditors and the mortgage payments on a recently purchased home in a relatively affluent middle-class neighborhood. Having no immediate kin in the United States, Willy contacted a creditor who was also a visa broker (*buscón*). In order to obtain a fraudulent visa from the broker, Willy transferred all the assets from his business (about 3,000 *pesos* or U.S. $2,200) to the *buscón*.

> "I knew I was taking a big risk," Willy told me. "If I had not made it in New York, perhaps all would have been lost. I wasn't doing this just for my own advancement, or even that of my wife and children. I was doing it for all my family; many of us had need, but no one was yet in New York to give us a helping hand."

Willy easily secured a job and housing in New York with the help of a family friend who had emigrated a few years earlier. Next he had to find a way to regularize his status so that he might begin petitioning for his other family members. He decided that his best alternative was to arrange what Dominicans call a *matrimonio de negocio*, a "business marriage." This is a method whereby an individual pays a legal immigrant or citizen a fee to enter into marriage and then uses the family reunification provision to acquire a legal resident visa. Such business marriages are meant to be undone; they are sealed by a civil ceremony frequently back in the Dominican Republic, and sexual relations between "business spouses" are proscribed (Georges 1990, 88). It took Willy three years of grueling work at two full-time jobs to save the $2,000 necessary to enter into a business marriage with a Dominican co-worker. It took one additional year before his petition for a temporary resident visa was granted. Willy then had to wait several more years, first to divorce his "business wife" and then to remarry his true spouse, Lidia. He and Lidia made sure to have a civil, as well as church, ceremony in the Dominican Republic in 1984 in order to have a legal marriage certificate to present to the U.S. consulate during the petition process. One year later Lidia's visa was granted. She joined Willy in the United States, reluctantly leaving her youngest children behind with her mother.

While Willy and Lidia had planned to save money to sponsor the migration of their youngest children first, unexpected events intervened. In 1986 the husband of Carmen, their twenty-four-year-old daughter was badly injured at work, and she was left with the responsibility to support her nuclear family. Unable to find suitable employment, Carmen implored her parents to help her acquire a tourist visa. They sent her funds to contact a local lawyer and plane fare. For a fee of several hundred U.S. dollars the lawyer was able to produce sufficient documentation for Carmen (e.g., bank statements and a deed to her home) to convince a consulate official that she was traveling for tourist purposes and would likely return due to strong financial and social ties back home. With tourist visa in hand, Carmen departed for New York where she moved in with her parents. She easily found employment and, as planned, remained after her tourist visa had expired. Carmen understood that her financial responsibilities now encompassed both her husband and young children back in the Dominican Republic and her own brothers and sisters who too sought visas. Her wages were apportioned to meet both sets of demands, as well as the operating expenses of the household in New York.

By 1988, some thirteen years after Willy's arrival in New York, he and Lidia were reunited with their two unmarried children. Willy would have liked to have petitioned the children at the time of their mother's emigration. Nonetheless, he chose not to complicate her petition by adding additional family members, lest the consular officials look too carefully into his previous divorce. Moreover, Willy was aware that consular officials often suspected that immigrant women with children planned to apply for welfare rather than seek employment in the United States. As a result, they often denied the children's petition until the mother could demonstrate a solid record of employment. Apparently, both parents' records were in order, because the children's immigration proved to be relatively easy and comparatively inexpensive.

Willy also fulfilled his pledge to help his own siblings. In 1990 he arranged for a poor, widowed sister to come to the United States. He paid $1,000 to a permanent returnee in the Dominican Republic who lent her "green card" to the widowed sister. The next step will be for Willy to become a U.S. citizen. As a citizen, Willy will have the right to legally sponsor the emigration of his remaining married children, siblings, and elderly parents.

The case of the Ramírez family contains several elements common to the immigration histories of many other Dominican families. First, the requirements for outmigration, whether it be legal or illegal, are costly. People from poorer families often cannot afford to migrate unless they can somehow forge social ties with more affluent immigrant families. This is apparently now occurring among some of the older and more established *cadenas* which have settled all their immediate kin who sought to emigrate. They are able to make loans to poorer "clients" of family members, such as trusted domestic servants and overseers of family property. Second, migration is for the most part a family project, and there is often an informal triage system which operates according to relative need. Since marriage among social equals is the norm, the use of marriage as a migration strategy tends to promote the predominance of the more economically secure within the migration stream. As one man in a small Dominican town told me, "Only the best families here have emigrated. And it is only a handful, because these families will only marry their children to each other." Third, while the Dominican population currently residing in the United States contains slightly more women than men, it is common for a man to be the pioneer of a migration chain. Owing to patriarchal beliefs and practices, women have often had to wait to be petitioned by a male immigrant. Finally, while the act of leaving children behind in the care of close kin is a wrenching emotional experience, this practice also highlights a more extended notion of the family than the one encoded in U.S. immigration law. The decision to leave children temporarily in the Dominican Republic can have negative consequences. Indeed, many parents fear that after years of separation, they will be reunited with children who are slow to respond to their love and authority. As one concerned father told me, "When I left they were babies. Now they're almost men. They have only known me as the father who sends dollars so they can eat and be clothed. I have not been there to gain their love and respect." School officials back in the Dominican Republic report their frustration, as well. Children who are temporarily separated from their parents sometimes refuse to apply themselves, arguing that their present schooling is irrelevant to their future education and work in the United States.[5] It should be added that an opposite migratory flow also operates: children who were born and/or raised in the United States are occasionally sent back to the Dominican Republic by their parents to be cared for by relatives there. This most commonly arises when the children have experienced behavioral problems, low academic performance at school, or drug addiction. According to one researcher, this strategy sometimes backfires and finds the youth even more disaffected and rebellious than they were prior to their return (Guarnizo 1996).

FORGING AN ETHNIC COMMUNITY IN THE UNITED STATES

Cadenas, as well as other social networks (based, for example, on membership in a particular sending community) are essential to the settlement process. They help Dominican immigrants locate jobs, learn "the ropes," and find receptive communities in which to settle. On this latter point, sociologists

Alejandro Portes and Rubén Rumbaut state, "Migration is a network-driven process, and the operation of kin and friendship ties is nowhere more effective than in guiding new arrivals toward preestablished ethnic communities" (Portes and Rumbaut 1990, 32). New York has always been a magnet for Dominican immigrants, with some 69 percent residing there in 1990, according to the last census. Neighboring New Jersey followed with 11 percent; Florida hosted 6 percent and Massachusetts was the home of another 5 percent. In other words, 91 percent of the Dominicans living in the United States in 1990 resided in only four states (U.S. Dept. of Commerce 1991).

Most Dominicans in the United States have made their homes in urban areas, with New York City being the first choice of many. Indeed, according to the 1990 census 206,719 Dominican immigrants were living there (Grasmuck and Pessar 1996, 32). This is a disputed figure, though, with many Dominican leaders insisting that the true number is twice or three times as large as the "official" count. What is undisputed is that the number of Dominicans in New York City has grown tremendously. A mere 9,223 were enumerated in the 1960 census, placing Dominicans in twenty-sixth place among immigrant populations in New York. In stark contrast, they currently enjoy first place (Guarnizo 1992).

While New York City is the locus of Dominican settlement, distinct settlement patterns within the greater metropolitan area have evolved over time. Like early immigrants before them, Dominicans first congregated in Manhattan's Lower East Side where they were attracted to cheap housing and jobs in manufacturing and services. This was also one of the sites of Puerto Rican settlement and many Dominican "pioneers" acknowledge the assistance Puerto Ricans extended to them in securing housing, jobs, and a general know-how about life in the City.

> "Now there is a Spanish-speaker on every corner," said one man who arrived in 1962, "but back then if you got lost, if you needed help, you might have to search for hours and even then it was likely that you would not find anyone who could understand you. . . . In those early years, we Dominicans were helped a lot by Puerto Ricans who already knew the ropes. I and most of my friends started out by living as boarders with Puerto Rican families. Puerto Ricans also helped us when we needed an apartment or a job. In fact I got one of my first jobs from a Puerto Rican neighbor."

Over the course of the 1960s, the more financially secure came to reject the squalor and decay of the Lower East Side and began to seek out middle-class neighborhoods in Queens (e.g., Corona) and Long Island (e.g., Rockville Centre) (Guarnizo 1992). Such pioneers in turn became magnets for others from their hometowns and villages. Indeed the mass resettlement of large numbers of Dominicans from specific locales has given rise to the "Dominicanization" of U.S. place names. For example Corona, Queens is fondly referred to as *Sabana Church* among Dominicans in recognition of the large number of residents originally from the Dominican community of Sabana Iglesias.[6]

Another locale whose name has been appropriated and Dominicanized is the Upper Manhattan neighborhood of Washington Heights. Stretching north on the west side of New York City from roughly 145th Street to 190th, "*Quisqueya Heights*"[7] is reputed to be the home of approximately one-third of all Dominicans in New York City and has emerged as the heart of the Dominican community in New York. Washington Heights has received successive waves of immigrants and migrants including Irish, Jews, Puerto Ricans, and Cubans; and it remains the home of many ethnic groups. Nonetheless, today it is Dominicans who largely shape the character of the community, as reflected in many of its cultural, social, political, and economic institutions.

Washington Heights has provided both a platform and inspiration for Dominican merengue bands, immigrant writers (see, e.g., Torres-Saillant 1991; Cocco de Filippis and Gutierrez 1994), and young filmmakers.[8] Dominicans have also put their own stamp on the religious life of the neighborhood. Several local Catholic churches which once labored to integrate earlier waves of Puerto Ricans into their predominately Irish and Italian fold have now emerged as national Dominican parishes. As national parishes, they serve as magnets and spiritual homes to all persons of Dominican ancestry regardless of where they reside, rather than ministering to all the faithful in a clearly defined geographical area (Goris-Rosario 1994). Indeed, a local parish has been named Our Lady of Altagracia, the patron saint of the Dominican Republic.

The community has also emerged as a site for political organizing and activism among Dominicans. One noteworthy effort involved a struggle for greater community control over the schools in northern Manhattan's Community School District 6. Of the 25,000 students attending elementary and intermediate schools in this district during the late 1980s, more than 80 percent were Dominican (Linares 1989, 78). At that time their schools were the most overcrowded in the city and the students' reading scores ranked the lowest (Linares 1989). The fight for community control and empowerment in District 6 began in 1980 when the Community Association of Progressive Dominicans confronted the school board and superintendent to demand bilingual education and programs for recently arrived immigrant families. Over the years Dominicans have gained a greater representation on the school board. This victory was the product of an aggressive program of voter registration, the creation of a parents' network throughout the district (based in the parent associations in each school), and the formation of a coalition of parents, community organizations, churches, and educators. Other subsequent gains have included the construction of additional public schools in the district and the appointment of a Dominican principal to head one of the community high schools.

The recent, successful campaign to redraw district lines in Washington Heights (District 10) is a striking example of the "coming of age" of Dominican community associations and of the collaboration between Dominicans and other area Latinos (see Graham 1996). Facilitated by federal legislation aimed at redressing the old practice of dividing geographic concentrations of ethnic groups to dilute their political influence, the newly created "Dominican district" reflects its Dominican majority and has created a jurisdiction in which Dominican officials might be more readily elected. Indeed, in the subsequent 1991 elections, Dominicans comprised the majority of candidates who ran for the district's seat in the New York City Council. Guillermo Linares, who earlier helped launch the movement for greater control over the neighborhood schools, was elected the first Dominican city councilman. Today Dominicans are also found in several other influential positions in city government, as well as in other agencies controlling local community development (Guarnizo 1994; Goris-Rosario 1994).

Dominicans' presence is clearly felt in the economic life of Washington Heights, where Dominican-owned businesses are burgeoning. One recent study of this neighborhood estimated between 1,500 and 2,000 visible Dominican-owned enterprises (Guarnizo 1992). These include scores of neighborhood *bodegas* (small, walk-in stores that stock food specialties of the Hispanic Caribbean), restaurants specializing in *comida criolla* (Dominican cuisine), travel agencies, money transfer agencies, and nonmedallion "gypsy" cab services. These ethnic-oriented business establishments help ease the transition between *aquí* ("here," the United States) and *allá* ("there," the Dominican Republic). The many Dominican-owned businesses in Washington Heights form part of a larger Dominican ethnic economy in New York. This is an economy ranging from ethnic-oriented, street vendors to medium-sized firms linked to the mainstream economy.[9] Many of the most successful Dominican returnees and "binationals" have gained their wealth through participating in this ethnic economy. Dominican subcontractors, who have extended their manufacturing base in New York to include factories in export processing zones in the Dominican Republic, exemplify this binational segment of the immigrant population. While the great majority of Dominican-owned businesses

are legal and contribute to the good of the local community, there are a minority who are involved in the drug trade. Among the drug industry's most unfortunate victims are those Dominican youth who participate in the distribution
and sale of cocaine in New York. In a study of a teenage drug ring located in
Washington Heights, the author had this to say:

> Money and drugs are the obvious immediate rewards for kids in the cocaine
> trade. But there is another strong motivating force, and that is the desire to
> show family and friends that they can succeed at something. Moving up a ca-
> reer ladder and making money is especially important where there are few
> visible opportunities. . . . Washington Heights, which the police call a "hot
> spot," is a battleground in the war on drugs. And as in all wars, it is the young
> who are the first casualties. (Williams 1989, 10, 26)

While a small segment of the Dominican population is involved in the
drug trade, the mass media has focused upon this activity to the detriment of
all Dominicans. Indeed, the stigma has been extended back to the island where
returnees have been disparaged as drug dealers by members of the Dominican
elite, and some have been excluded from exclusive neighborhoods, private
schools, and social clubs (Guarnizo 1996).

While sections of Washington Heights are considered "hot spots" by drug
enforcement agents, other sections of the community are considered "hot
spots" by developers and investors. As a result Dominicans have been gradually displaced from the more desirable sections of Washington Heights by
means of exorbitant rent-hikes, evictions, conversions of rental units into co-
ops and condominiums, as well as by a host of illegal practices. Those who
have "chosen" to relocate to less desirable locations within the neighborhood
face serious overcrowding, escalating crime, and deterioration of public services. For example, one woman living in a dilapidated building stated that she
lives as a virtual prisoner in her apartment afraid to open the door due to a rash
of recent robberies by individuals posing as police officers and employees of
the electrical company (Duany 1994). Moreover, as a result of overcrowded
schools, several thousand neighborhood children are bussed to districts in the
Bronx and other sections of Manhattan (Linares 1989).

In light of these negative trends, many working-class Dominicans are
again seeking to relocate within the city; the South Bronx appears to be
growing in popularity. As with earlier immigrant groups, the more financially secure have made their way to middle-class neighborhoods and communities in Queens, Long Island, Westchester County, and suburban New Jersey. The dispersal of Dominicans from Washington Heights to low-income and

middle-class neighborhoods both reflects and reinforces a growing social class stratification and polarization of the Dominican population in New York.[10] As has been a pattern with earlier immigrant populations, it is likely that the movement of the more affluent residents from the neighborhood will result in the loss of valuable resources which had earlier been channeled into the Dominican ethnic economy and community organizations.

ECONOMIC INTEGRATION

As the migration history of the Ramírez family shows, most Dominicans emigrate to the United States in search of economic opportunity and advancement. The decision to relocate to New York may seem at first perplexing in light of a general decrease in economic growth and decline in jobs over the last few decades. Nonetheless, the type of economic restructuring characterizing New York during this period has actually created economic opportunities in manufacturing and services for new immigrants (Sassen 1991, Waldinger 1987; Grasmuck and Pessar 1991).

In the face of heavy competition from other domestic and international markets, many New York manufacturers either would not or could not afford to retain native-born workers by increasing wages and improving working conditions. They also did not invest in modern equipment and technology, which might have reduced their reliance on labor. Many found a solution, though, in the supply of new immigrants who proved willing to accept prevailing wage levels and working conditions. Their actions placed a brake on escalating wages and operational costs. For example, the apparel industry—a major beneficiary of immigrant labor, in general, and Dominican immigrant labor, in particular—experienced a 10 percent decline in average hourly wages between 1965 and 1980 (Waldinger 1983). In addition, immigrants often possessed skills needed in traditional manufacturing industries. One study concludes that the large number of new immigrants has actually increased the demand in manufacturing for these workers (Marshall 1983). This is the case because employers have come to rely on labor-intensive techniques and older forms of production, such as subcontracting and industrial homework, that depend on a cheap and compliant workforce.

Dominicans have found a niche in New York City's restructured manufacturing industries. In 1979 almost one half (49%) of all Dominican workers, but only 18 percent of New York City's total labor force were engaged in manufacturing. A decade later the percentage of Dominicans working in manufacturing declined to 26 percent, yet it was still much higher than the percentage of all New York City workers in this sector (12%) (Hernández, Rivera-Batiz, and Agodini 1990, 42–45).

The restructuring of manufacturing has benefited immigrant entrepreneurs as well as immigrant workers. Operations, such as apparel subcontracting shops require relatively little start-up capital and thus are within the reach of the immigrant entrepreneur. In a recent study of Dominican entrepreneurs in New York, sociologist Luis Guarnizo found that 12 percent of the 92 firms he sampled were dedicated to manufacturing (1992, 121). The majority of these produced for the open market (especially in the garment and leather trades) and were owned by individuals who started as piece-rate workers, rose to supervisory positions, and finally set off on their own as subcontractors. Their operations ranged from home- or family-based micro-enterprises to mid-sized, stable plants (Guarnizo 1992, 113).

New immigrants cluster not only in New York City's restructured manufacturing sector, but also in the expanding service sector. Immigrants have found opportunities for low-paid employment in the advanced, highly specialized service sector and in other service activities meeting the needs of the city's high income professionals (Sassen-Koob 1986). In 1990 the service industry ranked as the largest employer of Dominican laborers, with over 28 percent of the entire Dominican workforce (Hernández et al. 1995, 43). It is also popular among Dominican entrepreneurs, as almost half of the Dominican-owned firms surveyed by Guarnizo were found in this sector (Guarnizo 1992, 121).

Dominicans, in comparison to other native-born and immigrant New Yorkers, have experienced a fair share of economic hardship. According to the 1990 census, Dominican New Yorkers were plagued with extremely high rates of poverty, 37 percent compared to 17 percent for the entire city, and 31 percent for all Hispanics (Hernández et al. 1995, 17). And while the per capita income of the overall New York immigrant population grew by 16 percent over the last decade, Dominicans lagged behind with only a 7 percent increase (Hernández et al. 1995, 22). Dominicans have been disadvantaged by their concentration in low-waged occupations as well as their comparatively low levels of education. While in 1990 virtually one-half (49 percent) of all Dominicans in the New York labor force were employed as operatives, laborers, and personal service workers, among other large Caribbean immigrant groups, only 37 percent of the Jamaicans, 45 percent of the Haitians, and 40 percent of the Cubans were concentrated in such low-wage occupations (Grasmuck and Pessar 1996, 283). One reason for the relatively low occupational attainment of Dominicans is their comparatively low levels of education. More than 60 percent of Dominicans over 25 have not completed high school compared to

34 percent of the Jamaicans, 35 percent of the Haitians, and 53 percent of the Cubans residing in New York City in 1990 (ibid.).

Compounding Dominicans' labor-market and educational disadvantages is evidence of considerable family disorganization. Almost 40 percent of all Dominican households in New York City are female-headed and more than half of these are living below the poverty line (ibid.). Clearly, research is needed to determine why Dominicans, who have much lower rates of female-headedness back home, are creating such large numbers of these units in New York (Gurak and Kritz 1988). My own work with Dominicans does point to one unsettling conclusion. On the one hand, Dominican women's regular access to wages has empowered them to challenge, and sometimes modify, patriarchal family practices. At its best, this challenge has led to more equitable forms of budgetary control and greater male participation in household duties and childcare. Yet, on the other hand, the refusal of many husbands to renegotiate gender relations has sometimes led to the disbanding of unions and the creation of female-headed households. A struggle that may have begun as a courageous act of female empowerment all too frequently ends in impoverishment. This is sadly attested to by the fact that in 1990, 52.4 percent of Dominican female householders were living below the poverty line, in comparison to 19.1 percent of the married Dominican householders (Grasmuck and Pessar 1990, 1996).

Finally, racial discrimination is yet another serious obstacle confronting Dominican immigrants. In the 1990 census the vast majority of Dominicans in New York City identified themselves as either mulatto, specified as "other" (50 percent) or "black" (25 percent). Skin color is a very significant predictor of poverty among Dominicans, with black and mulatto Dominicans having strikingly higher poverty levels than white Dominicans (Grasmuck and Pessar 1996, 285). Dominicans who are perceived as "white" by Caucasian Americans appear to enjoy a relative advantage in the labor market over darker-skinned workers. One fair-skinned Dominican woman explained, "When I got my job in the laundry, the owners said that even though I spoke Spanish, they would hire me because they didn't want any Blacks working for them." While she related this account with clear pride, the experience of racism has been denigrating and stinging for the majority of Dominicans who become the targets of racial discrimination. Consider the words of another dark-skinned Dominican:

> I was sitting in the waiting room of this big corporate office waiting for my interviewer to come out. A woman wandered out into the room I was sitting in, looked at me, looked around, and returned to her office. A few minutes later she did the same thing again. After the third time, she finally asked, "Are

you Luis Rodriguez?" I replied, "Yes," as the woman tried to explain her way out of the blunder she had just made. "I was looking for someone who looked different, I mean Hispanic, I mean . . ." (Carter 1994).

Such experiences as being "confused" with African Americans and being discriminated against because of their dark pigmentation are especially unsettling for Dominican immigrants. They come from a society where to be partly white (which includes most Dominicans) is to be nonblack.[11] The racial category of black is reserved for the highly disdained Haitian immigrants and ethnics in the Dominican Republic. As social scientists, José del Castillo and Martin F. Murphy write:

> Throughout Dominican history, the elite ideology has defined the dominican [sic] as a descendent of the Spanish and indigenous populations; the Dominican was considered a mestizo and when the color of his skin and other phenotypical characteristics of the African were noted, he was called a "blanco de la sierra," (white of the land). The Dominican systematically denied at the formal and official levels his African heritage and his condition as mulatto, to the extreme that officially and popularly he called himself "indio" (Indian). His Haitian neighbors were the descendants of Africans, but not the Dominicans. (del Castillo and Murphy 1987, 51)

Racial issues will undoubtedly remain salient for second-generation Dominicans who not only are exposed to contrasting cultural constructions of race in the United States, but are likely to experience both racial discrimination and racial pride in a different way than their parents. We see such signs of change emerging in the words of a second-generation Dominican college student who related her pride in being, in her words, "Afro-Caribbean." She told me she challenges her mother's advice to call herself *blanca* ("white"), to revere her father's light-skinned, blue-eyed ancestors, and to minimize her mother's much darker-skinned forbears. The politics of identity is, nonetheless, tricky. Many second-generation Dominicans, like one twenty-two-year-old male, feel ambivalent about identifying themselves as black, and instead often emphasize their "Latino-ness":

> All we see on television when we arrive is how bad blacks are, so we cling to our difference, our Latino-ness, in order to say we are not those blacks that you hear about in the streets or see on the news. We aren't bad. But at the same time, it feels ridiculous not to embrace our blackness because many dark Dominicans do live as other blacks, treated as blacks by white people, and other Latinos who act like there is one Latino phenotype, like there's a way to look Latino. . . . I'm black and Latino, a black Latino—we exist, you know. (Carter 1994, 28)

Finally, second-generation Dominicans are also far more likely than their parents to forge social and cultural ties with African Americans. Within the cultural sphere, Dominican youth have been especially attracted to African American styles of clothing, music, and dance (Canelo 1982).

CONCLUSION

Over the last few decades, Dominicans have come to assume first place numerically among all immigrant populations in New York City. Their prominence stems not only from their sheer numbers, but also from their contributions to the city's economic, political, and cultural life. Dominicans are forging a new ethnic community in New York—one that by all signs will keep growing as conditions in the Dominican Republic continue to deteriorate, leading yet larger numbers of Dominicans to "*buscar una mejora*" ("search for a better life"). Over the last few decades, this search for a better life has rewarded one segment of the community with economic advancement. Many of these have been professionals and entrepreneurs, who have either returned home permanently or have constructed binational lives. The majority of Dominican New Yorkers, however, have had to settle for far less. They have confronted declining local opportunities for stable, well-paying employment, severe overcrowding within low-income neighborhoods, deteriorating public services, and a mainstream America which is growing ever more intolerant of poor immigrants and their second-generation offspring. Against this backdrop, many have been further disadvantaged by such factors as low levels of education and membership in female-headed households.

In light of these hardships and disadvantages, the Dominican community in New York will need educated members and an educated leadership. In one respect, there is little room for optimism. Despite impressive community struggles, the inner-city schools in which Dominican youth predominate have not received the funding and programs they so desperately require. Programs for adult education and language training are also severely underfinanced. Nonetheless, there is also good reason for optimism. The proportion of college graduates among adult Dominican immigrants over twenty-five years of age has been increasing. For those arriving between 1985 and 1990, it went up 11 percent compared to 5 percent for the prior decades. Even more dramatic, some 27 percent of Dominicans born in the United States over the age of twenty-five are college graduates, a figure that compares favorably with national averages (Grasmuck and Pessar 1996, 282).

New community leaders are emerging out of the ranks of this well-educated, second generation. They differ from the previous cohort of Dominican immigrant leaders, who directed their efforts largely to political affairs back in the Dominican Republic (Georges 1987). This new brand of Dominican leader is concerned with *ethnic* politics "at home," in New York.[12]

Let me close with a reflection on how this process of ethnic leadership and ethnic mobilization may develop in the future. Restrictionists are fond of viewing such phenomena as, ethnic communities, ethnic economies, and ethnic politics as ominous signs of separatism. On this score, I find the historically informed arguments of immigration scholars, Alejandro Portes and Rubén Rumbaut, far more compelling. Regarding ethnic politics, they write:

> What held [this country] together then and continues to do so today is not cultural homogeneity, but the strength of its political institutions and the durable framework that they offered for the process of ethnic reaffirmation to play itself out. Defense of their own particular interests—defined along ethnic lines—was the school in which many immigrants and their descendants learned to identify with the interests of the nation as a whole. With different actors and in new languages, the process continues today. (Portes and Rumbaut 1990, 142)

NOTES

1. The only national sample identifying the volume of the return migration flow to the Dominican Republic available today comes from a 1974 survey conducted by the Dominican Ministry of Public Health. This survey indicated that a relatively high amount, 39 percent, of the total number of international migrants had returned at the time of the survey. Antonio Ugalde and Thomas C. Langham, "International Return Migration: Socio-Demographic Determinants of Return Migration to the Dominican Republic," in W. Stinner, K. de Albuquerque, and R. S. Bryce-Laporte, eds., *Return Migration and Remittances* (Washington, D.C.: Smithsonian Institution, 1982), pp. 73–95.

2. "Si saliera petroleo," Juan Luis Guerra 4:40.

3. At the time of this writing political repression and human rights abuses are again on the rise against opponents of the president, Joaquín Balaguer. At issue are well-substantiated allegations that he "won" the last election through fraud.

4. See also the pioneering work of Vivian Garrison and Carol I. Weiss on Dominican chain migration, "Dominican Family Networks and United States Immigration Policy: A Case Study," *International Migration Review* 12.2 (1979): 264–83.

5. See Glenn Hendricks, *The Dominican Diaspora*, pp. 37–39, for a discussion of the effect of emigration on schooling in one rural Dominican community.

6. The word for church in Spanish is "*iglesia*." For a study of immigrants from this Dominican community settled in New York, see Glenn Hendricks, *The Dominican*

Diaspora: From the Dominican Republic to New York City (New York: Teachers College Press, 1974).

7. Quisqueya is the indigenous name of the Dominican Republic.

8. An example is "Reaching the Heights" a video documentary about the lives of young Dominicans from Washington Heights. The film by Robert Guzman and Alexis Soto, two Dominican-American university students, is part of a project entitled, "Yo, T.V." produced by the Educational Video Center, New York City.

9. For more information on the Dominican ethnic economy, see Luis Guarnizo, "One Country in Two."

10. For a discussion of this phenomenon, see Luis Guarnizo, "Dominicanyorks," pp. 73–74.

11. For a more extensive treatment of racial discrimination against Dominicans in the United States, see Grasmuck and Pessar, "First and Second Generation."

12. For a discussion of the ways in which this new breed of Dominican leaders successfully combines political resources and alliances in both the United States and the Dominican Republic to further gains for the Dominican community in New York, see Pamela Graham, "Nationality and Political Participation" and Patricia Pessar, *A Visa for a Dream.*

REFERENCES

Bray, David. 1984. "Economic Development: The Middle Class and International Migration in the Dominican Republic." *International Migration Review* 18.2: 217–36.

Canelo, Juan de Frank. 1982. *Dónde, por que, de que, cómo viven los dominicanos en el extranjero*. Santo Domingo, Dominican Republic: Editora Alfa y Omega.

Carter, Sakinah. 1994. "Shades of Identity: Puerto Ricans and Dominicans Across Racial Paradigms." Senior thesis, Yale University.

Cocco de Filippis, Daisy, and Franklin Gutiérrez. 1994. *Stories from Washington Heights and Other Corners of the World*. New York: Latino Press.

del Castillo, José, and Martin F. Murphy. 1987. "Migration, National Identity and Cultural Policy." *The Journal of Ethnic Studies* 15.3: 51.

Duany, Jorge. 1994. *Quisqueya on the Hudson: The Transnational Identity of Dominicans in Washington Heights*. New York: Dominican Research Monographs, CUNY Dominican Studies Institute.

———. 1990. *Los dominicanos en Puerto Rico: migracíon en la semiperiferia*. Rio Piedras: Huricán.

Georges, Eugenia. 1990. *The Making of a Transnational Community: Migration, Development and Cultural Change in the Dominican Republic*. New York: Columbia University Press.

————. 1987. "A Comment on Dominican Ethnic Associations." In C. Sutton and E. Chaney, eds., *Caribbean Life in New York City: Sociocultural Dimensions*, 297–302. New York: Center for Migration Studies of New York.

Goris-Rosario, Anneris Altagracia. 1994. "The Role of the Ethnic Community and the Workplace in the Integration of Immigrants: A Case Study of Dominicans in New York City." Ph.D. dissertation, Fordham University.

Graham, Pamela. 1996. "Nationality and Political Participation in the Transnational Context of Dominican Migration." In P. Pessar, ed., *Caribbean Circuits*. New York: Center for Migration Studies.

Grasmuck, Sherri, and Patricia Pessar. 1996. "First and Second Generation Settlement of Dominicans in the United States: 1960–1990." In S. Pedraza and R. Rumbaut, eds., *Origins and Destinies: Immigration, Race and Ethnicity in America*. Belmont, Calif.: Wadsworth Press.

————. 1991. *Between Two Islands: Dominican International Migration*. Berkeley: University of California Press.

Guarnizo, Luis. 1996. "Going Home: Class, Gender, and Household Transformation Among Dominican Return Migrants." In P. Pessar, ed., *Caribbean Circuits*. New York: Center for Migration Studies.

————. 1994. "Los Dominicanyorks: The Making of a Binational Society," *ANNALS, AAPSS* 553: 70–86.

————. 1992. "One Country in Two: Dominican-Owned Firms in New York and the Dominican Republic." Ph.D. dissertation, Johns Hopkins University.

Gurak, Douglas, and Mary Kritz. 1988. "Household Composition and Employment of Dominican and Colombian Women in New York and Dominican Women in the Dominican Republic." Paper presented at the annual meeting of the American Sociological Association.

Hendricks, Glenn. 1974. *The Dominican Diaspora: From the Dominican Republic to New York City—Villagers in Transition*. New York: Teachers College Press.

Hernández, Ramona, Francisco Rivera-Batiz, and Roberto Agodini. 1995. *Dominican New Yorkers: A Socioeconomic Profile, 1990*. New York: Dominican Research Monographs, the CUNY Dominican Studies Institute.

Linares, Guillermo. 1989. "Dominicans in New York: Superando los Obstaculos y Aquiriendo Poder: The Struggle for Community Control in District 6." *Centro Bulletin* 2.5: 78.

Marshall, Adriana. 1983. "Immigration in a Surplus-Worker Labor Market: The Case of New York." Occasional Papers 39. New York: New York University, Center for Latin American and Caribbean Studies.

Martin, John Bartlow. 1966. *Overtaken by Events: The Dominican Crisis from the Fall of Trujillo to the Civil War*. New York: Doubleday.

Mitchell, Christopher. 1992. "U.S. Foreign Policy and Dominican Migration to the United States." In C. Mitchell, ed., *Western Hemisphere Immigration and United*

States Foreign Policy, 89–124. University Park: Pennsylvania State University Press.

Pessar, Patricia R. 1996. *A Visa for a Dream: Dominicans in the United States.* Boston: Allyn and Bacon.

Portes, Alejandro, and Rúben Rumbaut. 1990. *Immigrant America: A Portrait.* Berkeley: University of California Press.

Sassen, Saskia. 1991. *The Global City: New York, London, Tokyo.* Princeton, N.J.: Princeton University Press.

Torres-Saillant, Silvio. 1991. "La literature dominicana en los Estados Unidos y la periferia del margen." *Brujula/Compass* 9: 16–19.

U.S. Department of Commerce, Bureau of the Census. 1991. *Persons of Hispanic Origin in the United States: 1990.* Washington, D.C.: U.S. Government Printing Office.

Waldinger, Roger. 1987. "Changing Ladders and Musical Chairs: Ethnicity and Opportunity in Post-Industrial New York." *Politics and Society* 15.4: 369–402.

———. 1983. "Ethnic Enterprise and Industrial Change: A Case Study of the New York Garment Industry." Ph.D. dissertation, Harvard University.

Williams, Terry. 1989. *The Cocaine Kids.* New York: Addison-Wesley.

7

MICHEL S. LAGUERRE

Sex Education among
Haitian American Adolescents

The management of sexuality among Haitian American adolescents has not been the focus of attention of researchers specializing in the study of Haitian American immigrant communities. The emphasis in dealing with this ethnic minority group so far has been on unveiling four areas of academic and policy concerns, namely the social adaptation of the first generation immigrants in American society (Laguerre 1984), the articulation of their health practices with the formal American medical system (Weidman et al. 1978), the integration of the youngsters in the school system (Verdet 1976) and the appalling way the U.S. government has handled the Haitian refugee issue (DeWind 1990).

Haitian American adolescents have been studied so far from the angle of the school system with an emphasis on bilingual education (Glenn 1986). More recently, a timid effort was made to unravel the life history of a Haitian immigrant girl and her schooling experience in Maryland and Florida (Decker 1985). However, because of the spread of infectious diseases and the potential problem of teenage pregnancy the arena of adolescent sexuality has begun to be a growing area of concern for health providers and policymakers (White and DeBlassie 1992, 183).

In a study of thirty Haitian mothers living in Florida, DeSantis and Thomas (1987, 44) who investigated the issue in terms of "the education and health care systems, the parent-child interaction patterns and the immigrants' views of child development," have found that the girls "were introduced to the topic of menstruation at the onset of menses at a median age of thirteen. Only 26 percent of the Haitian mothers stated that parents or schools provided information about menstruation. When information was given by parents, it centered around the 'dangers' of menstruation." Furthermore, Farmer and Rim (1991, 213) report on the existence of a half-hour video produced by Haitian American teenagers in Cambridge who use it as a form of outreach to help prevent their peers from contracting HIV infection and also as a canvas for the discussion and sharing of information about sexuality in the various Haitian American neighborhoods of the Greater Boston Metropolitan Area. The exploratory research and findings mentioned above are useful in showing us pathways for further investigation of the issue of adolescent sexuality.

It is my view that the study of first- and second-generation Haitian American adolescent sexuality can be studied productively in the context of the family household as a multiproduct firm (Laguerre, 1994). By that, I mean to indicate that the family household is organized and operates like a firm in terms of maximizing its revenue, reducing its cost, establishing subsidiaries, taking risks, investing in human capital, preventing bankruptcy, and creating mergers (Laguerre 1990).

The expression of adolescent sexuality becomes then one component in the overall operation and long term strategy of the family household as an economic and social unit. The household attempts to control and orient the behavioral expression of adolescent sexuality so as to educate, prevent "problems," and reproduce the family system. The adolescent, however, attempts to express his or her sexuality in terms of the prevalent values of the mainstream American culture as a consequence of the Americanization process (the school system, the influence of the mass media, and the embrace of the American way of life). At the same time, he or she is still influenced by the premigrational values of the parents. Therefore, the management of adolescent sexuality is part of a negotiation process between various actors and cultural forces.

My view is that adolescent sexual behavior is the outcome of a negotiated order in a web of uncontrolled relationships that includes the premigrational views and the context of resettlement of the parents (with or without a residence visa, one or more relatives living in the household, one or both parents present), the learning experience in the school system and the wider system as a *laboratory of practice*. It is further my goal to locate the problem in its social context, while at the same time I attempt to decode the nature of this negotiated order. In this chapter, I limit the realm of this investigation to focus my attention exclusively "on the heterosexual behavior of adolescents that is most closely tied to reproduction" (Miller and Fox 1987, 269) and on Haitian American adolescents in a northeastern city.

THE RESEARCH PROCESS

This chapter is based on two sets of data: interviews with Haitian American parents (approximately ten individuals) and undirected group discussions in which both the professional staff of a Haitian Neighborhood Service Center and Haitian American adolescents participated.

In a study of the generational status of immigrant adolescents and adolescents born of first and second generation immigrant parents, Padilla and co-workers (1985) divided them into four categories comprising those who came to the United States before puberty, those who came during the period of their adolescence, those born in the United States of first-generation immigrant parents and those born of second-generation immigrant parents. This distinction was followed in my attempt to identify the group to be studied.

I am well aware of the class and generational diversity within the Haitian American community. This is why I selected adolescents who are in, or have gone to, high school here and not those who have recently arrived to the area and who have not yet learned English. The discussants whether born here or in Haiti are going through the American high school system or in a few exceptions are recent high school graduates. However, their parents have a common background in the sense that they are first generation immigrants.

This research is partly based on discussions conducted in 1992 in the locale of a Haitian American Neighborhood Service Center with a group of Haitian American adolescents. This discussion group had been meeting for a year and the participants knew each other fairly well because of a number of activities they organized throughout the year. I met with the group three times to discuss the various issues raised in this chapter.

The participants, as we mentioned earlier, were all attending high school or have just completed their high school training. Two of them were freshmen in college. The group comprises eight females and five males. Two staff members of the center—one a medical doctor and the other a social worker who has been working in the area of substance abuse among Haitian youth—were also present in those meetings.

For each discussion meeting, I presented the topic and the questions that the group was asked to discuss. This served as a way of orienting, not controlling the discussion. In fact, on several occasions other more pressing questions were brought in or my own questions were framed differently by members of the group. The three main foci of the discussion were on the context of the behavioral expression of sexuality in the household, the school environment and the peer group niche. In the following sections, I will show how Haitian American adolescent sexuality is negotiated and socially constructed in these three niches.

The students did not agree with each other on every single issue because of different family backgrounds and life experiences in the United States. Sometimes they brought their own personal and family experiences to bear on the point they wished to make and were willing to express their views on the areas where the perceptions of their parents clash with their own.

The group discussion allowed the participants an opportunity to pinpoint the different ways parents deal with their daughters' and sons' sexuality and the unspoken rules the latter are asked to adhere to. It also provided them an opportunity to voice their critical thoughts on the issue, to express freely their feelings and to contrast their views with those of their peers.

THE HOUSEHOLD AS WORKSHOP

In any firm, there is a possibility of conflict between management and personnel over certain policy issues. The reality is similar in the administration and governance of the family household. One policy issue that is conflict-ridden is that of the management of adolescent sexuality, that is, the extent of parental involvement in providing pertinent information or in controlling the adolescent's drives for self-expression and some form of autonomy.

The home is the central place where the Haitian American adolescents learn about themselves in general and how to manage their sexuality in particular. However, the home is by no means the only *laboratory* where sexual experimentation is carried out or the only *factory* where the production of active heterosexual behavior occurs. The home finds itself in competition with two other sources of knowledge about sexuality and arenas of practice, the school environment and the peer group.

It is, however, in the context of the household that the Haitian American adolescent learns both formally and informally about sexuality. It is there also that the mechanics of the body are learned in an unscientific manner. The way in which this formal and informal knowledge is shared with or communicated by parents to the adolescents varies considerably in the Haitian American community. This diversity is believed to be related to the social class, the generational status, and the education of the parents.

Adolescent sexuality must be seen on one level in the general context of parent-child relations. The cornerstone of the problem is located in two arenas which shed light on the conflicting views of both parties caused by upbringing and socialization in different cultural contexts. On the one hand, the parents are frustrated because the reproduction of family behavior is hindered by the new American environment. On the other hand, the attempt by families to raise children in the Haitian way collapses daily because the social contract and family orientation of the (backward looking) parents is different from the expectations of the (forward looking) teenagers who have been socialized in American ways. Adolescent behavior becomes then the outcome of the negotiation between these different and conflicting views and value systems. In these transactions, one witnesses a give and take attitude.

It is not enough to discuss the views of the parents about the management of sexuality of their children. It is as important to present the views of the adolescents themselves because their rationale may not be identical to that of their parents. Their views provide us an opportunity to understand the inner world of the Haitian American adolescents and possible clues in the search for creative policies to enhance their development, channel forward their aspirations and help alleviate their problems.

The adolescent girl informants argue that there is a symbolic wall between themselves and their parents that prevents them from asking questions about sexuality at home. It is their view that the Haitian American home does not provide an atmosphere where parent-child relations can be open, that is where these kinds of question can be voiced and where a satisfactory answer can be expected. One girl said that:

> I feel embarrassed to talk about sex with my folks. I do not know why. My mother did not tell me anything about menstruation before it happened. I learned about it from my older sister who used to have *vent fe mal* [cramps] before her periods. She is the one who told me about it.

In the home information about sexuality is not routinely shared by the mother with the daughter. If there is an older daughter, she may be the source of information for the younger one. If there is none, the other possibility would be eavesdropping. That is exactly how another adolescent learned about menstruation. She said that:

> I was cooking something in the kitchen and my aunt who lives next store to us and was visiting talked to my mother about her menses. They were talking at a low voice, but I heard it. At least part of the conversation. Since she was not talking to me and since it would have been inappropriate to ask questions, I left the room with a lot of questions in my mind but no answers.

Haitian American male adolescents have also developed their own understanding of the learning process that goes on in the home. They believe that the girls have learned more from their parents than they, the boys, do. But, they add, what the girls have learned is mostly the negative aspects of sexuality. One adolescent said, "The parents scare the girls about sex," *perhaps* referring to his inability to convince a Haitian American girlfriend to go on a date with him.

The male adolescents believe that their parents would feel embarrassed to talk about sex with them. While the girls blame themselves for being embarrassed to initiate such a conversation with their parents, the boys place the blame on their parents for not taking such an initiative. However, they acknowledge the fact that sometimes they garner bits and pieces of information from their fathers. The following adolescent voice seems to be a representative sample of the perceptions of the boys of what goes on at home. This discussant said that:

> My father is afraid to talk to us about sex. He tried once to tell us something. He did it by way of laughing and teased us about it. It was not a serious talk.

It is the views of the adolescents that their parents have a very limited knowledge of the range of issues around sexuality. One of the adolescents said:

> Parents feel that they do not know much. What they know about and are ready to talk about is how to prevent syphilis (advice for boys) and getting pregnant (advice to the girls). But they do not know much about the other aspects of sexuality.

The adolescents are struck by the lack of public display of affection at home between their fathers and mothers. Perhaps because of modesty, parents seldom hug each other warmly or show much affection toward each other in front of the children. On this score alone, the adolescents think they are different from their parents. For example, while they feel perfectly comfortable kissing their boyfriends or girlfriends in public, kissing in front of their parents, they believe, would be construed by the latter as unacceptable behavior.

The School Environment

The enrollment of the adolescents in school is seen by the family as an investment in human capital. It fulfills two major goals: one is preparation for the job market and the other is the achievement of personal maturity. The school is supposed to consolidate a positive return for the investment made by the headquarters-household. However, from the adolescents' perspective, the school also provides a means of escape from total parental control and opens a window on various aspects of social life.

If the role of the school is to educate students, one may assume that it does so also in the realm of sex education. The high schools attended by the informants all had sex education programs, and the Haitian American students do take advantage of this instruction.

The school provides an environment where two types of learning take place. One is formal whereby the students learn in biology and sex education classes about the physical makeup of their bodies, the trajectory of diseases, the physiology of pregnancy and the various modes of prevention of sexually transmitted diseases, among them the use of condoms. This information is not available in their homes and in this sense the school complements the household in the sexual education of Haitian American adolescents.

Unable to ask questions at home on sexual matters, the students take the opportunity to bring them to their sex education instructors. One Haitian American high school teacher laments that his Haitian American students have constantly bombarded him in the classroom and in the hallways with countless questions on sexuality; sometimes in view of acquiring new knowledge and some other times simply as a way of seeking his approval or endorsement for things they have done or intend to do. He believes that a lack of support at home to talk about these things and a lack of opportunity to express themselves motivates the students to bring their questions to the classroom. He said he is always surprised to hear an abundance of dirty Creole words referring to sexual organs that the students use in the bus, creating an atmosphere of carnival, when he takes them out for a day trip somewhere in the city.

The school also provides an environment where informal education takes place. It takes place mostly in the playground and the hallways where students meet to further discuss whatever they may have learned from their teachers about sex, discuss things among themselves, request clarification from their peers, and consolidate their knowledge. While the classroom provides the information which may be further discussed in the playground, sometimes the question is initiated there and brought to the classroom for a competent answer from the teacher.

The school plays, then, an important role in the sexual education of Haitian American adolescents that cannot be fulfilled elsewhere. The information that the parents are unable to share with their sons and daughters is provided by the school in a very objective and straightforward manner. In a sense, the school is one of the main arenas that helps shape the sexual identity of Haitian American adolescents.

THE PEER GROUP CONTEXT

In all formal settings, there is room for the emergence of informal organizations and activities allowing individuals to meet their personal and psychological needs. In the school, the peer group is just that kind of informal organization. The peer group provides a subterranean channel where new information can be learned and inner feelings expressed. It emerges to help members evade total parental control and structural constraints from the formal societal system as they contemplate alternative routes to fulfill their dreams.

By peer group I refer to the network of friends and acquaintances with whom an adolescent interacts routinely. It is in operation at the school, the neighborhood, and the city levels. It constitutes another arena where sex information is exchanged, where one's sexual prowess is debated, and where pressure to be sexually active is exerted.

The peer group provides that niche for concealment where nicknames or dirty words are learned and where information about one's intimate life can be discussed and ideas and values challenged. The peer group plays the role of a support group. In the various peer group ecologies (neighborhood, school), there are layers of interaction among participants in the sense that one speaks about different things with different friends because one seeks different outcomes.

Members of the group provide moral support and are the kinds of people one will turn to share personal sexual experiences and to seek advice. The support of the group makes it easier for the adolescent to decide whether or not to be sexually active. This choice may also depend on the moral orientation of the persons contacted on this question.

The peer group is also found to exert an influence in terms of the choice of one's partner and helps define or shape one's taste as well. The group is not only involved in matchmaking but also in breaking unfit pairs. It is so because members of the group are able to provide intelligence on the background of potential dates that may not be known to the party involved.

It is in the context of the interaction with the peer group that the Haitian American adolescent may decide to date a Creole-, French-, or English-speaking friend. Each type of dating requires different strategies, carries different assumptions, and is supposed to lead to different outcomes. Dating another Haitian American means that boundaries are known and the influence of the social network of friends can either enhance or undermine the relationship. Dating an outsider may occur because of personal preference, or as a way of adopting American mainstream ways and of adjusting to parental consent or dissent. However, in the process of selecting or continuing a date, the adolescent may request an opinion from a member of the peer group, or this opinion may be given even before asking for it. The peer group helps Haitian American adolescents to consolidate their feelings or confirm their hunches.

The peer group is a niche where news of sexual activities are spread, absorbed, and analyzed and where feedback is sought. This is done by way of informal communication and the physical presence of the adolescents in a specific locale is not necessary since a good deal of talking is done by way of telephone. The telephone is used to link the parties together so as to keep alive the network and the circuit of informal communication. The peer group is an important *informal* arena that helps shape the *formal* sexual identity of Haitian American adolescents.

THE INTERPRETIVE CONTEXT

The discussion has been so far less on the psychological aspects related to human development, and more on the social and relational aspects that influence adolescent behavior and their perception of the world around them in matters of sexuality. I am sympathetic to the Freudian paradigm about human sexuality that sees it "as a biological unfolding or emergence that presses for expression most urgently during adolescence" and Freud's suggestion concerning "the importance of opposing and largely unconscious motivations pitted in an inward struggle over gratifying sexual desires (id), on the one hand, and keeping such desires under control (superego) on the other" (Miller and Fox 1987, 270). However, I am more interested in the sociological paradigm that stresses the "learned behavior" aspect of adolescent sexuality. This second aspect can better account for gender and class diversity in the expression of adolescent sexuality.

The quality and quantity of information shared by parents with their adolescents was also a focus of the group discussion. It was revealed that there is more sharing between daughter and mother than between father and son in matters related to information on sexuality (see also Noller and Bagi 1985, 140). It is the view of the high school and college students who participated in the group discussion that only the bare minimum of information on sexuality is discussed at home.

Since sex education is not taught in the school system in Haiti, this leads to the following consequences in the Haitian American home.

1. The parents are ill-prepared to discuss the matter because of their lack of biomedical knowledge.

2. If and when the conversation on sexuality with the children takes place, the communication tends to focus on the dangers of getting pregnant (social and economic implications) and how to handle menstruation. Since most discussion about daily life tends to be carried out in the Haitian American household in a casual manner why should sexuality be handled differently.

3. Parents are sometimes confused as to the time when the daughters are supposed to start having their periods. The mother is always surprised to find out that the menses of her daughter begin at age 13 when they expect them around age 15 or 16 [*an ayti, ti moun nan te kon fome a 15 ou 16 zan* (in Haiti, the girls used to have their periods at age 15 or 16)] referring to the age brackets when they themselves experienced their first menstruation (see also DeSantis and Thomas 1987).

4. Since in their early age, the parents have learned through the church that sexuality is *sinful*, this religious background may be an hindrance to the transmission of sexual knowledge as it helps construct sexuality as a taboo topic for discussion at home.

Popular culture tends to reinforce this taboo. Sexual practice in Haitian American culture belongs to the domain of *disorder*, not order. Having sex is referred to, as in Haiti, as *fe dezod*, which in the Derridaean deconstruction mood means transgression and one's participation in a practice that *disorders* the natural order of things. Haitian American parents continue to look at sex in this old-fashion way and these pre- and postmigrational views tend to influence their postmigrational behaviors vis-à-vis the management of sexuality of their adolescent sons and daughters.

Furthermore, the peer group is the most important encounter for the learning of practical things about sexuality (Gebhard 1977). Evidently, there is the possibility that some misconceptions are passed along this line of communication as well (Onyehalu 1983, 627). The way the peer group shapes the perceptions of sexuality varies depending on the locus of interaction, whether at the school or the neighborhood level. It may again vary as to whether the encounter is with Haitian American youth or other ethnic American adolescents.

Some investigators have found that "many of the existing [sex education] programs are for some reason unappealing to adolescents as well as being generally ineffective" (Handelsman, Cabral, and Weisfeld 1987, 460). In contrast, Haitian American students have found sex education programs to be very useful because they provide information and answers to questions that neither the parents nor the peer group could answer in a straightforward and "scientific" manner. Also, such programs allow students to hear the questions their peers have, which may indirectly enhance their own knowledge base about sexuality. Sometimes these classroom questions are picked up for further discussion and clarification among the peer group. Or else questions initiated at the peer group level find their resolution later in the classroom. These multiple ecologies where new information is acquired contribute to the knowledge base and help shape the sexual identity of the Haitian American adolescents in many different ways.

Conflict between the parents and the adolescents over the management of adolescent sexuality arises because the parents look at it in terms of long range cost and benefit analysis while the adolescents tend to see it in terms of personal rewards and short term gains. The strategy of the parents to control the communication of sex information and the behavioral expression of the sexuality of their adolescents is in line with their long term goals to prevent "crisis" in the family. In contrast, the adolescents are in a risk-taken posture, trying to circumvent parental control and compete with peers in the free enterprise market of personal interactions. These different orientations play against each other in the realm of the Haitian American family household.

CONCLUSION

It is because the household is interested in its own reproduction that adolescent sexuality is seen in the long-term view of the establishment of a successful subsidiary household. Moreover, it is in view of gaining personal experience that the adolescent may adopt the short-term strategy with potential long-term results. While the ultimate goal may be the same for both parties, the strategy used to achieve this end is different and produces at times conflict in the household.

By and large, there is a lack of sex education within the Haitian American household. This is related to the fact that sex is not discussed formally at home, children are not welcome to ask "sexual" questions, and most parents are not knowledgeable about biology and biomedical terms so that they can hold a conversation that is relevant or meets the intellectual needs of their school age children. The majority of parents are not knowledgeable because they themselves never had sex education at home or at school.

According to Haitian American parents, in matters concerning the communication of sexual knowledge, there is a failure in the reproduction of the division of labor at home. By that, they mean, the husband believes it is his role to inform the male children about sex and concludes that there is no need to do so because there is no danger for the boys since they are not going to be pregnant. The husband fails to do so on the basis of his own experience that this education will take care of itself outside the household and among peers. The wife fails to inform the girls about sex, believing that too much sexual information could lead their "hot blooded" daughters (*ti fi-a gen yon chale nan kol*) to try things out. Controlling (instead of providing information on sexuality) is believed to be the best way of preventing unwanted pregnancies.

This problem of discussing (or not discussing) sexual matters with adolescents is compounded by problems related to migration and adjustment of the parents in the country. The fact that the wife may be going through her own middle life crisis and through menopause and the husband going through his own personal crisis of identity as well places the adolescent-parent communication in a special kind of context.

The words of parents on sexual matters are taken with skepticism by the adolescents because the former bring premigrational values that may not be what the youngsters aspire to. Youngsters may see the counsel as old-fashioned, not particularly practical in the new environment. Adolescents are afraid to ask questions in the family about sexuality because they know that these will not be welcome and probably not answered. When information about sexuality is given or discussed, it is done in general terms with metaphors and *sous-entendre* supposedly understood informally by both parties. Adolescents are getting much of their sex education through the school system formally and through peers, informally, but there is little evidence that they are able to discuss the matter with parents in a productive way, sometimes not even with brothers and sisters.

Sexuality is not manifested in a vacuum; it is a projection of what one wants for one's life. This is where the forward-looking orientation of the adolescents departs from the parental views. The expression of sexual behavior may differ whether one is dating for social purposes (to be seen as popular among peers), to gain sexual experience, or to look for a permanent mate (high school sweetheart).

Parent-adolescent communication is an area that needs improvement in the Haitian American household. Top-down communication is used by parents to pass orders to their children. The children use a bottom-up communication to make requests from their parents. Horizontal communication is often used to say idle things (jokes, for example). Personal communication is seldom directed toward providing information to help the adolescent manage his or her sexual needs, but more toward the management of illness and other social needs.

An aspect of everyday life in some households that contributes negatively to the management of adolescent sexuality is crowding. Crowding because of the presence of kin or friends in the household leads sometimes to sexual abuse (Laguerre 1984). This occurs because in the resettlement process individual friends may move in until they land a job or are able to find an apartment and move out. As parents leave the house to go to work, these additional adult members of the household—who are there in the absence of parents to help and protect the youngsters—may end up being abusers.

The Haitian American adolescent is experiencing confusion because of the clash of values in the household and because of his or her own fragility. There is a pull and push factor in the sexual identity formation of the adolescent as he or she tries to sort things out. At the very center of the construction of adolescent identity is on the one hand the premigrational experience of parents and on the other hand the socialization of teens in the school system and their internalization of American values. Adolescent sexual identity is negotiated to find a common ground for the meshing of these two magnetic poles.

REFERENCES

Decker, Phil. 1985. "Cleselia." *Migration Today* 13.2: 18–29.

DeSantis, Lydia, and Janice Thomas. 1987. "Parental Attitudes toward Adolescent Sexuality: Transcultural Perspectives." *The Nurse Practitioner* 12: 43–48.

DeWind, Josh, 1990. "Alien Justice: The Exclusion of Haitian Refugees." *Journal of Social Issues* 46.1: 121–32.

Farmer, Paul, and Jim Yong Kim. 1991. "Anthropology, Accountability, and the Prevention of AIDS." *The Journal of Sex Research* 28.2: 203–21.

Gebhard, P. H. 1977. "The Acquisition of Basic Sex Information." *Journal of Sex Research* 13: 148–69.

Glenn, Charles L. 1986. "How We Are Failing 'Linguistic Minority' Students." *Equity and Choice* 2.3: 79–86.

Handelsman, Carol Damoth, Rebecca J. Cabral, and Glenn E. Weisfeld. 1987. "Sources of Information and Adolescent Sexual Knowledge and Behavior." *Journal of Adolescent Research* 2.4: 455–63.

Laguerre, Michel S. 1984. *American Odyssey: Haitians in New York City.* Ithaca, N.Y.: Cornell University Press.

———. 1990. *Urban Poverty in the Caribbean: French Martinique as a Social Laboratory.* London: Macmillan, and New York: St. Martin's Press.

———. 1994. "Headquarters and Subsidiaries: Haitian Immigrant Family Households in New York City." In Ronald L. Taylor, ed., *Minority Families in the United States: A Multicultural Perspective.* Engelwood Cliffs, N.J.: Prentice-Hall.

Miller, Brent C., and Greer Litton Fox. 1987. "Theories of Adolescent Heterosexual Behavior." *Journal of Adolescent Research* 2.3: 269–82.

Noller, Patricia, and Stephen Bagi. 1985. "Parent-Adolescent Communication." *Journal of Adolescence* 8: 125–44.

Onyehalu, Anthony S. 1983. "Inadequacy of Sex Knowledge of Adolescents: Implication for Counseling and Sex Education." *Adolescence* 18.71: 627–30.

Padilla, A. M., Alvarez, M., and Lindholm, R. J. 1985. "Generational Status and Personality Factors as Predictors of Stress in Students." In A. M. Padilla, R. J. Lindholm, M. Alvarez, and Y. Wagatsuma, eds. *Acculturative Stress in Immigrant Students: Three Papers.* Occasional Paper no. 20. Los Angeles: University of California, Spanish Speaking Mental Health Research Center.

Verdet, Paule. 1976. "Trying Times: Haitian Youth in an Inner City High School." *Social Problems* 23.2: 228–33.

Weidman, Hazel H., et al. 1978. *Miami Health Ecology Project Report: A Statement on Ethnicity and Health.* Miami: University of Miami School of Medicine, Department of Psychiatry.

White, Sharon D., and Richard R. DeBlassie. 1992. "Adolescent Sexual Behavior." *Adolescence* 27.105: 183–91.

8

Karen Leonard _____

Changing South Asian Identities
in the United States

For South Asian migrants, context, generation, and gender have significantly shaped new constructions of identity in the diaspora, in the United States and elsewhere. Identities are formed in interaction with others in particular economic, political and social settings, and South Asian identities are sure to be changing and many-layered[1] in their American settings. Through engagements with the very different contexts in which they are settling, these immigrants are transforming their personal, ethnic, and national identities in the United States. Many writers remind us of the power relations embedded in the "politics of location" and the local, regional, and national aspects of "situatedness" and "cultural location."[2] New conceptions of identity are especially rich among members of the second generation. The youngsters, even if born in South Asia, are brought up in, and can position themselves in, the history, culture and language of the United States. Already based in the new society, but sometimes reluctant to reveal how fully to their own parents, their voices are surprisingly muted but inventive and diverse. Even more than their parents, they can help to build new conceptions of ethnic and national identities for themselves and for America.[3]

Consideration of the generational and gender issues confronting South Asian immigrants in the United States comes at a time when the concept of "culture" is being reexamined. Anthropologists and other social scientists are turning from the old concept of "cultures" marching in bounded units through time and space, and their new theories talk more about "connected social fields"[4] which can be moved, stretched, and interwoven in multiple ways. We know that people migrating are "changed by their travel but marked by places of origin,"[5] and it is time to direct attention to the first part of that statement rather than the last.

There are striking differences between the "old" and "new" South Asian immigrants, yet the earliest South Asian pioneers in the United States well illustrate the changes brought about by travel, the construction and transformation of identities in a new context. South Asians have been coming to the United States since the late nineteenth century, but their numbers were relatively small in the early twentieth century. The first migrants were almost all men and from only one part of India, the Punjab province along the northwestern frontier. From farming backgrounds, these men settled in California and other western states in the early 1900s and worked in agriculture. All of the early South Asians coming to the United States encountered discriminatory laws which effectively ended immigration in 1917. Other discriminatory laws affected their rights to gain citizenship, hold agricultural land, and marry whom they chose,[6] yet they worked hard to become citizens, acquire land and status, and establish families in the United States. They were called "Hindus" by others in their localities, and this simply meant "people from Hindustan" or India. Because of legal constraints, most of them married women of Mexican background and thus produced a biethnic second generation. Christian by religion and bilingual in English and Spanish, these "Mexican-Hindu" children were nonetheless extremely proud of their Indian heritage.[7] Later South Asian immigrants, unable to imagine the conditions in which the pioneers lived, have found it hard to acknowledge these biethnic descendants as "Hindus."

South Asian immigration opened up again after 1946, as political changes at the national level in both the United States and British India made it possible for the old immigrants to reestablish connections with their homeland and for new immigrants to come. In 1946, South Asians gained the right to become naturalized U.S. citizens,[8] and in 1947 Great Britain's Indian empire gave way to the independent nations of India, Pakistan, Sri Lanka, and Burma. As American citizens, the pioneers could revisit their places of origin and sponsor relatives as immigrants, and their pride in their newly independent South Asian nations was an impetus to such reconnections.

An even greater spur to new migration came with the 1965 U.S. Immigration and Naturalization Act, which reversed decades of discrimination against Asians.[9] The new pattern of South Asian migration and settlement is quite unlike the earlier one, in terms of both places of origin in South Asia and places of residence in the United States. The recent immigrants come from all over South Asia, and they are predominantly urban, highly educated professionals, migrating in family units. All the diversity of the subcontinent is now represented in the United States: in India alone there are some nineteen vernacular languages, on which that country's political structure (the linguistic states' reorganization of 1956) is based. The most numerous regional groups in the United States are Gujeratis, Punjabis, and Malayalis (from Kerala). Diverse religions are represented as well, including many kinds of Hindus, Muslims, Buddhists, Christians, Sikhs, and Parsis (or Zoroastrians).

Also, many "traditional" caste and community categories still have some significance in the lives of the immigrants, particularly for purposes of marriage. While many people from South Asia can tell a fellow immigrant's background (language, religion, perhaps caste) from his or her name, it is not always possible to do so. Now, it is the complexity and diversity of the community, and its settlement all across the United States, that strikes one.

Like other Asians, South Asians slightly favor California (Asians formed some 10 percent of the state population in 1993), with New York, Texas, and Florida close behind in popularity.[10] South Asians are doing very well in the United States, with those born in India having the highest median household income, family income, and per capita income of any foreign-born group in the 1990 Census. The immigrants born in India also had the highest percentage with a bachelor's degree or higher and the highest percentage in managerial and professional fields.[11] Among the skilled South Asian professionals, many are doctors. One estimate puts Indian doctors at more than 20,000, or nearly 4 percent of the nation's medical doctors, and the largest ethnic body of doctors in the United States is the American Association of Physicians from India.[12] In terms of family stability, the immigrants from India lead the foreign-born in percentage of population married and are at the bottom in percentage of those separated and divorced. The most common household size is four.[13] Despite this high-status profile, a 1992 compilation of social science surveys shows that Asian Indians are perceived by Americans as relatively low in social standing,[14] a finding that must be attributed to prejudice.

The first wave of post-1965 immigrants set the high standards measured above, while those arriving since the mid-1980s have brought the averages and medians down somewhat. Many of these later arrivals are coming in under the Family Reunification Act and are not so well qualified as the earlier ones; they have also been coming in during a recession in the U.S. economy.[15] Thus the percentage of South Asian families in poverty is also high, putting those born in India twelfth on the lists of both families in poverty and individuals in poverty.[16] The U.S. Immigration Act of 1990 should reverse this downward trend, since it has sharply increased the numbers of highly skilled immigrants from India (and Asia generally) at the expense of unskilled workers and non-employed immigrants (parents and spouses of citizens). In 1991 and 1992, India was the seventh-ranked place of origin for newcomers to the United States, helping along a prediction that South Asian Americans will be the third largest Asian American group by the year 2000.[17]

Participation in American political life was a goal for the early South Asian immigrants and is becoming one for the newcomers. After the Luce-Celler bill made them eligible for citizenship in 1946, the Punjabi pioneers helped elect Dalip Singh Saund from California's Imperial Valley in 1956, the first congressman from India.[18] After some hesitation, the newer South Asian immigrants also are becoming engaged in U.S. politics. About half of those migrating from India since 1977 have become naturalized U.S. citizens, although they must give up their Indian citizenship to do so (the U.S. allows dual citizenship but India does not).[19] Initially, immigrants pressured India to change its policy and allow dual citizenship, like Pakistan, but India's leaders have recently encouraged its NRIs (nonresident Indians) to become American citizens and work for themselves and India through the U.S. political system.[20] South Asians are becoming active in both Democratic and Republican party political funding and campaigning.

The South Asian organizations show a progression over time from the individual-level adaptations made by the first migrants to early organizations based on national origin (India, Pakistan, Sri Lanka) or ecumenical religious categories (incorporating South Asians into various Christian churches or Muslim mosques). As the South Asian immigrant population has grown, a variety of linguistic associations, ethnic organizations, and sectarian or guru-centered religious groups have been formed.[21] Some of these organizations reproduce divisions important back in South Asia,[22] but at the same time, the organizations are federating at the national level on the basis of South Asian ancestry. Several competing national federations[23] reflect not only rivalry among leaders but uncertainty over the best term for the community—Asian Indian is the Census term, while Indian American and Indo-American are the other leading contenders. Political mobilization is based on issues like crimes against South Asians,[24] individual or institutional discrimination in higher education and business, and problems with municipalities. Thus merchants may fight to achieve "minority" business preference status or to name a business area "Little India," while those seeking to establish Hindu temples or other religious institutions often must work hard for local permission.[25]

Coalition-building with other groups, such as Asian Americans and/or Muslim Americans, is a promising political strategy. Among Asian Americans, Asian Indians soon will move from being the fourth-largest group, after the Chinese, Filipinos, and Southeast Asians, to third largest, overtaking the Southeast Asians. The Asian Indian group includes Indians, Pakistanis, Bangladeshis, Sri Lankans, and Fijians and Guyanese of Indian origin, and while it has been behind most other Asian American groups in participation in educational and political coalitions, that situation is changing fast.[26] Similarly, Islam either already is or will by 2000 be the second largest religion in the United States, and South Asian Muslims provide the intellectual and political leadership for Muslim Americans.[27]

South Asians are settling into the United States in ways unanticipated a decade ago. Not only are the young people moving into the American mainstream, elderly parents are following their adult children to the United States. This major demographic trend is a mixed blessing for these parents, who feel isolated from their old friends and former lives. Stuck in the suburbs without access to shops or other people, oftentimes they serve as babysitters, phone answerers, perhaps even cooks, for their children. However, some of them contribute to changes in American life, helping to make South Asian culture more available. The founder of the "Kwality" ice cream and restaurants, a chain famous throughout India, migrated to California in the late 1970s and helped set the standard for Indian restaurants there, symbolizing the explosion of Indian fast foods and packaged foods being distributed in South Asian ethnic groceries throughout the country.[28] South Asian religious and cultural festivals are observed in the United States, their timings adjusted to those of American holidays; one Indian entrepreneur markets Hallmark cards for Diwali, an Indian festival, in southern California. Shops now supply almost everything needed to produce South Asian weddings satisfactorily in America.[29]

Indian music and dance abounds in the United States, with many signs of integration into the American cultural landscape. Indian dance academies offer classical Bharatanatyam and regional folk dances like Punjabi *bhangra* and Gujarati *giddha*, along with dances from Hindi films and "hip-hop bhangra." In northern California, Ali Akbar Khan's College of Music's 1994 summer concert featured five apparently Euro-American *kathak* dancers, while the master musician Ravi Shankar has settled down in southern California.[30] In Cleveland, Ohio, the annual Thyagaraja Aradhana, or Karnatic music festival, draws more Karnatic artists than any other festival outside India, and probably more than many in India now. Swami Chinmayananda, one of India's most popular spiritual leaders, died in 1993 in San Diego, California, on one of the extensive overseas lecturing tours he had undertaken in recent years; this is just one indication of an intensification of South Asian religious activity in the United States.[31]

Despite all the signs of their own adaptation to, and, indeed, of South Asian impact upon, American life, some South Asian immigrants are concerned about negative aspects of American life. Fearing that their children will "lose" South Asian culture, and perhaps feeling that they themselves cannot ever be more than second-class citizens of the United States, some older people are returning to their homelands upon retirement.[32] Their return is to some extent a recognition of the importance of context in the shaping of identity, yet the return presents a considerable problem to their children who were born or brought up largely in America.

For first-generation immigrants from South Asia, "the youth problem" looms large. Many conference sessions, public talks, and private conversations are devoted to worrying about the children of South Asian descent being raised in the United States. Parental ambitions are high with respect to the economic success of their offspring: children are encouraged to undertake higher education and professional training, particularly in medicine and engineering. Parents also tend to stress "tradition," the retention and transmission of South Asian culture, rather than the adoption of American culture. This places the children in a difficult position, since they are inevitably products of their American cultural context and are comfortable in that context in ways that their parents are not. As one article title indicates, "It Ain't Where You're From, It's Where You're At,"[33] and both parents and youngsters make this point repeatedly. One Hindu grandmother in Hyderabad, India, asked if her grandchildren, who are being brought up in Texas, are in any way Hyderabadi, replied despairingly, "Hyderabadi? They're not even Indian," and then cried as she told how her granddaughter asked her to wear some other clothing, not a sari, when accompanying her to school. One adult son settled near San Diego, California, made his identity clear by insisting on watching the Super Bowl in the main living room while I talked to his aging parents, visiting from Karachi, Pakistan, in a smaller room. His rudeness was atypical; sent to the United States at an early age for schooling, his were not South Asian manners.

The second generation's difference, its participation in American culture in all its contemporary diversity and intensity, is borne out in many ways. A young lawyer whose father may have worked only in partnership with coethnics has a Vietnamese American partner in his law office, and young women of the second generation are moving beyond the South Asian ethnic beauty contests to compete in more general ones. In the 1994 South Asian Youth Conference at UCLA, discussion topics included Interracial Marriage, South Asians and Hip Hop Culture, Homosexuality, Premarital Sex, and Violence against Women, as well as Identity Formation, Discrimination in Corporate America, and Racism. And a recent full-page ad for the Northern California Youth Awards Night at the India Cultural Center featured a conspicuously printed dress code specifying that no jeans, sneakers, or jackets with gang symbols would be allowed. Only a few years ago, perhaps even now, it is hard to imagine that this announcement would be needed.[34]

Some of the "youth problem" concern comes from religious leaders and organizations, both Hindu and Muslim. This concern is ostensibly about the continuity of family, caste, and community religious traditions, but just as clearly, it is about sexuality and marriage, in particular about parental arrangement of marriages and parental control of family life. In a North American edition of *Hinduism Today*, the publisher discussed the threat to Hindu families represented by marriages not arranged by the parents, marriages most often with non-Hindus in the United States. Stating that 80 percent of the young Hindu women in Texas are marrying "outside of Indian tradition," he blamed parents for not arranging marriages soon enough, for permitting their children to pursue personal fulfillment rather than fulfillment of duty.[35] In the *Pakistan Link,* a medical doctor from Pakistan presented an Islamic perspective on dating, opposing it on the grounds that it inevitably leads to having sex or to date rape.[36] This echoes the South Asian parental view of dating as inevitably involving sex, the view which prevailed in a survey of post-1965 Indian immigrants carried out in 1990.[37]

While the experience of growing up in America has not been a uniform one, most youngsters of South Asian descent go through a cycle of early identification with American culture and then, later, identification with Indian culture.[38] Even after they become more interested in their heritage, these young people do not necessarily see themselves as part of a larger community of Indo-Americans. But, one writer asserts, what they do have in common with other Indo-Americans is their parents, "parents who are overinvolved, overworried, overprotective. Parents who have an opinion on every minor life decision, who make demands, impose guilt, withhold approval." She goes on: "We entered the world the axis around which our parents' lives revolved, their source of fulfillment, their contract with the future . . . as children of immigrants, the promise we fulfill is our parents' own promise, long-deferred and transmuted now into the stuff of American dreams (and nightmares). So we must become respectable, make money, buy a house, bear children. . . . My parents' love supports me and enfolds me, but sometimes also weighs me down. . . . Still I carry the burden of their unhappiness." She writes of becoming interested in her Indian heritage, but "as this Indian fire flickered and grew—it shed light on my American self, too. . . . I see that I am in love with the complexity of the American culture I grew up in, and cherish my easy familiarity with it . . . that I love to defend it against detractors, revel in its excesses . . . that after attending many Indian dinner parties . . . I long to be with American friends, because with them I relax and return to myself."[39]

It is the young women of South Asian background, not the young men, who are of most concern. As a young Indian Muslim woman wrote, "in my culture, it's O.K. for a man to marry outside our Muslim community, go away to college, stay out at night, do whatever he pleases. A girl, on the other hand, must learn to cook, not say what's on her mind, and repress sexual desires. . . .

Moslem boys brought up in America integrate much faster into American society than Muslim girls."[40] And in a "Focus on Youth" feature in *India West*, a young Hindu woman made a similar point, citing a father who stated that because daughters can get pregnant they are controlled much more strictly than sons, since it is they who can damage the family's reputation. This writer asserted that it was time to face up to the issue of sex in her Indo-American generation, and she quoted a Hindu woman doctor who said that 40 percent of her Indo-American patients are sexually active. The writer and the doctor both termed the refusal of parents to accept this possibility as "extreme denial."[41] Sexuality is a major theme in a powerful new anthology of writings by predominantly young women of South Asian descent in America, not only heterosexual feelings and activities but lesbian ones as well.[42] Intergenerational conflict and anger are evident in these short stories, poems, and analytical essays. These emotions were echoed in papers given at a recent conference on South Asian women, a conference which took up issues still controversial among South Asians such as sexuality, divorce, lesbianism, and physical and verbal abuse of women.[43]

Both the dangers of raising girls in America and the double standard are constantly emphasized in the South Asian ethnic press. During Women's History Month in 1993, a series in *India West* had a finale focused on this. A young woman said that "one of the healthy aspects of living in America is that you are taught to question and you are taught to think. In India you don't question your parents, while in the American culture you do." Another testified that while parents get changed by America more the longer they are here, the generational clash is strongest on the issue of marriage. "Parents have frozen some vision of the India they grew up in which necessarily does not exist today at all in terms of today's youth." A third young woman, commenting on how young Indo-American women deal with the pressure for an arranged marriage, said "A lot of kids just do things and [do] not tell their parents."[44]

The strategy of nondisclosure, not telling one's parents about the significant choices one is making in life, is a common one. In her book, Priya Agarwal discusses social issues for second generation Indo-Americans, and she opens with a quote from a young man about going with a girl for four years without telling his parents anything about the relationship. More than half the young people in Agarwal's survey preferred to date without telling their parents.[45] In a recent ethnic press column on dating, a young man, while saying that guys have it easier than girls, cited a male friend of his who had not told his parents about a girlfriend of three years standing. "If he tells his parents, his relationship is basically over. Yet, on the other hand, going against his parents is something he does not want to do. It goes against everything he believes in." In the same column, a young woman testified that while most of her friends date, "their parents do not come into play until the relationship is serious. . . . Indian parents have difficulty grasping the concept of a boyfriend-girlfriend relationship. . . . Many Indian parents tend to overanalyze or underestimate the seriousness of their daughter's relationships. . . . I must give credit to Indian parents for being so concerned with their daughter's well-being. However, there is a limit. I don't believe in overprotective parenting." She advocated simply bringing a boyfriend into the home and confronting one's parents with the fact of an existing relationship.[46]

It is with respect to that very important life event, marriage, that the gender and generational differences become magnified. A recent photograph in *India West*, a South Asian ethnic newspaper published in California, stood out as most unusual: one looked directly into the eyes of a happy young bride, her address a California one, seated next to her groom. The contrast with the literally hundreds of photographs of brides from/in India and Pakistan was striking: this girl looked straight into the camera and her smile was dazzlingly broad.[47] South Asian brides, however, on video or in photo albums, look down modestly and often are covered with a veil of one sort or another. But this girl, like many of the second and later generations of South Asians born or brought up in America, is not like the women of her parents' generation.

Marriage is sometimes the occasion for crisis in these South Asian immigrant families. Because of parental opposition to dating and "love-marriages," the children of South Asian immigrants are usually put into an either/or situation. They must trust their parents to arrange their marriages, or they must trust themselves. One second generation woman trying to understand the first generation's view wrote: "[South Asian] Society is clearly worried about the conduct of women not strictly confined within limited boundaries. It is to perpetuate these boundaries that the arranged marriage system is still strongly encouraged for . . . even Indo-Americans. The concept of a father deciding on a spouse for his daughter with no input from her is *deplorable* [emphasis added]."[48]

In response to the prospect of an arranged marriage, perceived by some as "deplorable," a few young people are making secret marriages. That is, they are marrying, often with partners who are not South Asian, and keeping the marriages secret from their parents. While they are trusting themselves, acting in accordance with their own wishes in this important decision, they are reluctant to publicly betray their parents' trust, to acknowledge that they have made their own decision in a matter so crucial to each generation's sense of itself.[49]

Thus they gain the spouse they want, but they do not lose (or they delay the loss of) their families. The stakes are high here, for one knows of many marriages made by parents for their children which have not worked out, and the consequences have been tragic. Divorce is now a distinct possibility for Indo-Americans, and the frequently transglobal marriage and family networks add international legal complications to the emotional costs of divorce for South Asians.[50]

We have come full circle, and it is time to remember the experiences of the Punjabi pioneers and their Punjabi Mexican families, experiences which emphasize the flexibility of ethnic identity and of culture. For the new immigrants from South Asia as well, we need to recognize the historical construction of identity in "connected social fields," with that phrase's implication that there will be several levels of intersecting fields or contexts. To look at South Asian culture and identity in the United States in this new and more flexible way, we do not really need to employ language like the "invention of culture" or "imaginary homelands," phrases which somehow hint at an "inauthenticity" of certain constructions or voices.[51] We do need to recognize that time and place are very important components in our studies, because changes in the historical context have powerful consequences for individual, family, and "community" identity. The turnabouts in United States citizenship and immigration policies in the 1940s and 1960s had dramatic consequences for Punjabi Mexican family life in California,[52] and the changing global economy and society are having dramatic consequences for the much larger and more diverse population of South Asian immigrants in the United States now. "South Asian" will have very different meanings in the many places South Asians are now living, and for older and younger South Asians. Just as identities and communities have been constituted and reconstituted over time back in the South Asian homelands, new concepts of identity and community will be produced in the United States by South Asian immigrants and their descendants.

NOTES

1. Here, Stuart Hall's remarks on identities are useful: he discusses the sociological subject and the postmodern subject, the former constituted by an interaction between the self and society, the latter far more fragmented, shifting, contextually and constantly reformulated. I find these "postmodern" qualities particularly apt (although since they characterize the Hyderabad Kayasths in the eighteenth and nineteenth centuries and the Punjabi Mexicans in the early twentieth century, I am not enthusiastic about the "postmodern" label and a necessary link to [recent] globalization). Stuart Hall, "The Question of Cultural Identity," especially 275–77, in Stuart Hall, David

Held, and Tony McGrew, eds., *Modernity and Its Futures* (London: Open University, Polity Press, 1992); Karen Isaksen Leonard, *Social History of an Indian Caste: The Kayasths of Hyderabad* (Berkeley: University of California Press, 1978); and Karen Isaksen Leonard, *Making Ethnic Choices: California's Punjabi Mexican Americans* (Philadelphia: Temple University Press, 1992).

2. Michael Keith and Steve Pile in the introduction to their edited volume *Place and the Politics of Identity* (London: Routledge, 1993), 18. In the same volume, David Harvey reminds us of the power relations embedded in "situatedness" (57–59) and Neil Smith and Cindi Katz also discuss there the "disruptive politics of location," a phrase from Adrienne Rich, and they distinguish her dynamic concepts from James Clifford's more static concept of travel from space to space (76–79).

3. Stuart Hall, "New Ethnicities," *Black Film British Cinema* (London: Institute of Contemporary Arts, 1988), 27–31.

4. The phrase is Sally Falk Moore's, *Social Facts and Fabrications* (New York: Cambridge University Press, 1986), 4–5; and see James Ferguson and Akhil Gupta, "Beyond 'Culture': Space, Identity, and the Politics of Difference," *Cultural Anthropology* 7.1 (1992): 6–23.

5. James Clifford, "Notes on Theory and Travel," in James Clifford and Vivek Dhareshwar, eds., *Traveling Theory Traveling Theorists* (Santa Cruz: Center for Cultural Studies, 1989), 188.

6. The relevant federal and state policies and laws (the 1917 Barred Zone Act, the 1924 National Origins Quota Act, the 1923 U.S. Supreme Court Third Decision, California's Alien Land Laws, and state anti-miscegenation laws), are covered in Leonard, *Ethnic Choices,* and in Bruce La Brack, *The Sikhs of Northern California 1904–1975: A Socio-Historical Study* (New York: AMS Press, 1988) and Joan M. Jensen, *Passage from India: Asian Indian Immigrants in North America* (New Haven: Yale University Press, 1988).

7. Leonard, *Ethnic Choices.*

8. The result of extensive lobbying by the Indians in the United States, the Luce-Celler bill allowed citizenship by naturalization and allowed use of the quota of 105 per year set by the 1924 National Origins Quota Act (used only for whites born in India until 1946, due to the Supreme Court Thind decision in 1923 declaring Indians Caucasians but not "white" and therefore ineligible for U.S. citizenship).

9. The 1965 Immigration and Naturalization Act took effect in 1968: for general coverage, see Sucheng Chan, *Asian Americans: An Interpretive History* (Boston: Twayne, 1991), 145–65.

10. The projected percentage of Asians in California will be 20 percent in 2020: *India West*, May 6, 1994.

11. See U.S. 1990 Census releases reported in *India West*, October 1, 1993, February 4, 1994. A 1991 five-group survey of Asian American groups showed that Indians held the most IRAs and stocks and were the most highly educated: *India West*, January 25, 1991. Census data released in 1994 showed Indian American families

with the second-highest median incomes among major Asian groups, second only to the Japanese: *India West*, February 4, 1994. A study on foreign-born professionals, by Leon Bouvier and David Simcox for the Center for Immigration Studies, was released April 15, 1994, and showed foreign-born Indians to be the highest paid among foreign-born professionals (with an annual median income of $40,625). Foreign-born Indians numbered 593,423 in the 1990 Census, while 450,406 were born in India: *India West*, April 22, 1994.

12. For the 4 percent figure, see *India West*, February 26, 1993; for the AAPI, see *India Today*, August 15, 1994, p. 481. There is also an Association of Pakistani Physicians of North America, which overlaps with the Islamic Medical Association of Canada: *The News*, August 21, 1993. In 1980, of the 400,000 Indians in the United States, 11 percent of the men and 8 percent of the women were physicians, while 17 percent of the men were engineers, architects, or surveyors and 7 percent of the women were nurses: *India West*, November 27, 1992. There are also the Association of Indian Pharmacists in America (*India West*, September 10, 1993), an Indo-American Physicians and Dentists Political Association (*India West*, November 27, 1992), and many Indian computer professionals working in the U.S. (*India Today*, December 31, 1993, p. 48c).

13. For the married and divorced percentages, see *India West*, Oct 1, 1993; for the most common household size (for 29 percent), see *India West*, October 8, 1993.

14. This national study used polls done over several years by seven national polling organizations and compared 33 ethnic and religious groups (in some tables, 58 groups); of the 33 groups, Indians were highest in educational level, fifth in household income, but 28th in socioeconomic standing (of the 58 groups, they were 38th in social standing): *India West*, January 17, 1992.

15. Forty-four percent of Indian immigrants came before 1980, and those arriving since 1985 show a much lower percentage in managerial and professional jobs, a much lower median income, and a much higher unemployment rate. *India Today*, January 31, 1994, p. 60 c-d-f.

16. *India West*, October 1, 1993.

17. *India West*, December 17, 1993: 45,064 admitted in 1991, 36,755 admitted in 1992. For the prediction, *India West*, March 19, 1993, quoting LEAP (Leadership Education for Asian Pacifics), *The State of Asian Pacific America: Policy Issues to the Year 2020* (Los Angeles: LEAP, 1993).

18. See Dalip Singh Saund's autobiography, *Congressman from India* (New York: E. P. Dutton & Co., 1960).

19. For Indians admitted from 1977 to 1991, the naturalization rate was 49.8 percent: *India West*, December 3, 1993.

20. India actively encourages the NRIs to invest financially in the homeland, but it has not welcomed some of its overseas citizens' political involvements (in particular, the movements for Sikh or Kashmiri independence). Abid Hussain, India's ambassador to the United States in 1992, told Indo-American associations to work for America,

terming India the "Janam bhoomi (birthland)" and America the "Karam bhoomi (livelihood land)": *India West*, February 14. And India's next ambassador to the United States, Siddhartha Shankar Ray, told NRIs to "think twice" about dual citizenship and to participate in U.S. politics: *India West*, July 30, 1993.

21. This typology was developed by Raymond Brady Williams, ed., *A Sacred Thread: Modern Transmission of Hindu Traditions in India and Abroad* (Chambersburg, Pa.: Anima Publications, 1992), 228–57.

22. For example, the Telugu Association of North America is dominated by members of the Kamma caste, while their rivals in the countryside of Andhra Pradesh (the Telugu-speaking state in South India), members of the Reddy caste, have formed the American Telugu Association: *India West*, February 25, 1994, citing research by Rukmini Timmaraju.

23. The leading four national associations are the Association of Indians in America, the NFIA or National Federation of Indian Associations, the Indian American Forum for Political Education, and the National Association of Americans of Indian Descent.

24. Crime impacts specific South Asian populations, for example, New York's cabbies, news-stand attendants, and gas station attendants, 40 percent of whom are from the subcontinent: *India Today*, March 15, 1994.

25. In Norwalk, California, a Hindu temple could be built only after being re-designed to look like a Spanish mission!

26. South Asians are beginning to ally with Asian Americans: see *India West*, March 6, 1992, for a special session on Indo-Americans and other "hidden Asians" at a conference on Asian and Pacific Americans in Higher Education.

27. See Omar Khalidi, ed., *Indian Muslims in North America* (Watertown, Mass: South Asia Press, n.d. [c. 1991]), particularly the article by Raymond Brady Williams.

28. The "Kwality" founder, Kapal Dev Kapoor, died in Los Angeles in 1991: *India West*, October 18, 1991.

29. Astrologers find dates which coincide with Labor Day and the Fourth of July. For the Diwali cards, *India West*, November 12, 1993; and for the wedding economy, see Karen Leonard and Chandra Sekhar Tibrewal, "Asian Indians in Southern California: Occupations and Ethnicity," in Parminder Bhachu and Ivan Light, eds., *Comparative Immigration and Entrepreneurship: Culture, Capital and Ethnic Networks* (New Brunswick, N.J.: Transaction, 1993).

30. Rahesh Thakkar argues that Indian classical dance plays a major role in winning a place for Indian culture in the North American scene: "Transfer of Culture through Arts: The South Asian Experience in North America," in Milton Israel and N. K. Wagle, eds., *Ethnicity, Identity, and Migration* (Toronto: University of Toronto Center for South Asian Studies, 1992). For Ali Akbar Khan's College, ads in *India West*, August 1994 various issues; for Ravi Shankar's move, *India West*, August 13, 1993.

31. For the festival, *India Today*, April 30, 1994 p. 44i; for the Swami's death,

India West, August 13, 1993. On religion, see Williams, *Sacred Thread*, and also Raymond Brady Williams, *Religions of Immigrants from India and Pakistan: New Threads in the American Tapestry* (New York: Cambridge University Press, 1988); Fred W. Clothey, *Rhythm and Intent* (Madras: Blackie and Sons, 1983); John Y. Fenton, *Transplanting Religious Traditions: Asian Indians in America* (New York: Praeger, 1988); and Khalidi, ed., *Indian Muslims*.

32. On going back to India, see *India Today*, May 31, 1994. Complexes are being built for senior citizens returning from the United States, and Social Security payments can be sent to India, after ten years of employment.

33. Paul Gilroy, "It Ain't Where You're From, It's Where You're At . . . : The Dialectics of Diasporic Identification," *Third Text* (c. 1987), pp. 3–16.

34. For the law firm of Bhakhri and Nguyen, *India West*, ads in 1993; for beauty pageants, *India Today*, September 30, 1993; p. 52 f–g. The India Festival Committee organized many pageants from 1980 on within the ethnic community, but the current Miss Iowa is an Indo-American, and the current Miss Universe is from India itself. For the UCLA conference, flyers distributed; for the dress code, *India West*, August 12, 1994, p. 71.

35. Satguru Sivaya Subramuniyaswami, *Hinduism Today*, June 1993, p. 2.

36. Dr. Shahid Athar called for an Islamic perspective on America's problems, which he listed as abortion, teenage pregnancy, alcohol and drugs, homosexuality, AIDS, right to life [sic], poverty, and child and wife abuse: *Pakistan Link*, May 20, 1994, p. 44.

37. Priya Agarwal, *Passage from India: Post-1965 Indian Immigrants and Their Children* (Palos Verdes, Calif.: Yuvati Publications, 1991), 48–49.

38. That is my impression, based on personal experiences and the field research papers produced over the last ten years in an undergraduate field research class I have been teaching at UC Irvine.

39. Gauri Bhat, "Tending the Flame: Thoughts on Being Indian-American," in *COSAW* [Committee on South Asian Women] *Bulletin* 7.3–4 (1992): 1–6.

40. Saba, "Reflections of a Young Feminist," *COSAW Bulletin* 7.3–4 (1992): 8.

41. Smriti Aggarwal, *India West*, July 30, 1993, p. 62. The doctor is clearly speaking of her adolescent patients.

42. The Women of South Asian Descent Collective, eds., *Our Feet Walk the Sky: Women of the South Asian Diaspora* (San Francisco: Aunt Lute Books, 1993).

43. This conference was put together by a determined student, Sangeeta Gupta, and was perhaps the first one in the United States of its type; she hopes to publish a volume of the conference papers.

44. Lavina Melwani, "Voices of a New Generation," *India West*, March 26, 1993, pp. 49, 57–58.

45. See Agarwal, *Passage from India*, 50–59, on inadequate communication between parents and children, and 48–49, for the dating quote and statistics.

46. The columnists were Sunil Bagai and Monica Doshi: *India West*, September 23, 1994, p. 55.

47. *India West*, March 18, 1994, p. 84.

48. Sangeeta Gupta, "Indo-American Women and Divorce," p. 25, paper given at the South Asian Women's Conference, Los Angeles, October 1994.

49. Perhaps it is not their own parents whom they fear to lose, but the wider family, in the United States and/or South Asia, and therefore this fear of disapproval and being cut off may be on behalf of their parents as well as themselves. I explored the reasons for such secret marriages in a paper, "The Management of Desire: Sexuality and Marriage for Young South Asian Women in America," given at the South Asian Women's Conference, Los Angeles, October 1994.

50. Sangeeta Gupta, "Indo-American Women and Divorce," above, and Asha Singh, "Adjustments to Divorce for Women of an Indian Background," at the same conference.

51. Not that Benedict Anderson and Salman Rushdie are not stimulating instigators of thought about transnational migration, they are—but these particular phrases constitute a barrier for those uninitiated into this kind of discourse: Anderson, *Imagined Communities: Reflections on the Origin and Spread of Nationalism* (London: Verso, 1983); Rushdie, *Imaginary Homelands* (New York: Penguin, 1992).

52. The possibilities opened up by U.S. citizenship and the sponsorship of relatives from South Asia endangered the inheritance rights of some spouses and children in the United States, while also changing the pool of potential spouses for both first- and second-generation "Hindus." See Leonard, *Ethnic Choices*, especially pp. 174–202.

9

MIN ZHOU

Social Capital in Chinatown
The Role of Community-Based
Organizations and Families in the
Adaptation of the Younger Generation

Chinese Americans are by far the largest subgroup of Asian Americans. As a direct result of the liberalization of the U.S. immigration law in 1965, which abolished the national quotas system, they have become one of the fastest-growing minority groups in the United States. Over the past fifty years, their numbers have increased fifteen times. Between 1970 and 1990, in particular, the number of Chinese Americans more than tripled, from 435,062 to 1,645,472. Much of this growth has been attributed to immigration. According to the U.S. Immigration and Naturalization Service (1991), a total number of 682,755 immigrants were admitted to the United States from China, Hong Kong, and Taiwan as permanent residents between 1971 and 1990. The 1990 U.S. Census also attests to the big part played by immigration: foreign-born persons account for 69.8 percent of Chinese Americans nationwide and 78.7 percent in New York City.

Parallel to the rapid growth in sheer numbers is the extraordinarily high educational achievement of immigrant Chinese and their offspring. In recent years, Chinese American children have scored exceptionally high in standardized tests, have been overrepresented in the nation's most prestigious high schools and universities, and have disproportionately made the top lists of many national or regional academic contests. They have, for example, appeared repeatedly in the top-ten award winners' list of the Westinghouse Science Talent Search, one of the country's most prestigious high school academic contests. In 1991, four of the top ten winners were Chinese Americans. Although fewer than a third of Chinese American school-aged children were born outside the United States, a majority of them grew up in immigrant households. Why are younger-generation Chinese Americans so well adapted to U.S. society? Into what specific social contexts are they adapting? How do their community and families affect their adaptational experience? This chapter attempts to address these questions by focusing on the role of community-based organizations and families in New York City's Chinatown.[1]

CHINATOWN:
THE BASIS OF SOCIAL CAPITAL

Adaptation to the U.S. society is a complex process depending not only upon individual motivation and abilities but also upon specific contexts of reception. Preexisting ethnic communities represent the most immediate dimension of the context of reception (Portes and Rumbaut 1990), serving as the basis of a unique form of social capital to facilitate immigrant adaptation. This social capital is defined as "expectations for action within a collectivity that affect the economic goals and goal-seeking behavior of its members, even if these expectations are not oriented toward the economic sphere" (Portes and Sensenbrenner 1993), or as closed systems of social networks in a community, which allow parents to "establish norms and reinforce each other's sanctioning of the children" (Coleman 1990). In fact, the social capital thesis touches on one of the oldest sociological theories, Durkheim's theory of social integration. Durkheim maintains that individual behavior should be seen as the product of the degree of integration of individuals in their society (Durkheim 1951). The greater the integration of individuals into a social group, the greater the control of the group over the individual. In the context of immigrant adaptation, children who are more highly integrated into their ethnic group are likely to follow the forms of behavior prescribed by the group, such as studying or working hard, and to avoid the forms of behavior proscribed by the group.

If ethnic communities are interpreted in terms of social capital, it becomes possible to suggest a mechanism by which the adherence to community-based support systems and positive cultural orientations can provide an adaptive advantage for immigrants and their offspring in their strive to achieve their goals in American society. However, this mechanism is never stagnant; it constantly accommodates changes in the process of immigration. Social capital should thus be treated as "a process," rather than as a concrete object, that facilitates access to benefits and resources (Fernandez-Kelly 1995), that best suit the goals of specific immigrant groups. Chinatown, with its networks of support and social control mechanisms, serves as a prime example for understanding the meaning of social capital.

New York City's Chinatown started as a bachelors' society at the turn of the century. By the 1940s, Chinatown, still a bachelors' shelter with a sex ratio of 603 men per 100 women, had grown into a ten-block enclave, accommodating almost all Chinese immigrants in the city. The old-timers were motivated by a sojourning goal of making a fortune in America and returning home with "gold." They left their families behind in China and were drawn to this community by extensive kinship networks. During the time when legal and institutional exclusion set barriers and American society made available few options of life to these Chinese sojourners, they had to isolate themselves socially in Chinatown and to work at odd jobs that few Americans wanted. Since they had no families with them and had no intention to stay a long time, they built Chinatown initially as a place of refuge that resembled home. In Old Chinatown, immigrant workers could speak their own language, eat their own food, play their own games, exchange news from home, and share common experiences with fellow countrymen day in and day out. The level of social interaction was fairly high through various tongs (merchants' associations) and kinship or family associations (Kuo 1977; Wong 1979).

After World War II, the bachelors' society began to dissolve when Chinese women were allowed into the United States to join their husbands and families. Resulting from the repeal of the Chinese Exclusion Act and passage of the War Bride Act, immigrant Chinese women composed more than half of the postwar arrivals from China. However, the number of Chinese immigrants entering the United States each year was quite small because the annual quota was set at 105 (Sung 1987). After 1965, when Congress amended the immigration law abolishing the national origins quota system, the number of Chinese in New York City increased rapidly, from 33,000 in 1960 to 240,014 in 1990.

As Chinese immigrants and their families pour into New York City, Old Chinatown has undergone a series of dramatic transformations. These transformations have been physical, social, and economic. Once confined to a ten-block area in Lower East Manhattan, Chinatown has expanded in all directions beyond its traditional boundaries, taking over decaying neighborhoods and giving rise to "satellite" Chinatowns in Queens and Brooklyn (Zhou 1992). Unlike the old-timers who were predominantly from rural Canton, immigrant Chinese in recent years have come from other parts of mainland China, Hong Kong, Taiwan, and elsewhere in Asia and Latin America. Upon arrival, they have tended to bypass Old Chinatown in Manhattan to settle in outer boroughs. Immigrants from mainland China have been fairly evenly distributed across Manhattan, Queens, and Brooklyn; those from Hong Kong have tended to reside in Queens or Brooklyn; and those from Taiwan have overwhelmingly concentrated in Queens. Cantonese is no longer the sole language spoken in Chinatowns. In such newly established Chinatowns such as the one in Flushing, Queens, Mandarin is now the most commonly used language among immigrant Chinese.

Today's Chinese Americans in New York City have become more diverse in their socioeconomic backgrounds than the earlier arrivals, who were uniformly unskilled laborers. According to the 1990 U.S. Census, immigrant Chinese born in Taiwan displayed the highest proportion of college graduates (four times as high as the U.S. average), the highest proportion of workers in professional specialty occupations, and the highest median household income compared to those born in mainland China, Hong Kong, and other countries. Mainland-born Chinese were the most disadvantaged, except for their citizenship status. Fewer than half of them showed proficiency in English; fewer than half had completed high school; and only 13.8 percent held professional occupations. Their median household income was at least $7,000 less than that of their counterparts born elsewhere. In contrast, U.S.-born Chinese showed exceptionally high levels of educational and occupational achievements. However, regardless of differences in socioeconomic status, over 80 percent of Chinese spoke a language other than English at home, indicating that not only immigrants but also the younger generation lived in a bilingual environment.

Recent immigrant Chinese are not only more diverse than earlier arrivals, they also come with goals that are vastly different from those of the old-timers, who were here to sojourn rather than to settle and assimilate. They are characterized by their strong desire to become integrated into the mainstream society and to make America their new home. Many of them have immigrated to the United States to secure their already well-established lives, and more importantly, to provide their children with a future without fear and uncertainty, in which the children can realize their full potential. The demands of immigrant Chinese for speeding up the process of assimilation have brought about important changes in the economic and social structures of Chinatown.

Since 1965, the stereotypical Chinatown has been withering away, and a full-fledged family community with a strong ethnic economy has gradually and steadily taken its place. During the 1930s and 1940s, Chinatown's ethnic economy was highly concentrated in restaurant and laundry businesses. By the 1970s, the laundry business had shrunk substantially and had been replaced by the garment industry, which has become one of the backbone industries in Chinatown. Today, the garment industry, estimated at over 500 factories run by Chinese entrepreneurs, provides jobs for more than 20,000 immigrant Chinese, mostly women. It is estimated that three out of five immigrant Chinese women in Chinatown work in the garment industry. The restaurant business, another backbone industry in Chinatown, has continued to grow and prosper. Listed restaurants run by Chinese grew from 304 in 1958 to 781 in 1988, employing at least 15,000 immigrant Chinese workers (Kwong 1987; Zhou and Logan 1989). In addition to garment and restaurant businesses, various industries, ranging from grocery stores, import/export companies, barber shops, and beauty salons to such professional services as banks, law firms, financial, insurance, and real estate agencies, and doctors' and herbalists' clinics also experienced tremendous growth. These ethnic economies have created ample job opportunities for immigrant Chinese and have provided convenient and easy alternatives to meet ethnically specific consumer demands.

Changes in Chinatown's economic structure have had a lasting impact on the adaptation of the younger generation. On the one hand, jobs made available in ethnic economies and goods and services provided by the community tend to tie immigrant Chinese and their offspring to Chinatown despite spatial dispersion. These ties have directly or indirectly broadened the base of ethnic interaction and thus increased the degree of ethnic cohesion, which in turn sustains a sense of identity, community, and ethnic solidarity. On the other hand, despite the low wages and long working hours typical of many jobs in Chinatown, immigrants take pride in being able to work and support their families. The work ethic and the capacity for delayed gratification in parents is explicitly or implicitly passed on to children, who are expected by their parents to appreciate the value of schooling as a means to move out of Chinatown. Moreover, the prosperity of ethnic economies in Chinatown offers material support for the establishment and operation of many community-based voluntary organizations. These community-based organizations, in turn, furnish a protective social environment, which shields off adversaries, such as drugs, crime, teenage pregnancies, prevalent in inner-city poor neighborhoods where immigrants tend to concentrate, and provides them with access to resources that can help them move ahead in mainstream American society.

THE CHANGING ROLE OF COMMUNITY-BASED ORGANIZATIONS

The transformation of Chinatown from a bachelors' society into a family-oriented community has increased the number and broadened the role of community organizations. The rapid change in the nature of Chinese immigration has created pressing demands for services associated with resettlement and adjustment problems which have overwhelmed the ability of the existing traditional organizations (Sung 1987). To accommodate these changes, traditional organizations have been pressured to redefine their role, and various new organizations have been established in Chinatown. By glancing at one of the Chinese business directories, for example, one can easily come up with a list of over 100 voluntary associations, 61 community service organizations, 41 community-based employment agencies, 16 daycare centers, 27 career training schools, 28 Chinese and English language schools, and 9 dancing and music schools (Chinatown Today Publishing 1993—note that the actual number of community organizations in Chinatown was approximately twice as many as this list because many were not listed in this particular directory). Most of these organizations are located in Manhattan's Chinatown; some are located in new satellite Chinatowns in Flushing and Sunset Park.

In Old Chinatown, family or clan associations and merchants' associations (tongs) were the major community-based organizations. These organizations functioned primarily to meet the basic needs of fellow countrymen, such as helping workers obtain employment and offering different levels of social support, and to organize economic activities. Powerful tongs controlled most of the economic resources in the community and were oriented toward shielding Chinatown from outsiders and preserving the status quo within the community (Kuo 1977). Some of the tongs capitalized on the demands of the sojourning Chinese, mostly males, by running brothels, opium dens, and gambling parlors. Because of the illicit nature of some of the tongs' operations, Chinatown was often stereotyped as an unruly den of vice and co-ethnic exploitation, and immigrant Chinese as inassimilable aliens with an imputed "filthy" and "immoral" second nature.

The single most important social organization was the Chinese Consolidated Benevolent Association (CCBA). The CCBA was established as an apex group representing some sixty organizations in Chinatown, including different family and district associations, the guilds, the tongs, the Chamber of Commerce, and the Nationalist Party, and it operated as an unofficial government in Chinatown (Sung 1987, 42–46). The CCBA was mainly controlled by tongs but cooperated with all voluntary association (Kuo 1977).

While traditional organizations functioned to secure the standing of Chinatown in the larger society and to provide a refuge for sojourning laborers, some of them formed underground societies to profit from such illicit activities as partitioning territories, extortion for business protection, gambling, prostitution, and drugs (Dillon 1962; Kuo 1977; Sung 1987). Tong wars were frequent; and youth gangs, consisting almost entirely of immigrants, arose as tongs needed lookouts for raids, guards, escorts, and debt collectors (Sung 1987). Although youth gangs come and go, they have formed a disruptive segment of the community to which new immigrant youth, mainly boys, are extremely vulnerable.

Since the 1960s, as the community has become more and more family-oriented, the concerns and needs of community members have broadened and diversified. Not only do the immigrants themselves have strong desires to integrate into American society, they overwhelmingly expect their children to become successful. Many immigrants have experienced considerable downward mobility, but they accept the sacrifices to win better futures for their children. The more diversified resettlement concerns and needs of newcomers have pressured Chinatown's traditional social organizations to change and expand. To appeal to new immigrants and their families, the CCBA has established a Chinese language school, an adult English evening school, and a career training center, and has instituted a variety of social service programs, including employment referral and job training services.

The CCBA-operated New York Chinese School is perhaps the largest children- and youth-oriented organization in Chinatown. The school has annually (not including summer) enrolled about 4,000 Chinese children, from preschool to 12th grade, in their 137 Chinese language classes and over 10 specialty classes (e.g., band, choir, piano, cello, violin, T'ai chi, *ikebana*, dancing, and Chinese painting). The Chinese language classes run from 3:00 to 6:30 P.M. daily after regular school hours. Students usually spend one hour on regular school homework and two hours on Chinese language or other selected specialties. The school also has English classes for immigrant youth and adult immigrant workers.

The Chinese-American Planning Council (CPC) is another important organization that has been established since the late 1960s in Chinatown. Although not as influential and deeply rooted in Chinatown as the CCBA, the CPC has utilized a grass-root community effort and has managed to draw upon government funds to provide services to immigrant Chinese. The CPC's mission is to provide "access to services, skills and resources toward the goal of economic self sufficiency and integration into the American mainstream" (CPC 1993).

During the 1970s, the CPC, then the Chinatown Planning Council, initiated a number of youth-targeted programs, such as drug-prevention, outreach, and various recreational programs to help immigrant children and youth to adapt to their new environment. These programs targeted high-risk youth not only by offering counseling and opportunities for young people to voice their concerns and problems, but also by providing recreational activities, such as renting places where they could read, party, and play pool, video or ballgames, and furnishing free field trips, shows, and museum visits (Kuo 1977). Most of these programs have continued, expanded, and diversified into the 1990s.

In 1995, the CPC has three branch offices in the Lower East Side of Manhattan, Sunset Park, Brooklyn, and Flushing, Queens. It is operating over 40 programs, including 12 daycare services, 8 youth programs, and 17 multiservice programs associated with youth. Within each of the programs, there are various subprograms. For example, the Manhattan branch of the CPC-Youth Program offers five specific services to young people, especially those from low-income families, including the career educational program, after-school ESL classes, the theater workshop, and in-school counseling. The main purpose of the CPC's youth-oriented programs is to enhance new immigrant students' well-being, class attendance, and academic performance, and, in turn, to prevent students from dropping out of school and to help them become aware of future educational opportunities and career options.

In addition to large, well-established organizations such as the CCBA and the CPC, many smaller voluntary organizations have been established to address concerns and demands of new immigrants and their children. The Chinatown History Museum (CHM), a community-based, member-support organization, was established in 1980 primarily as a history project for reclaiming, preserving, and sharing Chinese American history and culture with a broad audience. The museum offers historical walking tours, lectures, readings, symposia, workshops, and family events year-round, not only to Chinese Americans but also to the general public. The museum also provides school programs for grades K to 12, guided and self-guided visits for college-level students, and a variety of videotapes, slide presentations, and exhibits.

Recently, the CHM has formed the Exhibition Planning Student Committee, depending mainly on voluntary efforts of Chinese American students, to create a permanent exhibition entitled "Who's Chinese American?" The purpose of the museum in mobilizing student volunteers is to stimulate input from the second generation and to incorporate the experiences of children of immigrants, in addition to the more widely recognized experiences of the old-timers, into Chinese American history. The Student Committee has attracted an increasing number of concerned Chinese American youth. For example, at their first meeting, organizers only expected a handful of students; but some forty students showed up despite a citywide social event, a dance party for high school students, happening the same evening.

Ethnic religious institutions have also played an important role in helping immigrants adjust to life in the United States. In the larger Chinese community in New York City, the number of churches or temples has doubled since 1965 including over 80 churches and 18 Buddhist and Taoist temples; about three-quarters of which are located in Manhattan's Chinatown. While Buddhist and

Taoist temples tend to attract adults, including some college students and the elderly, Christian churches generally have well-established after-school youth programs, in addition to their regular Sunday Bible classes. The Youth Center of the Chinese Christian Herald Crusade, for example, has established an after-school program and an ongoing intensive program for high-risk youth. Located conveniently across from a public high school in Chinatown, the Youth Center annually provides services to about 200 high school students, most of whom are immigrant youth. The center's after-school program, which is preventive in orientation, offers tutoring, counseling, and language aid to students whose major adjustment problem is English.

Since 1992, the center has started a small, intensive, crisis-oriented program for high-risk youth, referred to or sent to the center either by parents or by social workers. This crisis-oriented program is aimed at youth who frequently play truant and "hang out" with other truants on streets or in video game shops. According to the center director, "these kids have serious adjustment problems besides language. Since they are not interested in school, we have to approach them differently. Our purpose is not to brainwash them but to influence them with compassion, sympathy, and understanding, and to help them find their own selves." The crisis-oriented program offers daily escorts to participants from home to school, organizes basketball games on Saturdays, and arranges weekend overnight trips.

The center also runs a summer camp in upstate New York, where "problem" youth are offered a free four-week camp in exchange for their help with maintenance, cleanup, and landscaping work in the camp. During their stay at the summer camp, youth are also given the opportunity to voice their concerns and feelings in voluntary study groups. "It is very important to allow youth to express themselves in their own terms without parental pressures. Chinese parents usually have very high expectations of their children. When children find it difficult to meet these expectations and do not have an outlet for their frustration and anxiety, they tend to become alienated and lost on streets." The center director estimated that over half of these participants had shown improvement in their school attendance and that at least half of them had become Christian after a two-year intensive involvement in the program.

Social organizations in Chinatown, whether they are formal or informal, government-funded or community-rooted, have played a vital role in meeting the social and economic needs of the Chinese community. Interviews with community leaders, organizers, and activists indicate that the functions of new community organizations specific to the younger generation are manyfold. Instrumentally, community organizations provide a safe, healthy, and stimulating environment where youngsters, especially those whose parents are at work, can go after school. The after-school programs not only ensure the time spent on homework or on other constructive activities, but also help to keep children off the streets and to reduce the anxieties and worries of working parents.

These organizations also serve as bridges between a closed immigrant community and the mainstream society. Immigrant children and youth growing up in Chinatown are relatively isolated. Their daily exposure to the larger American society is limited; they generally come from low-income families, live in crowded housing, attend inner-city public schools, walk on streets surrounding primarily by small, family-based businesses, and are vulnerable to ghetto youth subcultures. Their parents, usually too busy working just to make ends meet, tend to expect their children to do well in school and to have successful careers in the future; but the parents are unable to give specific directions to their children's educational and career plans, leaving a gap between high expectations and realistically feasible means of meeting these expectations. Community-based organizations fill this gap to help young people to become more aware of their choices and potentials and to help them find realistic means of moving up socioeconomically into mainstream society instead of being stuck in Chinatown.

Culturally, these organizations function as ethnic centers, where Chinese traditional values and a sense of ethnic-identity are nurtured. Students participating in the after-school programs, especially the U.S.-born and reared, often speak English to one another in their Chinese classes, and they actually learn a limited number of Chinese words each day. However, they are exposed to something which is quite different from what they learn in school and are able to relate to Chinese "stuff" without being teased about it. They also listen to stories and sing songs in Chinese, which reveal different aspects of Chinese history and culture. Children and youth learn to write in Chinese such phrases as "I am Chinese," "My home country is in China"; and to recite classical Chinese poems and Confucius sayings about family values, behavioral and moral guidelines, and the importance of schooling. A Chinese school principal made it clear that, "these kids are here because their parents sent them. They are usually not very motivated in learning Chinese per se, and we do not push them too hard. Language teaching is only part of our mission. An essential part of our mission is to enlighten these kids about their own cultural heritage, so that they show respect for their parents and feel proud of being Chinese."

A latent function of these community organizations is that they create a common bond between immigrants, their children and the community at large. Participation in after-school programs enables not only children but also their parents to directly interact with each other and with the community. The increasing contact among co-ethnic members and with the community can strengthen the social networks in a community. The involvement in the community-based organizations not only enables parents to establish norms and reinforce each other's sanctioning of the children, but also provides some space where children and youth can express themselves, easing intergenerational conflicts. In this sense, community organizations furnish resources of support and direction that promote value consensus and behavioral conformity among individual families and build bridges between immigrant, often non-English-speaking parents and their U.S.-born or reared children. Next, we discuss the role of the family in the adaptation of second-generation immigrants.

THE FAMILY: VALUES, BEHAVIORAL STANDARDS, AND EXPECTATIONS

The 1965 amendment to the U.S. Immigration and Naturalization Act, which emphasizes family reunification, has provided the end link to a system of chain migration. Because 80 percent of the quota is allocated to relatives, post-1965 Chinese immigrants are not only vertically (spouses, parents and children) but also horizontally (brothers and sisters and their immediate families) related to their sponsors within an extended family network. This family-chain migration suggests that, unlike the old-timers who intended to return to China, the newcomers are here to stay and to assimilate (although much of the assimilation may take place through the children) into U.S. society. As a result, the base of the kinship structure in Chinatown has been broadened (Sung 1987).

Chinese immigrants arriving after 1965 have mostly been family-sponsored immigrants, about 75 percent of whom were admitted as immediate family members (spouses, unmarried children, and parents) or as close relatives (married children, brothers, or sisters of U.S. citizens). Some 20 percent have been employment-based immigrants (whose admission was sponsored by a U.S. employer). Consequently, about 80 percent of the Chinese in New York City live in married-couple households and only 5 percent live in female-headed households. The family has stabilized the community and become the most important institution, furnishing an immediate source of social capital for facilitating the adaptation of immigrant children to American society in a unique way.

In New York City, as in other parts of the United States, the majority of Chinese American youngsters grow up in intact families. However, the socioeconomic status of Chinese families varies by length of stay since immigration. Based on the 1990 U.S. Census, only 15 percent of the children had parents who were U.S.-born or immigrated before 1965, about 40 percent of them had parents who immigrated between 1965 and 1979, and 46 percent of them had parents who immigrated after 1980. Among these three groups, children of post-1980 immigrant parents were more likely to reside in Brooklyn, children of immigrant parents arriving between 1965 and 1979 disproportionately resided in Queens, and children of U.S.-born or pre-1965 immigrant parents were geographically dispersed throughout the city. The proportion of female-headed households was generally low for all three groups. Children of post-1980 immigrant parents tended to live in the homes where Chinese was spoken and most lived in linguistically isolated neighborhoods. This residential pattern implied that children from post-1980 immigrant families were the most isolated group and had the least exposure of the larger society.

The economic gap between the three groups was fairly large. Close to two-thirds of the children of most recent immigrant parents lived in rental housing whereas almost two-thirds of the children of U.S.-born or pre-1965 immigrant parents lived in owner-occupied housing. Moreover, children of post-1980 immigrant parents were most economically disadvantaged with a poverty rate of 27 percent, more than four times as high as that among children of U.S.-born or pre-1965 immigrant parents. Furthermore, parents who immigrated after 1980 had much lower levels of education, were less likely to be in executive or professional occupations, and had much lower average earnings comparing to parents who immigrated earlier or who were U.S.-born. However, regardless of the length of stay since immigration, most of these parents were married and stayed married and were employed full time. Dependence on public assistance was uncommon among them.

Despite socioeconomic variations, Chinese American families, no matter how integrated they may be into the larger society, do not function in isolation. They are embedded in a long-standing cultural tradition and in the social structure of the larger Chinese American community. Comparing the Chinese American family to the traditional Chinese family, Betty Lee Sung (1987, chapter 7) has specified several distinctive characteristics of the Chinese American family. First, the Chinese family in the United States carries a long history of dismemberment, where immigrant men crossed the Pacific to seek fortunes, leaving their parents, wives, and children behind in China. After 1965, family reunification has been in relays, generally with the men arriving much earlier, and wives and children arriving at later times. Consequently, many immigrant families have suffered varied length of family separation, and once reunited, they have to adapt to the norm of the nuclear family. Second, women in Chinese American families have taken a more independent role than they did in the traditional family; working outside the home has become a norm and an economic necessity for women in Chinatown. The work role gives women some measures of power and makes them less exclusively dependent upon their husbands. Third, the size of a Chinese American family is generally much smaller with an age gap between children and with older children who are foreign-born. Fourth, kinship or clan ties become weakened in the process of migration, and face-to-face interaction among family members decreases as both men and women are out working for long hours.

However, the Chinese American family remains culturally distinct from the mainstream American family despite the alterations specified above. The Chinese American family has not simply retained its "Chineseness," but has also incorporated a set of characteristics associated with adaptational strategies for coping with uprooting and assimilation. While assimilation is the ultimate goal for the Chinese American family, parents are constantly caught in the conflict between maintenance of cultural identity in children and the adoption of desirable mainstream cultural ways.

In general, the Chinese American family has continued to be influenced by Confucianism. Confucianism emphasizes traditional values, such as ancestor worship, a respect for authority (e.g., the ruler, the elder, the parent, and the teacher), a belief in consensus, a willingness to put society's or the family's interests before the individual's interest, an emphasis on education as a means of mobility, clear rules of conduct, constant self-examination, and the importance of face-saving. These values have been carried over to America with few modifications and have been essential for the Chinese American family to socialize the younger generation.

For the younger generation, obedience, hard work, and success in school are matter-of-fact expectations. These values and family expectations are not only instilled in individual families, but also reinforced in the Chinese community. Illustrative are some of the most common adult-child greetings observed in the homes, streets, and restaurants in Chinatown. Parents frequently greet children with, "How was school?" "Did you behave in school in today?" "Have you got your grades yet? How good are they?" or "Have you done your homework?" Relatives or adult family friends often greet children with, "Have you been obeying your parents?" "Have you been good?" "Have you been working hard in school?" "Have you been making good grades?" These simple everyday adult-children greetings reflect the Chinese values of obedience, respect, hard work, and education; and children are expected to give positive answers. As a continuation of the long-standing Chinese tradition, Confucius values have been transplanted to America and become the normative behavioral standards in Chinese American families. Deviation from these standards is considered shameful or "face lost" and thus sanctioned by the family and the community.

Specifically, we can summarize the following distinctive characteristics of the Chinese American family. First, Chinese parents believe that discipline and hard work, rather than natural ability or innate intelligence, are the keys to educational success. Regardless of socioeconomic backgrounds, they tend to think (also tend to make their children believe) that their children can all get A's in their tests in school if they are disciplined and hard working. Many folk tales make the point that diligence can achieve any goal, such as the tale of a woman who ground a piece of iron by hand into a needle and that of an old man who removed a mountain with just a hoe. There is also a saying that dullness can be overcome by industriousness. Because of the cultural influence, Chinese children are pushed to work at least twice as hard as their American counterparts, which has indeed brought about remarkable results. A downside of this cultural emphasis, however, is that Chinese parents tend to be less sensitive than American parents to individual ability of their children, such as varied degrees in their ability to master English, to adjust to the new school and social environments, and to interact effectively with teachers and fellow students. Children fear their parents and are hesitant to discuss these problems with them. Even if they do, they may be misunderstood as "finding excuses for being lazy."

Second, unlike the American family, which emphasizes individual responsibilities, the Chinese American family values collective responsibilities. The success of children in school is very much tied to face-saving for the family. Parents themselves are expected to bring up their children in ways that honor the family. In Chinatown, one frequently hears parents brag about their children's success but seldom hears them talk about problems. Children are constantly reminded that if they fail, they will bring shame to the family. According to several school counselors, this collective orientation works both ways. On the one hand, children's education is given priority with social and material support from their family and community and children are pushed to their full potential, which contribute to their success. On the other hand, however, children act like "little adults," sacrificing the opportunities of being children, exploring and developing their own selves (Sung 1987, 91).

Third, the parent-child relationship in Chinese American families tends to be more formal and rigid and less emotionally expressive than the mainstream family. Chinese culture emphasizes submission to authority. The parent is the authority in the home, as is the teacher in the school. The parent, often the father, is not supposed to show too much affection, to play with children, or to treat children as equals. The stone-faced authoritative image of the parent often inhibits children from questioning, much less challenging, their parents. Moreover, there is a general lack of demonstrative affection in the Chinese American family, which applies not only to children but to the spouse and friends as well. Chinese parents are not expected to show emotions or express love in a direct way. Children rarely hear their parents say, "I love you." They seldom receive kisses or hugs from their parents in public. In a culture where physical intimacy and affection are publicly displayed, children tend to feel deprived and to interpret the lack of demonstrative affection as, "My parents don't love me" (Sung 1987, 116). Therefore, while parental authority effectively reinforces behavioral standards, which are constructive to the adaptation of children to school, it intensifies cultural conflicts and thus increases the level of anxiety in children.

Fourth, most of the Chinese American families have both parents working. Working parents, particularly those in immigrant families, tend to work long hours each day, six days a week. Although parents are very concerned about their children's schooling, they have very little time to be physically involved, to help their children with their homework, much less to talk with them or play with them. Moreover, the contact between school and parents is minimal, not because parents do not want to get involved, but because they can't find time and their English is not proficient enough for such contact. Some children do not even bother to pass teachers' notes to their parents about conference arrangements or participation in school events. Or they simply pass the notes to their parents and then say, "Never mind. I know you can't go."

Many immigrant parents are struggling for survival in the hope that their children will appreciate their hard work and repay them by doing well in school. Many children do understand the pain and struggle their parents have had to endure. One teenager wrote in her essay at school,

> [Our] ancestors came to this country hoping to make a better life for themselves and generations thereafter. Although they did not find much gold or money in the "Gold Mountain" at first, they succeeded in staying together and making their children's lives and grand-children's lives a much easier one to endure.[2]

Still, long working hours and exhaustion from work make some parents over-look the specific needs of their children. When serious problems occur, they are surprised and puzzled. A parent reacted with shock and disappointment after learning that his child had been absent from school for more than a week, "I don't understand why this has happened. He never mentioned to me that he didn't like school. I work, and work, and work. For what? Isn't it just for my boy to be able to finish high school and to go to college? I have given him everything I can possibly afford. What else does he want?" The bilingual counselor in school explained, "This parent apparently did not understand what his child really wanted." According to this counselor, many Chinatown children are aware of their parents' expectations and try to meet them.[3] How-ever, they encounter a lot of adjustment problems daily in school, such as lan-guage difficulties, inability to express themselves, frequent teasing or harass-ment by other students because of their different look, accent, and dress, misunderstanding by the teacher or fellow students; and they fear to bring these problems up at the dinner table for fear that their parents will get upset or blame them. When their problems are unaddressed, they become discouraged, and discouragement is sometimes followed by loss of interest, dropping grades, and dropping out of school.

In sum, the Chinese culture in which the family is embedded is a double-edged sword. While it provides specific goals, behavioral guidelines, and a so-cial basis of support to facilitate adaptation of immigrant children to school and the society, it does not always deal adequately with the problems facing the younger generation. In Chinatown, however, voluntary organizations have started to address the new challenges by initiating family-oriented programs. The CPC, for example, has several ongoing programs, providing services to immigrant families, including crisis-prevention, parental skills, counseling, re-ferral, and family recreational activities. In this sense, the community and the families are connected to establish a unique social context in which the younger generation is brought up. Next, we take a close look at this younger generation.

THE YOUNG GENERATION:
THE PROCESS OF BECOMING AMERICAN

Although Chinese American children are generally considered by public school teachers to be well-adjusted, motivated, hard-working, disciplined, and respectful, they are burdened with a number of bicultural and adjustment prob-lems, including issues of identity, perceptions of parental affection, conflicting values and behavioral standards, the gang subculture, and the problem of achieving. The question of "Who am I?" or "Who's Chinese American?" is sometimes ambiguous among children of Chinese immigrants. The following is an excerpt from a student paper that reflects the feelings of many Chinese American children:

> His ten minute long speech [at a family dinner table] was apparently comprehensible to all but my parents and me. I watched my cousins' attentive faces with interest as my great uncle spoke. I know that to them, what I spoke was the foreign language. I was amazed that I was in a room with twenty-five relatives and felt like such an outsider. When my uncle was finished and dared to release his grasp of the table to fall quite gracefully back into his seat, everyone exchanged cheers in Chinese. I just smiled back at every one as they addressed me, and for the first time, I saw myself through their eyes. I saw an Americanized teenager who had casted off her Chinese identity in order to conform more to American ways. Suddenly, I became aware of overwhelming feelings of guilt, anger and confusion. . . . These conflicting emotions threw me into a state of confusion and wonder, a confusion and wonder I have yet to figure out.[4]

Apparently, growing up in America is a difficult process for children of immigrants, as they are constantly torn between conflicting cultural goals and demands at home and in the larger society. An immediate bicultural conflict in the Chinese American family is the difference in the perception of affection between parents and children. As discussed in the previous section, parent-child relationships in immigrant Chinese families are not as emotionally expressive as those in American families. In the countries of origin, Chinese children are socialized into this pattern of relationships and seldom feel deprived. Since immigrant children, even those who are isolated in the enclave, are increasingly exposed to the television, movies, magazines, books, and the popular culture, they become aware of the different ways of expressing affection in different families and tend to interpret their parents' way as insufficient (Sung 1987). A Chinatown teenager recalled, "My mom never kissed me 'good night' or said 'I love you.' When I told her what American moms did, she answered, 'We Chinese don't do it this way.' For a long time, I felt that I was not loved." While this particular pattern of parent-child interaction may help maintain parental authority, the cost is often an emotional detachment from parents and a reduction of communication with parents on the part of the children.

Another cultural dilemma in which immigrant Chinese children often find themselves is that of conflicting values and behavioral standards. First, immigrant Chinese families tend to rely on the value of thrift as an important means of achieving future goals. In immigrant Chinese families, where parents are struggling to make ends meet and to attempt to save as much money as possible for the future—buying a home, opening up a small business, and sending children to college—children are taught the values of thrift and the importance of saving. However, influenced by the mass media and the larger consumer market, immigrant children tend to pick up quickly what is "in," or what is "cool," which is unquestionably at odds with the Chinese cultural value of thrift.

Parents bluntly reject material possessions and conspicuous consumption on the part of children and perceive spending money on name brand clothes, luxurious accessories, and fashionable hairstyles as a sign of corruption, which they often term as becoming "too American." Commonly heard from parents are, "You shouldn't have spent $35 on this stupid haircut when you can spend $5 on a much nicer cut"; "How can you spend like this when you don't even know how to make money?" "What if you had a family to feed?" When they do work, immigrant Chinese children are expected to hand over the wages to their parents.

In an interview with a group of eighth and ninth graders who participated in one of the youth programs in Chinatown, the young people indicated that their major concerns were the lack of spending money and the lack of understanding from their parents. "My mother didn't care what people think of me," said a fourteen-year-old boy. "She used to force me to wear a jacket, which she bought two years ago from China and which had become too small for me, not to mention the outdated style and the kiddy patterns. She would say to me, 'It still fits and you can wear it for another spring.' I was so embarrassed that I took it off and packed it in my book sack the minute I got out of the house." Another boy said, "My mother never bought me clothes from Gap or Levi's. I had to save my meager allowance for months to buy what I want and then told her that I bought it cheap from a street vendor." An immigrant girl echoed, "My mother did not know what I have to go through in school everyday. I was made fun of or looked down on by my peers because I couldn't speak English well, had a strange haircut, and wore weird and cheap clothes. I used to be called 'nerdy' and 'boring.' I was so ashamed." When children complain, parents simply reply, "Just ignore them and concentrate on your study. When you make good grades, make it to an elite college, and eventually get a good job, you can afford whatever you want."

While immigrant parents value thrift and denounce luxurious consumption, they never hesitate spending on whatever they consider good for their children, such as books, after-school programs, Chinese lessons, private tutors, private lessons on the violin or the piano, and other educational-oriented activities. At a family counseling session, a mother puzzled at why her daughter would insist on going to a party instead of going to a scheduled piano lesson, "I only make $5 an hour, but pay $20 an hour for my daughter's piano lessons. I do this for her own good. Can't she understand?" This is a common parent-child problem in immigrant Chinese families, where parents are too driven by the mentality of "turning sons into dragons" and do what they think is good for their children, but tend to ignore what their children think is good for themselves.

The American cultural values of individualism and personal freedom are also downplayed in immigrant Chinese families. Chinese culture gives priority to the family as a whole rather than individual self-gratification. Parents fear that too much individualism would undermine their authority and the moral basis of their families. They consistently remind their children that achievement is a duty and an obligation to the family rather than to the individual. Moreover, they expect their children to respect authority, to be polite and modest, to refrain from aggression, and to stay away from trouble. Chinese children are generally stereotyped as hard-working, respectful, and well-disciplined. In terms of parent-child interaction, this stereotype works to ensure effective control and sanctioning of children. In terms of student-teacher interaction, the stereotype can also work as an advantage, for high teacher expectations generally result in high student performance (Sung 1987). The major drawbacks, however, are children's reluctance to express their own views in class or at home, a lack of creative and independent thinking, and the "little adult" syndrome (accepting too much responsibility and acting like an adult).

A third major problem immigrant Chinese children are facing is the fear and the appeal of the gang subculture. Street gangs have been a common problem in many immigrant and minority neighborhoods since the nineteenth century. In Chinatown, gangs were formed for the same reasons as other gangs in Little Italy, Little Saigon, Mexican American *barrios*, or South Central Los Angeles (Kuo 1977; Sung 1987; Vigil 1990; Vigil and Yun 1990). Kuo (1977) points out some of the mains reasons why immigrant youth join gangs: the lack of a sense of home because parents are too busy working or are unemployed, overcrowded housing, language deficiency, the lack of recreational facilities, the existence of gambling houses offering "easy money" and status, ghetto segregation, peer pressure for recognition, searching for identity and self-esteem, and the need for self-protection. Immigrant children, especially boys, are extremely vulnerable to the gang subculture in Chinatown.

On the one hand, many immigrant children fear being involved in gangs because of the stigma and the rule of conduct prescribed by the community. A Chinatown teenage boy said, "I am afraid of walking on certain streets by myself because people tend to identify boys hanging out there as gangsters and I don't want to be so identified. On the other hand, the real gangsters would approach you, put their arms around you, check you out, and try to kick you in." On the pressure of gang subculture, a community organizer commented,

> Youngsters have to spend a lot of energy trying to interpret whom other people think they are. They have to constantly prove certain things and unprove certain things. A student volunteer was once asked to take some fliers to streets that were gang dominated. He had to go with some girls because he was afraid of being identified as gang or being approached by gangsters. The pressure of coming to Chinatown is certainly real. But young people still come to Chinatown to see families and friends, to eat at the restaurants, and to do other things.[5]

On the other hand, street gangs are appealing to some immigrant youth in that they correspond to the desire for affiliation and achievement (Vigil 1990). In Chinatown, new gang recruits are typically those immigrant youth having severe adjustment problems, especially problems due to English language deficiency, which makes adaptation to school extremely difficult, resulting in frequent truancy and high dropout. This community organizer also pointed out another dimension of the problem: "It is sometimes easier to be a gangster. These kids were generally considered 'losers' by their teachers, parents, and peers in school. In school or at home, they feel uncomfortable, isolated, and rejected, which fosters a sense of hopelessness and powerlessness and a yearning for recognition. In the streets, they feel free from all the normative pressures. It is out there that they feel free to be themselves and to do things wherever and whenever they want, giving them a sort of identity and a sense of power."

While youth gangs continue to be a major concern in Chinatown, there are conscious and grass-roots effects to redirect them to more productive activities. Since the early 1970s, many community-based organizations, such as the CCBA, the CPC, and the Chinese Christian Herald Crusade, established various types of high-risk youth rehabilitation or prevention programs. Drawing on government and private funds and community resources, these programs have met with considerable success. Some gangs have agreed to make peace; some members of the gangs were provided with jobs or enrolled in English language and other job training classes by the CCBA; and still others reformed and enrolled in a preparatory school in Chinatown aiming at preparing high school dropouts and ex-gang members to enter college (Kuo 1977).

Although youth gangs are still a threatening force in the streets of Chinatown that is not going to go away in the near future, community organizers have been persistent and optimistic in their efforts to run and expand the existing preventive and targeted youth programs. "We can't reform them all, but we can do something good for these youngsters in ways that can be accepted by them. Most of the gangsters have a lot of energy and a strong desire to get recognized. Our goal is to redirect their energy to more productive activities," said the director of the Youth Center of the Chinese Christian Herald Crusade.

Finally, the problem of achieving is perhaps the most profound conflict confronting immigrant Chinese children. In recent years, the emphasis on education has paid off. Even though they are a small fraction of the total population (less than one percent) in the United States, Chinese Americans, many of whom are immigrants themselves or the children of immigrants, have surpassed other ethnic minorities in school attendance, grades, conduct, high school graduation rates, standardized tests, college admission rates, and other major indicators of academic achievement. In New York City, Chinese make up only 3 percent of the city's population; but in the city's most prestigious public high schools, such as the Hunter College High School, the Stuyvesant High School, and the Bronx High School of Science, where admission is based on standardized tests, Chinese American children are disproportionately represented.[6]

The academic achievement of Chinese American children has gained public attention, resulting in a positive stereotype as a model minority (Bell 1985; Kasindorf 1982). A school administrator commented,

> This positive stereotype has both positive and negative impacts. On the positive side, it helps develop a favorable attitude of the public and school teachers toward Chinese American children, leading to expected results like what is predicted by the self-fulfilling prophecy. On the negative side, it creates tremendous pressures for achieving both on parents and on children, leading to withdrawal from school and rebellious behavior, especially among those who have adjustment problems.[7]

The pressure for achieving also comes from within the community. "The pressure comes from the mothers and from those whom their mothers work with," said a community organizer. "When a mother hears that other mothers are sending their sons or daughters to the Hunter College High School, or to the Stuyvesant High School, or to the Bronx High School of Science, she would naturally think, 'Why shouldn't my child go to that school?' It's the peer pressure of the parents."[8]

Immigrant mothers, most of whom work in garment shops or other ethnic economies in Chinatown, are very aware which public high school is the best in the city. At work, if a mother hears that another's child is going to one of the best schools, she will go home and tell her children to prepare for that school. Many working mothers work all day and are isolated in Chinatown, and all they see is that many of the graduates at the public elementary school in Chinatown (with 90 percent of the students being Chinese) go to the Hunter College High School each year. This information is circulated among mothers, and going to Hunter becomes a standard. "My mother used to scold me and called me a dummy because I couldn't get into Hunter. She didn't have a clue how hard it was to get in these elite schools," said a college freshman who grew up in Chinatown.

Parental pressure is combined with accessible ethnic resources in Chinatown to push children to move ahead in school. Afterschool programs, tutor services, and test preparation programs are run by Chinese parents or entrepreneurs and are readily available in the community. School after school has become an accepted norm. An educator said, "when you think of how much time these Chinese kids put in their studies after regular school, you won't be surprised why they succeed in such a high rate."

From the children's perspective, they are motivated to learn and do well in school because they believe that education is their only way to get out of their parents' status. Also, many children do well in school hoping to make their parents happy and proud. "But that never happens. My mother is never satisfied no matter what you do and how well you do it," said a student, echoing a frustration felt by many other Chinese youth, who voiced how much they wish not to be compared with other children and how much they wish to rebel. Following success, however, many Chinese American youth return or go to Chinatown to find their paths and identities. Some of them have become actively involved in the community to help another generation of immigrant youth in their struggle to become "Chinese American." As one youngster from Brooklyn remarked, "I am certainly Chinese American, because I feel that, being exposed to Chinese and American cultures, I have the best of both worlds."[9]

CONCLUSION

This chapter examines how the process of adaptation of young Chinese Americans is affected by tangible forms of social relations between the community, immigrant families and the younger generation. We have shown that Chinatown serves as the basis of social capital that facilitates, rather than inhibits, the assimilation of immigrant children in the expected directions. Although today's immigrant Chinese overwhelmingly desire to ultimately assimilate into the mainstream society, the majority of them have only limited resources and face structural barriers, making assimilation an extremely difficult and lengthy process. In order to prevent immigrants and their children from assimilating into the margins of the American society, Chinatown has broadened its economic and social bases and has established various economic and social organizations to provide jobs, job referral services, career training, language learning facilities, childcare, after-school programs, family counseling, and various youth-oriented crisis-prevention and rehabilitation programs. Because many parents and children are involved, in one way or another, in these intense ethnic networks in Chinatown, it becomes possible for the community to reinforce norms and to promote a high level of communication among group members and a high level of consistency among standards. In this sense, the community, as an important source of social capital, not only makes resources available to parents and children, but serves to direct children's behavior. This type of social capital helps many of Chinatown's children to overcome intense adjustment difficulties and unfavorable conditions, such as linguistic and social isolation, bicultural conflicts, poverty, gang subculture, and close proximity to other underprivileged minority neighborhoods, and to ensure successful adaptation.

This case study provides useful insight into the role of community-based organizations and families in promoting adjustment and success of immigrant children and offers a point of departure for studying the process of adaptation for the second and later generations. The generalizability of our findings, however, may be limited since we have focused only on children in Chinatown. Because different social contexts and different dynamics may affect different sets of immigrants and their offspring, the theoretical issues of social capital and social integration will require more elaboration and refinement than we have been able to give in this case study of a specific social setting. It will be necessary, also, to delve in greater detail into how and under what circumstances our findings may be generalized to other situations. Therefore, additional research is needed to examine in greater detail the ways in which children and their families are connected to one another by ethnically concentrated communities, and how these connections between families and community-based organizations facilitate the adaptation of young people.

NOTES

1. The study relied on the 1980 and 1990 U.S. Census data and fieldwork in New York City's Chinatowns in Lower East Manhattan, Flushing, and Sunset Park. The field observations were conducted by the author sporadically in selected homes, streets, community-based organizations, restaurants, and garment factories during the months of September and October in 1994. Face-to-face or telephone interviews (lasting half an hour to an hour) were conducted by the author in English or in Chinese on a convenient sample of 4 community-based Chinese schools, 6 youth-oriented programs run by various organizations, 3 family associations, 2 Christian churches, and 2 Buddhist temples, in addition to Chinese Consolidated Benevolent Association, Chinese American Planning Council, and Chinatown History Museum. Pseudonyms are used when individuals' names were mentioned. The author wish to thank all informants who provided generous help in this study. This chapter was written while the author was in residence at the Russell Sage Foundation, whose support is also gratefully acknowledged. The author is exclusively responsible for the contents of the chapter.

2. Excerpt from "Yellow Discrimination" written in 1994 by Eunyang Theresa Oh, a member of the Student Committee of the Chinatown History Museum, as part of the exhibition entitled "Who's Chinese American?"

3. Recorded from one of the parent-counselor conferences and a conversation with the counselor at a public high school in Chinatown, October 1994.

4. Excerpt from "The Smell of the Wet Grass" written in 1994 by Carla Shen, a member of the Student Committee of the Chinatown History Museum, as part of the exhibition entitled "Who's Chinese American?"

5. Personal interview with a community organizer at the Chinatown History Museum, September 1994.

6. Telephone inquiries of the staff of the schools mentioned, October 1994.

7. Personal interview with an administrator of a public high school in Chinatown, September 1994.

8. Personal interview, September 1994.

9. Recorded from a discussion at one of the youth sessions, October 1994.

REFERENCES

Bell, D. A. 1985. "An American Success Story: The Triumph of Asian Americans." *The New Republic* 3677 (July 15): 24–31.

Chinese-American Planning Council (CPC). 1993 (October). *Chinese-American Planning Council: Program List*. New York: CPC.

Chinatown Today Publishing. 1993. *Chinese-American Life Guide*. Hong Kong: Chinatown Today Publishing.

Coleman, James. 1990. *Foundations of Social Theory.* Cambridge, Mass.: The Belknap Press of the Harvard University Press.

Dillon, R. H. 1962. *The Hatchetmen: Tong Wars in San Francisco.* New York: Coward McCann.

Durkheim, É. 1951 [1897]. *Suicide: A Study in Sociology,* John A. Spaulding and George Simpson, tr., G. Simpson, ed. New York: Free Press.

Fernandez-Kelly, M. Patricia. 1995. "Social Capital and Cultural Capital in the Urban Ghetto: Implications for the Economic Sociology and Immigration." In Alejandro Portes, ed., *Economic Sociology.* New York: Russell Sage Foundation.

Immigration and Naturalization Service. 1991. *Statistical Yearbook of the Immigration and Naturalization Service 1990.* Washington, D.C.: U.S. Government Printing Office.

Kasindorf, Martin. 1982. "Asian Americans: A Model Minority." *Newsweek* (December 6): 39–51.

Kuo, Chia-Ling. 1977. *Social and Political Change in New York's Chinatown: The Role of Voluntary Associations.* New York: Praeger.

Kwong, Peter. 1987. *The New Chinatown.* New York: Hill and Wang.

Portes, Alejandro, and Rubén G. Rumbaut. 1990. *Immigrant America: A Portrait.* Berkeley: University of California Press.

Portes, Alejandro, and Julia Sensenbrenner. 1993. "Embeddedness and Immigration: Notes on the Social Determinants of Economic Action." *American Journal of Sociology* 98: 1320–50.

Sung, Betty Lee. 1987. *The Adjustment Experience of Chinese Immigrant Children in New York City.* New York: Center for Migration Studies.

Vigil, James Diego. 1990. "Gangs, Social Control, and Ethnicity: Ways to Redirect." In Shirley Brice Heath and Milbrey W. McLaughlin, eds., *Identity and Inner-City Youth: Beyond Ethnicity and Gender,* 94–119. New York: Teachers College Press.

Vigil, James Diego, and S. Yun. 1990. "Vietnamese Youth Gangs in Southern California." In R. Huff, ed., *Gangs in America: Diffusion, Diversity, and Public Policy,* 146–62. Beverly Hills, Calif.: Sage.

Wong, Bernard P. 1979. *A Chinese American Community: Ethnicity and Survival Strategies.* Singapore: Chopmen Enterprise.

Zhou, Min. 1992. *Chinatown: The Socioeconomic Potential of an Urban Enclave.* Philadelphia: Temple University Press.

Zhou, Min, and John R. Logan. 1989. "Returns on Human Capital in Ethnic Enclaves: New York City's Chinatown." *American Sociological Review* 54: 809–20.

10

CARL L. BANKSTON III _____

Education and Ethnicity in an
Urban Vietnamese Village
The Role of Ethnic Community Involvement
in Academic Achievement

VIETNAMESE AMERICAN COMMUNITIES

On April 18, 1975, less than two weeks before the fall of Saigon, President
Ford authorized the entry of 130,000 refugees from the three countries of In-
dochina into the United States, 125,000 of whom were Vietnamese (Haines
1989, 3). Five years later, according to the U.S. Census, this new American
ethnic group had grown to 245,025. The 1990 U.S. Census found 614,545
Vietnamese, an increase of over 150 percent in a ten-year period. This made
the Vietnamese, almost nonexistent in the census twenty years before, the fifth
largest Asian group in the country.

Since the early 1980s, a number of scholars have called attention to the
fact that Vietnamese Americans have not simply grown in numbers and increased in geographical concentrations, they have also formed definable communities. Christine R. Finnan and Rhonda Ann Cooperstein, in 1983, produced a report for the Office of Refugee Resettlement that has become
influential among resettlement officials who work with the Vietnamese.
Finnan and Cooperstein suggest that three phases can be identified in the resettlement process.

The first phase occurred from 1975 to 1978, when about 150,000 Indochinese arrived in the United States. "These refugees," the authors note,

> tended to be well-educated and many spoke English at the time of their ar-
> rival. Refugees were initially placed in localities scattered across the United
> States. There were very few Southeast Asians living in the United States
> prior to 1975, so refugees had to form new communities rather than rely on
> existing communities for support. Refugees formed small communities; for-
> mal organizations began to develop, and leaders emerged. Members of these

communities primarily provided intangible support to each other. Secondary migration to areas of refugee concentration began to occur during the end of this phase. (Finnan and Cooperstein 1983, 16)

The second phase identified by Finnan and Cooperstein lasted from 1979 to 1982, when about 400,000 Southeast Asians from all socioeconomic backgrounds flooded into the U.S. These newcomers were drawn to the ethnic concentrations that had already been established. As Vietnamese communities put down deeper roots and grew in size, ethnic businesses began to be established and community structures, such as formal organizations and patterns of leadership, took definite form (Finnan and Cooperstein 1983, 17).

In the third phase, the flood of refugees became a trickle and the newcomers arrived in well-established communities. "Refugee leaders and self-help organizations have become integral parts of the resettlement program on many localities. During this phase, the refugee communities have continued to provide intangible support to their members, and are becoming increasingly capable of providing tangible support" (Finnan and Cooperstein 1983, 18).

In contrast to the Chinatowns that developed earlier in American history (see Zhou 1992), hostility from the larger society did not play a large part in creating Vietnamese communities. The emerging Vietnamese communities resulted from attempts to draw on the social relations formed in the homeland to adapt to a new and strange environment. In this way, the Vietnamese created communities in the United States both as means of self-help and as efforts to retain some aspects of familiar ways of life (on this point, see Kibria 1993 and Muzny 1989).

Finnan and Cooperstein argue that the development of Southeast Asian communities in the United States has major policy implications for government programs directed toward the Vietnamese and the much smaller groups from Laos and Cambodia. First, they argue that the U.S. government must shift its focus from a concern with the short-term economic adjustment of individual Southeast Asians to a focus on long-term adaptation of those in specific localities. Second, they maintain that the individual orientation must change to a community orientation. Such an orientation would involve "recognizing refugee communities as viable ethnic communities similar to nonrefugee ethnic communities in the locality" (Finnan and Cooperstein 1983, 19). Moreover, business development in Southeast Asian neighborhoods should become part of federal policy (Finnan and Cooperstein 1983, 30).

In *The Vietnamese Experience in America* (1992), Paul Rutledge interviews Vietnamese Americans in virtually all parts of the United States. "One of the foremost strengths affecting Vietnamese refugee adaptation and adjustment to the United States," he observes on the basis of these interviews, "has been the formation of communities. Vietnamese communities are proving to be strong pillars for assisting refugees in their adjustment economically, spiritually, psychologically, and symbolically. Their communities are supportive through continuing many of the traditional practices of Vietnam, while simultaneously encouraging changes necessary to adapt successfully" (Rutledge 1992, 58).

Studying the Vietnamese community in Oklahoma City, anthropologist Charles Muzny finds that on the individual level Vietnamese made some adaptive changes to life in America, but that individual lives continued to be dominated by the family (Muzny 1989, 184–85). For the purposes of the present study, however, the most interesting developments in the Vietnamese community of Oklahoma City occurred at the group level. "On the group level," Muzny reports, "it was observed that a small nucleus of elites assumed leadership positions among the Vietnamese of Oklahoma City. The same group of leaders were mainly responsible for the development of the Vietnamese American Association (VAA), the Vietnamese Buddhist Association, the Vietnamese Catholic Association, and the Vietnamese Baptist Association. Through the programs of the VAA, other Vietnamese were able to study English, find jobs, and make advances in public sector areas of work and school" (Muzny 1989, 186). Thus, to Rutledge's observations of the importance of community life for Vietnamese Americans, Muzny adds the insight of a particular structure of social relations within this community life, a structure dominated by an elite exercising its influence through multiple, interlocking formal ethnic associations that are created by strong informal ties and a highly developed sense of group identity.

This does not mean that competition among elites in Vietnamese communities has been completely absent. Kibria (1993) sees the competition of Vietnamese groups, expressed in elite-run associations, as a threat to the solidarity to many of these communities. However, the relatively small numbers of leaders, and the tendency of Vietnamese community leaders to hold multiple positions in different ethnic organizations, as well as the sense of common identity, has usually made cooperation more prevalent than conflict and factionalism.

VIETNAMESE AMERICAN YOUTH IN THE SCHOOL ENVIRONMENT

Rutledge remarks, "educationally, Vietnamese refugees are succeeding at an exponential rate" (Rutledge 1992, 148). After citing numerous examples of individual Vietnamese students who have shown outstanding performance in American schools, he concludes that "the success of Vietnamese Americans in high schools and universities across America forecasts the benefits gained from the resettlement of refugee peoples. Within a short period of time, the costs necessitated in the resettlement process will be overshadowed by the financial benefits, both direct and indirect, derived from the contributions made to the economic development of America by refugee-Americans" (Rutledge 1992, 148).

Rutledge's glowing praise for Vietnamese American students, and their potential contribution to American society, is regularly echoed by teachers who have contact with these students. However, the evidence of Vietnamese American academic success is by no means limited to generalizations from anecdotes. Vietnamese students have been found to receive an average score above the national average on standardized achievement tests such as the California Achievement Test. In math, especially, they seem to have outstripped other young people. "Half the [Vietnamese] children studied obtained [math] scores in the top quartile," reports one study. "Even more spectacularly, 27 percent of them scored in the 10th decile—better than 90 percent of the students across the country and almost three times higher than the national norm" (Caplan et al. 1992, 38; see also Caplan et al. 1989, and Caplan et al. 1991, for detailed evidence of the academic accomplishments of Vietnamese children in the United States).

The 1990 U.S. Census of Population and Housing shows that failure to complete high school is much less common among Vietnamese Americans than other American groups: only 6.5 percent of Vietnamese Americans from 16 to 19 were neither enrolled in high school nor high school graduates, compared to 9.8 percent of white American youth and 13.7 percent of black American youth. Moreover, Census data indicates that Vietnamese Americans have unusually high rates of continuing education beyond high school: 49.3 percent of Vietnamese Americans between the ages of 18 and 24 were enrolled in college or another form of higher education beyond the high school level. By contrast, only 39.5 percent of white Americans and only 28.1 percent of black Americans in the same age group were in college or another form of education beyond high school (U.S. Census of Population and Housing 1990, Detailed Population Characteristics).

The development of socially integrated, highly interrelated Vietnamese communities, then, has taken place in the same period of time that the scholastic performance of Vietnamese students has begun to draw attention. This study will argue that these two phenomena are connected: that Vietnamese ethnic communities have provided students with systems of social supports and constraints that encourage academic excellence. In order to make this argument, it will be helpful to focus on a particular community in order to examine the characteristics it fosters in its young.

VERSAILLES:

A VIETNAMESE COMMUNITY ON THE BAYOU:

FOUNDING OF A COMMUNITY

The Vietnamese residential enclave in New Orleans East, often referred to as "Versailles," after the apartment complexes at the center of the neighborhood, is bounded by the Chef Menteur Highway, Michoud Boulevard, and the Bayou Sauvage Wildlife Refugee, near the Michoud exit from the I-10 expressway, about 10 miles from the bridge over Lake Pontchartrain to Slidell (cf. Bankston 1991, 14). This Vietnamese community began in 1975, after the fall of Saigon, when about 1,000 refugees from Vietnam were settled on the eastern edge of New Orleans by Associated Catholic Charities, one of the volunteer agencies in charge of refugee resettlement, with offices in New Orleans (Ashton 1985a, A13). "These neighborhoods were seeded by chance," writes a reporter for the *Times-Picayune* newspaper. "Their location reflects the city's rental vacancies a decade ago when Associated Catholic Charities began looking for housing for the refugees" (Ashton 1985a, A1). The Versailles Arms apartments, near Michoud Boulevard and the Chef Menteur Highway, offered ample room for new residents. The apartments were considered undesirable by most New Orleanians, since they were a long way from the city itself and were provided with inadequate bus service (Ashton 1985b, A12). According to the Melanie Ottaway, manager of Versailles Arms Apartments, the apartment complex had been built in 1970, when the neighborhood of New Orleans East was still expected to expand, along with the local NASA plant (Ottaway, personal communication, February 17, 1994). By 1975, however, economic hardship had hit the plant and the management of Versailles Arms was eager to find residents.

These initial 1,000 residents provided the end link in a system of chain migration. In 1976, another 2,000 Vietnamese arrived on their own. While Associated Catholic Charities has continued to settle Vietnamese in this area, many of the residents have been drawn by ties to friends, relatives, and former neighbors. According to Sister Ann Devaney, head of refugee social services for Catholic Charities, three-fifths of those who have settled in the community have been secondary migrants from other states.

The religious and historical backgrounds of those in this neighborhood attest to the importance of established networks in directing living patterns, even among those who have migrated around the world. Ninety percent of the

Vietnamese in this community are Catholics. The late Rev. Michael Viet-Anh, a priest who lived in the Versailles area, has estimated that "about 60 percent of the Vietnamese in the Versailles community once lived in Bui Chu province in North Vietnam and later moved to Vung Tau (a coastal town in former South Vietnam)" (Ashton 1985a, A12). Phuc Tinh, another fishing village in South Vietnam was also settled in 1954 by North Vietnamese from Bui Chu, so that there are a variety of kinship ties between the people of Phuc Tinh and those of Vung Tau.

Most of the residents of this neighborhood who do not trace their origins back to Bui Chu are from families deriving from Nghe An, another Catholic area that moved south in 1954. The Nghe An people settled on the island of Phu Quoc or in the coastal town of Nha Trang. This reconstruction of Vietnamese villages on the banks of the bayous has resulted from channeling by ethnic networks, rather than from official resettlement policy. "Despite the appearances, no villages were resettled . . . in New Orleans by Associated Catholic Charities. The villagers apparently regrouped on their own" (Ashton 1985a, A12).

Much of the factionalism that has occurred in this neighborhood has taken place along the lines of village of origin. The Bui Chu people and the Nghe An people are still often able to recognize one another by accent and they tend to form separate cliques. The local Catholic church mitigates this potential conflict by including priests and nuns stemming from both villages of origin. Since it is an overwhelmingly Catholic neighborhood, open religious conflicts are not found, although some young Vietnamese Buddhists in the area have expressed to me a sense of being somewhat "left out" of the many activities that take place at the church.

In a manner reminiscent of the Mexican kinship networks in Douglas Massey and co-workers' *Return to Aztlan* (1987), family networks provided the means for conveying to Vietnamese in other states that a large concentration existed in New Orleans East. By the time of the second wave of Vietnamese refugees, the Vietnamese settled in the United States had themselves become sponsors for newly arrived refugees, replacing the organizational sponsorship of the first years. Since they generally sponsored their relatives, this means that Vietnamese increasingly came directly to New Orleans from Vietnam. At present, as the overseas refugee camps are being closed down, almost all primary migrants are coming directly from Vietnam, into the homes of their kinspeople (Tony Tran, personal communication, April 13, 1994).

In interviews that I conducted with fifty-three residents of the area in 1993 and 1994, all interviewees reported that they had been drawn to New Orleans by of some sort of family connection. When I asked, "why did you come to

New Orleans?," the most common answers were "Because my brother was here" or "Because my uncle was here," or because some other relative was already in the New Orleans area. Other answers that were frequently given were, "Because I heard the weather was like the weather in Vietnam," or "Because I heard there were jobs for fishermen." These answers might, on the face of it, seem to suggest that at least some of the residents of New Orleans East had not migrated along lines provided by family networks. However, when I would ask them, "How did you hear about the weather?" or "How did you hear about the job?" the answers were, invariably, "My wife's uncle, who was already here, told us about it in a letter," or "I heard about it from my cousin." Thus, even those who did not have family reunification as a motivation for moving to New Orleans moved as a result of information provided by family communication channels. The result of this type of settlement, typical of many U.S. Vietnamese communities, is that an extended kinship network underlies the formal community structure.

FORMAL ORGANIZATIONS

Muzny notes that "when one investigates the leadership of the Vietnamese organizations in Oklahoma City, it becomes apparent that there is a limited core of 'elites' within the Vietnamese groups" (Muzny 1989, 171–72). Those familiar with Vietnamese communities around the United States have observed this tendency to form task-oriented organizations around individuals who have both prestige and special abilities to achieve tasks. For example, Diana Bui, director of the Southeast Asia Resource Action Center in Washington, D.C. (formerly known as the Indochinese Refugee Action Center), which coordinates activities among the U.S. government–recognized self-help groups known as Mutual Assistance Organizations, remarked in a telephone interview in June 1994, that "the Vietnamese are forever forming organizations, and it's always just a few people who run them" (Bui, personal communication, June 6, 1994).

As in other Vietnamese communities, the leaders tend to be well-educated males who arrived in the United States in 1975 or shortly thereafter. They tend to be professionals, rather than shopowners, fishing boat owners, or other small businessmen, although the businessmen provide the organizations with most of their funding and may be presumed therefore to have some influence over organization goals and activities. All of these community leaders know one another and maintain cooperative relations.

The Catholic church provides the physical location for many meetings and other activities. However, Buddhist leaders from the much smaller Vietnamese communities elsewhere in the New Orleans participate in several of the organizations, such as the Vietnamese Educational Association, and the Catholic priests and major Buddhist figures, such as Luong Truong of Marrero, General Secretary of the Buddhist Fellowship of Louisiana, maintain personal ties with one another (Msgr. Dominic Luong, personal communication, May 24, 1993). In this way, religious institutions are not simply normative in nature, providing abstract symbols of ethnic identity, but they also provide connecting pathways among ethnic group members. A few of the ethnic organizations that meet at the Vietnamese Catholic Church are the Vietnamese American Voters' Association, the H. O. Union (an organization of former political prisoners), the Mother-Daughter Association, a Vietnamese Boy Scout troop, and the Vietnamese Educational Association.

The Vietnamese Educational Association, formed in 1985, may serve as an example of the kind of formal organization that leads to such impressive results on the part of Vietnamese students. It was the brainchild of the pastor of the Vietnamese Catholic Church and it is primarily managed by two local Vietnamese teachers, one a high school teacher and the other an elementary school teacher.

The two chief projects of the Vietnamese Educational Association are: (1) after-school classes held in the Child Development Center behind the church, and (2) yearly awards granted to Vietnamese students who have excelled in the public school system in a ceremony usually held on church grounds on a Sunday in May or June, immediately after school has closed for the summer. Until about 1992, after-school classes were offered, on a voluntary basis to high school students. The subjects that were emphasized in these classes were English language and Vietnamese language, although other academic subjects were also offered from time to time. After 1992, the after-school classes began to shift their attention from high school students to students in the elementary schools. One of the volunteer teachers involved with the after-school classes explained that "we feel that it's best to start when they're young, and that way we can have more of an effect." He also said that preparing students to take entrance tests to get into magnet schools or honors programs within the local public schools was one of the major reasons for focusing on younger children (Ngoc Thanh Nguyen, personal communication, November 21, 1993).

INFORMAL SUPPORTS AND CONSTRAINTS

The Vietnamese Educational Association is just one of many ethnic organizations in this community, but it may serve as an example of how ethnicity serves as a basis for providing guidance and assistance to the local youth. However, the informal structure of the community is at least as important as the formal organizations in directing the behavior of adolescents. As Nash (1992) reports, children in the Vietnamese neighborhood find themselves in a dense web of relationships consisting of all of their neighbors as well as their individual family members. To illustrate this point, Nash quotes the Vietnamese proverb, "Parents may be far away, but the neighbors are always near" (Nash 1992, 53).

Interviews with parents and students in the neighborhood support this view of the ethnic community as a major influence on the behavior of young people. A father of four daughters and one son expressed a common attitude when he observed, "When my children do well, everyone knows and they think I have done well. When my children do something bad, everyone knows that too, and I have the blame." A young woman of seventeen, a high school student, offered another perspective on this same state of affairs: "The Vietnamese people here, they're are always minding everyone else's business, so you really can't get away with anything. Anything I do, everybody knows, and there's so much gossip that you have to watch your step all the time." Another student, a young man of eighteen, told me, "if you graduate at the top of your class and it looks like you're going to become a doctor or an engineer, you're like a hero to everyone."

It would, of course, be a mistake to suggest that Vietnamese students are uniformly excellent, all conforming to a stereotype of a "model minority." Teachers, parents, and students all report the existence of a number of disaffected Vietnamese students, known as troublemakers in school, often suspected of being gang members or hangers-on. These are the culturally marginal young people, those who feel at home neither in the Vietnamese community nor in the larger American society (on this point, see Bankston 1995)." You can tell the problem kids by their language," remarks one Vietnamese community leader, "they speak in bits of Vietnamese and bits of English, and they don't use either one very well." Dr. Joseph Vuong, a local school counselor and adjunct professor of Vietnamese at Tulane University, attributes the problems of this group of young people to their alienation from their own ethnicity. "A branch broken off from its tree cannot live," Dr. Vuong observes, explaining that the troubled young of the Vietnamese neighborhood are anomic and isolated because they have rejected the culture of their elders (Joseph Vuong, personal communication, November 2, 1993). Tony Tran, a Vietnamese social worker active in the community essentially agrees with Dr. Vuong, but places some of the blame on the community itself: "They put a lot of effort into helping the 'good kids' here, but they just want the 'bad' ones to go away. They just want to give up on these kids" (Tony Tran, April 13, 1994). The picture that emerges from these descriptions of the Vietnamese youth in the New Orleans community is one of a group for whom the relationship to their own ethnic community is a defining characteristic. Those who are well integrated into the ethnic community and are guided and supported by the community's formal and informal support systems tend to be high achievers in the school system of the surrounding American society. Those who are alienated from the organizations and social networks of the community tend to be also the ones who have the greatest difficulty in the American school system and will also, therefore, experience the greatest difficulty in becoming part of the mainstream American society. A bit paradoxically, involvement with an ethnic community appears not only as the chief source of identity for these young people, but also as their primary vehicle for successful entry into the world beyond their ethnic community.

THE STUDENTS OF VERSAILLES:
INVOLVEMENT IN AN ETHNIC COMMUNITY
AND ACADEMIC ACHIEVEMENT

Most of the high school students in the Versailles area attend two high schools: one is located in the immediate vicinity of the Vietnamese community, within walking distance of students' homes; the other is on the outer edge of the area of New Orleans East where the Vietnamese have settled. The second school contains what is referred to as a "magnet component." This means that 10 percent of the students in the school are in the honors program, composed of classes that follow a special, challenging curriculum. Students from outside the boundaries of the school district may enter the honors program, but they must have a B average or better in their previous school, and they must pass an entry test that covers all subjects.

Roughly 80 percent of the students in the honors program are Vietnamese and about 90 percent of the Vietnamese students who attend the school on the outer edge of the Vietnamese community are in the honors program.[1] Even in the school located in the neighborhood itself, attended by new arrivals to the United States or simply by those whose families want them close by, however, Vietnamese students have acquired a reputation for excellence. As a physical education and science teacher at the neighborhood school told me, "those Vietnamese kids are the ones that keep me coming here each morning. They really care and work hard." These sentiments are echoed by almost all the teachers in schools with Vietnamese students.

In order to examine the connections between the ethnic community and the scholastic performance of its students, I administered a survey in three school with Vietnamese students in April 1993. These surveys were given out in English classes and completed in school, with the assistance of teachers in the schools. Two of the schools are those that primarily serve the Vietnamese community. The first, the one located close to the center of the Versailles neighborhood, is approximately 77 percent black and approximately 20 percent Vietnamese. The other, the school with the 10 percent magnet or honors component, is approximately 85 percent black and 12 percent Vietnamese. In addition to Vietnamese students at these two schools, I also surveyed the fifteen Vietnamese from this neighborhood who have won entry into the elite public school for high achievers from all of Orleans Parish that is located on the campus of the University of New Orleans. This school has a somewhat different population, since its students tend to come from higher socioeconomic ranks than other New Orleans public schools, and it is approximately 69 percent white and 15 percent black.

Table 1 gives selected characteristics of the Vietnamese students at these three schools. Vietnamese language skills tend to be fairly high. All respondents can speak some Vietnamese and over half report being able to speak the language well. As we might expect, reading and writing abilities are somewhat less developed than speaking abilities, but a majority of respondents can read and write their ancestral language at least fairly well. Use of Vietnamese in daily life is also common. Most students report always speaking Vietnamese with their parents, nearly three-quarters usually or always speak Vietnamese with siblings, and over half always or usually speak Vietnamese with friends. These linguistic characteristics suggest a distinctive community in which ethnicity plays an important part in the daily lives of students.

Commitment to endogamy is an important aspect of ethnicity, since ethnic groups maintain their existence through in-group marriage and choice of spouse is an essential part of personal identity. Over 60 percent of the Vietnamese students at least prefer a Vietnamese spouse and over one in five is firmly committed to ingroup marriage. This represents a theoretical commitment to endogamy, an unwillingness to marry outside the group under any hypothetical conditions. Actual rates of endogamy are much higher, since 80 percent of students say that all or most of their friends are Vietnamese and, in another item not reported in this table, over 80 percent report that their parents want them to marry a Vietnamese person.

Self-description, another aspect of ethnic identity, also shows a sense of belonging to the ethnic group of the community. About 64 percent of teenagers describe themselves unequivocally as "Vietnamese," and most of the others describe themselves as "Vietnamese American."

Friendship networks tend to be circumscribed by the ethnicity. Eighty

TABLE 1. Characteristics[1] of Vietnamese American Adolescents in the Versailles Community

Vietnamese language abilities:

	Not at all	A little	Fairly well	Well
Speak Vietnamese	0.0%	8.5%	36.6%	55.0%
Read Vietnamese	10.4	23.6	26.9	39.1
Write Vietnamese	13.2	22.9	28.1	35.8

Vietnamese language use:

	Never	Seldom	Sometimes	Usually	Always
Speak with parents	1.0%	2.2%	11.9%	26.6%	58.2%
Speak with siblings	4.7	7.7	21.6	40.8	25.1
Speak with friends	3.7	10.2	31.3	39.1	15.7

Extent to which respondents prefer a Vietnamese spouse:

Definitely does not want Vietnamese spouse	1.7%
Prefers non-Vietnamese spouse	1.0
Not important	34.8
Prefers Vietnamese spouse	39.6
Definitely wants Vietnamese spouse	22.9

Self-description:

American	3.2%
Vietnamese American	33.1
Vietnamese	63.7

Proportion of friends who are Vietnamese:

None	1.2%
Very few	4.5
Some	4.2
About half	10.0
Most	24.1
Almost all	56.0

Averaged reported grade received:

D or F	5.7%
C	13.7
B	55.7
A	24.9

Perceived importance of college:[2]

Doesn't want to go	5.1%
Not important	5.6
Fairly important	16.5
Very important	72.8

1. $N = 402$ on all variables, unless otherwise noted.
2. $N = 394$.

TABLE 1. *(continued)*

Time spent daily on homework: [3]

Don't do	4.8%
Less than 30 minutes	16.3
1/2 to 1 hr	24.2
1 to 2 hrs	28.5
Over 2 hrs	26.2

Substance abuse:

	Never	Once	2–5 times	More than 5 times
Alcohol abuse	77.4%	4.2%	12.5%	6.5%
Illegal drug use	89.3	0.5	1.2	9.0

Number of times stopped by police:

Never	77.9%
Once	6.5
Twice	2.7
Three times	5.7
Four or more	7.2

Mean age: 16.3

Percent Female: 53.4%

Year of arrival in U.S.:

Before 1980 or U.S.-born	54.5%
1981–1985	14.7
1986–1990	11.9
1991–1993	18.9

Living with both parents: 82.1%

Living with grandparents in the home: 18.2%

Mean number of siblings: 4.9

Education of parents:

	Less than high school	High school graduate	Some college	College graduate	Grad. degree
Father	38.1%	44.5%	10.7%	4.5%	2.2%
Mother	58.0	37.1	3.0	1.7	0.2

Weekly work hours of parents:

	None	Less than 20 hrs	20 to 40 hrs	Over 40 hrs
Father[4]	23.5%	11.9%	29.1%	35.4%
Mother[5]	31.3	15.9	33.6	19.3

3. $N = 393$.

4. $N = 378$.

5. $N = 384$.

percent of Vietnamese students in this area report that most or all of their friends are Vietnamese. In these statistics, we see a group of young people for whom an ethnic community is a central aspect of their lives, determining patterns of communication by developing a minority language and encouraging its daily use, channeling the choice of marriage partners, shaping a sense of personal identity, and directing relationships with peers. A brief look at statistics on academic achievement can tell us about how students coming from this distinctive community function in the world outside of it.

The overwhelming majority of these students report grades that average to a B, and a quarter of them report grades averaging to an A.[2] Most of them see college attendance as very important. They tend to spend a great deal of time on homework, supporting current performance and making future educational plans realistic goals. Over half report spending more than an hour every day and one in four spends over two hours every day on homework.

In order to look also at how young people in this community deal with some of the difficulties confronting contemporary adolescents, I have also included indicators of problematic behavior in this table: the number of times students report using alcohol to the point of drunkenness, the number of times they report using illegal drugs, and the number of times they report being stopped by the police.

The types of problematic behavior indicated by these items are not common among the students of the Versailles community, but they do occur. Responses to the question about illegal drug use are particularly interesting, since they suggest that while most students (89.3 percent) do not use drugs at all, most of those who have used drugs have used them more than five times. Similarly, although most students have never been stopped by the police, the modal category for those who have been stopped is four times or more. These statistics provide some preliminary corroboration of the view offered by interviewees, that these problems among these young people occur disproportionately within a distinct minority. Self-reports of socially unacceptable behavior are always problematic, but I think that these statistics are reasonably valid, if perhaps somewhat conservative. Respondents were assured of the survey's complete anonymity, and conversations with respondents in days after the survey convinced me that they had generally answered the questions honestly. Some underreporting of drug and alcohol use would not present a serious problem for analysis, unless there were a systematic bias in this underreporting.

These Vietnamese students have a mean age of just over sixteen, which is similar to other ninth- through twelfth-graders, and there are slightly more females than males. The majority either arrived in the United States before 1980 or were born in this country, but new arrivals have continued to arrive since 1981. The vast majority of them (82 percent) live with both of their parents and almost one out of every five has a grandparent in the home. Families are quite large by American standards: the mean number of siblings reported by respondents is almost five.

The high levels of academic achievement seen above do not seem to be the result of coming from highly educated families. Most fathers have no more than a high school education and most mothers are not high school graduates. Parents of these young people show high levels of unemployment (24 percent for fathers and 31 percent for mothers), but those who work tend to work long hours, since the modal category for fathers was working over forty hours per week and the modal category for mothers was working twenty to forty hours per week, with almost 20 percent of mothers working over forty hours per week.

Tables 2 through 4 provide a preliminary examination of the relationship between involvement with the Vietnamese community and important indicators of academic achievement, using simple cross-tabular analysis. I employ three indicators of academic achievement here: an average of past and present grades received by respondents reported in the survey, students' reports of the importance of college for them, and reports of amount of time spent daily on homework. These three indicators provide us with three separate dimensions of academic achievement, which may be considered as the dimension of current performance, that of dedication to continuing education, and that of the effort expended to attain favorable results in current and future educational endeavors.

Once again, indicators of involvement in the ethnic community and identification with it include facility in the ethnic language, use of the ethnic language with family and peers, commitment to endogamy, self-description as a member of the ethnic group, and social networks composed primarily of ethnic group members. For the sake of clear interpretation in cross-tabulation, each of these indicators of ethnicity has been recoded into two values and the higher value is reported.

Table 2 reports the cross-tabulation of reported averaged grades with the various indicators of ethnicity. Averaged grades have been recoded here into three categories: an average of C and below, an average of B, and an average of A. Column percentages are reported in each cell.

Among those with a C average or less, 33.3 percent reported the ability to speak Vietnamese well, rather than not at all, a little, or fairly well, and 54.5 percent of those with a B average or less reported the ability to speak

TABLE 2.   Cross-tabulations of Average Grade Received by Vietnamese High School Students with Indicators of Identification with the Ethnic Community

Indicators of Ethnic Identification	Average Grade			
	C or less	B	A	Chi-Square
Speak Vietnamese well	33.3 (26)	54.5 (122)	73.0 (73)	27.91[*]
Read Vietnamese well	15.4 (12)	36.6 (82)	63.0 (63)	43.01[*]
Write Vietnamese well	16.7 (13)	32.6 (73)	58.0 (58)	34.86[*]
Usually speak Vietnamese with parents	69.2 (54)	87.9 (197)	90.0 (90)	18.51[*]
Usually speak Vietnamese with siblings	38.5 (30)	69.2 (155)	80.0 (80)	36.07[*]
Usually speak Vietnamese with friends	30.8 (24)	54.9 (123)	73.0 (73)	31.55[*]
Definitely want to marry a Vietnamese	39.7 (31)	65.2 (146)	74.0 (74)	23.55[*]
Describe self as "Vietnamese"	42.3 (33)	65.2 (146)	77.0 (77)	23.29[*]
Almost all friends are Vietnamese	65.4 (51)	81.7 (88)	88.0 (88)	14.869[*]

Note: Number of respondents reported in parentheses.
[*] $p \leq .001$.

Vietnamese well. By contrast, nearly three-quarters of those with an A average reported the ability to speak Vietnamese well. Reading and writing abilities follow much the same pattern. The higher the grade, the more likely it is that the student the student will show advanced skills in Vietnamese.

It is possible that Vietnamese language skills are related to academic performance because the cognitive skills developed in the acquisition of language skills may be transferred to other areas of intellectual performance (for a discussion of this argument regarding the relationship between language skills and academic skills, see Bankston and Zhou 1995). However, this would not appear to be the only reason for this relationship, since language skills are produced by particular systems of social relations, and since other indicators of ethnicity show much the same pattern.

A majority of Vietnamese students within each grade category reported that they usually or always speak Vietnamese with their parents (rather than "never," "rarely," or "sometimes"). However, the higher the average grade received by the student, the more likely it is that she or he speaks Vietnamese with her or his parents. Among students with A averages, 90 percent usually rely on Vietnamese in speaking with their parents, compared to only about 70 percent of those with C averages or less. Use of Vietnamese with siblings and friends, as we might expect, is much less common than with parents, but again we see a linear relationship between language use and grades.

Three-fourths of respondents with an A average report that they "definitely want to marry someone who is Vietnamese" (rather than " . . . prefer to marry a Vietnamese," "don't care," "prefer to marry someone who is not Vietnamese," or "definitely want to marry someone who is not Vietnamese"). By contrast, only 65 percent of those with a B average and only 40 percent of those with a C average or less express a strong commitment to in-group marriage. Self-description as "Vietnamese" (rather than "American" or "Vietnamese American"), a subjective dimension of ethnic group membership, also increases as grades become higher, in a manner almost identical to commitment to in-group marriage. Finally, those who reported receiving higher grades were more likely to report that almost all or all of their friends were Vietnamese. All dimensions of ethnic group identification and involvement show relationships to grades that are positive, linear, and significant.

Table 3 considers the relation between the various aspects of involvement and identification with the ethnic community and another dimension of academic achievement, that of perceived importance of college attendance. Since only a few students reported that they did not want to attend college or that college was not very important to them, this variable has been recoded here into two values. Those who report that college attendance is very important to them are more likely to have advanced Vietnamese speaking, reading and writing skills, to speak Vietnamese with family and peers, to be committed to marrying someone of their own ethnicity, to describe themselves unequivocally as "Vietnamese," and to have friendship groups that are almost all or all Vietnamese. The strength of relationship, as indicated by percentage differences, is smallest in the case of speaking Vietnamese with parents and in the case of having Vietnamese friends, apparently because the vast majority of these students usually speak Vietnamese with their parents and have mostly Vietnamese friends, regardless of their commitment to future education.

Table 4 examines a final dimension of academic achievement, that of effort put into schoolwork, indicated by time spent daily on homework. The numbers of those who don't do homework at all are relatively small. Nevertheless, in general we see the same linear relationship between time spent on homework and ethnic community involvement seen in the cases of the two other dimensions of academic achievement.

**TABLE 3.   Cross-tabulation of Perceived Importance of College Attendance
Reported by Vietnamese High School Students with Indicators of
Identification with the Ethnic Community**

Indicators of Ethnic Identification	Perceived Importance of College Attendance		Chi-square
	Less than "very important"	"Very important"	
Speak Vietnamese well	40.0 (46)	61.0 (175)	14.5***
Read Vietnamese well	23.5 (27)	45.3 (130)	16.42***
Write Vietnamese well	21.7 (25)	41.5 (119)	13.89***
Usually speak Vietnamese with parents	76.5 (88)	88.2 (253)	8.63**
Usually speak Vietnamese with siblings	47.8 (55)	73.2 (210)	23.48***
Usually speak Vietnamese with friends	35.7 (41)	62.4 (179)	23.65***
Definitely want to marry a Vietnamese	47.8 (55)	68.3 (196)	14.66***
Describe self as "Vietnamese"'	50.0 (58)	69.0 (198)	12.22***
Almost all friends are Vietnamese	73.9 (85)	82.6 (237)	3.87*

Note: Number of respondents reported in parentheses.
* $p < .05$.   ** $p < .01$.   *** $p < .001$.

The slight exception to the general rule that those who spend more time on homework are more likely to score highly on indicators of ethnic community involvement occurs in the case of ethnicity of friends, where the highest percentage of those who said that almost all or all of their friends are Vietnamese is in $\frac{1}{2}$ to 1 hour category, but even this variable shows the same general trend.

These cross-tabulations provide good evidence that academic achievement among these young people is positively related to their involvement in this distinctive ethnic community. However, it must still be considered whether ethnic community involvement is the chief influence on scholastic performance, as suggested above. In order to examine this point, Table 5 introduces the results of OLS regression equations. Here, all of the indicators of ethnic community involvement discussed individually above are added together to

TABLE 4. **Cross-tabulation of Time Spent on Homework Daily by Vietnamese High School Students with Indicators of Identification with the Ethnic Community**

		Time Spent on Homework				
Indicators of Ethnic Identification	Don't do	Less than 30 min.	$\frac{1}{2}$–1 hr.	1–2 hrs.	Over 2 hrs.	Chi-square
Speak Vietnamese well	15.8 (3)	37.5 (24)	41.1 (39)	65.2 (73)	75.7 (78)	49.79**
Read Vietnamese well	5.3 (1)	14.1 (9)	18.9 (18)	51.8 (58)	67.0 (69)	83.13**
Write Vietnamese well	5.3 (1)	12.5 (8)	16.8 (16)	46.4 (52)	63.1 (65)	76.27**
Usually speak Vietnamese with parents	57.9 (11)	79.7 (51)	86.3 (82)	84.8 (95)	91.3 (94)	15.42**
Usually speak Vietnamese with siblings	15.8 (3)	53.1 (34)	52.6 (50)	74.1 (83)	85.4 (88)	53.97**
Usually speak Vietnamese with friends	10.5 (2)	46.9 (30)	42.1 (40)	63.4 (71)	68.0 (71)	33.25**
Definitely want to marry a Vietnamese	42.1 (8)	39.1 (25)	57.9 (55)	73.2 (82)	72.8 (75)	29.34**
Describe self as "Vietnamese"	31.6 (6)	48.4 (31)	51.6 (49)	78.6 (88)	73.8 (76)	36.17**
Almost all friends are Vietnamese	47.4 (9)	71.9 (46)	88.4 (84)	79.5 (89)	83.5 (86)	20.22**

Note: Number of respondents reported in parentheses.
* $p < .01$.   ** $p < .001$.

create an index of community involvement, which is utilized as an independent variable. Dependent variables indicating academic achievement are, again, averaged overall grades, perceived importance of college, and time spent on homework. In order to consider whether ethnic community involvement may be seen as a major force in directing students away from behavior that can have diminish their opportunities for success in school and in later life, as well as in directing them toward accomplishments, attitudes, and behavior that can enhance opportunities for success, the number of times respondents report engaging in substance abuse[3] and the number of times they

TABLE 5. Standardized Regression Coefficients and Standard Errors of Predictors of Indicators of Academic Achievement and Problematic Behavior by Vietnamese Adolescents

	Dependent Variables				
Independent Variables	Average grades	Importance of college	Time spent on homework	Substance abuse	Times stopped by police
Ethnic community involvement	.536**	.256**	.372**	−.334**	−.236**
	(.007)	(.008)	(.011)	(.019)	(.012)
Two-parent family	.038	.120*	.030	−.021	−.073
	(.096)	(.117)	(.162)	(.274)	(.172)
Grandparents in home	.051	.082	.057	−.010	−.028
	(.084)	(.104)	(.141)	(.239)	(.150)
Number of siblings	.002	−.055	.034	.031	.028
	(.014)	(.017)	(.023)	(.039)	(.024)
Father's education	−.117*	−.066	.039	.051	−.034
	(.041)	(.051)	(.070)	(.118)	(.074)
Mother's education	.019	.036	.019	−.064	.124*
	(.058)	(.072)	(.098)	(.165)	(.103)
Father's weekly work hours	.112*	.086	−.025	−.078	−.138*
	(.032)	(.039)	(.054)	(.091)	(.057)
Mother's weekly work hours	.015	−.005	.027	−.010	−.028
	(.032)	(.039)	(.054)	(.091)	(.057)
Age	−.049	−.009	−.020	−.082	−.052
	(.020)	(.025)	(.034)	(.058)	(.037)
Sex	.138**	.093	.118*	−.275**	−.202**
	(.066)	(.080)	(.110)	(.187)	(.118)
Recency of arrival	−.011	.140*	.150**	−.066	−.169**
	(.006)	(.007)	(.010)	(.016)	(.010)
R^2	.337	.159	.250	.231	.202
N	378	378	378	378	378

Note: Standard errors reported in parentheses.
* $p < .05$.   ** $p < .01$.

report being stopped by police are also used as dependent variables. Control variables include indicators of family structure, parental education, weekly work hours of parents, age, sex, and recency of arrival.

Not only is ethnic community involvement the greatest influence among the variables on averaged reported grades, the magnitude of the regression coefficient is striking. Father's education, curiously, has a slight negative influence on grades, which may indicate that fathers from educationally limited backgrounds in Vietnam push their children more to take advantage of opportunities that the fathers themselves did not have. Father's weekly working hours are positively related to grades. This is probably due to the greater control over children exercised by fathers who understand mainstream American society well enough to be employed full-time. Females tended to make higher grades than males.

The only significant influences on perceived importance of college are ethnic community involvement and recency of arrival. The educational ambitions of the more recently arrived may be interpreted as part of an "immigrant ethos," the tendency of new immigrants to place a heavy emphasis on upward mobility. Ethnic community involvement also has by far the greatest influence on hours spent on homework. Females, again, put more time into their schoolwork. It is interesting that recency of arrival has a fairly strong influence on time spent on schoolwork, although more recent arrivals do not actually do better in school. This makes sense, since more recent arrivals need to work harder to catch up with those who have been raised in the United States.

Influences on the two indicators of problematic behavior are virtually the inverse of influences on academic achievement. Ethnic community involvement is the strongest negative influence on both substance abuse and run-ins with the police. It is interesting that mother's education has a slight positive influence on dealings with the police. These may be a result of the fact that those with more highly educated mothers live in more "Americanized" families, but this is only speculation. Those whose fathers have longer work weeks are less likely to have been stopped by the police, which may be explained in the same manner as the influence of father's working hours on grades. Females are significantly less likely to engage in these types problematic behavior than males, a trend that is similar to relationship between sex and delinquency in other ethnic groups. More recent arrivals are less likely to have been stopped by the police, in part because they have had less time in the United States to get into trouble.

CONCLUSION

I have suggested that the development of distinctive Vietnamese American communities, with their own formal and informal support systems, has been a major part of the history of Vietnamese people in the United States since 1975. I have maintained, moreover, that the exceptional academic performance of Vietnamese American youth noted by a number of scholars is, in large part, a result of the development of communities that provide networks of supports and constraints to their young.

Focusing on a single Vietnamese community has made it possible to briefly describe its young people and their school and neighborhood environment. The relationship of young people to the Vietnamese community itself appears to be a critical part of their general adaptation to American schools and other areas of life. Those with stronger connections to the Vietnamese community tend to be those who are pointed out as "success stories." Those with weak connections to the ethnic community, on the other hand, are seen by the Vietnamese community itself as the problem children, the gang members, the poor students.

Examination of quantitative evidence has supported the view that involvement in the Vietnamese community is the chief determinant of success in school for Vietnamese American young people. The frequencies of selected characteristics have shown that Vietnamese adolescents in New Orleans East have shown high rates of ethnic community involvement, as indicated by language abilities and use, commitment to endogamy, self-description, and friendship networks. They have also shown that, in general, the students of this area have high rates of academic performance. Cross-tabulations have established a clear, positive, linear relationship between academic achievement and ethnic community involvement. Finally, Ordinary Least Square regression results have shown that integration into the ethnic community is by far the most important factor in determining the scholastic performance of Vietnamese students.

This description of the role of Vietnamese communities in the lives of Vietnamese young people in the United States and the analysis of survey results suggest a number of ways that we should consider the academic and general social adaptation of immigrant and other minority group members. First, it is not enough to think about ethnic groups only in terms of their individual members and the places of those individual members in the larger society. We must also take into account the internal structures of the groups themselves, their social integration, and the extent to which they have formed coherent communities. Second, the role of ethnicity in the lives of young people can vary depending on the kinds of supports and controls ethnic communities can provide to their young. Third, when a cohesive ethnic community exists, this can exercise a greater influence than many of the determinants of educational success more traditionally considered by sociologists and educators, such as individual characteristics, family background, or even family structure.

NOTES

1. One unfortunate result of the Vietnamese predominance in the honors program is that many African American students appear to have been led to believe that

academic excellence is somehow "not black." During my fieldwork in the school in question, several outstanding African American students complained to me that they had been teased by their co-ethnic peers for being in classes that were perceived as Asian classes. I sensed little active resentment toward the Vietnamese by African American students, but the Vietnamese concentration in the magnet component of this school does seem to have contributed to the social distance between the two groups.

2. In order to obtain the greatest possible validity in self-reporting of grades, students were asked for the grade received the previous year in English, math, and social studies; and, at different places in the questionnaire, they were asked what grade they currently received most often, and what grade they received most often in their years in school. These were averaged. As a further check, I compared the variation in these reported averaged grades with the variation in actual midterm grades of a sample of students and found that the two matched well.

3. The variable "substance abuse" is an index created by adding together the number of times respondents report drinking alcohol to the point of drunkenness and the number of times they report using illegal drugs.

REFERENCE

Ashton, Gail. 1985a. "Carving a Slice of American Dream." *Times-Picayune,* April 1, Al.

———. 1985b. "Refugees Showed They Are Survivors." *Times-Picayune,* April 1, Al.

Bankston, Carl L. III. 1991. "Landfill on the Bayou." *The Progressive* 54, 13–14.

———. 1995. "Vietnamese Ethnicity and Adolescent Substance Abuse: Evidence for a Community-Level Approach." *Deviant Behavior* 16.1: 59–80.

Bankston, Carl L. III, and Min Zhou. 1995. "The Effects of Minority Language Literacy on Academic Achievement: The Case of Vietnamese Youth in New Orleans." *Sociology of Education* 68: 1–17.

Caplan, Nathan, John K. Whitmore, and Marcella H. Choy. 1989. *The Boat People and Achievement in America: A Study of Family Life, Hard Work, and Cultural Values.* Ann Arbor: University of Michigan Press.

———. 1991. *Children of the Boat People.* Ann Arbor: University of Michigan Press.

———. 1992. "Indochinese Refugee Families and Academic Achievement." *Scientific American* 266 (February): 36–42.

Finnan, Christine R., and Rhonda Ann Cooperstein. 1983. "Southeast Asian refugee resettlement at the local level: the role of the ethnic community and the nature of refugee Impact." Report prepared for the Office of Refugee Resettlement, Social Security Administration, Department of Health and Human Services. Menlo Park, Calif.: Social Sciences Center, SRI International.

Kibria, Nazli. 1993. *Family Tightrope: The Changing Lives of Vietnamese Americans.* Princeton, N.J.: Princeton University Press.

Massey, Douglas, Rafael Alarcon, Jorge Durand, and Humberto Gonzalez. 1987. *Return to Aztlan: The Social Process of International Migration from Western Mexico*. Berkeley: University of California Press.

Muzny, Charles C. 1989. *The Vietnamese in Oklahoma City: A Study in Ethnic Change*. New York: AMS Press.

Nash, Jesse S. 1992. *Vietnamese Catholicism*. Harvey, La.: Art Review Press.

Rutledge, Paul. 1992. *The Vietnamese Experience in America*. Bloomington and Indianapolis: Indiana University Press.

U.S. Bureau of the Census. 1990. *Census of Population and Housing, 1990*. Washington, D.C.: U.S. Bureau of the Census.

Zhou, Min. 1992. *Chinatown: The Socioeconomic Potential of an Urban Enclave*. Philadelphia: Temple University Press.

PART
III

Hearing Silenced Voices
Other "Minorities"

11

Dennis Carlson _____

Gayness, Multicultural Education, and Community

While public schools have long been viewed by progressive educators as embryonic communities that should engage young people in building a democratic community of mutual support and respect, gay people have for the most part been made absent, invisible, and silent within this community and at the same time represented as the deviant and pathological "Other." In what follows, I not only want to point to some of the ways gay people and "gayness" have been "kept in their place" in the school community; more importantly I want to argue that these practices are increasingly hard to sustain. Public schools are being drawn into the battle brewing between "new right" fundamentalists and progressives in American culture as older forms of community and family are beginning to disappear and cultural diversity is increasing. Within this unsettling context, I want to suggest that public schools may play an important role in helping build a new democratic, multicultural community, one in which sexual identity (like other markers of difference including class, gender, and race) is recognized, in which inequities are challenged, and where dialogue across difference replaces silencing and invisibility practices (Burbules and Rice 1991).

Throughout much of this century, the dominant idea of community in America was represented by what I will call the *normalizing community*. Within normalizing communities, some individuals and subject positions (i.e., white, middle class, male, heterosexual, etc.) get privileged and represented as "normal" while other individuals and subject positions (i.e., black, working class, female, homosexual, etc.) are disempowered and represented as deviant, sick, neurotic, criminal, lazy, lacking in intelligence, and in other ways "abnormal." Public schools in particular have often promoted such "normalizing" conceptualizations of community that are based on defining a cultural center

233

or "norm" and positioning class, gender, race, and sexual Others at the margins. In particular, marginalization may be associated with tracking and ability grouping practices, with "deficit" theories of the child and his or her family, and with curriculum practices that exclude the contributions and voices of various Others. However, as those marginalized within this normalizing discourse on community have begun to "speak out" and challenge their marginalization, and have also begun to develop collective movements and communities of support, the modernist idea of homogeneous, normalizing community is being more seriously disrupted than ever before.

In the struggle brewing in American culture over the reconstruction of community, three divergent perspectives have emerged. The first of these may be associated with the notion of a "community of interest." As the idea of a cohesive, monolithic community is collapsing, new social movements of identity are forming their own, relatively autonomous communities, speaking their own discourses. I see some merit to this idea of community although I also believe it is fundamentally limited. It has helped marginalized groups find their own voices and create a space of their own; and it seems to me consistent with the extension of human freedom and the renewed emphasis on identity in the postmodern. But this comes at a cost. Community gets redefined in a noninclusive manner so that we are unable to articulate a common or "public" interest. A second emergent discourse on community in America is that associated with the new right and cultural neoconservatism. This is a discourse about recapturing a romanticized lost American community, a "Father Knows Best" community where authority was respected, everybody "knew their places," and culture was homogenous. It is also a community with a less benign face, one that maintains a dominant culture through oppressive tactics used to keep Others "in their places." Arthur and Marilouise Kroker refer to this as a community organized around the "will to purity," involving a "vengeance-seeking search for scapegoats on whom expiation can be found for the absence at the center of society; . . . and a panic fear of viral contamination by swirling impurities: exchanges of bodily fluids, transgressionary thoughts, women rebelling against the sovereignty of lines, [etc.]" (Kroker and Kroker 1993, 3). In unsettling times, such hypernormalizing constructions of community have a wide, popular appeal. Yet a third discourse on community to emerge over the past decade or so in America is associated with the notion of a community of difference and diversity—what I will call a democratic multicultural community. Within this discourse community gets redefined so that difference is recognized outside of binary oppositions, space is provided for identity groups to form their own communities of interest, and at the same time a common, public culture is continuously being constructed and reconstructed through dialogue across difference. With all of the unresolved tensions presented by this reconceptualization of community, I think it may serve as a useful framework for articulating a new progressive agenda for educational renewal, one organized around the process of "becoming somebody" in a democratic, multicultural community (Wexler 1993).

Before proceeding, it seems important that I say something more about my use of the terms "gay" and "gayness" in this essay. The commonsense perspective on language is that words refer to or stand for things, so that it does not really matter what you call these things. But words do not merely stand in for "things." They emerge out of and take on meaning within particular discourses and practices. Thus, the words "homosexual," "gay," "lesbian," and "queer" have histories we have to consider when we invoke them. Homosexual is an ostensibly neutral category, one designed by scientists; and yet its usage may involve a scientific distancing from the homosexual object of study and a refusal to see the political and cultural elements of sexual identity. "Gay" and "lesbian" or "gay men" and "lesbians" are the most "politically correct" labels, although their usage tends to further divide and separate men and women when in fact homophobia and oppression are directed against homosexuals as a group. I thus rely most frequently on the term "gay" to refer to both men and women in a way that has become common in popular culture. Of course, this term, to the extent that it invokes a bipolar construct "straight/gay" may serve to police its own boundaries and set up its own oppositions. "Queer" has become a term recently reappropriated from its oppressive context of usage to support a militant form of standing outside of conventional roles, and its usage is creeping into gay culture generally and into gay studies in the academy (Corey 1993; Leck 1993–94). Yet "queerness" represents a celebration of the outsider that may not effectively link-up with a democratic progressive politics of inclusion. Finally, I want to distinguish between a homosexual orientation or preference, and gay identity. The former I take to refer to the more-or-less natural direction of one's sexual desires while the latter refers to the active construction of a gay self identity and visible gay presence within culture— what I am referring to as gayness.

THE NORMALIZING
SCHOOL COMMUNITY AND GAYNESS

I want to begin by mapping out in more specificity some of the ways in which gayness has been marginalized within the modern, normalizing school community that has predominated throughout much of the twentieth century in America. Since all normalizing communities maintain a center and margin in the face of opposition and resistance from those being marginalized, analysis needs to proceed through an account of the specific techniques and apparatuses of power that have been employed in the school to keep gayness "in its place" as an invisible presence. Three techniques of normalization and (hence) marginalization have been of primary importance in this regard: (1) the erasure of gayness in the curriculum, (2) the "closeting" and "witch hunting" of gay teachers, and (3) verbal and physical intimidation of gay teachers and students.

One way that a normalizing curriculum or text works is by presenting students with a "selective tradition."[1] To some degree, all traditions of culture and knowledge must be selective, even multicultural traditions, for the production of a text always involves a selection process in which something must be left out. Nevertheless, normalizing texts systematically exclude and neglect the culture of those outside the norm for the purpose of ratifying or legitimating the dominant culture as the only significant culture worth studying. This exclusionary aspect of the construction of a selective tradition is particularly important in understanding how texts have worked with regard to gayness. For we do not get very far if we look for what *is* said about gayness in educational texts. We get much farther if we pay attention to what Susan Sellers calls the "silent spaces" or the "not said" of the text, and what Mike Cormack and others have called the "structuring silences" within texts (Sellers 1991, 143–44; Cormack 1992, 31). Not only do these silent spaces work to make those on the margins invisible and silent; they also, and at the same time, make the cultural center invisible as a center since it never has to "speak its own name" (Ferguson 1990, 9–14). At the level of state educational policy, it is noteworthy that no state currently recognizes gays and lesbians as legitimate minority or cultural groups to be considered in textbook adoption or to be included in multicultural education; and a number of states explicitly prohibit teaching about homosexuality. In 1993, for example, the gay rights movement claimed a major victory in the signing into law of a Minnesota bill that makes it illegal to discriminate against lesbians and gay men in employment and housing. Yet what got ignored in all the celebrating was a provision in the bill that prohibits teaching about homosexuality in the public schools (Kielwasser and Wolf 1993–94, 62). In such an environment, it should hardly be surprising that major textbook publishers avoid gayness like the plague. English literature anthologies still go out of their way to avoid acknowledging that certain famous writers were gay, such as Gertrude Stein, Walt Whitman, or James Baldwin. This cleansing of gayness from the literary canon is often defended as an effort to maintain the reputation or "good name" of authors by not "outing" them. Yet such concern is, of course, another way of affirming that being gay is cause for a loss of respect. Aside from being an absence in the curriculum, gayness has been made visible in some various limited and marginalized contexts. To the extent that gayness is recognized in the curriculum, it is likely to be in the health curriculum, where it is associated with disease. For example, one of the most popular health texts on the high school market is *Health: A Guide to Wellness*, which mentions homosexuals or homosexuality once in acknowledging that "the first group in the United States diagnosed with AIDS were male homosexuals."[2]

Normalizing practices, however, must reach beyond curriculum texts if they are to be effective in constructing a normalizing school community. Throughout this century, one of the primary means of ensuring that gayness was an invisible presence in the school was through the dismissal of teachers who were found out to be homosexuals. Early in this century, the dismissal of gay teachers was legitimated as a way of keeping young people from being exposed to improper role models, lechery, and child molestation. Willard Waller, in his 1932 classic *The Sociology of Teaching*, argued that homosexuals should not be allowed to teach for several reasons. First, employing a disease metaphor, he argued that homosexual teachers represented a danger to their students since "nothing seems more certain than that homosexuality is contagious" (Waller 1932, 147–48). Much as communist teachers were to be drummed out of the teaching corps because communism was "contagious," so gay teachers were to be fired because they too were understood as contagious—and in the height of the McCarthy era in the late 1940s and early 1950s, homosexuality and communism were closely linked as threats to the "American way of life." In both cases, the association with sickness and disease provided a means of legitimating isolation from impressionable young people. Second, homosexual teachers were presumed to be lecherous and develop "ridiculous crushes" on students. Waller observed: "the homosexual teacher develops an indelicate soppiness in his relations with his [sic] favorites . . . and makes minor tragedies of little incidents when the recipient of his attentions shows himself indifferent." Waller went on to suggest that because homosexual teachers were always victims of such "crushes," that this was inevitably "fatal to school discipline." Since homosexuals were therefore ineffective as teachers, Waller encouraged administrators to be on the lookout for "latent homosexuals" when they are hiring teachers. Among the best diagnostic procedures for identifying a homosexual, according to Waller, were "such personality traits as carriage, mannerisms, voice, speech, etc." (1932, 148). Waller thus provides a good example of how "expert" knowledge on homosexuality as a pathological disorder was used to legitimate "witch hunts" in the schools for homosexual teachers. Today, witch hunts against gay teachers are (for the most part) a thing of the past and many lesbian and gay male teachers are relatively "out" among a select group of co-workers. Yet the intimidation continues, much as it does in the military. The official policy in most school districts is in fact identical to that of the U.S. military, namely: "Don't ask, don't tell." Interestingly, while this policy is being challenged by gays in the military, it has not been forcefully challenged by gay teachers in public schools yet, perhaps because they feel (probably rightly so) they could not win if they pushed their case.

One of the effects of this closeting of gay teachers may be an overzealous effort by gay teachers themselves to avoid any class discussion in which gayness may come up, since they presume that to be publicly "out" at school would cost them their jobs. In his study of *Growing Up Gay in the South* in the 1980s, James Sears reports a case of a gay high school English teacher who went out of his way in introducing Walt Whitman's poetry to avoid discussing recent scholarly interpretations of his work that emphasize its homoerotic themes. The teacher remarked, "There is a kind of terror that runs through my mind when I think about that [mentioning gay themes in Whitman's poetry]. There's a Pandora's Box that's opened with that. . . . I just don't know if students are mature enough or whether that's a subject that in this environment we can deal with."[3] In this case, the fear is not only of acknowledging Whitman's sexual identity, but having to acknowledge the homoerotic desire within his poetry—the ultimate taboo. Straight teachers often participate in silencing practices because they are fearful of raising a controversial issue that might provoke conflict in the classroom. One young man Sears interviewed recalled a class discussion in high school: "In my sociology class we were talking about AIDS. One guy said, 'I think gay guys are just sick. How could they do that? It's wrong!' . . . Well, everyone looks over to Miss L., our teacher, for what she thinks. She says, 'I have no comment. I'm not even going to get into this discussion. I'm going to keep my opinion to myself'" (Sears 1991, 391). On the other hand, Sears found that it was okay in many schools to condemn homosexuality if you are a teacher without facing any criticism. Of a high school physics teacher, one interviewee recalled: "Mr. Jenson would usually drift away from the subject. He'd often bring up homosexuality. He mainly talked about the wrongs of it and how it was such a sin and that they should be condemned" (Sears 1991, 390).

A final important technique of power used to keep gayness "in its place" in the school community has been sanctioning of the verbal and physical intimidation of gay teachers and students. Michelle Fine, for example, reports in her ethnographic study of an urban alternative high school in New York City that: "A male substitute teacher was greeted by [one of the students] as she shouted across her English classroom: 'That man's a faggot, right? Look at how he talks!' Arriving at her seat she yelled, 'Hey, Mr. Faggot, I mean Sir, you got a pencil?'" (Fine 1991, 41). Elsewhere she writes: "Dismissed as adolescent behavior, screams of 'Faggot!' echo down the hall, terrifying, stigmatizing, and isolating" (42). In Sears study, one young man remembers: "When I was changing classes I had all the books in my hands looking down and walking up. I'd hear someone mutter 'Faggot' and have my books knocked down. People were walking over me as I am trying to gather my books" (Sears 1991, 240). These abuses get tolerated because gay teachers and students operate in an environment where they feel afraid to stand up for themselves, and because any discussion of gay people continues to be absent in the curriculum so that homophobia is not interrogated. All of this also takes a considerable toll. It no doubt drives many good teachers out of the profession, and it furthers the alienation of gay youth who remain in schools. For example, it is now estimated that up to one-third of all adolescent suicide victims are gay, approximately one-quarter of all homeless youth in the United States are gay, and dropout and drug abuse rates among gay youth are likewise high (Gibson 1989).

The Representation of Gayness
in Popular Culture

Public schools have attempted to be "total institutions" in that everything students do during the school day and are exposed to in the curriculum is controllable.[4] Like communist states, they have been based on the presumption that if students in the school community can be kept shielded from "bad influences" and provided only "positive" representations of community life, that they can be molded into "good," "well-adjusted" citizens and workers. The problem with this strategy, in the public school community as in the communist state, is that "big brother" control does not work in a world increasingly bound together with popular culture and electronic images. A number of postmodern theorists have made the point that the public school curriculum is becoming less important and relevant to young people as they have access to a broad array of information, discourses, and cultural "texts" outside of school. We might think of this as the *popular culture curriculum*: films, videos, TV, MTV, magazines, newspapers, rock music and events, and so forth. Whereas gayness was largely or completely invisible in popular culture throughout most of the century, over the past several decades representations of lesbians and gay men have begun to surface. The effect of this is that the technologies of power and knowledge used to keep gayness invisible have become more and more ineffective and out of sync with cultural developments that are making gayness more visible and talked about. How, then, does the popular culture curriculum represent gayness and gay people, and what images of "being gay" are young people—both gay and straight—bringing with them to schools?

Rather than attempt to map out a broad overview of popular cultural representations of gayness, let me limit my comments, for the most part, to film representations, and more particularly, several film representations of gayness to appear in the 1980s. The first of these is the film *Personal Best*, released by Warner Brothers in 1982, and the subject of a critical essay review by Elizabeth Ellsworth (1988). The movie tells the story of two women athletes, Chris and Tory, who meet at the 1976 Olympic Track Trials and become friends and then lovers. They live together for three years, but break up after their male coach places them in competition with one another for a place on the Olympic team and after Chris has an affair with a male Olympic swimmer. The two women meet again at the 1980 Olympic Track Trials and reaffirm their friendship through a refusal to compete with one another. Ellsworth focuses on *Personal Best's* reception in the mainstream and feminist press, and suggests that the film was open to multiple readings by multiple audiences. She finds that the film was generally viewed in the mainstream press as providing a positive representation of lesbianism, although because the film placed lesbianism within the context of the athletic world, one traditionally and conventionally defined as a "man's world," some cultural stereotypes were not seriously challenged. Mainstream reviewers of the film also "consistently assigned the lesbian relationship the status of a simple filmic plot device for drawing out more worthy, primary themes, like competition, coming of age, and goal-seeking" (112).

Yet Ellsworth suggests that *Personal Best* was read and viewed in some quite divergent ways—some of them transgressive or oppositional—so that the text eluded being assigned any fixed or stable meaning. Liberal feminist reviewers, for example, emphasized an intellectual deconstruction of the text's meaning which saw positive achievements in the film, such as "the achievement of women in male-dominated fields, and the representation of women athletes as beautiful, graceful, and strong" (113). Lesbian-feminist reviewers "resisted the narrative's heterosexist closure and imagined what would happen to the characters in a lesbian future." This involved a subversive rewriting of the film, a rewriting which saw the two women as really in love and committed to each other, despite the film's attempt to trivialize their commitment.

Another common strategy for rewriting relied on by lesbian reviewers was to ignore large sections of narrative material that focused on heterosexual romance, making no reference to their existence or implications for the film's authorized meaning (113). All of this, she says, "raises the possibility for films like *Personal Best* to 'get it right' unintentionally," that is, to provide a space for the construction of meaning that was not intended and that subverts or inflects conventional roles and dominative power relations, for readings that go "against the grain" (Ellsworth 1988, 115; see also Simon 1992).

This is also the case with another representation of gayness that was influential in the 1980s, *La Cage aux Folles*. The French play by Jean Poiret was made into a highly successful movie in 1979, a sequel followed, and it went on to become a long-running Broadway play. So, as a popular cultural representation of gayness, it assumed special significance in the 1980s. The movie and play tell the story of an aging transvestite, Albin, who performs "drag" in a ritzy, glitzy Paris nightclub, and his partner and business manager of twenty years, Renato. The latter's son has become engaged to a girl whose parents are very conventionally "straight" and represent traditional, aristocratic values regarding the importance of "high moral standards" in society. The father, in fact, is the Secretary General of the "Union for Moral Order" within the government and views himself as a personal symbol of all it stands for. In order to gain the support of the young woman's parents, the son arranges a visit by them to meet his father. Renato agrees to pretend to be straight, and Albin is to play his mother. The setting for all of this is the nightclub, "La Cage aux Folles," which Renato owns, and more particularly the sumptuous if somewhat flamboyant suites upstairs where Renato and Albin live.

On one level, *La Cage aux Folles* may be read as a very conventional text on gayness, constructed within the normalizing discourse of the time. Gay men are confirmed in their role as the Other—a bit silly, prone to emotional and hysterical outbursts, narcissistic, obsessed with sex and fancy clothes, and inhabiting an exotic and "decadent" life on the margins. This was the image of the gay male that Liberace so well represented for America in this period as well. As a politically conscious gay man watching this film for the first time in a crowded theater, I found myself choking in shock and anger at these outrageous representations of gay men, unable to laugh even as the mixed straight and gay audience around me kept erupting into laughter. But my shock finally gave way to laughter as well, a laughter based on the recognition that the joke was not on Albin and Renato but on the "straight" or conventional world that judged them. Within the film, the world of Renato and Albin is linked to a deep-rooted desire for a space in which all people are free to "be themselves," and in which diversity is not only tolerated but celebrated. In promotional material for the home video of the movie, MGM quotes a reviewer from the *Los Angeles Times* as writing that "the film makes its point: Be yourself no matter who or what you are."

This authorized message—be yourself—has begun to surface as one of the primary codes within commercial popular cultural texts, and it is a message that, like so many postmodern messages and codes, is open to contradictory readings. "Being yourself" celebrates individualism and the autonomy of individuals to construct their own lives according to their own values and achieve goals they set for themselves—a deep foundational value in American culture. Hardly a subversive theme, it would seem. Yet it becomes so to the extent that we take it seriously and begin to resist the representatives of the "Union for Moral Order" in our own communities—those who seek to rid the community of "moral decay" and "perverts," cleanse the public school library shelves of "immoral" literature, and prevent us from seeing art or films that are presumed to violate "public decency" (as Robert Mapplethorpe's photographs were presumed to in several U S. cities in the early 1990s). The problem with the message, "Be yourself," is that it fails to account for the fact that the "self" is at least partially an historical, cultural, and discursive production, which set limits upon, even if they do not determine, one's "possibilities of existence" (see de Lauretis 1986, 8; Simon 1992, 90–91). This means that we need to interrogate the particular ways that gay people have learned to "be themselves" in different historical periods and the historical conditions that make possible the constructing of empowering or disempowering identities. Throughout much of this century, one dominant, socially sanctioned way of "being gay" was to be a flamboyant, emotionally unstable, feminized male; and Albin may be said to represent this historical construction of gayness, a construction that legitimated keeping gays in their place as the deviant and neurotic Other.

Another dominant message in *La Cage aux Folles* that may be read in contradictory ways has to do with celebration of life as a carnival. It is not coincidental that the play and film is set in the world of the nightclub, where transvestite "drag queens" perform to a mixed crowd of straight and gay customers, easily rubbing against one another in friendly camaraderie—a carnivalesque world of role reversals, the suspension of conventional norms, and the transgression of established borders and boundaries. It is a world of night, of desires unleashed, and of individuals who inhabit a kind of permanent carnival of the margins. The medieval European carnival, as Mikhail Bakhtin saw it, "celebrated temporary liberation from the prevailing truth and from the established order; it marked the suspension of all hierarchical rank, privileges, norms and prohibitions" (1984, 10, quoted in Quantz and O'Connor 1988, 101). Within the carnival time and life came out of its usual, legalized and consecrated forrows and entered the sphere of utopian freedom (Bakhtin 1984, 89). In one sense, most all movies are designed to provide a safe carnival experience and viewing them in a darkened theater on big screen becomes part of the carnival. Within this space and time, established symbolic orders can be challenged and new ones tried out. This, indeed, has always been the subversive potential within film. Of course, we need to be careful not to overstate the transformative potential in carnival, especially the kind produced and packaged by Hollywood. As with all carnivals, when this film ends, everyone is expected to return to the "normal" or "real" world outside, the normality of which has been confirmed and affirmed by the safe experience of briefly escaping to a marginalized world. Still, we may take something with us from carnival—such as a vision of a more equitable and humane world, or a certain empathy for those who transgress the norms of "straight" culture.

In recent years, popular cultural representations of gayness have moved beyond the stereotypes embodied in *La Cage aux Folles*, much as representations of blackness have moved beyond the stereotypes of *Amos and Andy*. Yet in both cases we may legitimately question just how much progress has been made. Black males are now often represented as either the athlete Other (all physicality with little in the way of intellect) or the criminal, drug-addicted Other (and thus as prime candidates for being shot and killed in films). Similarly, if gay men are less likely to be the brunt of jokes about their effeminacy, or treated as desperate and pathetic, they are more and more represented as diseased and dying Others. Even though major films such as *Philadelphia, Longtime Companion,* and *The Band Played On* "take sides" with AIDS victims, and even though it is important to focus attention on the relationship between the struggles of those with HIV and AIDS and gays and lesbians generally, the linkage between gayness and AIDS in popular culture must also be called into question. Simon Watney reminds us that AIDS is associated not only with gay males but with blackness and with the African continent, and that "blacks and gay men remain curiously linked—the two great indispensable Others. . . . Hence the widespread tendency of Western governments to emphasize the 'threat' of HIV 'leaking' from the social constituencies affected most severely by AIDS" (Watney 1990, 98; see also Hammonds 1992). Through the representation of AIDS in popular culture, Watney argues that "Africa becomes a 'deviant' continent, just as gay men are effectively Africanized" (92). Furthermore, even though the popular cultural representation of gayness has changed somewhat, much remains the same. Thus, the major "gay film" of 1996 was *The Bird Cage*, an Americanized version of *La Cage aux Folles*, with all the earlier film's campy stereotypes intact.

Because popular cultural texts work in so many contradictory ways and are open to multiple and competing readings, it is difficult to predict their precise impact on young people's evolving conceptions of self and Other. However, since silencing and invisibility are so central to the maintenance of the closeted, normalizing community, popular culture may be subversive even when it reinforces stereotypes. Furthermore, all popular cultural texts are open to multiple interpretations. Finally, some popular cultural forms which I have not discussed here, such as the television talk show, seem to potentially open up even more room to challenge normalizing conceptions of community. Richard Mohr has recently argued that "the clearest sign that gays are winning the cultural wars is the near total collapse in the mainstream [press and popular culture] of the taboo covering the discussion of gay issues. . . . The effect of this structural change in public life cannot be overestimated. . . . With the collapse of the taboo, straight people can for the first time really listen to gay lives, change their views, and, in turn, express publicly their own feelings" (Mohr 1994, 6; see also Mohr 1993). Gay people, including gay youth, become part of the everydayness of our lives when they appear on Donahue or Oprah. Mohr even goes so far as to suggest that the New Right is contributing to this process by promoting discourse on sexuality and gayness. "For the more they talk about things gay, the more the taboo collapses" (Mohr 1994, 6). Merely by representing gayness and making it part of everyday discourse, TV talk shows and other forms of commercialized popular culture challenge the worst forms of oppression associated with silencing and invisibility and make it more difficult for public schools to continue their own silencing practices. At the same time, however, by failing to help students deconstruct popular cultural texts to reveal how they work to represent the Other, and by failing to engage them in critical readings and rewritings of popular cultural texts, public schools may encourage young people to read popular cultural texts in a noncritical way, merely consuming images and fitting them within their preexisting stereotypes and biases.

IDENTITY FORMATION AND "COMING OUT" AS GAY

Popular culture may represent identity, but identity also is represented in corporeal form, as individuals actively "live" their identities and make these identities visible in their everyday relations with others. Identity formation in this sense involves several processes. First, it involves identification with groups or collectivities and with the subcultures and discourses these groups have produced as part of the process of defining themselves. Second, it involves some understanding of self in relation to Others. In normalizing communities, identity is typically constructed in rigidly oppositional ways, with one pole of identity privileged and viewed as "normal" and the other pole viewed as deficient and "abnormal." "Being gay" thus involves some level of identification with a "gay community," "gay culture," and/or "gay struggle," and also some understanding of oneself as different from "straight" women or men. Within the normalizing American community, this has also tended to mean oppositional to "straight"—in lifestyle, definition of femininity and masculinity, and so on. This means that an analysis of gay identity is never to be understood as separable from an analysis of straight identity, just as an analysis of the meaning of "blackness" in American culture necessarily involves an analysis of the historical construction of "whiteness." How, then, are young people learning to "be gay" in the nineties? And, to what extent does gay identity and culture pose an existing or potential challenge to heterosexist constructions of gay and straight identity?

To begin to unpack these questions, we must begin with the recognition that gay culture is not all of one piece, but rather provides gay-identified individuals with alternative ways of "being gay," some of which are consistent with keeping gays in their place at the margins and others of which are more individually and collectively empowering and counterhegemonic—that is, linkable to a new democratic discourse and social movement. The most counterhegemonic way of "being gay" may be associated with the gay rights movement, although that broad movement involves more than an assertion of rights to equal protection under the law. Among other things, it involves the constitution of a whole network of support services and organizations designed to help individuals "come out" in a supportive environment and participate in the gay community, including gay counseling services, drop-in centers, support groups, athletic leagues, choruses, and political organizations. "Coming out" may be appreciated as an important cultural ritual or rite of passive in that it involves the reconstruction of self in terms of identification with a collective, historical struggle. As a process of reconstructing the self, coming out also involves adopting a new way of "being in the world" and a new way of knowing. Worldviews that normalize the world and that define homosexual desire as "bad" or "sick" must be rejected in the process. A politicized identity is promoted within the gay community through the use of visible gay icons and symbols such as the "rainbow" flag and banner, pink triangles and gay churches, and the quilt of the "Names Project," commemorating those who have died of AIDS. One of the most powerful of these symbols, featuring a pink triangle under which is written the slogan "Silence = Death," is associated with the most militant and itself marginalized group in the movement, ACT UP. The call, then, is to speak out and be seen.

For the most part the institutions that make up the gay community are not open to adolescents, so that most gay youth continue to stay unattached and even unaware of this potential community of support. This may be changing, however. There is some limited evidence that an increasing number of youth, particularly in big cities, are "coming out" as gay within their high schools, at least to close friends, a process that disrupts closeting and silencing practices essential to the maintenance of the normalizing school community. One inter-esting study of identity formation among gay youth that looks at the influence of this politicized gay movement and community is Gilbert Herdt and Andrew Boxer's, *Children of Horizons* (1993). Horizons Social Services in Chicago began serving as a community-based social service agency for the gay men and lesbians of Chicago in the early 1970s; and Herdt and Boxer studied a gay youth support group sponsored by Horizons in the mid-1980s, a support group that enrolled young gay men and lesbians between the ages of fourteen and twenty. Unlike the stereotype of the suicidal or runaway gay youth, these youth, the authors found, had strong self-concepts and generally viewed their gayness positively. Coming from middle-class homes for the most part, the youth aspired to have what they called a "normal life." According to the au-thors, "They [the support group members] not only want to be gay but expect to be accepted by society as gay and lesbian. They do not know if they can achieve such a cultural lifeway, but they are trying very hard to find out" (xiv). The support group was a transformative experience for the youth, in that, as the authors note: "for the first time in their lives, they begin to talk openly about sexual feelings with peers and friends of their own age who show them respect, finding others like themselves, and adult role models, whom they can admire. Their worst fears are that they are 'out of their minds,' full of sin and sickness, that they are doomed to dress as transvestites, molest children, hate the opposite sex, or contract AIDS" (xv). Herdt and Boxer conclude that such support groups, and other support networks in the gay community, provide a needed ritualistic context for "coming out" in empowering ways.

Some young people, particularly in big cities, are beginning to bring their "out" identities to high school, affirming who they are and asserting their rights. For example, in the study by Fine that I referred to earlier of a Manhat-tan alternative high school, she points to the existence of a Gay and Lesbian Alliance (GALA) in the school started by "a small group of very sophisticated and very 'out' gay males and lesbian females." These students "quite publicly raised questions, doing the complex intellectual and political work with and for their teachers and their peers." Still, Fine notes that the majority of lesbian, gay, and bisexual students in the school remained closeted, ever aware of threats to their physical and psychological well-being (Fine 1991, 40). Given the realities of being "out" in high school, this strategic closeting of one's gay identity unfortunately continues to be a safe response, even if it comes at the cost of lying about one's life.

It is also the case that many, perhaps most, gay-identified youth are constructing a less politicized and publicly "out" identity than those who have been most influenced by the gay rights movement and community. For these youth, being gay may mean identification with a gay community that offers an exciting life on the margins, of "partying," of constructing a "buffed" and sexually marketable body, and of celebrating life in the middle of an oppressive culture. Among adults, this is a way of "being gay" closely linked to "bar culture." Gay bars were long the only spaces gay people had carved out within pre-Stonewall America, and I do not want to be overly critical of their influence on gay identity formation. By providing a space for people to come together and build a sense of collective identification, gay bars played a significant role in the early gay rights movement; and it is not coincidental that the beginning of the modern gay rights movement is marked by a riot at a Greenwich Village bar in 1969. As African Americans had their churches as free spaces, the gay community had its bars. Still, gay bar culture has not on the whole served as an important site for building an empowering, nonmarginalized gay identity. One major reason is that gay bar culture is grounded in the commercialization of gayness, which means that its primary motivation is to make money through the selling of a particular way of being gay that is relatively apolitical in its implications. "Bar culture," although it serves important positive roles, allows gay people only a brief escape from the normalizing community, and in a space hidden from public view, so that in some ways it has helped keep gay people in their place.

A related way of being gay represented in gay culture, especially for gay men, has been that of "sexual outlaw" (to use John Rechy's term) (Rechy 1985). If, in popular culture, being straight meant being "normal," that is, affirming (if not always practicing) bourgeois, traditional, repressive, monogamous, married sexuality, then being gay meant—by definition—the opposite. Gay identity was constructed around the experience of being a sexual outsider, deviant, and (quite literally) outlaw. One dominant way to affirm one's gayness in pre-AIDS America and to some degree today has been to accentuate an unrepressed sexuality with multiple partners. While some degree of desublimation of sexuality has been consistent with the advancement of human freedom, gay identity has meant, for some, an obsessive desublimation, a desublimation that reached its peak in the late seventies and early 1980s, in a pre-AIDS

America. Some gay males growing up in major urban areas may even feel that getting AIDS is inevitable and part of being gay; or they may feel guilty that they have been spared when others have not, and as a consequence put themselves at risk. Consequently, growing up to affirm a gay identity is not without its dangers, particularly if that gay identity continues to be organized primarily around notions of "living dangerously."[5]

Other features of gay culture in America currently limit its potential as a site for locating gayness within the reconstruction of a democratic, multicultural community. One of these is that gay culture has tended to be organized around an upper middle-class "yuppie" identity and lifestyle. Certainly, the great majority of gay men and lesbians are not members of the upper middle class in either income or lifestyle, although new right representations of gayness have emphasized the supposed fact that all gay people are economically privileged.[6] But if most lesbians and gay men in America are not economically privileged, gay culture has tended to be overwhelmingly middle class in orientation and values. To some extent this is because gay people have found more acceptance within the middle class and among the college-educated than within the working class. The problem is thus not merely one of gay culture constructing gay identity in opposition to working-class identity, but of working-class culture failing to come to terms with homophobia, along with sexism. Similarly, gay culture has been overwhelmingly "white," and this makes it difficult for many young black gay people to affirm both their gayness and their blackness. Furthermore, in black culture (and Latino and Asian culture for that matter) gayness often has been positioned as a "white problem" or a contaminant from European culture (West 1993, 89).

Gay culture, then, like all subcultures forged within the context of oppression, has contained contradictory currents. It contains, on the one hand, elements of a radical critique of normalizing constructions of sexuality and sexual identity and it provides space for individuals to affirm both a positive sense of self and a collective identification with a cultural and political struggle. Yet currents in gay culture have also played a part in keeping gay people in their place through the promotion of forms of resistance to "being straight. that can be self-destructive (such as the "sexual outlaw" identity); and it has tended to promote a middle-class, white construction of gayness. At the present time, there are several ways in which gay identity is impacting on the school community and disrupting or unsettling established practices. First, regardless of how young people construct a gay identity, the very existence of more-or-less "out" gay-identified youth in schools poses a threat to silencing practices. It remains to be seen how long public schools can fail to respond to the existence of "out" gay youth, and gay teachers. Second, by failing to help gay youth (and all youth, for that matter) to critically reflect on the process of "becoming somebody," and by seeking to erase gayness from the curriculum and everyday school life, schools promote alienating responses among gay youth. The high levels of drug use, high dropout rates, and high suicide rates among gay youth are at least partially understandable both as manifestations of alienation and as socially sanctioned, self-destructive ways of "being gay." We need to start holding the school accountable for failing to meet the needs of these youth. Third, as gay-identified youth are beginning to surface in schools, we are seeing an increase in incidents of verbal and physical harassment or "gay bashing" which the schools are pressured to respond to. Finally, as gay identity has surfaced in the community and gays have begun organizing to advance an empowerment agenda, and as a strong and virulent backlash movement has developed on the political right, public schools have been caught in the crossfire and are seemingly unwilling or unable to move in any decisive direction.

PUBLIC SCHOOLS AND COMMUNITY
IN THE POSTMODERN

One thing we can conclude about the emerging shape of community in America is that because it is more fragmented, it is becoming more difficult to construct a "public" curriculum that has broad-based support. This represents a problem for both democratic progressive and neoconservative or new right forces. The new right has not been successful in building a broad-based power bloc or articulating a "public" discourse on educational and social problems with broad appeal. However, neither have any of the new social movements on the political left. For the time being, at least, this means that the public schools are caught in a dilemma over gayness, unable to please anyone, and unable to act without inviting attack from one side or the other. The recent battle over the "Children of the Rainbow" multicultural curriculum in New York City provides a good example. The so-called "Rainbow Curriculum" was developed as part of a 1989 resolution by the New York City Board of Education requiring lessons in the appreciation of racial, ethnic, religious, and sexual diversity ("Teaching" 1992). The Gay and Lesbian Teachers Association, an increasingly visible presence in the district in the nineties, had been instrumental in pushing for the inclusion of language on sexual orientation into the proposed curriculum, and the final report of the drafting committee was "gay friendly." For example, as part of the first-grade curriculum the report recommended that teachers "include references to lesbians and gays in all curriculum areas and . . . avoid exclusionary practices by presuming a person's sexual orientation, reinforcing stereotypes, or speaking of lesbians/gays as 'they' or 'other.'" The report included a bibliography with three books that depict children in families headed by homosexual partners: *Daddy's Roommate, Heather Has Two Mommies,* and *Gloria Goes to Gay Pride.*

Once an initial draft of the proposed curriculum was released, the controversy began almost immediately. The president of District 24 local school board in Queens declared, among other things, that the board would not "accept two people of the same sex engaged in deviant sexual practices as 'families'" ("Diversifying" 1992). Ultimately, the New York City school district became embroiled in an internal battle that led to the rejection of the Rainbow Curriculum by the school board, at which point Chancellor Fernandez threatened to override the board's rejection. In the compromise that followed, Fernandez agreed to eliminate references to "lesbian/gay families" and replaced this with "same gender couples." A statement recommending the inclusion of "references to lesbian/gay people in all curriculum areas" was eliminated. *Heather Has Two Mommies* was taken off the suggested reading list. Interestingly, other language in the curriculum was also modified to appeal to traditionalist and religious fundamentalist groups. Out came a section suggesting teachers challenge conventional gender stereotypes by "purposely making pink or red name tags for boys and blue tags for girls," along with a section on how people with AIDS have been unfairly stigmatized (Fernandez 1993). Major church groups also lined up against the Rainbow Curriculum including the Bronx Hispanic Clergy Association, the Catholic Archdiocese of New York, Christian fundamentalists, and Orthodox Jews. Yet twenty-five Protestant and Jewish clergy formed a council to counter the attack from the Right ("Liberal Groups" 1993). This points to the growing battle *within* the religious community over sexuality.

It may be that the final "compromise" multicultural curriculum constructed in New York City is the best that progressive forces can hope for in the current situation. Part of the problem to begin with was that the curriculum was developed by school district staff in the central office with relatively little input from the communities that were to "implement" the imposed plan for multicultural education. If the Rainbow Curriculum had emerged out of community-based dialogue, it would have taken much longer to construct, and it would certainly have emerged as a compromised document. But at least the community would have been involved in a necessary dialogue across difference on sexual identity, along with gender, race, ethnicity, religion, and so on. This points to the need to forge a democratic multicultural curriculum in ways that maximize public participation, provide room for divergent perspectives, and are sensitive to the concerns of all—including New Right constituencies.

At the same time, democratic progressivism must stand for something in the way of a moral or ethical vision for the reconstruction of community. Here is where I think the discourses of critical pedagogy and feminist pedagogy, as they have developed in the liberal arts academy over the past decade or so, provide an important framework for talking about multicultural education in democratic, empowering ways and for integrating the study of gay identity and gay culture within the curriculum (Giroux 1992; Luke and Gore 1992; McLaren 1993–94; Weiler and Mitchell 1992). Within these discourses, a number of interrelated concerns have been raised that are relevant to the construction of a democratic multicultural curriculum and pedagogy. Let me then identify some of these concerns and their implications for the study of gay identity. First, and at the most basic level, multicultural education is linked to the protection and extension of certain democratic "virtues," including the protection of minority rights and individual freedoms, equity, respect for difference, and (in its fullest form) the development of interlocking webs of caring, supportive relations among individuals. This implies at the very least that educators involve young people in a discussion of gay identity within the context of a discussion of human rights in a democratic community, and it may extend to a discussion of caring for others, including the gay Other, in community. Second, democratic multicultural education must challenge "essentialistic" worldviews that take categories such as gender, sexual identity, and race for granted as "natural" categories having fixed meaning. While our race, gender, and sexuality may, at least to a good degree, be fairly fixed or given, what we make of being gay or straight, man or woman, black or white, is very much cultural as well as personal. Third, and related to this last point, multicultural education is reconceptualized in terms of crossing or rupturing the borders that separate individuals into neat categories and camps. As Russell Ferguson puts it: "As we enter into language we must simultaneously negotiate the crude classifications which are imposed upon us and create our own identities out of the twisted skins of our backgrounds" (1990, 13). One way to rupture the boundaries between groups is to emphasize the multiple subject positions (class, race, gender, sexuality, etc.) we all occupy. Thus, I am not merely a gay person, but rather a gay, white, male with a particular working-class background and middle-class status and occupation. As an individual, my identity is multifaceted and this means that I am freer to "make myself" as a unique subjectivity.

Fourth, it also means that I am inextricably involved in multiple cultural struggles rather than merely one. Democratic multicultural education must be directed toward helping young people build alliances and see the interconnectedness between different arenas of identity formation and cultural struggle. This is absolutely essential if we are to rekindle a sense of community in America. I have suggested in this essay that all marginalized groups in American culture share a common source of oppression in the ideology of the normalizing community that constructs a cultural center and relegates Others to the margins. But there are more specific cultural and historical linkages between identity struggles as well. When we examine gayness, for example, we are inevitably drawn into an examination of gender, and thus "maleness" and "femaleness" as well, for the historical treatment and representation of women and gays has been very similar in this culture and may be related to a common patriarchal worldview. Within this worldview, "real men" are separated from all women and from gay men. This is the reason why it so important for many straight men to "see" gay men as the Other, and this has been accomplished by understanding gay men as less than men, as feminized men, and as sissies. Thus, the gay and lesbian movements, with their challenge to these stereotypical constructions of gayness, are part of something much bigger than sexual identity. Straight women, because they have developed their own critique of patriarchy and because they can relate to marginalization, have generally been most supportive of the gay movement. The challenge is to engage straight men in a deconstructive analysis of how they understand "being straight" in ways that involve treating women and gays as Others. This is a challenge since, as William Pinar observes, "men have no theoretical apparatus, no parallel to feminism, to help them to understand what has happened and is happening to them" (Pinar 1995, 187). The public schools, it seems to me, have a responsibility to help young men begin to develop such a theoretical apparatus.

Finally a democratic multicultural education must become a dialogue in which all "voices" are heard and all "truths" are understood as partial and positioned. The objective of classroom discourse is thus not so much to achieve consensus on one "true" or "objective" depiction of reality, but rather to clarify differences and agreements, work toward coalition-building across difference when possible, and build relationships based on caring and equity. This will require learning to live with the contradictions and ambiguities of supporting democratic beliefs and values in ways that are not coercive or overbearing. We cannot and should not attempt to impose "politically correct" beliefs on students; but we have a responsibility as public educators in a democratic society to engage them in a dialogue in which all voices get heard or represented and in which gay students and teachers feel free to "come out" and find their own voices.

NOTES

1. This is the term coined by Raymond Williams, the neo-Marxist literary critic. For an example of "selective tradition" research in curriculum, see Joel Taxel, "Children's Literature: A Research Proposal from the Perspective of the Sociology of Knowledge," in Suzanne De Castell, Allan Luke, and Carmen Luke, eds., *Language, Authority, and Criticism* (New York: Falmer Press, 1988), 32–45.

2. For a critical discussion of this health text, see Kielwasser and Wolf (1993–94).

3. James Sears, *Growing Up Gay in the South: Race, Gender, and Journeys of the Spirit* (New York: Haworth 1991), p. 399. Sears's book weaves together the narratives of thirty-six Southern lesbians and gay men coming of age in the 1970s and 1980s.

4. The term "total institution" is used by Erving Goffman, *Asylums: Essays on the Social Situation of Mental Patients and Other Inmates* (Garden City, N.Y.: Anchor Books, 1961).

5. A recent study of gay men in four cities—Baltimore, Chicago, Los Angeles, and Pittsburgh—concluded that one-third of all currently uninfected twenty-year-old gay and bisexual men will become HIV-positive by the time they are thirty, and that the majority of twenty-year-old gay men in the sample will eventually contract AIDS. See Michelangelo Signorile, "Unsafe Like Me," *Out*, October 1994, pp. 22–24.

6. For all the talk from New Right activists about how gay people are economic elites, the evidence paints a different picture. According to one recent study at the University of Maryland conducted by Lee Badgett, a labor economist, gay men make 11 to 27 percent less than heterosexual men in comparable jobs. Lesbians earn 5 to 14 percent less than heterosexual women. While studies such as this are based on small samples and conclusions are thus tentative, they do counter the general stereotype of gays as elites. See Mary Pemberton, "Study Finds There Is No 'Gay Elite,'" *Gay People's Chronicle* (Columbus, Ohio), 10.5 (1994): 1–2. See also Garry Boulard, "Numbers," *Advocate*, October 4, 1994, pp. 30–31.

REFERENCES

Bakhtin, Mikhail. 1984. *Rabelais and His World*. Helene Iswolsky, trans. Bloomington: Indiana University Press.

Burbules, Nicholas, and Suzanne Rice. 1991. "Dialogue across Differences: Continuing the Conversation." *Harvard Educational Review* 61.4: 393–416.

Corey, Richard. 1993. "Gay Life/Queer Art." In Arthur and Marilouise Kroker, eds., *The Last Sex: Feminism and Outlaw Bodies*. New York: St. Martin's Press.

Cormack, Mike. 1992. *Ideology*. Ann Arbor: Michigan: University of Michigan Press.

de Lauretis, Teresa. 1986. "Issues, Terms, Contexts." In Teresa de Lauretis, ed., *Feminist Studies/Critical Studies*. Bloomington: Indiana University Press.

"Diversifying Schools' Golden Rules." *New York Times*, October 6, 1992, B1–B6.

Ellsworth, Elizabeth. 1988. "Illicit Pleasures: Feminist Spectators and *Personal Best.*" In Leslie Roman and Linda Christian Smith with Elizabeth Ellsworth, eds., *Becoming Feminine: The Politics of Popular Culture.* New York: Falmer Press.

Ferguson, Russell. 1990. "Introduction: Invisible Center." In Russell Ferguson, Martha Gever, Trinh Minh-ha, and Cornell West, eds., *Out There: Marginalization and Contemporary Cultures.* Cambridge, Mass.: MIT Press.

"Fernandez Modifies Parts of Curriculum about Gay Parents." *New York Times*, January 27, 1993, A1; B3.

Fine, Michelle. 1991. *Framing Dropouts: Notes on the Politics of an Urban High School.* Albany: State University of New York Press.

Gibson, Paul. 1989. *Gay Male and Lesbian Youth Suicide.* Washington, D.C.: U.S. Department of Health and Human Services, Secretary's Task Force on Youth Suicide.

Giroux, Henry. 1992. *Border Crossings: Cultural Workers and the Politics of Education.* New York: Routledge.

Hammonds, Evelynn. 1992. "Race, Sex, AIDS: The Construction of 'Other.'" In Margaret Andersen and Patricia Collins, eds., *Race, Class, and Gender: An Anthology.* Belmont, Calif.: Wadsworth.

Herdt, Gilbert, and Andrew Boxer. 1993. *Children of Horizons: How Gay and Lesbian Teens Are Leading a New Way Out of the Closet.* Boston: Beacon Press.

Kielwasser, Alfred, and Michelle Wolf. 1993–94. "Silence, Difference, and Annihilation: Understanding the Impact of Mediated Heterosexism on High School Students." *High School Journal* 77.1–2.

Kroker, Arthur, and Marilouise Kroker. 1993. "Scenes from the Last Sex: Feminism and Outlaw Bodies." In Arthur and Marilouise Kroker, eds., *The Last Sex: Feminism and Outlaw Bodies.* New York: St. Martin's Press.

Leck, Glorianne. 1993–94. "Politics of Adolescent Sexual Identity and Queer Responses." *High School Journal* 77.1–2: 186–92.

"Liberal Groups Are Cooperating in New York School Panel Races. *New York Times*, April 21, 1993, A1; B9.

Luke, Carmen, and Jennifer Gore, eds. 1992. *Feminisms and Critical Pedagogy.* New York: Routledge.

McLaren, Peter, 1993–94. "Moral Panic, Schooling, and Gay Identity: Critical Pedagogy and the Politics of Resistance." *High School Journal* 77.1–2 157–68.

Mohr, Richard. 1994. "How Things Stand for Gays in America." *Gay People's Chronicle.* Columbus, Ohio, September 2, 1994.

———. 1993. *A More Perfect Union: Why Straight America Must Stand Up for Gay Rights.* Boston: Beacon Press.

Pinar, William. 1994. "Understanding Curriculum as Gender Text: Notes on Reproduction, Resistance, and Male-Male Relations." In William Pinar, *Autobiography,*

Politics, and Sexuality: Essays in Curriculum Theory, 1972–1992. New York: Peter Lang.

Quantz, Richard, and Terence O'Connor. 1988. "Writing Critical Ethnography: Dialogue, Multivoicedness, and Carnival in Cultural Texts." *Educational Theory* 38.1.

Rechy, John. 1985. *The Sexual Outlaw: A Documentary.* New York: Grove Press.

Sears, James. 1991. *Growing Up Gay in the South: Race, Gender, and Journeys of the Spirit.* New York: Haworth.

Sellers, Susan. 1991. *Language and Sexual Difference: Feminist Writing in France.* New York: St. Martin's Press.

Simon, Roger. 1992. *Teaching Against the Grain: Texts for a Pedagogy of Possibility.* New York: Bergin and Garvey.

"Teaching about Gay Life Is Pressed by Chancellor." *New York Times,* November 17, 1992, B3.

Waller, Willard. 1932. *The Sociology of Teaching.* New York: John Wiley & Sons.

Watney, Simon. 1990. "Missionary Positions: AIDS, Africa, and Race." In Ferguson, Gever, Minh-ha, and West, eds., *Out There: Marginalization and Contemporary Cultures.* Cambridge, Mass.: MIT Press.

Weiler, Kathleen, and Candace Mitchell, eds., *What Schools Can Do: Critical Pedagogy and Practice.* Albany: State University of New York Press.

West, Cornell. 1993. *Race Matters.* Boston: Beacon Press.

Wexler, Philip. 1993. *Becoming Somebody.* New York: Falmer Press.

12

PATRICIA TIMM AND KATHRYN BORMAN _____

"The Soup Pot Don't
Stretch That Far No More"

*Intergenerational Patterns of School Leaving
in an Urban Appalachian Neighborhood*

Currently, federal, state, and local policymakers and practitioners across the United States are feverishly engaged in a common effort to reform education. With the passage of federal legislative mandates under the rubric of President Clinton's Goals 2000 plan, attention is focused upon such issues as how to assure the best learning environments for all students; how to assess student outcomes; and what constitutes the best practice in the professional development of teachers.

While states and local educational authorities (LEAs) work out how Goals 2000 funding should be made equitable among districts as well as how to prioritize initiatives ranging from early childhood education reform to the School to Work Opportunities Act, issues such as addressing the particular needs of specific ethnic groups remain outside these discussions perhaps because these matters are usually regarded as the province of teachers, counselors, and others at the local school level.

The aim of our paper is to provide a background understanding of a particular, often neglected group—urban Appalachian girls and young women. In addition, we will offer intervention strategies aimed at creating more favorable outcomes. In doing so, our analysis relies on case examples drawn from the first author's intergenerational analysis of the early school leaving of urban Appalachian girls and young women. We also identify examples from regional fiction. Many novels about the Appalachian region over the past several decades have provided particularly rich accounts of children's school, family, and community lives. Our analysis is enriched by the inclusion of selected material from this literature.

Conceptualizing the experiences of those individuals whom sociologists might term "downwardly mobile" in a culturally sensitive manner provides a way of understanding those whose opportunities for success under present conditions are in peril. Dropping out of school, for example, is often seen as an individual problem and rarely as an adaptive strategy. However, from the native perspective, leaving high school before graduation can be and frequently is an appropriate action, particularly for members of racial and ethnic groups who value family solidarity above individual accomplishment (Deyhle and Margonis, forthcoming; Stack 1972). When early school leaving is considered in this light, implications for the formulation of intervention strategies become clear.

A SOCIOCULTURAL UNDERSTANDING OF FAMILIES AND COMMUNITIES

In U.S. schools educational attainment continues to fall below national goals despite the priority placed on it by school reform movements of the past decade. In midwestern cities, descendants of the more than 3 million Appalachian migrants who came to cities such as Chicago, Detroit, Cincinnati, and Columbus in the forties, fifties, and sixties have disproportionately high rates of early school leaving. Recent (1990) census data show that 67 percent of white Appalachians in Cincinnati lack a high school education (Maloney 1991). In many central cities, Appalachian students leave school before graduation at higher rates than African Americans and other whites.

Dropout studies and community ethnographies have attempted to explain why so many poor and minority group members' educational attainment continues to fall behind that of other students (LeCompte and Dworkin 1991; Fine 1991; Natriello 1986). These analyses are in contrast to less thoughtful approaches following a politically expedient agenda and that variously blame the parents, the students, the schools, and the taxpayers for students' failure to persist in school. We view explanations grounded in a sociocultural understanding of the family and neighborhood as particularly useful. Thus we provide analyses of: (1) structural barriers, (2) cultural dissonance, and (3) school attachment as factors contributing to alienation from school generally and to the early school leaving of Appalachian girls and young women specifically.

Structural barriers in the form of inadequate or no access to schools are apparent in the life histories of mothers and grandmothers whose formal education was cut short because public schools denied them as pregnant young women the opportunity to complete high school. Their histories also demonstrate that structural barriers rise and fall over time. According to most local public school policies, today's young women may attend school if they are pregnant, although a particular school and curriculum still may be inaccessible to them. They are often warehoused in special schools for pregnant teens and made to feel both "different" and inferior.

Cultural dissonance or lack of synchrony between that which is valued by schools and that which is valued in families is also apparent in these life histories and is present in the fiction of the Appalachian region, particularly in those novels focused on strong, resourceful, and resilient mountain women. Theories of cultural dissonance to explain school failure have been hotly debated for at least thirty years.

Our understanding of the dissonance between families and schools is that such dissonance has little to do with deficiencies in the cultural capital children bring to school and much to do with the limited number of intersections between the worlds constructed in schools and those constructed in families and among young urban Appalachians. Because the overlap between the school and family is slight, the *attachment* to school is limited. Generally sets of push and pull factors contribute to an individual's decision to leave school. For schools to become attractive sites for urban Appalachian students (and others), school policy that creates environments supportive of affirmation and activity must take the values, memories, narratives, and systems of meaning of individuals into account if we wish schools to be meaningful places (Heath and McLaughlin 1993).

In the United States, social structural factors, such as deteriorating neighborhood conditions; opportunity constraints associated with race, ethnicity, gender and socioeconomic status; and unstable labor market conditions persist in the last decade of the twentieth century. These factors interact with individual, family, and school characteristics to shape young people's educational achievement, out of school activities, and attitudes toward self and society. Neighborhood conditions, as an illustration, have a clear impact on both leaving school before graduation and teenage childbearing.

Two national studies illustrate the importance of social structure in affecting human lives in urban, suburban and rural places. In the first case, using the percentage of workers in a neighborhood who held professional and managerial jobs as an index of neighborhood quality, Crane (1991) determined in a sample of 92,512 adolescents that the neighborhood effect is extremely large for both blacks and whites in urban ghettos. In all cases the jump in adolescent pregnancy and school leaving occurred at the same point in the distribution, that is, neighborhoods where only 4 percent of the workers held high-status jobs.

The second example is drawn from an analysis of "High School and Beyond," a national longitudinal survey initiated in 1980 with high school sophomores.

Researchers followed this cohort through five waves of data collection. The students who eventually left school before completing twelfth grade differed from those who remained in a number of ways. The dropouts had lower test scores, did less homework, came from homes with weaker educational support, had poorer school performance, exhibited more behavior problems in school, were more alienated from school life, and had more friends who were themselves alienated from school (Ekstrom, Goertz, Pollack, and Rock 1986).

While the findings of these two studies may not be surprising, they do illustrate that factors beyond individual characteristics such as intelligence and personality variables strongly influence success in school. Social structures in which human lives are embedded, including neighborhoods, families, and peer groups, are relentless in their impacts. Nonetheless, individual lives can display great strength and resilience in the face of alienation, structural constraints, and family hardships.

An Urban Appalachian Neighborhood: Riverbend

Despite difficulties associated with life in Riverbend[1] and communities like it, enclaved groups of urban Appalachians continue to live in the poorer neighborhoods of midwestern cities (Borman, Mueninghoff and Piazza 1988). Families will often stay even if they can afford to move away. Riverbend is geographically bounded and socially cohesive. It is located on a long, narrow strip of land on the flood plain of the Ohio River. The steep hillside on its northern border and the river to the south contribute to the isolation of the community.

Many residents have been in the neighborhood for three to four generations. They are descendants of farmers and miners who migrated from the Appalachian region[2] between 1940 and 1960 in search of employment in Cincinnati's machine shops and large manufacturing firms including GE and Cincinnati Milacron. Currently the neighborhood is a site for urban development—housing for the upper middle class is being constructed and existing structures are being renovated. The median annual income of Riverbend residents in 1990 was $5,000, below that of other neighborhoods in the city. Census data between 1940 and 1970 show that only ten percent of the adults in the community had completed twelve years of school.

Riverbend is geographically, socially, and economically similar to enclaved Appalachian neighborhoods in the city and in cities such as Dayton, Cleveland, and Detroit. Although per capita income is extremely low, Riverbend's location provides residents with rather generous lots, access to several parks and playgrounds, and proximity to a handful of shops and stores, including a gas station, bar, and restaurant managed (but not owned) by community residents.

Compared to Lower Price Hill, an urban Appalachian neighborhood on the city's west side, Riverbend's inhabitants have been at least equally if not more engaged in community-based political action. For example, Riverbend's community council under the leadership of two of the community's most powerful women actively opposed the construction of high-rise condominiums priced outside the range of housing affordable to the large majority of community residents. These efforts were widely discussed by the city's two major daily newspapers in stories that often portrayed community activism as both justifiable and admirable.

Similarly, Lower Price Hill's battle with the city's health department and with the manufacturing firm whose toxic processes the city refused to regulate was also taken up by the media. Lower Price Hill's case was actively supported by the Urban Appalachian Council, a neighborhood-based advocacy and social services agency. In addition, a highly detailed report documenting effects of the manufacturer's processes on the toxicity of soil and air as well as the action steps to correct the situation was authored by experts at the University of Cincinnati's College of Medicine.

Contributors to the report also included a somewhat marginal political hopeful who headed a small but influential environmental organization. Roxanne Qualls would be elected to city council the year the report was published (1989) and became mayor of Cincinnati in 1993. At this writing, urban Appalachian communities in Cincinnati seem particularly well positioned politically, with a mayor in office sympathetic to their concerns, the strong advocacy of the United Way–funded Urban Appalachian Council and the commitment of a number of University of Cincinnati (and other) professionals, in addition to politically adept talent pools at the neighborhood level.

The Women and Their Stories

Why, then, given their obvious strengths, do many urban Appalachian communities harbor girls and women who by the standards of the larger society are not economically successful? At least part of the answer to this question resides in the firm commitment many of them have to their immediate social context. The women whose stories the first author gathered are strongly attached to their families, to extended kin, and to their neighborhood. Their views and experiences can be understood only from this orientation. The pull of family, kin, and neighbors generally prevails over other forces and has in some cases for four generations.

The following sections are organized to tell the stories of three generations of three families: The Adamses, the Lewises, and the McGradys. The narrative accounts provided here were gathered in connection with a larger-scale project investigating the impact of redevelopment on the working-class and poor residents of the community. Over the course of eight months in 1990, the first author spent many hours in the kitchens and living rooms of the women whose narratives are presented here. Later we offer a sociocultural analysis of these families, particularly with respect to decisions to leave school, and a brief set of conclusions.

Throughout the chapter we rely on the narrative voices of Appalachian women whose experiences are chronicled in the fiction of the region. In concert with Borman, Mueninghoff, and Piazza (1988), we see the task of the social scientist to be at least in part to understand the fabric of human lives. Lives are often beautifully realized in fiction. Good fiction is a useful foil for life history data analyzed here.

The Adams Family: Alienation

Grace Adams was born in the study neighborhood in 1916. Her father's family came from Cold Spring, Kentucky, some fifty miles southwest of Cincinnati. Grace completed the sixth grade at Riverbend's only public elementary school; the family subsequently moved to another Cincinnati neighborhood where she completed seventh and eighth grades. Grace registered at the Sewing Trade School downtown for the ninth grade, but was forced to leave after only a few months because of the family's financial reversals. It was the Depression and the family had neither adequate food nor clothing. When Grace turned sixteen, a sick neighbor with two young children signed her work permit, formally paving the way for Grace's exodus from school. Grace loved school, and remembers her experiences and her teachers fondly. She had dreams of becoming a musician or a dress designer. After leaving school, in addition to assisting her neighbor, Grace helped raise her own eleven siblings. At nineteen she married and left the family home.

Grace and her husband settled in the neighborhood where she was born. Her husband had graduated from high school in New York before moving to Cincinnati in 1924. He worked in printing and was involved in the organization of the printer's union in the city. Together he and Grace raised two daughters and a son. Their son completed tenth grade. When he married, he moved from the city; both daughters completed the twelfth grade. Grace's first daughter, Ann, graduated from District High School, married and moved to Kentucky.

Ann's five children are high school graduates. Grace's second daughter, Gladys, is the subject of this account.

Gladys and Gina

Gladys was born in 1942 in Riverbend. She attended several different neighborhood public elementary schools as the family moved several times between a downtown neighborhood and Riverbend and back again. She especially liked Riverbend's elementary school, which had now been attended by four generations of her family. This school was closed in 1979. After completing elementary school, she registered each fall first at District Middle School, and later at District High School and District Vocational School, but never attended any of them for long: "I just hated school after I got out of that elementary school. I liked my elementary teachers, but after I got out of the elementary, they were snobbish." When she went to school, Gladys attended only the classes that she liked: sewing and crafts. In the ninth grade she was assigned to a gym class with senior girls.

> So I attended that class one time and then I set down in the locker room. . . . I didn't know them, and they weren't interested in me. . . . Even the teacher wasn't interested in me. . . . She came down in the locker room and seen me and she never said nothing. . . . I'd just sit there. Then I finally got tired of doing that. Then I quit going."

Gladys expressed no regrets about having quit school. Although she had never been bored with school, she experienced considerable alienation and therefore little attachment to it; Gladys subsequently became an enthusiastic adult learner and has dreams of studying computers and business practices in hopes of starting her own small enterprise after retirement from the printing industry where she has worked since she was sixteen.

Gladys and her ex-husband have one son and three daughters. They each completed eighth grade at District Middle School, but never registered for high school. The two older children earned their GEDs through a neighborhood-based program and now live outside the neighborhood. The youngest daughter Gina is twenty-one. She attended the same neighborhood elementary school as her grandmother and mother. She explained that she liked the school because teachers took the time with her she needed when learning something new. "Even the math teacher, which I hate . . . math. She was mean, but I still liked her [pause]. She wasn't mean. She disciplined, and she made sure you had your homework done."

The last grade Gina completed was seventh at District Middle School. She explained that she hated the school: "I was always looking at a sheriff for skipping and not going to school." She moved in with her sister who lived in the country and attended the school there for several months, but she was unhappy away from her mother and her home neighborhood. She got a work permit signed by her sister, for whom she baby-sat while the sister worked the day shift at a fast food restaurant. Gina worked the night shift at the same place. She has worked in fast food restaurants, convenience stores, and a factory. She wants to learn a trade—auto mechanics or veterinary medicine—and she believes that she could be successful since her interests in these areas are much stronger than her interests in academics.

In sum, each generation of Adams women has exhibited considerable talent and skill in the manual trades—talent and skill that schools have traditionally devalued. It is not surprising that each generation of these women has felt so alienated from school that they have withdrawn from it in the end, maintaining a love of learning and desire to develop and use their skills in vocations such as printing, auto mechanics, and veterinary medicine.

Carrie, Flora, and Rondal

Women as portrayed in the fiction of the region, like many of the Adams women, are powerful, devoted to family, enjoy reading at home, and, in the case of Carrie Bishop, the narrator of Denise Giardina's *Storming Heaven*, are not "deferrin'." In describing her father's views, Carrie says, "He told me he didn't expect me to find a husband. I was not 'deferrin'' enough, my tongue was too sharp and I was too forward in my ways. I didn't believe him. Aunt Jane was not 'defferin'' and she had been married. Most of the women I knew on the creeks were strong and feisty and they all had men."

In the same novel, the local teacher, Ben Honaker, tries to encourage Carrie's sister Flora to seek an education outside the community. He asks,

> "Why are you still in school?"
> "Because I like to learn." Flora's voice was soft and shy.
> "A girl as smart as you should be off to the normal school, or maybe even to Berea."
> "I don't want to go way far off from home. Don't want to teach neither. Hit would upset me too much when the younguns did wrong. When I was helping them with their lessons today, I couldn't stand to have them make a mistake. I felt like hit was my fault. And I couldn't never fuss at them."
> "What do you like to do?"
> "I like to grow flowers. I like to take care of the animals. And I like to read. I like to read a pretty word and say it out loud. Me and my brother and sister all likes to read."

Gladys is similar to Flora who places her concern for family above personal ambition. Gladys' school experience alienated her from formal academic study. Although she did not provide many details beyond describing her teachers after elementary school as "snobbish" and not interested in her, Gladys's experience in junior high seems parallel to another of Giardina's protagonists, Rondal Loyd, in an incident involving a teacher, Miss Radcliffe, from his boyhood in Winco, West Virginia, an American Coal Company town:

> I attended the Winco School and did well. When I was in the third grade, the teacher, Miss Radcliffe, invited the ten best students to her apartment for oatmeal cookies. She lived in the clubhouse, a building most of us had never entered. It was reserved for the unmarried teachers, nurses, and bookkeepers of the company.
>
> Miss Radcliffe, tall and gray-headed, led us single-file up the stairs and ushered us into her rooms with the air of a genie revealing a treasure. We tiptoed across a rug Miss Radcliffe said was oriental and settled in miserable silence upon her purple-striped sofa and chairs. Miss Radcliffe smiled proudly as we craned our heads to take in the high cherry bookcases with glass doors, the purple-flowered wallpaper, the grandfather clock with gold trim on the door.
>
> She served the cookies on bone-white china, and we had hot tea served in delicate cups with handles so small that even a child could not get a proper grip without being burned. Miss Radcliffe talked about the importance of an education, about how we had the obligation to raise ourselves above our parents and save our mountain people from ignorance. She reminded us that Abraham Lincoln had been as poor as we were. . . .
>
> Cookie crumbs kept falling down the front of my overalls and I couldn't fish them out without spilling my tea. I was afraid they would drop on Miss Radcliffe's carpet when I stood up, and she would call me "slovenly," one of her favorite terms of disdain. When the grandfather clock struck four, we escaped. I wrapped three cookies in my bandanna to share with my brothers after supper, and ran down the hill to our house. When I went inside, I smelled grease. Mommy was scraping the bacon leavings in the iron skillet for gravy. I scuffed my base feet across the gritty wood floor, sprinkled with coal dust despite Mommy's daily scrubbing. Yellowing newspaper plastered the wall to keep out the cold.

As we noted at the outset, schools and the teachers who strongly influence young lives, those whom Sleeter (1992) calls the "keepers of the American dream," are not likely to value the talents and interests brought by those outside the mainstream even after they have been trained to accept, nurture, and utilize them. The negative consequences for members of Gladys's family including Gladys herself are paralleled in Giardina's novel. The shame and self pity expressed in Rondal and Flora's alienating experiences in particular are, unfortunately, mirrored in the life experiences of Gladys and her family.

THE LEWIS FAMILY:
OPPORTUNITIES AND CONSTRAINTS

Louise Lewis was born in 1918 in Riverbend. Her parents before her were raised in the neighborhood. She, her two sisters, and her two brothers attended the neighborhood parochial school through the eighth grade. Louise went to District Vocational School for ninth and tenth grades and received a certificate in sales and retailing; however, she did not complete high school. Instead, she worked for a short while in a downtown department store, but had to quit to take care of the children of a sick neighbor. She married a neighborhood boy who also attended the parochial school and had graduated from high school. They raised their nine children on worker's compensation following his accident as a forklift operator. The first seven children graduated from high school between 1968 and 1975. The last two daughters, Lois and Linda, left school in their senior years. Linda earned her GED after leaving high school.

Lois, Laney, and Linda

Lois attended the same neighborhood parochial school that her mother had attended. At this time, however, the school had classes only through the sixth grade. Lois later enrolled in seventh and eighth grades at a parochial school in the city. She subsequently went to District Middle School for the tenth and eleventh grades. In the eleventh grade she became pregnant and was required to go to a special school with other students who were pregnant or had other "social problems." Her baby was stillborn, and Lois "lost the spirit of going back to school." She and her husband later had five children who are now six to sixteen years old. Separated from her husband at this writing, Lois and the children are dependent on her two jobs. A newspaper carrier in her neighborhood since she was sixteen, Lois now delivers the afternoon paper to the downtown racks; she also works as a nurse's aide on the night shift. Lois explains that while most of her siblings graduated from high school, none of her neighborhood friends had: "At that time the students from the neighborhood were uncomfortable at District High School and nobody at the high school cared whether they were in school or not."

Lois' first child, Laney, attended a preschool Montessori program that had been organized by middle-class hillside dwellers and was located in the building that had been occupied by the parochial school attended by her parents. Fifty percent of the enrollment slots in the Montessori program were reserved for Riverbend children. The school organizers were committed to providing the tuition for these students. Laney went to an alternative (magnet) school from kindergarten through eighth grade. She loved the school and her teachers, and described it as one great family. The school is a thirty-minute bus ride from Laney's neighborhood.

After her graduation from the eighth grade, Laney registered at District High School, the school her mother, aunts, and uncles had also attended. She is an honor student there, an eleventh grader, majoring in accounting and computing. Recently Laney dropped her geometry class because it was pulling down her grade point average. She does not have plans yet for post–high school studies. Laney enjoys the social life at her high school, hanging out with friends from other neighborhoods before, during lunch, and after school. She no longer has much contact with friends from Riverbend, and explains that many have had to leave as housing conditions in the neighborhood have worsened. There are no other kids from her immediate neighborhood at District High School. Three neighborhood friends who are still at District Middle School are pregnant. Others decided at the seventh and eighth grades that they didn't like school and weren't going to go anymore, sometimes getting into fights on purpose to get suspended. This pattern was also observed by Borman and Mueninghoff (1984) in their study of urban Appalachian girls and young women who grew up in Lower Price Hill, the west side neighborhood mentioned previously. The young women who persisted in the high school outside their neighborhood and who were also academically successful lost touch with friends from their Lower Price Hill, explaining somewhat defensively to us that they had gone their separate ways.

As we also discussed earlier, Laney's Aunt Linda, Lois's younger sister, like Lois left District High School in the eleventh grade. She was unwilling to dissect a frog in biology class, and, believing that she could not be excused from the required assignment, didn't go to school that day, and never went back. Linda speculated that unless you had the money to get a college degree, a high school education is not enough to get a job in today's competitive marketplace.

Aunt Linda and Aunt Alma

Aunt Linda speculated about the constraints of the local job market, which demands, she believes, a degree beyond the high school diploma. Indeed, job markets are conditioned by local and regional opportunities and constraints. Linda and the other women interviewed in Riverbend made careful observations of local economic conditions and the future opportunities and constraints present in the market with reference to their own opportunities for mobility. Similarly, girls and young women in regional fiction take stock of the limits and possibilities of their economic futures. A wry, deprecating "analysis" of the local labor market in the formerly booming textile mills located in the foothills of South Carolina is provided by Bone, Dorothy Allison's tough heroine in *Bastard out of Carolina*. She reflects:

> Aunt Alma joked that the twins were too lazy to fart on their own, and sometimes I thought she was right. They were certainly dumb enough. Neither of them ever read a book or talked about anything but how rich they were gonna be "someday." Mama said you could tell they were starting to grow up by how silly they had become, that teenagers always got stupid before they got smart. I wondered if that was what was happening to me, if I had already started to get stupid and just didn't know it. Not that it mattered. Stupid or smart, there wasn't much choice about what was going to happen to me, or to Grey and Garvey, or to any of us. Growing up was like falling into a hole. The boys would quit school and sooner or later go to jail for something silly. I might not quit school, not while Mama had any say in the matter, but what difference would that make? What was I going to do in five years? Work in the textile mill? Join Mama at the diner? It all looked bleak to me. No wonder people got crazy as they grew up.

The Lewis family and the parallel example from Allison's *Bastard out of Carolina* serve to illustrate how individuals take into account structural constraints including current labor market conditions in considering their education and career options. Young women, in fact, rationalize their diminished contact with girlhood friends if they are in serious pursuit of academic success. We can conclude that becoming economically mobile requires a self-conscious examination of the benefits and costs associated with such a decision. Some, like Bone, the fictional heroine in Allison's novel, correctly observed that her choices were highly limited and that staying in place meant rather grimly resolving to accept one's limited horizons. Others such as Laney may sacrifice close emotional ties with girlhood friends to pursue individual achievement.

Guidance counselors, teachers, school psychologists, and others must become sensitive to the particular cultural strains and mismatches between remaining close to kin and neighborhood friends and aiming at achievement through educational attainment. Some including Helton, Barnes, and Borman (1994) have put forward models for educators and social service providers to utilize in their work with urban Appalachian clients. Such models emphasize the importance of practical, direct, clearly stated information in connection with a wide range of personal issues especially if information is provided in the context of open communication and mutual goal setting. Others, however, are less sanguine. After months of well-designed instruction carried off in a collegial manner, the teachers with whom Christine Sleeter worked continued to hold negative stereotypes about their African American students.

THE MCGRADY FAMILY:
THE STRENGTH OF FAMILY TIES

Marie McGrady was born in 1918. Raised in the study neighborhood, she attended the same school, District Elementary School, attended by members of the Adams family. She exclaimed:

> Oh, I graduated. that's been a long while ago. I graduated at the end of the eighth grade. I loved school, and I made good grades. We went everyday. If we had a temperature or a cough, that was nothing. I could . . . [still] name almost all of my teachers.

During the summer after the eighth grade her parents separated, and their drinking got out of hand. Then, she laments, "*me* and my sister got left out of high school. Oh, I wanted to go." But instead, they had to pick up the pieces of their family life and take on adult responsibilities.

Marie, Madge, and Missy

Marie was married to a friend from the neighborhood who had also completed the eighth grade. They had six children: four daughters and two sons. The two boys left school after the eighth grade; one has five children all of whom left school after the eighth grade; the other has three children still in school, one who left at the tenth grade and one (the first) who completed the twelfth grade but was denied a diploma because he could not pay his school fees. All of these children and grandchildren live in Riverbend.

The first of Marie's daughters completed the eighth grade; the second one graduated from the District High School; the third one, Madge, left school after the eleventh grade; and the fourth left following ninth grade. Seventeen of Marie's twenty-six grandchildren live in the neighborhood. All but one of these grandchildren left school between the eighth and tenth grades. Seven of her grandchildren are attending elementary school.

Madge was born in 1954. She left the District High School after the eleventh grade because she was pregnant and was forbidden by the district to return to school. "I knew they wouldn't let me come back to school. I called

them. They told me 'No.' They couldn't be responsible for me over there."
After the baby was born, Madge and her boyfriend were married and had two
more children before they were divorced. She could not return to school because she had to take care of the babies. She had liked school and said she
got along well with her teachers. Her sons attended District High School;
one left in the tenth grade frustrated by learning disabilities; the other, an
honor student, left in the eleventh grade after disagreements with a teacher.
Her daughter, Missy, withdrew from the District High School in the fall of
1993. She had been repeating the ninth grade.

Marie, Madge, and Missy live in the same household. Madge had been enrolled at the community college, studying to be a practical nurse. When
Missy's personal problems disrupted Madge's studies, she lost the C average
required to keep her financial aid. Missy has been hospitalized several times
during this year after overdosing on pills prescribed to her grandmother Marie.
Missy is now pregnant, and Madge is worrying about how to take care of her
aging mother as well as her despondent daughter. They subsist on social security income from Marie's deceased husband and ADC for Missy. Madge's
dreams of a nursing degree and meaningful work have been disrupted by her
family responsibilities.

Missy attended the neighborhood elementary school, two middle schools,
and the District High School. She does not like school, nor does she like the
teachers. "And they don't like me," she exclaims. She would like to get into
District School for the Creative and Performing Arts, but needs a C average to
audition. She's also interested in going to the Academy, a special program for
students sixteen and over who have "dropped out" of school previously. She
likes the fact that the school is in the neighborhood.

Missy has had a history of incidents with the juvenile justice system. According to Madge and Marie, the first one was provoked by the principal of
Missy's elementary school after Missy had gone on to middle school. A
school office worker had called the household with a message for a neighbor.
The neighbor's child was waiting at the school for someone to pick her up.
Madge said that Missy could come to collect the child, and that the child
could wait in their home until her mother returned from work. When Missy
arrived at the school, the "principal went off on her." The principal told Missy
that she no longer went to the school, and that she was not wanted in *her*
building. The police were called and arrested Missy for criminal trespassing.
She was found guilty by the juvenile court and sentenced to ten days of work
detail. That was Missy's first encounter with the justice system. She subsequently has been back in court five or six times, charged at the middle school

with unruly conduct for "talking back." Now she is sixteen, officially withdrawn from school, and three months pregnant.

The McGrady family's commitment to one another and to neighborhood friends and kin helps maintain the cycle of limited or no success in undertaking traditional educational careers. In addition, in Missy's case a pattern of behavior regarded by the justice system as defiant to authority in the context of the school does not bode well for any future contact with a formal system of schooling. Carol Stack's (1972) classic ethnography of an African American community located in a large midwestern city and inhabited by migrants from the black South describes a similar pattern of behavior in that context. Poor families typically respond to relatives who are experiencing financial hardships by assisting family members, sacrificing individual success for the survival of the group.

A Sociocultural Analysis of
Riverbend Families and Children

At the outset of this chapter we described factors which contribute to an understanding of the lives we have presented here. We did so under the rubric of what we have termed a sociocultural understanding of families and communities. Structural factors including poverty measured at the neighborhood as opposed to the individual level as well as cultural dissonance, notably the mismatch between home and school, contribute to the outcomes across generations of urban Appalachian girls and young women. In this section we summarize our findings across the three cases: the Adams, Lewis, and McGrady families.

Structural Barriers

All the Riverbend grandmothers we interviewed in this study cited poverty as a condition of their early school leaving. In the case of the Lewises, as an example, Louise Lewis was forced by her family's economic plight to leave in the ninth grade when the Depression set in and the family couldn't afford clothes or food. She laments,

> We had to grow up, because it was the Depression. And my mother had to go to work; and I knew that my dad had lost his job after thirty-some years. And he was having a hard time finding more employment, which everybody did. So we had to grow up fast. It's not that the parents . . . [today] don't care that the kids go to school. It's that when you're getting your kid up at 5:30 in the morning to send them to school, and they say they're tired, you can relate to

being tired . . . and to send your kid out in the dark, on the bus for an hour. . . . [You ask yourself] Is it worth it?

Although economic indicators in 1994 suggest a modest rebounding of the national economy, Lois believes that hard times have persistently interfered with her own and her children's school completion:

Everything is so bad that the parents are scrambling to find money to just feed and house the kids . . . [as a consequence] the parents are so far out of touch with the kids. . . . There's a lot of people out . . . [of work] or afraid of losing their jobs. You don't want to borrow off somebody that's already struggling.

The general sense of current and prevailing economic conditions is that times are tougher now than when Lois, Madge, and other members of the second generation were "coming up" in the 1950s. Lois recalled that her Mom was always home and knew pretty much where her kids were and how they were doing. Her mother, Louise, told stories of neighborhood kids coming to her house after school for a bowl of soup before baseball practice.

Their soup and all was sitting on the table when they walked in. Everyday was soup day. Our house was handy. The soup pot don't stretch that far no more.

Madge McGrady often spoke of the difficulties of making ends meet, such as the time when she had to come up with the money to stay in nurse's training. Her mother Marie suggested that she should take a loan against Marie's insurance. Madge resisted pursuing this strategy:

No. I won't let her do that. She's talking about the death insurance she has. She doesn't have that much, and when she is gone, we're going to have to put to that. You know, for her to be buried properly.

Marie adds, "They'll bury me for love. They will. First thing."

Families in Riverbend have historically moved with frequency, changing residences from sheer necessity as families were forced from rundown housing by city decrees or evicted bodily by landlords after falling behind in their rent. For example, the Adams family home was passed down to Gladys by her father; she and her daughter were able to remain in it because the mortgage had been paid off long before. During her childhood, however, Gladys moved back and forth between her neighborhood and cramped space in a downtown apartment building. The Lewis family made do by living in a neighborhood apartment building owned by an uncle. Like the McGradys, they have lived in numerous apartments in Riverbend as they adjusted to their own worsening economic circumstances, conditions that mirror those in the neighborhood overall. Another ramification of the persistently poor housing conditions and ongoing gentrification is the impact upon social networks. As Lois Lewis sees it, "People are just coming in and taking the houses. Their friends have to move away, and there's no reason for it."

Two families had the additional financial burden of chronically ill relatives. Louise Lewis left her retailing job when her aunt took sick. She has never returned to formal employment. Marie McGrady abandoned high school studies to assume adult responsibilities when her folks started drinking. Madge McGrady left nurse's training to care for Missy. The pull of family responsibilities is a fact of life for low-income people, placing enormous constraints on personal ambition.

Cultural Dissonance

In addition to these often overwhelming structural constraints, the values and beliefs of urban Appalachian community residents frequently undergird decisions to leave school. Riverbend's households, like many in the mountain region, usually include both parents and often a single aunt or uncle, widowed parent, or orphaned cousin. Additional relatives frequently live in adjacent or nearby households.

Seventy-two percent of the fifty families we interviewed reported having relatives in the neighborhood. Neighborhoods like Riverbend and Lower Price Hill are frequently referred to as urban "hollers" by community-based activists who recognize how these communities remain incubators of Appalachian culture across the generations. Throughout the conversations held by the first author with the women whose stories are told here, neighbors and kin frequently passed through the homes to check in, to exchange money or food, or just to visit. Extended kinship networks and friendship ties are the principal means by which these residents gain social support. Maintaining close ties and relying on kin and neighbors for support is a strong and constant value among mountain people and among their counterparts in urban places.

Advocates for Appalachians who have moved to inner-city neighborhoods hold the view that values such as loyalty to kin and others including neighborliness, identification with place, and person rather than goal orientation are fundamentally in conflict with school values and practices. The skills, strengths, and values of minority and poor children are maladaptive in schools operated by representatives of the middle class. Insensitive school policies and practices such as those reported by the McGradys and the Lewises serve as examples of how students have been pushed out of school.

Madge McGrady, for example, could not return to school after she became pregnant because school policy prevented her attendance. Maureen Sullivan, the Urban Appalachian Council's executive director, explains that a culturally held view links childbearing to one's status as a woman (Borman et al. 1988). Excluding pregnant teenagers from school is no longer school policy; however, the consequences for the McGrady family persist. Madge's son, although an honor student, gave up school after being embarrassed by a teacher in front of his peers. His efforts to sort out the disagreement were rebuffed; after he dropped the required course, he unsuccessfully tried to schedule it the following year with another teacher, and subsequently left school without the necessary credit. Like Linda Lewis who never came back after skipping school the day of the frog dissection, Madge's son never recovered from the embarrassment he suffered as a result of his teacher's insensitive comments. After Madge's nephew completed his graduation requirements, he was nevertheless denied a diploma when he could not pay school fees. Madge herself was forced to give up nurse's training when school policy required her to pay her fees in cash rather than through loans after her grade point average dropped as she dealt with her daughter's suicide attempts. School policies and practices such as those mentioned here that result in early departure can be viewed as "push out" practices.

All three families reported many efforts by the women to intervene at the schools on behalf of their children. Often when the women went to school seeking to understand their children's academic and behavioral difficulties, they endured long waits to get an administrator's time. On one occasion as Madge reports:

> The [assistant principal] and I went to war. I mean, I threatened to have his job on a silver platter. And that's what I told him. I told him, I said "You don't scare me. No. Nobody in this building scares me. And come hell or high water, I'll have your job on a silver platter, Buddy, if you don't lay off of my kid.". . . And after that incident with him and my going off on him over there, he was very nice to me. But, up until that point, he had his attitude out on me. So I called town. I called the board of education on him. I called their area director. I called the superintendent. I called and talked with him, and we got it squared away.
>
> They called a big meeting. And everything was laid out on the table. [The assistant principal] told them he wasn't going to put up with my calling there everyday, and my coming in everyday taking up his time, that he was

not going to put up with that. And they told him that's what he was there for. And that if he didn't like that, that he needed a job elsewhere.

I was just determined that, you know, I knew what [my son's] problem was. And I was not going to let any of these people walk on [him]. And I didn't. I mean, there were many occasions where I went to the schools [where he went], and I just took [my son] by the hand, and I just simply walked out of the building with him and dared them to do anything about it.

Lois reported difficulties getting her ten-year-old daughter into summer school after the child had failed the fourth grade: "You'd think they would be beggin' kids to get in summer school. I took her to summer school the first day. They kept her in the office all day. I went back. He said, 'No. She couldn't get in. You missed the deadline.'"

Administrators and counselors both in the local schools and "downtown" were seen as unhelpful and, in many cases, disparaged them and their cultural background. Madge said of district school administrators:

You know, they had attitudes. I always though that when you had a problem, you went into your assistant principal or your counselor's [office] to talk to 'em about. That they was there to help you. Instead, you know we usually always got. . . . I thought that the white kids always got pushed out the door.

Madge's observations reflect the concern that administrators and other school personnel often treated her and others with indifference, and that district policies and practices were often biased in favor of blacks whose successful political action had resulted in their more favorable treatment. The white Appalachians in Riverbend do not hold racist views. In fact, whites and blacks in the community worked together to block the erosion of the neighborhood by developers intent on erecting housing beyond the means of "native" residents to afford. Rather, the parents we interviewed understood that their lack of political mobilization in the area of schools and the education of their children constituted a real problem.

A MIXED MESSAGE ABOUT SUCCESS IN SCHOOL

Urban Appalachian parents often present a mixed message to their children about school performance and school attendance. Messages reflect the conflict between parents' aspirations for their children and deeply rooted cultural values. On the one hand, they wish their children to graduate, but also to value active engagement with life over bookishness. They wish for their children to complete college and enter professions, but they also feel that these aspirations are unrealistic and thus expect their children will actually work in trades or industry. They want their children to get along at school, but they expect them to stand up for themselves when challenged by schoolyard bullies. In the end, individual achievement is not as important as what is best for the family.

The grandmothers also believed that it was essential that their kids and grandkids graduate from high school; however, none of them was herself a high school graduate. Marie McGrady's comment about her position with her children on the importance of formal schooling is typical: "I was strict on school. I wanted my kids to have an education. That was the most important thing." Nonetheless, one of her three sons was sent up to the penitentiary for stealing a car, two gave up on school after the eighth grade; one of her daughters was prohibited from returning to school after she got pregnant; and one was despondent after being raped in the neighborhood. Only one of her children graduated. Marie's strong desire to have her children complete high school could not overcome the problems besetting the family. We must conclude that attachment to traditional high school practice is slight.

Nurturant Teachers and Attachment to School

Bonding to school and attachment to school peers and professionals is a requisite for persistent educational effort in school (Wehlage 1986, 1988, 1989). The four conditions of school bonding that Wehlage and his colleagues and others posit are (1) commitment to what one must do to achieve goals of school completion expressed through (2) conformity to school rules and participation in the school's demands, (3) involvement in the activities of the school (engagement), and (4) belief in the legitimacy and efficacy of the institution. School attachment is an issue for both students and their parents. The women whose stories we have told here are attached to their families, their extended kin, and their neighborhood. Attachment to school is a rarity, however, and accomplished only when neighborhood commitments are forsaken.

Most of Riverbend's children experience discomfort being away from home and family; they may feel insecure in competition with youth from other neighborhoods at schools outside the community; their parents may experience difficulty monitoring school attendance; and, finally, parents may lack the opportunity to engage actively in their children's day-to-day education experiences. Nonetheless, all of the women talked about their fondness for the neighborhood elementary schools they attended. Lois Lewis described the special character of her school:

> I can remember first grade. I could not do Ss right. You know. So one of the kids that could do Ss right, gets up to the board and shows you. The class

didn't go on until every kid mastered that thing. You know. That was the nicest part about it. Nobody, you know, nowadays, if the kid is doing bad, that teacher will not help that kid at all.

The close, nurturing involvement and support of the classroom teacher and engagement of the entire class in learning are critical. This is not surprising. As the literature of the region illustrates, these are the very qualities in mountain teachers which assured their ability to be embraced by their students and, indeed, by the entire community. What is said in *Dove, Women of the Mountains* by author Florence Bush is true for the women of Riverbend:

> Each generation is a step further away from the mountains, but, still, in each of us is a spirit that longs to soar like an eagle back to the place of our beginning, our home. In years to come, we can look back toward the Smokies and remember our heritage. Many ancestors lived, worked, and died under the smoky haze, leaving us a legacy of determination, courage, intelligence, and the knowledge that God is always near.

Another sympathetic account of teachers and teaching in Janice Holt Giles's *Miss Willie*, a novel set in the 1940s in Piney Ridge, a chain of hills in southeastern Kentucky. Miss Willie had come from her home in Texas to establish a school in the mountains. Her classroom is appealing and homelike.

> [Miss Willie] had always taken pride in the comfortable, homelike atmosphere of her schoolroom, believing ardently that for small children, venturing so insecurely into the wider world, the school room should offer a measure of the feeling of home. So she had brought her little rocker and her hooked rug and her pots and green plants to school to give it a warmer and a snugger look, to draw in the horizons of the new world to a safer, more enfolding circle. She brought her knitting also, and many times when she sat in her little rocker, knitting, she watched a feeling of contentment, security, safeness, spread over the room, the purring, satisfied contentment of a child who can sprawl happily over his work because his mother sits nearby with her sewing. She believed all this was good.

However, even the dedicated Miss Willie remains an outsider and because of her devotion to "book logic" she is judged to be rather "quare." The town trustee, Wills Pierce, who was instrumental in bringing Miss Willie to Piney Ridge, explains,

> Miss Willie, hit'll take the rest o'yer life to learn the ways of the ridge. You have to be borned here to know 'em all, an' to fit ever' time. Ifen you stay

here the rest o'yer life, you'll get easylike with 'em, but they's things that'll allus puzzle you. But it don't matter, Miss Willie. Jist keep this in mind. They think yer quare, but that ain't goin' to keep 'em from likin' you, an' being' proud yer their teacher. Hit won't keep 'em from buckin' you when what you want don't suit, neither.

It is difficult to imagine most teachers in urban places being "schooled" by their students' parents as Miss Willie was by the folk in the mountains. Yet something close to the kind of intimate understanding of folkways, beliefs, and practices is essential if school people are to hold urban Applachian children and families in esteem. Most of the women in Riverbend spoke about difficult transitions from small, sometimes elementary schools in the neighborhood, transitions that often were so rocky that they led to the women's departure from school altogether. Madge McGrady relates:

> You know, I was the kind of kid that was afraid to ask the teacher to explain this or that or the other; because I didn't want the other kids thinking I was stupid. I think that probably started when I was in junior high school. You know, I had done okay all through elementary school with my math. It just seemed like when I started junior high school, I was . . . I was shy and backward. I was afraid to say, "Well [to the teacher] could you explain this to me more, so I can understand it better?"

Lois Lewis talked about the difficult switch to middle school:

> Because, at the [elementary school] you had everybody from the neighborhood. So you were all doing the same thing, and you were all together. So, you know, you just did it, because everybody else was doing it, and it was fun, because all your friends were in school and, you know, you helped one another out with the stuff that the other one didn't do, or couldn't do, the other one helped. And then we went to [middle school], and that was like nobody cared whether you were there or not.

Lois and Linda Lewis talked about their own and their friends' experiences at District High School. "There were a lot of fights, and you just felt uncomfortable at the school. And nobody cared if you were there or not." Their parents cared, but they did not know. Louise relates, "I sent them out to school. They all went out at the same time." The girls respond,

> Everybody went until like the eleventh grade, and then it was just the common thing. We didn't all drop out at the same time. There was no social at school. Maybe that was one of the problems. You went to your classes, and,

basically, that was it. [The District Middle School] was different because when you went [there] you seen your friends and you were in classes with your friends and you still had contact. So everybody was doing the same thing.

Without the strong attachment to school that comes from feelings of solidarity and a sense of shared joy, misery, or even indifference, individuals are likely to leave school. When friends from childhood are left behind in what is tantamount to a self-conscious break with former friends and neighbors, students from Riverbend and other similar urban Applachian neighborhoods have access to careers as successful students. They do, however, pay a heavy price.

CONCLUSIONS AND RECOMMENDATIONS

The views presented in this chapter of the women from three families of an urban Appalachian neighborhood about the circumstances of their lives and their decisions regarding school completion underscore the different types of response to the same institution that are possible from members of the same ethnic group. Some, notably the members of the Adams family, were severely alienated from school even while valuing reading and learning; others hated school. For all, an identity as a woman in a family and a neighborhood had a stronger pull than any identification of themselves as students in most of the schools they attended. School was disliked because of its distance from their homes and the attitudes conveyed to them about themselves by school teachers and administrators. What they loved was neighborhood classrooms with teachers who expressed their caring and their commitment.

Urban Appalachian women's self-esteem, considerable energy, and competence were evident in their narratives about their own schooling and that of their children. They have persisted despite constraints of poverty and public policy, even as the social infrastructure of their neighborhood was disrupted. Their emotional strength and their capacity to keep control of their families as well as their refusal to give control to the distant schools remain the underpinning of the community life.

What recommendations do these findings suggest for school policy and practice? For one, placing students in schools removed from a neighborhood social context should be discontinued if the children of urban Appalachian poor families are to be well served. New policies that seek to extend and improve the educational experiences of urban Appalachian students can also strengthen recreational, health, and employment services in the neighborhood. We must focus on the requirements of children and reconstruct the institutions that assist children to move toward adulthood successfully. A relatively large investment of resources will be required to reverse damages caused by the removal from the community over the years of its educational and social institutions. The extended kinship network and friendship ties of neighborhood residents should be the foundation on which new institutions are constructed.

NOTES

1. Riverbend is the name we have given the neighborhood in which this study took place.

2. The Appalachian Region, as designated by Congress, comprises 397 mountainous counties from rural Maine to Tennessee.

REFERENCES

Borman, K., and E. Mueninghoff. 1983. "Lower Price Hill's Children: Family, School, and Neighborhood." In A. Batteau, ed., *Appalachia and America*, 210–55. Lexington: University of Kentucky Press.

Borman, K., E. Mueninghoff, and S. Piazza. 1988. "Urban Appalachian Girls and Young Women: Bowing to No One." In L. Weis, ed., *Class, Race and Gender in U.S. Schools*, 230–47. Albany: State University of New York Press.

Coleman, J. 1988. "Social Capital in the Creation of Human Capital." *American Journal of Sociology* 94 (supplement): S95–S120.

Crane, J. 1991. "Effects of Neighborhoods on Dropping Out of School and Teenage Childbearing." In C. Jencks and P. E. Peterson, eds., *The Urban Underclass*. Washington, D.C.: The Brookings Institution.

Deyhle, D., and S. Margonis. (in press).

Ekstrom, R. B., M. E. Goertz, J. M. Pollack, and D. A. Rock. 1986. "Who Drops Out of High School and Why? Findings from a National Study." *Teachers College Record* 87.3: 356–73.

Fine, M. 1991. *Framing Dropouts*. Albany: State University of New York Press.

Fine, M., and P. Rosenberg. 1983. "Dropping Out of High School: The Ideology of School and Work." *Journal of Education* 165, 257–72.

Fine, M., and N. Zane. 1989. "Bein' Wrapped Too Tight: When Low-Income Women Drop Out of High School." In L. Weis, E. Farrar, and H. G. Petrie, eds., *Dropouts from School: Issues, Dilemmas, and Solution*. Albany: State University of New York Press.

Heath, S. B. 1983. *Ways with Words: Language, Life and Work in Communities and Classrooms*. New York: Cambridge University Press.

Heath, S. B., and M. McLaughlin. 1987. "A Child Resource Policy: Moving Beyond Dependence on School and Family." *Phi Delta Kappan* (April), 576–80.

Lareau, A. 1989. *Home Advantage*. Philadelphia: Falmer Press.

LeCompte, M., and G. Dworkin. 1991. *Giving Up on School*. Newbury Park, Calif.: Corwin Press.

Maloney, M., and K. Borman. 1987. "Effects of Schools and Schooling upon Appalachian Children in Cincinnati." In P. Obermiller and W. Philliber, eds., *Too Few Tomorrows: Urban Appalachians in the 1980's*, 89–98. Boone, N.C.: Appalachian Consortium Press.

Natriello, G. 1986. *School Dropouts*. New York: Teachers College Press.

Ogbu, J. 1974. *The Next Generation*. New York: Academic Press.

———. 1982. "Cultural Discontinuity and Schooling." *Anthropology and Education Quarterly* 13.4: 290–307.

———. 1987. "Opportunity Structure, Cultural Boundaries, and Literacy." In Langer, J., ed., *Language, Literacy, and Culture: Issues of Society and Schooling*, 149–77. Norwood, N.J.: Ablex Publishing.

Sleeter, C. 1992. *Keepers of the American Dream: A Study of Staff Development and Multicultural Education*. Washington, D.C.: Falmer Press.

Stack, C. 1972. *All Our Kin: Strategies for Survival in a Black Community*. 1st edition. New York: Harper and Row.

Taylor, D., and C. Dorsey-Gaines. 1988. *Growing Up Literate: Learning from Inner-City Families*. Portsmouth, N.H.: Heineman Educational Books.

Wagner, T. 1974. Report of the Appalachian School Study Project. Working Paper No. 4. Cincinnati, Ohio: The Urban Appalachian Council.

———. 1977. "Urban Schools and Appalachian Children." *Urban Education* 11.3: 283–96.

———. 1981. "Urban Appalachian School Children: The Least Understood of All." Working Paper No. 6. Cincinnati, Ohio: The Urban Appalachian Council.

Wehlage, G. 1986. "Dropping Out: How Much Do Schools Contribute to the Problem?" In G. Natriello, ed., *School Dropouts: Patterns and Policies*. New York: Teachers College Press.

———. 1989. "Dropping Out: Can Schools Be Expected to Prevent It?" In L. Weis, E. Farrar, and H. G. Petrie, eds., *Dropouts from School: Issues Dilemmas, and Solution*. Albany: State University of New York Press.

Wehlage, G., R. A. Rutter, G. A. Smith, N. Lesko, and R. R. Fernandez. 1989. *Reducing the Risk: Schools as Communities of Support*. Philadelphia: Falmer Press. Taylor and Francis, Inc.

13

MICHELLE FINE, LOIS WEIS, JUDI ADDELSTON,
AND JULIA MARUSZA

White Loss

The 1980s and 1990s have been decades in which white males have, indeed, lost a good bit of their privilege. Those most squeezed have been white working-class males, with the progress of Title IX, Affirmative Action, the shrinking of unionized and public sector jobs, the vibrant (if sometimes muzzled) energy of feminism, civil rights, and the unstoppable "coming out" of gay/lesbian rights. In our interviews with poor and working-class males in Jersey City, Buffalo, and Charleston, South Carolina, we hear a mantra of losses that they narrate, angrily, bitterly, with pointed fingers. From days gone by, they have lost wives whom they thought would stay home and cater to them, good jobs in the public sector and those protected by labor unions. Their schools and communities have been "invaded" by people of color. Their monopoly on power and privilege has been pierced. They are not happy. Their stories of loss are voiced in a discourse of property rights. While it is the case that they have been economically dethroned, re-gendered, and re-raced in the past two decades, they feel only mugged. Not by the global treachery of late capitalism, the flight of manufacturing jobs from the United States, or the erosion of strong labor unions, all of which are the real cause of their present circumstances. Instead, they feel erased by white women, men of color, gays and lesbians. Unable/unwilling to critique boldly and broadly, these men, for the most part, rehearse a noble loyalty to their American dreams.

From these men we hear similar narrations of identities perched in opposition to white women, men and women of color, gays and lesbians. We hear about "them" taking away "our" women, "our" jobs, "our" streets and communities. These men have been strong supporters and, ironically, big losers under the Reagan-Bush years. While their "Brahman" elite brothers have been barely touched by economic hard times, and poor people of color continue to struggle, these men have, as Kathryn Newman eloquently describes, "fallen from grace." Through anger and bitterness we hear pain and we watch these men surveil "downward," scanning furiously the Darwinian gender/race/class

283

scale, searching below for who robbed them of their privileges. When did their women decide to work? When did their factories leave the country? When did their unions dismantle? When did their neighborhoods color? When did they fall out of the seat of within-class privilege?

We open, in this chapter, a conversation about how white males, working-class in particular, make sense of their dwindling bases of power. For these men the very hierarchies within they once anointed themselves and assumed their seats to be guaranteed are corroding beneath their feet. These men dare not challenge the beliefs of meritocracy and progress, but instead sponsor social "block watches," patrolling for *who* shattered their dreams. With no social movement to attach to, ripped from the nostalgic moorings of the nuclear family, church, and trade unionism, with little prospect of mortgages, of Catholic schools for their children, or of residing in a "safe community," these men are looking for someone to blame. While the workings of capital, the flight of jobs, and the devastation of the public sector escape largely unnoticed, black men, white women, and gays/lesbians are held accountable for their white misery.

We take you into a pool of data—constructed by combining narratives from listening to white boys and men searching desperately for an explanation and someone to blame. The data derive from Weis's study of a high school, Weis and Fine's analysis of working-class young adults in Jersey City and Buffalo, Addelston and Fine interviews at the Military University, an all-male public college, and Marusza's interviews in white working-class bars. Across these sites we hear stories of what Gerald Suttles (1972, 21) would call "undefended neighborhoods," or spaces where these men attempt to seal themselves off and defend against encroachment. But now these spaces appear to be under double siege. First they are no longer mono-demographic— that is, white and male. Their schools are desegregated. The military includes women. The fire/police departments have changed their tests and recruit men (and sometimes women) of color. Even their bars are no longer "safe," that is, assuredly filled with "real men." Second, these spaces are threatened because the identities that they once guaranteed—stud, cadet, husband, provider, laborer, or a well-paid public servant—are neither secure nor sacred. Invaded and "emasculated," old sites for white, working-class male identity formation are being renovated—often in pink, lavender, or the colors of race nationalism.

As we listen to the words of white working-class male protest, we notice two things. First, we hear the frightened refusal by these men to analyze critically the macro relations of labor, race, or gender that have sold them out. Second, we hear a constricted search for the culprit who took "my place." We hear these protests lodged in categories of "loss"—women, jobs, communities, and schools. It is in these categories that we review the data.

Loss of "Our" Women

An ethnographic study conducted by Lois Weis in a community called "Freeway" provides insight into how some white working-class males of high school age translate an understanding of their devalued social and economic status into their lives. Freeway is a divided town and a small number of Arabs and Hispanics live among African Americans largely on one side of the "tracks," and whites on the other, although there are whites living in one section of Freeway just adjacent to the steel mill, which is in the area populated by people of color. Virtually no people of color live in the white area, unlike large American cities where there are pockets of considerable mix. Most African Americans came up from the South during and after World War II, drawn by the lure of jobs in the steel plant. Having been relegated to the dirtiest and lowest paid jobs, most are now living in large public housing projects, never having been able to amass the necessary capital to live elsewhere.

Here, among these white adolescent males, people of color are used reliably as a foil against which acceptable moral and particularly sexual standards are established. The goodness of white is always contrasted with the badness of black—blacks are scripted as being involved with drugs; blacks are unacceptable sexually; black men attempt to "invade" white sexual space by talking with white women; black women are simply filthy. The constructed binary translates in ways that compliment white boys. There is a virtual denial of anything at all good being identified with blackness, and of anything bad identified with whiteness. Much expressed racism centers on "white males'" spoken or unspoken sense of entitled access to white women, thus serving the dual purpose of fixing blacks *and* white women on a ladder of social relations:

> JIM: The minorities are really bad into drugs. You're talking everything. Anything you want, you get from them. A prime example, the ward of Freeway; about twenty years ago the ward was predominantly white, my grandfather used to live there. Then Italians, Polish, the Irish people, everything was fine. The houses were maintained; there was a good standard of living. . . . The blacks brought drugs. I'm not saying white people didn't have drugs, they had drugs, but to a certain extent. But drugs were like a social thing. But now you go down to the ward; it's amazing, it's a ghetto. Some of the houses are okay. They try to keep them up. Most of the homes are really, really terrible. They throw garbage on the front lawn, it's sickening. You talk to people from [surrounding suburbs]. Anywhere you talk to people, they

tend to think the majority of our school is black. They think you hang with black people, listen to black music. . . . A few of them [blacks] are starting to go into the ward now [the white side], so they're moving around. My parents will be around there when that happens, but I'd like to be out of there.

•

LW: There's no fighting and stuff here [school], is there?

CLINT: Yeah, a lot between blacks and whites.

LW: Who starts them?

CLINT: Blacks.

LW: Do blacks and whites hang out in the same place?

CLINT: Some do. [The blacks] live on the other side of town. . . . A lot of it [fights] starts with blacks messing with white girls. That's how a lot of them start. Even if they [white guys] don't know the white girl, they don't like to see . . .

LW: How do you feel about that yourself?

CLINT: I don't like it. If I catch them [blacks] near my sister, they'll get it. I don't like to see it like that. Most of them [his friends] see it that way [the same way he does].

LW: How about the other way around? White guys and black girls?

CLINT: There's a few that do. There's people that I know of, but no one I hang around with. I don't know many white kids that date black girls.

•

BILL: Like my brother, he's in ninth grade. He's in trouble all the time. Last year he got jumped in school . . . about his girlfriend. He don't like blacks. They come up to her and go, "Nice ass," and all that shit. My brother don't like that when they call her "nice ass" and stuff like that. He got suspended for saying "fucking nigger," but it's all right for a black guy to go up to whites and say stuff like that ["nice ass"]. . . . Sometimes the principals aren't doing their job. Like when my brother told [the assistant principal] that something is going to happen, Mr. _____ just said, "leave it alone, just turn your head." . . . Like they [the administrators] don't know when fights start in this school. Like there's this one guy's kid sister, a nigger [correction]—a black guy—grabbed her ass. He hit him a couple of times. Did the principal know about it?

LW: What if a white guy did that [grabbed the girl's ass]?

BILL: He'd probably have punched him. But a lot of it's 'cause they're black.

It is important to note that these white boys are constructing white females as being in need of their protection; the young men fight for their young women. The complaint is communicated through a language of property rights; others, specifically black males, are intruding onto *white property*. It is the fact that *black* boys are invading *white* girls, the assumed property of *white* boys, that is at issue here, not a broader concern with the behavior of males vis-à-vis females. The discursive construction of black men as oversexualized enables white men to elaborate their own "appropriate" and tamed heterosexuality. At a time of heightened concern with homosexuality, by virtue of their age, the collective nature of their lives, the fear of being labeled homosexual and the violence that often accompanies such labeling in high school, these boys assert virulently and publicly their concern with black men, while expressing their own heterosexuality and their ability to "take care of their women." This intersection of race, racism, and "acting straight" has not, to our knowledge, been explored, but it is in serious need of analysis. Black males provide the foil around which all these constructions can unfold. There is a complete social distortion about this particular set of interactions, a distortion which enables white men to write themselves as pure, straight, and superior, while authoring black men as dirty, oversexualized, and almost animal-like.

It is most interesting that not one female in this study ever discussed young black men as a "problem" in this regard. This is not to say that white females were not racist, but this discursive rendering of black males was quite noticeably the terrain of white men. Not insignificantly, it is always fathers, according to young white women, who oppose interracial dating. This is, of course, tied to the history of racism and race relations in a white working-class community, where blacks were used to break strikes and, therefore, pitted against white men economically. In a de-industrializing economy, these young Freeway males are aware that the hard labor or traditional "male" jobs no longer exist. Instead of swallowing their rage, they displace it toward others. By constructing a moral subclass for African American males out of old stereotypes, the Freeway boys effectively maintain a sense of superiority.

Loss of "Our" Jobs

Anger over the loss of social power among white working-class males is not only articulated in the sexual realm, it is also targeted in the world of work, and what are considered by some to be unfair hiring practices. This theme emerged in interviews with poor and working-class white males as part of a larger ongoing study of poor and working-class young urban adults who grew up in the Reagan-Bush years, conducted by Michelle Fine, Lois Weis, and a group of graduate students. In broad strokes we are investigating constructions of gender, race, ethnic, and class identities; participation in social and community-based movements for change; participation in self-help groups and religious institutions; experiences within and outside the family; and experiences within and outside the new economy. We have adopted a quasi–life history approach in which a series of in-depth interviews are conducted with young people between the ages of 24 and 35, poor and working-class, of varying racial backgrounds. Interviewees were split more or less evenly among African Americans, Latinos, and white men and women in Buffalo and Jersey City. In Jersey City an Asian sample was added due to the relatively large population of Asians in that community.

As with the Freeway boys, we hear from these young white males identities that are bordered by white women, African Americans, and gays. While most of these somewhat older men narrate hostile comparisons with others, some offer sympathetic, but still bordered, views. Like cartographers working with different tools on the same geopolitical space, all these men—from western New York and northern New Jersey—sculpt identities as if they were discernably framed by and contrasted through race, gender, and sexuality. As with the teens, reported above, the critique voiced by young adult white men declares the boundaries of acceptable behavior at themselves. By young adulthood, the target site for white male critique shifts from sexuality to work, circling in particular around concerns of Affirmative Action.

INTERVIEWER: What has the experience been for you as a white male?

PETE: For the most part, it hasn't been bad. It's just that right now with these minority quotas, I think more or less, the white male has become the new minority. And that's not to point a finger at the blacks, Hispanics or the women. It's just with all these quotas, instead of hiring the best for the job, you have to hire according to your quota system, which is still wrong.

INTERVIEWER: Do you have any sense of social movements? Like the Civil Rights Movement?

PETE: Civil Rights, as far as I'm concerned, is being way out of proportion.

INTERVIEWER: Talk to me more about that.

PETE: Well, um, granted, um, the Afro-Americans were slaves over two hundred years ago. They were given their freedom. We as a country, I guess you could say, has tried to, well, I can't say all of us, but most of us, have tried to, like, make things a little more equal. Try to smooth over some of the rough spots. You have some of these other, you have some of these militants who are now claiming that after all these years, we still owe them. I think the owing time is over for everybody. Because if we go into that, then the Poles are still owed [he is Polish]. The Germans are still owed. I mean, you're, you're getting cremated, everybody wants to owe somebody. I think it's time to wipe that slate clean.

INTERVIEWER: Umm. Do you think that movement has hurt you as a white male?

PETE: To a small extent.

INTERVIEWER: In what way?

PETE: Because it's, it's all that, um, you have to hire a quota of minorities. And they don't take the best qualified, they take the quota number first . . . so that kind of puts you behind the eight ball before you even start.

INTERVIEWER: Um, um. Has the movement helped you in any way, do you think?

PETE: Not at all. I'm not a minority. So they really didn't do much for me. Well, I'm a minority according to some people now, because they consider the white male now a minority.

•

JOHN: I mean in theory, a whole lot of it [Civil Rights Movement] is good. I feel that it is worthwhile, and there has to be some, not some, there has to be equality between people. And just because of . . . I feel that the federal government sometimes makes these laws or thinks that there's laws that are bad, but they themselves break them. I mean, I look it as where—this is something that has always irked me—taking civil service exams. I feel that, I mean, I should be given a job based on my abilities and knowledge, my background, my schooling, everything as a whole, rather than sometimes a black man has to have a job just because he's black. And really you're saying, you're not just basing it on being black or whether you're a male or female, but that's exactly what they're doing, so it's almost like a double . . .

INTERVIEWER: Do you feel that these movements have helped or hurt you?

JOHN: I would say hurt me.

INTERVIEWER: In what ways?

JOHN: That would be one of them—quotas. I really, I completely disagree with quotas. I don't feel it's, they're fair. I mean, me as a white male, I'm really being pushed, turned into a minority. I mean, it doesn't matter. We have so many blacks working in the police department or in the fire department, or women. And even though, well, say, I'm not just saying this because I'm a white male, but white males, you know, will be pushed, you know, pushed away from the jobs or not given the jobs even thought hey might qualify more so for them, and have more of the capabilities to do the job. And they just won't get it because they are white males. That's the majority; there's a lot of white males, so we're going to give it to the black males or females.

INTERVIEWER: Do you think these movements are important or relevant despite what you've said to me?

JOHN: Yes, yes because, um, I feel they have their place. I wouldn't say completely it should be out of the question. They have their place, where I feel that women can speak with women or children a lot better than men can sometimes, and um, really with the areas of the crime, you have to have blacks and Hispanics working in community programs, so you have to have certain jobs and responsibilities where they can deal with people, like say, with people of their own background, more so than someone who is Irish or German or Polish or something else, because you have to have some of the common background, or maybe say the same upbringing or values, traditions, traditions is a big part of it.

•

TOM: It goes into another subject where blacks, um, I have nothing against blacks. Um, whether you're black, white, you know, yellow, whatever color, whatever race. But I don't like the black movement where, I have black friends. I talk to them and they agree. You know, they consider themselves, you know, there's white trash and there's white, and there's black trash and there's blacks. And the same in any, you know, any race. But as soon as they don't get a job, they right away call, you know, they yell discrimination. That's where I think some of our, you know, politicians come in, too. You have your [council members in Buffalo], and I think they do that. They like to, um, [say] the bad word of discrimination and that. But I think maybe if you went out there and educated yourself—and you know, there's a lot of educated blacks, and you don't hear them yelling discrimination because they've got good jobs. Because they got the knowhow behind them. But the ones that are really lazy don't want it, they, they start yelling discrimination so they can just get the job and they're not even qualified for it. And then they might take it away from, whether it's a, you know, a woman or a guy.

The white male critique of Affirmative Action is that it is not "fair." Privileging blacks, Hispanics, and at times white women, above white males, white men are being set up as the "new minority." It is noteworthy that nowhere in these narratives is there any recognition that white men as a group have historically been privileged, irrespective of individual merit. Mark, for example, is a white firefighter who describes the firehouse as a relatively protected and defended space for working-class whiteness and masculinity. He is certain that minorities have gained access unfairly, but sure that white men gained access through "merit:"

Q: What would you like to see changed about the job?

A: Have probably testing be more well rounded. More straightforward and

fair. It seems to be a court fight every time to take a test. Everybody takes the
same test. I just don't understand why it's so difficult. I understand you have
to have certain minorities on the job and that's only fair, but sometimes I
think that's not fair. It's not the fire department, it's the people that fight it . . .
I think everybody should take the same test and that's it. The way you score
is the way you score.

We hear, from these young white males, a set of identities carved inside,
and against, demographic and political territories. While all of our interviewees are fluent in these comparisons, those who sit at the collapsing "bottom"
of the economy or in sites of fragile employment, rehearse identities splintered
with despair, verbal violence, and hostile comparisons of Self and Other. Others, including those more economically secure, also speak through these traditional contours of identity, but insist that they have detached from the moorings of hostile attitudes and oppositional identities. Even this last group,
however, has little social experience from which to invent novel constructions
of self, as white, working-class, male, and positively engaged with others.
While some men are more generous in their views of race and gender, they
tend to be the more stably employed. Our worry is that they are simply one job
away from the narrations of their more desperate white brothers. With few
noticing that the economy has engendered hostile raced, classed, and gendered
relations of scarcity, these white men are the mouths that speak the American
economic lie. Without an analysis of shifting relations of capital, gender, or
race, they hold black and Latino men, and to a certain extent, white women,
accountable for their white financial disappointments.

THREATENED LOSS OF A
PUBLIC–ALL MALE SCHOOL

The notion of masculinity under siege is not just a part of the lived realities of
poor and working-class white males. Data collected at a public, paramilitary,
southern college present a striking example of how an historically male-only
institution and the young white males with middle-class aspirations who attend, are tenaciously involved in litigation to maintain its tradition of excluding women. We will call this college Military University. This struggle at Military U. illuminates a delicate gender order precariously built upon the the
oppression, denigration, and exclusion of relevant outgroups, and in this case,
namely white women. This understanding is unknowingly narrated by cadets
and administrators and claim that boys can only develop into men in singularly
male spaces. Women are viewed as both weak and powerful objects in who

contaminate and threaten the transition to manhood. Echoing the Freeway data and the Jersey City/Buffalo narratives, the legal defense of the Military University as all-male articulates an institutional discourse of white male entitlement and fragility. A graduate of the Military U., now a law student, laid out this stance critically in his deposition:

> The idea is we have created something virtually perfect, something that creates a whole man, a real man, and there are only certain people who can do this and those people who can't do this are less of a man than you are and you have got to become part of this group. . . . They set up a system by excluding others and making other people feel inferior. (Vergnolle 1992, 70–71)

Two faculty members submitted into evidence a document they titled "The Case for Single Gender Education" in which they wrote:

> The critical issue for the effectiveness of the [Military U.] system is that the components . . . of the system be all male in terms of peer membership. . . . There are at least three elements to this process which are significant for understanding [Military U.]: the breaking away from the mother-dominant home; the establishment of a place within the group; the freedom to explore and discover within the security of the group and safe from female reaction. (Mahan and Mahan, 3)

Located on the southeast coast, with a 150-year-old tradition, this school is viewed as one of the most prestigious colleges in the South. In many cases, there are family histories at this institution, with grandfathers, fathers, and sons among former students. Students and alumni claim that graduates were "insured employment" through the tightly controlled Military U. alumni network and, of course, women "flock like bees to pollen" to Military U. boys. Cadets who graduate are assured successful work and heterosexual relations.

In the Spring of 1993, a young woman then still in high school, had just been accepted for admission. The woman had intentionally omitted any reference to gender on her application, and asked that her teachers and counsellors do the same in their letters of recommendation. Upon "discovering" her gender, the Military U. revoked her acceptance and she, with the ACLU, sued the school for sex discrimination. During the defense, a faculty member described the university as "one of the last bastions of true masculinity left in the United States," a place to be "macho, masculine and objective." Sociologist David Reisman testified to the dangers of admitting women, in the Virginia Military Institute case (a case directly analogous to this lawsuit):

I think that if women were admitted to V.M.I. the whole program would collapse. I cannot imagine women, given the executive qualities we were talking about earlier with reference to Carol Gilligan's work and my own parallel work, that women would, for example, treat rats [first-year men] as rats are treated now at the Virginia Military Institute. They simply wouldn't. Women would not go through the shaving of the head, the other reductions of previous attributes. They can't shed their gender. (1991, 193)

Faculty members also argue that cadets require a "women-free" environment . . . away from the mother dominant home . . . and safe from female reaction" (3). For men to be strong, women need to be absent. Alumni Ronald Vergnolle described how ritualistically these oppositional identities were exercised against women and gays. "[To insult a cadet, others call him] a fag, a woman . . . a sally or a skirt" (1993, 70).

You spend your entire career . . . connoting women with negativism. When you screw up, you are a woman. (81)

•

Every time I did anything wrong at the [Military U.] someone made a point of telling me that I was—with expletives—a woman; you're weak, why don't you go to a woman's school?; you belong in a woman's school. What is the matter, are you having your period? Why can't you do the pushups? Are you a woman? Why don't we get a skirt for you? (84)

Confirming this student's experience, a counselor at the counseling center says:

It's like *Lord of the Flies*. Every group has at least two knobs [first-year men] they harass and intimidate. Ones that are the least bit feminine become "IT" and are treated like shit. If they come to the counseling center for help, and return to the barracks, their commanding officer can demand to know—"Knob, where have you been?" Unable to lie, he would say "Counseling center, Sir!" only to hear, "What, are you a wimp, a fag, or a woman?"

As the boys from Military U. sat at the trial wearing their "Save the Males" buttons, we reflected on their fragility. The 1980s and 1990s marked a time when their women became independent, their jobs became scarce, and their privileged access to public institutions, even Military U., was compromised by the success of equal rights and Affirmative Action. Additionally, traditional bases of white male material power—head of the family, productive worker, and exclusive access to "good" public sector jobs—are disappearing rapidly. Sold out by elites, these young men are in panic and despair. Their reassertions of status reveal a profound fragility masked in the protection of "their women," their fight for "fairness" in the workplace, and their demand for "diversity" among (but not within) educational institutions.

THREATENED LOSS OF COMMUNITY

Thus far, our data have evidenced an eroded sense or privilege among white males which coalesces around formidable sites of identity construction—such as the spheres of sexuality and work. Anger over the felt loss of entitlement, however, does not just occur in single moments in time and space. The battle at Military University, for instance, was to continue to keep the journey from boyhood to manhood intact for future generations of cadets. An ethnographic study conducted by Julia Marusza inside bars located in a white working-class urban neighborhood reveals that white males incorporate their rage into how they have historically come to make sense of their communities and their own place within that continuum.

Due to the large Irish population in this section of the city, we refer to the neighborhood as the Riley Road community. Because of its central location to large steel mills and railroad yards, the Riley Road area was a center of economic prosperity from the turn of the century to the mid to late seventies. Of the men Julia Marusza interviewed in Buffalo for this ethnographic study, all had fathers, uncles, or grandfathers who worked their entire lives in various occupations revolving around steel production or transport. Now the steel mills and railroads are defunct and the area has suffered economically. Today there are very few skilled and unskilled jobs to which these displaced workers and their children can turn. The men that were interviewed work as seasonal landscapers, cleaners, dishwashers, salespeople, part-time window installers, and part-time messengers. All of the men complained of low wages and limited or nonexistent benefits. Interestingly, six out of the seven want to eventually get into careers in law enforcement.

In Halle's (1984) ethnographic study of blue-collar workers at a New Jersey chemical plant, he found that workers from the same plant, by living in a blue-collar neighborhood, were at least partially able to develop a working-class consciousness through their communities. In the case of the Riley Road men who do not have jobs at plants, they are not able to establish a working-class consciousness through their neighborhood. They are, however, aware of their community as defining a large part of who they are and how they live their lives:

MAX: The neighborhood is exactly the same as it has always been. Basically the younger generation coming up is getting the same kind of trouble we were. They are making the same kind of mistakes. I see them on the street corners and they remind me of myself hanging at that same spot five, maybe ten, years ago with my friends.

•

DARRYL: It is a good place to raise a family. Me and my friends used to run around the streets . . . we still do this now, and we probably will when we are fifty. . . . That is how I learned all about life and people. This is our neighborhood.

•

JACK: The neighborhood hasn't changed. We won't let it. The young kids get into trouble; they steal cars at fourteen and fifteen. Then they grow out of it. I learned most of what I know in these streets. I hope to raise my kids here someday. . . . We did all our growing up on Riley.

•

RUSTY: This is a great neighborhood, a real family place. We used to play in the streets, games like release the peddler. It's a fun neighborhood, quiet. . . . I didn't pay much attention in school, but I learned on Riley.

•

PETER: Riley hasn't changed at all. Everybody grew up together. It makes you think; you look down on the little kids and you call them punks. But then you think you were the same way. You see them jumping into trouble. But it's a good neighborhood. It will always be a good place to grow up. . . . We love our neighborhood on Riley.

The Riley Road men feel a sense of history in the streets, ownership of the neighborhood. They also hope to live out their lives in the spaces that comprise the Riley Road community. In addition, the dialogue shows Riley Road men tend to identify with a group of friends at an early age. When asked about their past, they often answer in terms of a group experience. As the men talk about life in the present, it becomes apparent they still consider themselves as a part of a group of friends. On the whole, for these men, community is experienced through a group of friends of similar age and circumstance.

The men of Riley Road reveal that they live with their parents, other family members, and friends. Although their living expenses are relatively low, the men complain of their jobs which they see as dead-end, and their salaries which they see as meager. The men continuously compare themselves to their fathers who in many cases had good plant jobs, were married, and were homeowners by this time in life:

RUSTY: [age 27] I only work part-time, as a messenger for an insurance agency on Riley. It's a crappy job, but I can't find anything better. . . . I still live with my parents because I can't afford anything else. I am glad I have a place to live, but I am really trapped, I guess. Women aren't too impressed if you live at home at my age. . . . My dad was able to get married and buy a house when he was 27. . . . Of course there were good jobs at Republic [steel mill] back then.

•

CHARLIE: [26] I hate my job; it's nothing I can get into. Work the night shift cleaning offices on Riley. . . . [I] would quit, only I have to pay my sister and her husband $200 bucks a month because I live with them. . . . I worry how I will ever be able to buy my own house.

•

JACK: [29] I work full-time washing dishes at Journey's End Suites [motel]. I hate my job, plus there are no benefits. But I have to work to pay the rent. . . . I live above this bar with my brother. My landlord gives me a good deal because I spend so much money at the bar. . . . I am too old for this lifestyle. . . . By this age my dad had a house, a wife, and three kids. . . . I haven't made it because there are no jobs anymore. . . . I never have any extra money.

•

DARRYL: [27] I work installing windows. I got laid off late last fall, but started up again this April. It's an okay job; I work all day with friends and the job is easy. . . . But the job doesn't pay that well, which is a problem because me and my girlfriend and our two-year-old kid rent a house from Sharon's [girlfriend] parents on Riley. . . . I wish I could just buy my own house, but I don't see that happening. . . . I am really just scraping by.

•

PETER: [27] I've been at Murphy's [hardware store] for five years. I started getting benefits two years ago, but not dental, though. . . . I've been renting a place on Riley with a buddy of mine for two years now. . . . I'm glad my rent is cheap and all, but my father was making a lot more than me when he was 27. . . . I never have any spare money.

•

MAX: [26] Working at the dock for Hy-Grade Distributors [paper supplier] is not an ideal job. It's only part-time, so I never have enough cash. . . . My cousin works alongside me on the docks and we rent together, too. . . . What I really want is a good job, a house, and a wife and kids, but I'm not making enough money to save. . . . It makes me so mad.

•

NICK: [30] I can only find part-time junk jobs. It's not the same like during my dad's day, when you could go to any plant and get hired. Even if you were fired, could go to another plant and get hired again. . . . I install windows and load docks for a total of about 35 hours a week and no benefits. . . . I live with a couple of friends. . . . At this rate I'll never be able to buy a house and get married. . . . I'm pissed because I'm thirty and still can't find a job and get my life together.

These men are bitter about their work situations and how their underemployment translates to their lives. With the absence of steady labor jobs, the men of Riley Road complain about what they consider the impossibilities of establishing personal and financial independence. If buying a house and getting married is the true indicator of "making it," they do not foresee this in their immediate future. For the most part, they have a cushion in being able to live, currently, with family or friends. But as far as they see things, that cushion is not going to help them get jobs, get married, or to buy houses.

As Halle (1984) explains, the chemical plant workers he interviewed all saw owning a home as a major goal. Many of those workers were the same as as the Riley Road men, but they had steady plant jobs and many were married and owned homes. Largely, the chemical workers saw owning a home as freedom from a landlord's restrictions. Halle also points out that owning a home seemed to validate the workers' felt economic status. The men he interviewed constantly deferred to discussion on what their homes were worth on today's market, and how their property was appreciating in value; thus, according to Halle, the workers saw themselves as worth something. The chemical workers also proudly talked about the improvements they made to their homes. As they remodeled, they were shaping the space in their houses to conform to the needs of their own personal space. Because the Riley Road men cannot find steady employment, they are, perhaps, denied access to this area of material self-validation and personal expression that the chemical workers found goes with owning a home. Instead, the men of Riley Road are dependent on their family and friends and, as they say, live from paycheck to paycheck.

Among the chemical workers in Halle's (1984) study, there was also a distinction between work time and free time. For the men of Riley Road, the edges are decidedly blurred. Having such an abundance of undefinable time, the group at the bar may provide Riley Road men with a structure that is missing in their lives. Adding more strength to their counterculture, outside of the occasional hunting trip, these men rarely leave their community. It seems their thoughts, as well, mostly center around their bar and street culture. Although there is a tendency for collectivity among these men who are angry at their devalued economic status, without a sense of a collective cultural or labor history, they are not able to constructively critique their place within the larger context of economic restructuring. To this end, the Riley Road men both individually and collectively displace their anger onto others.

The majority of the Riley Road men interviewed say they want jobs in law enforcement. In the group interviews, they talked about what it would be like to be a police officer. These men, however, do not seem to be realistically working toward that goal. Instead, they appear to partially construct masculine identities out of self-created roles as community police. As personally appointed police, they enforce their own laws, demarcated and bordered by race. When asked why they wanted to get into policing, some of the answers were:

DARRYL: Well, jerks come in, drug dealers, thieves, everyone. Most of my friends want to get into law enforcement. . . . I'd love to carry a gun . . . like the show *COPS* . . . that's my idea of power.

•

PETER: Every now and then someone gets chased. The way it is, the people protecting are seen as the bad ones. . . . I'm not racist, but the ones doing the right thing are seen as doing the wrong thing, when they are the ones protecting.

Me and my buddies do this. . . . If I were a cop, then people would see this as right. . . .

•

CHARLIE: The Irish guy with the red hair on *NYPD Blue* is really cool. Women seem to like him.

•

RUSTY: I want to make sure the neighborhood gets cleaned up. Scummy people coming in give a bad impression, a bad image. . . . Everything should look the same, not run-down. Places are going downhill at the ends of the streets. Why should a few people be allowed to lower the property value?

•

JACK: Cop shows got me into it—you know, police enactment TV.

•

NICK: I am not closed minded or anything, but I want violence out of here. Today the East side of [section of Buffalo predominantly populated by African American residents] is like south central Los Angeles. This is why I want to get into law enforcement.

Some of these responses appear to be media inspired. Aronowitz (1992) argues the media cannot be ignored in discussions about identity formation. He contends a working-class identity has been eroded to such a degree that presently there is no working-class identity in the media for white working-class males to identify with. This group's representation is displaced into the realm of police TV shows, according to Aronowitz, in which overly masculine characters convene in bars, torn between fighting crime, talking about women, and controlling the streets.

The Riley Road men are not seeing their daily economic and personal struggles on the screen. Instead, they are seeing the familiar barrooms and the friendship the policemen share. Aronowitz claims these free spaces in bars with male friends reflect the kind of working-class male solidarity of days past, when men would stop at the bar after their shift and discuss life and union talk. Today, these overly masculine representations of police in the media are what the Riley Road men aspire toward, as they finally find a venue in which their embattled masculine and white identities can be embodied. It is frightening, indeed, to think about how these men may enact their reappropriated police roles.

CONCLUSIONS

Our data worry us. Across data sets, we hear these young white men in pain from economic and social dislocations, and blaming those most socially disempowered for their displacement. We worry that white working-class men have been robbed, not by people of color, white women, or gays/lesbians, but by a culture that promised them a modest spot on the social ladder and then changed the rules. We worry that these white men have little substance out of which to craft alternative identities and fill it instead with the noise of opposition, denigration and raced/gendered violence. They mimic, all too well, Cheryl Harris's critical analysis, *Whiteness as Property!*

> Within the worlds of de jure and de facto segregation, whiteness has value, whiteness is valued, and whiteness is expected to be valued in law. The legal affirmation of whiteness and white privilege allowed expectations that originated in injustice to be naturalized and legitimated. The relative economic, political, and social advantages dispensed to whites under systematic white supremacy in the United States were reinforced through patterns of oppression of Blacks and Native Americans. Materially, these advantages became institutionalized privileges, and ideologically, they became part of the settled expectations of the whites—a product of the unalterable original bargain. The law masks what is chosen as natural; it obscures the consequences of social selection as inevitable. The result is that the distortions in social relations are immunized from truly effective intervention, because the existing inequities are obscured and rendered nearly invisible. The existing state of affairs is considered neutral and fair, however unequal and unjust it is in substance. (1777, 1778)

The white males in these studies arguably consider the privilege that has historically accompanied their whiteness and maleness as "natural law." They contend, therefore, that they are just and right in their anger over the collapse of the "natural order." This theme strongly pulls across all our data, and it is not difficult to imagine as the logic among white working-class males in other communities. Due to institutionalized racism in the United States, which structures public schooling, the military, the legal system, and so on, it is not surprising that the men of Riley Road felt that they were sanctioned to create and enforce their own laws for the "good" of their community, laws which work toward the maintenance of white power. In the final analysis, none of these narrations should be ignored, as white working-class male anger toward loss can and does manifest in violent ways.

We are, however, at the same time challenged by these data. The time has come to shift the sands so that whiteness and maleness are reinvented. Adult women and men must invite and invent pedagogies that begin to unscramble various forms of masculinities for young boys and men. We can imagine such talk within schools but also much beyond. Across generations and within them. Carving out safe spaces, white males need to analyze critically the banner of privilege they once carried, and have now lost, and the sites of white masculinity from which productive identities can be spawned. All other "demographic groups" have begun this work of consciousness raising and critical identity reformation. Time has come for analysis by white males and critical coalition work. We look to community based organizations, athletic clubs, churches, arts and theater groups to provoke such conversations for and with boys and men. At the same time that institutions must hold males accountable for their supremacist behaviors across gender and race, they must create occasions in which the tough talk of identity work can happen for the young boys who were merely "doing the white thing," were sold out, and remain ever loyal to the American dream.

NOTE

This study was partly funded by the Spenser Foundation.

REFERENCES

Aronowitz, F. 1992. *The Politics of Identity: Class, Culture and Social Movements.* New York: Routledge.

Halle, D. 1984. *America's Working Man.* Chicago: University of Chicago Press.

Fine, M., and J. Addelston. In press. "On sameness and difference." In S. Wilkenson, ed., *Feminist Social Psychology II*. London: Sage.

Harris, Cheryl. *Whiteness as Property.*

Marusza, J. 1994. "White Working Class Males and the Possibilities of Collective Anger: Patroling Reilly Road." Unpublished manuscript.

Newman, K. 1993. *Declining Fortunes: The Withering of the American Dream*. New York: Basic Books.

Suttles, G. 1972. *The Social Construction of Communities*. Chicago: University of Chicago Press.

Mahan, A., and T. Mahan. 1993. "The Citadel: The Case for Single Gender Education." Unpublished manuscript submitted on behalf of the defendants in *Johnson v. Jones*. United States District Court: Charleston Division.

Riesman, D. 1991. Deposition in *United States of America v. Commonwealth of Virginia et al.* United States District Court: Roanoke Division.

Vergnolle, R. 1993. Deposition in *Johnson v. Jones*. United States District Court: Charleston Division.

Weis, L. 1993. "White Male Working-Class Youth: An Exploration of Relative Privilege and Loss." In L. Weis and M. Fine, eds., *Beyond Silenced Voices: Class, Race, and Gender in United States Schools*. Albany: State University of New York Press.

CONTRIBUTORS

JUDI ADDELSTON is a Visiting Assistant Professor of Social Psychology and Women's Studies at Rollins College.

CARL L. BANKSTON III is Assistant Professor of Sociology at the University of Southwestern Louisiana.

DAVID R. M. BECK is Assistant Professor of History and Director of the Tribal Research Center at NAES (Native American Educational Services) College, Chicago.

KATHRYN BORMAN is Professor of Anthropology at the University of South Florida.

DENNIS CARLSON is Associate Professor of Educational Leadership and Director of the Center for Education and Cultural Studies at Miami University.

ANN LOCKE DAVIDSON is a Postdoctoral Fellow at the Learning Research and Development Center at the University of Pittsburgh.

MICHELLE FINE is Professor of Social Psychology at the City University of New York Graduate Center.

SIGNITHIA FORDHAM is Assistant Professor of Education at the University of Maryland, Baltimore County.

MICHEL S. LAGUERRE is Professor of African American Studies at the University of California, Berkeley.

KAREN LEONARD is Professor of Anthropology at the University of California, Irvine.

JULIA MARUSZA is a Graduate Student in Sociology of Education at the State University of New York, Buffalo.

PATRICIA PESSAR is Associate Professor of American Studies at Yale University.

MAXINE SELLER is Professor of History of Education at the State University of New York, Buffalo.

MARCELO M. SUAREZ-OROZCO is Professor of Education for Learning and Teaching and Professor of Human Development and Psychology at Harvard University.

PATRICIA TIMM is a Public Policy Mediator at the Center for the Resolution of Disputes, Cincinnati.

IRENE VILLANUEVA is a Lecturer/Supervisor in Teacher Education at the University of California, San Diego.

LOIS WEIS is Professor of Sociology of Education at the State University of New York, Buffalo.

MIN ZHOU is Assistant Professor of Sociology at the University of California, Los Angeles.

INDEX

JOHN
CIARDI

a bibliography

John Ciardi at Bread Loaf in 1955

JOHN CIARDI

a bibliography

by *William White*

with a note by John Ciardi

DETROIT
WAYNE STATE UNIVERSITY PRESS
1959

•

Of this edition, 550 copies have been issued
in connection with an exhibition of Mr. Ciardi's
MSS and books (from the Feinberg Collection)
in the Wayne State University Library, 1 to 14
May 1959, and Mr. Ciardi's lecture, sponsored
by the Detroit Public Library, 5 May 1959.

Contents

Introduction

Although Ernest Hemingway wrote Louis Henry Cohn, ' I think it is all balls to publish bibliographies of living writers,' the novelist did help Captain Cohn with *A Bibliography of the Works of Ernest Hemingway* (New York: Random House, 1931) ; and such compilations of living authors are certainly no new things. Witness Louis and Esther Mertins's *The Intervals of Robert Frost: A Critical Bibliography* (Berkeley and Los Angeles: University of California Press, 1947) ; Jack Potter's *A Bibliography of John Dos Passos* (Chicago: Normandie House, 1950) ; Raymond Toole Stott's *Maughamiana: The Writings of W. Somerset Maugham* (Garden City: Doubleday & Company, Inc., 1950) ; and Donald Gallup's *T. S. Eliot: A Bibliography* (London: Faber & Faber Limited, 1952). So now that John Ciardi has written six collections of poetry, translated into English verse Dante's *Inferno,* and edited a successful anthology of modern American poems, it is well for his own bibliography to be published. And as he is making an address at the Detroit Public Library on 5 May 1959 and his MSS and books (from the Feinberg Collection) are on exhibit at the Wayne State University Library from 1 to 14 May 1959, ' If it were done when 'tis done, then 'twere well / It were done quickly.'

5

The present bibliography is not complete: the briefest bibliographical descriptions are given of Mr. Ciardi's eight books, only the poems and criticism in the most easily available periodicals are listed, only a selective list of biographical and critical material is included, and the MSS which are described are from the collection of Mr. Charles E. Feinberg of Detroit. But it is hoped all this will give a representative view of Mr. Ciardi's work to date.

In the preparation of this bibliography, Mr. Ciardi has been very helpful, but wrote:

> When I first broke into the magazines, I saved every thin little issue of every evanescent little magazine that had immortalized itself with a couple of my lines—magazines, newspapers, incidentalia. Before very long I had more feet of paper than I could afford shelf space to, and I threw the whole bloody batch out. Never since have I kept a record of little magazine publications. I usually remember which poems have been published in the little mags, and I always of course remember which I have been paid for—once or twice I've been afraid I had let the same thing out to two places, but it always worked out I hadn't—and that's about all I've had to work on.
>
> I'm not a very systematic person. I do have some pack-rat instincts but they are slovenly, too. Over the course of two years, I could prowl various boxes and set aside forgotten copies of magazines in which I have had poems; but I simply have no way of guiding anything like a complete bibliography of my things in little mags—in any organized way, that is.

Thus the list of poems in periodicals begins with the first one he was paid for, in *Poetry* in 1939, followed by a *Yale Review* poem in 1940. Before these there were a lot of juvenilia in undergraduate magazines at Bates College in 1933 and 1934 and at Tufts, to which Mr. Ciardi transferred in 1935. At the University of Michigan, he published in *Perspectives*. In 1940 Louis Adamic, one of the founders of *Common Ground*, reprinted a poem from *Homeward to America,* followed by three other poems in the same magazine in the next two years. Among other periodicals in which Ciardi material has been published, but which are not listed below, are *Poetry* (Australia), *The Poet* (Scotland), and *Yank.* There may well be others.

Finally, the poet writes: 'I have had some pieces translated into French (*Journal des Poètes,* Brussels), into Greek in 1957 in something called *Nea Estia,* into various Italian mags (no trace) and newspapers (less trace).'

These things are mentioned here as evidence of Mr. Ciardi's versatility and productiveness—if such evidence were needed for the Poetry Editor of *The Saturday Review,* the Director of the Bread Loaf Writers Conference, Professor of English at Rutgers University, critic, translator, and most important of all, poet.

WILLIAM WHITE

Wayne State University
30 March 1959

Note

by John Ciardi

When a friend of mine heard that Charles Feinberg was arranging for a bibliography of my writing, he said: 'But you're not even dead yet!'

'Knowing Charles Feinberg,' I told him, 'is better than being dead.'

A good friend is not only better than being dead; he is the best thing to be alive for. If Charles Feinberg's enthusiasm for this bibliography does nothing to establish him as a critic, it will do that much more to testify to his love of the arts.

A bibliography does seem a portentous thing to carry around the neck. Or is it more like incipient rigor mortis? It is in any case a recognition, and because no artist gets enough recognition ever, I must endorse all that comes—to me, or to anyone else who—whether he works badly or well—works seriously to make something.

And suddenly I realise I am paraphrasing Aaron Copeland. A few years ago, when he received a Gold Medal from the American Academy he said (approximately): 'Had anyone told me when I was a student in Paris that an Academy would some day give me a Gold Medal, I'd have laughed. Now, how-

9

ever, I find myself thinking every artist deserves a Gold Medal—and I'm very happy to get mine today.'

A bibliography is a bit more nearly like a bronze casket than it is like a gold medal, but I get one bonus out of it. I have always been poor at keeping files and records. I seem always to have lived in an avalanche of paper, and periodically I have flared up and chucked the whole mess out. Then, from time to time, I'd come on a little piece I had completely forgotten, and that always troubled me. No artist should throw away anything. Good or bad, what he does is part of himself, and he needs it all to know himself by. I am especially curious, therefore, to see what William White has dug up for inclusion. I hope his listing will help me remember some things I have lost. To him and to Charles Feinberg, my warm gratitude. I am looking forward to the finished work—how many people, after all, get a chance to go to their own funeral?

Chronology

1916   Born, Boston, Mass., 24 June

1921   Moved with mother and three sisters to Medford, Mass., two years after his father's death

1933–34   Attended Bates College, Lewiston, Maine, leaving in sophomore year

1935–38   Attended Tufts College, Medford, Mass., B. A., *magna cum laude*, 1938

1938–39   Attended University of Michigan, M. A., 1939

1939   Avery Hopwood Award in Poetry, University of Michigan

1940   *Homeward to America*

1940–42   Instructor in English, University of Kansas City

1942–45   United States Army Air Corps, including combat service on Saipan as aerial gunner; discharged October 1945 as technical sergeant

1943   Oscar Blumenthal Prize, *Poetry Magazine*

1944   Eunice Tietjens Memorial Prize, *Poetry Magazine*

1945–46   Instructor in English, University of Kansas City

1946   Married Judith Hostetter, 28 July

11

1946	Levinson Prize, *Poetry Magazine*
1946–48	Instructor in English, Harvard University
1947	*Other Skies*
1948–53	Briggs-Copeland Assistant Professor of English, Harvard University
1949–	Poetry Editor, Twayne Publishers, later Executive Editor
1949	*Live Another Day*
1950	*Mid-Century American Poets*
1951	Lecturer, Salzburg Seminar in American Studies
1951	*From Time to Time*
1952	Phi Beta Kappa Poem, Harvard University
1952	Elected Fellow, American Academy of Arts and Sciences
1954	Dante's *Inferno*
1955	*As If*
1955–	Director, Bread Loaf Writers Conference (on staff since 1947)
1956	Prix de Rome
1956–	Poetry Editor, *Saturday Review*
1957	Elected Fellow, National Institute of Arts and Letters
1957–	Professor of English, Rutgers University (on staff since 1953)
1958	*I Marry You*
1958	Elected President, College English Association
1959	*How Does a Poem Mean?*

Books by John Ciardi

Homeward to America
1940

JOHN CIARDI / HOMEWARD (in red) / TO AMERICA
(in red) / Winner / of the / Hopwood Poetry Prize /
1939 / NEW YORK / HENRY HOLT AND COMPANY /

x, 62 pp. $8\frac{5}{8}$ by $5\frac{5}{8}$ inches. Issued in red cloth. Stamped in
gold on front cover: (decoration) / HOMEWARD / TO /
AMERICA / (decoration) /. Stamped in gold on spine, reading
downwards: (star) HOMEWARD TO AMERICA · CIARDI ·
HOLT (star) /.

Contains:
    Letter to Mother
    Man Stranded
    The Foolish Wing
    Winter Music
    Native Only
    Continent's Edge
    To Westward
    Night Freight, Michigan

Note: Certain poems in this collection first appeared in *Poetry* and *Perspectives*. Most of the poems are from a MS awarded the major poetry prize in the Avery Hopwood and Jule Hopwood Awards Contest for 1939 at the University of Michigan.

Other Skies
1947

Other Skies / *by* JOHN CIARDI / The Innocent keep other
skies. / We have much to learn. / SUDDENLY WHERE / SQUAD-
RONS TURN / *An Atlantic Monthly Press Book* / Little,
Brown and Company · Boston / 1947 / (The whole enclosed within a rule within a decorated rule)

[x], 84 pp. 8⅛ by 5½ inches. Issued in blue cloth. Stamped
in dark blue on front cover: publisher's device. Stamped in
dark blue on spine, reading downwards: *Other Skies POEMS
BY* JOHN CIARDI / *Atlantic* / Little, / Brown / (Last three
lines read across spine).

Contains:

Record Crowds at Beaches
Song
Cryptogram for My Students
Ode for School Convocation
The Sound Track Jumps
Suddenly Where Squadrons Turn
On Sending Home My Civilian Clothes
Camptown
Night Piece for My Twenty-seventh Birthday
Poem for a Soldier's Girl
Mechanic
Take-off over Kansas
Goodmorning with Light
Reveille for My Twenty-eighth Birthday
Reflections While Oiling a Machine Gun
Death of a Bomber
Reverie During Briefing
Port of Aerial Embarkation
Saipan
Ritual for Singing Bat

15

Note: Certain poems in this collection first appeared in *The Atlantic Monthly, The New Republic, The New Yorker, Poetry* (Australia), *Poetry, The Tuftonian, The University of Kansas City Review, War Poets, The Yale Review,* and *Yank.* Some of the poems were awarded by *Poetry* the Blumenthal Prize (1943), the Eunice Tietjens Memorial Prize (1944), and the Levinson Prize (1946).

Live Another Day
1949

Live Another Day / POEMS / BY / JOHN CIARDI / *I have
eaten all my bait but my line is out:* / *If some foolish fish
will bite metal* / *I may live another day.* / TWAYNE PUB-
LISHERS / 42 BROADWAY .. NEW YORK 4 /.

88 pp. 8½ by 5⅜ inches. Issued in reddish brown cloth.
Stamped in gold on front cover: LIVE ANOTHER DAY /
John Ciardi /. Stamped in gold on spine, reading downwards:
John Ciardi · LIVE ANOTHER DAY · *Twayne Publishers* /.

Contains:

> Foreword to the Reader of (Some) General Culture [prose]
> To Judith Asleep
> A Drive Through Spring
> Union Station
> Three Eggs Up
> Dead Pigeon on South Street
> Metropolitan Ice Co.
> Sunday Afternoon Near the Naval Air Base
> Rock Island Line
> The Pilot in the Jungle
> Stone Works
> Chorus
> The Captain Is Asleep
> Letter from a Rubber Raft
> Results of an Action
> Homecoming—Massachusetts
> To My Students: Last Class, Last Words
> Vale
> Philosophical Poem
> A Visit to Aunt Francesca
> Prologue for a Play
> For My Nephew Going to Bed

17

Morning in the Park
In the Year of Many Conversions and the Private Soul
The Convert
On Flying to a Political Convention
Poem for My Thirty-Second Birthday
A Christmas Carol
Christmas Eve
New Year's Eve
Composition for a Nativity
Portrait—The Men of the Family
Mule
.22
Harvest
Survival in Missouri
Hawk
Letter from a Metaphysical Countryside
Letter to Virginia Johnson
Filippo Argenti
Letter to Dante
A Guide to Poetry
Notes [prose]

Note: This collection also contains poems in the dedication and in four of the section headings. Certain poems in the collection first appeared in *The Atlantic, The New Yorker, Poetry,* and *The University of Kansas City Review.*

Mid-Century American Poets
1950

EDITED *by* JOHN CIARDI / *Mid-Century* / *American* / *Poets* / (dot) / (rule) / *Twayne Publishers, Inc. New York 4* / (The whole enclosed within a rule within a rule)

xxxv, 300 pp. $8\frac{3}{8}$ by $5\frac{1}{4}$ inches. Stamped in pale blue on front cover: MID-CENTURY / AMERICAN / POETS /. Stamped in white on spine, reading downwards: MID-CENTURY AMERICAN POETS /.

Contains:

Foreword [prose]

[Poems and introductory remarks by Richard Wilbur, Peter
  Viereck, Muriel Rukeyser, Theodore Roethke, Karl
  Shapiro, Winfield Townley Scott, John Frederick
  Nims, E. L. Mayo, Robert Lowell, Randall Jarrell,
  John Holmes, Richard Eberhart, Elizabeth Bishop,
  Delmore Schwartz]

To the Reader of (Some) General Culture [prose]

Elegy Just in Case

To Judith Asleep

V-J Day

On a Photo of Sgt. Ciardi a Year Later

Ode for the Burial of a Citizen

The Pilot in the Jungle

Poem for My Thirty-Second Birthday

Vale

Morning in the Park

In the Year of Many Conversions and the Private Soul

Composition for a Nativity

Note: Mr. Ciardi's poems in this volume, which he edited,
and his introductory remarks to them are from *Other Skies*
and *Live Another Day*. His long foreword is printed here for
the first time.

From Time to Time

1951

THE TWAYNE LIBRARY OF MODERN POETRY / FROM
TIME TO TIME / JOHN CIARDI / TWAYNE PUB-
LISHERS, INC. / NEW YORK /

84 pp. 8 by 5¼ inches. Issued in blue cloth. Stamped in gold
on spine, reading downwards: JOHN CIARDI FROM TIME
TO TIME TWAYNE /.

Contains:

Foreword
The Lamb
Home Revisted: Midnight
Manocalzata (Gloved Hand)
The Evil Eye
Three Photos of Me on My Mother's Dresser, My Image
    in Her Mirror
Mystic River
Image of Man as a Gardner after Two World Wars
Monday Morning: London
Elegy I
Elegy II
Elegy III, Cavalcante
Fragment of a Bas Relief
Credo
The Extraction of Concept from Nature
At a Concert of Music Honoring the Dead in Korea
Midnight on a Side Street
Man in Bed with Asthma
Newsreel
A Box Comes Home
The Cow
The Cartographer of Meadows
Annals
The History of Something
Elegy in a Cube
My General's Face
Love Poem
Gulls from a Fantail
Improvisation at Marblehead
High Tension Lines Across a Landscape
Shore Piece
The Size of a Universe
The Clock in the Mirror
Two Songs for a Gunner

March Morning
My Father's Watch
Landscapes of My Name
Anatomy Lab
Joe with a Wooden Leg
Heatwave
Elegy for Sam
Childe Horvald to the Dark Tower Came
Memorial Day
Laing's Goat
Another Comedy

Note: Certain poems in this collection first appeared in *The Atlantic, The Beloit Quarterly, Harper's, The New Yorker, The University of Kansas City Review,* and *The Harvard Advocate.*

Dante's Inferno
1954

DANTE ALIGHIERI / The / Inferno / *Translated in Verse by* / JOHN CIARDI / Historical Introduction by A. T. M[a]cAllister / 1954 / *Rutgers University Press* / NEW BRUNSWICK NEW JERSEY /.

288 pp. 8 by $5\frac{1}{4}$ inches. Issued in brown marbled paper covered boards with a black cloth backstrip. Lettered in gold on front cover: DANTE'S / *Inferno* /. Stamped in gold on spine: (decoration) / DANTE'S / *Inferno* / (decoration) / CIARDI / (three decorations) / RUTGERS / (decoration) /.

Note: A paperback edition from the same plates was issued at the same time: DANTE ALIGHIERI / (decorated rule) / THE INFERNO / *a verse rendering for the modern reader* / *by* JOHN CIARDI / Historical Introduction by A. T. Mac-Allister / (publisher's device) / A MENTOR BOOK / Published by THE NEW AMERICAN LIBRARY /.

As If
1955

AS IF / *Poems New and Selected* / John Ciardi / RUTGERS UNIVERSITY PRESS / *New Brunswick, New Jersey,* 1955 /.

ix, 143 pp. $8\frac{1}{4}$ by $5\frac{1}{4}$ inches. Issued in half gray paper covered boards and half red cloth. Stamped in white on spine, reading downwards: Ciardi AS IF RUTGERS /.

Contains:

To Judith
The Health of Captains
Poem for My Twenty-Ninth Birthday
Elegy for Kurt Porjescz
Elegy Just in Case
Sea Burial
V-J Day
On a Photo of Sgt. Ciardi a Year Later
Two Songs for a Gunner
The Lamb
The Evil Eye
My Father's Watch
Mystic River
Elegy
Home Revisted: Midnight
Days
Elegy for Sandro
Thursday
A Variation on Some Lines
Survival in Missouri
To My Father
Three Views of a Mother
Poem for My Thirty-Ninth Birthday
Doctor Faustus

A Shore, Half in a Dream
Fragments from Italy
Gray Sand, Black Stone, Steel Water, and Figures
Naples

Note: Certain poems in this collection first appeared in *Antioch Review, Atlantic, Beloit Quarterly, Colorado Review, Epoch, Harper's, Inventario* (Naples), *Kenyon Review, Ladies Home Journal, Nation, New Orleans Poetry Journal, New Yorker, Patterns, Pennsylvania Literary Review, Poetry, Quixote, Venture I, Volusia Review*, and *Yale Review*. Others were selected from Mr. Ciardi's *Other Skies, Live Another Day*, and *From Time to Time*. There have been two editions of *As If*.

I Marry You
1958

I MARRY YOU / *A Sheaf of Love Poems* / John Ciardi / RUTGERS UNIVERSITY PRESS / *New Brunswick, New Jersey*, 1958 /.

viii, 44 pp. 8¼ by 5¼ inches. Issued in half tan decorated paper covered boards and half brown cloth. Stamped in white on spine, reading downwards: Ciardi I MARRY YOU RUTGERS /.

Contains:

Men Marry What They Need. I Marry You
Snowy Heron
Epithalamion After a War
To Judith Asleep
Morning: I Know Perfectly How in a Minute You Will
    Stretch and Smile
Sometimes the Foundering Fury
The Stills and Rapids of Your Nakedness
The Deaths about You When You Stir in Sleep

24

Looking over the Rail of Ponte Sant' Angelo as a Guide
 Goes By with His Flock in Trail
I Look through My Dead Friend's Eyes at the House of Love
March Morning
Two Egrets
A Thanks That Flesh is Sad
In the Rich Farmer's Field
The Deaths They Are, Those Great Eyes from the Air
Most Like an Arch This Marriage
The Stone without Edges Has Not Been Mined
For My Son John
Two Poems for Benn
That Summer's Shore
Ten Years Ago When I Played at Being Brave
A Dawn Twelve Years After a War: I Sit, the Children
 Sleep
Letter from an Empty House
A Suite for Love
What World It Is the Crocodile May Know
Letter from a Death Bed

Note: Certain poems in this collection first appeared in the *Atlantic, Ladies Home Journal*, and *Poetry*. Others were selected from Mr. Ciardi's *Live Another Day, From Time to Time*, and *As If*. There have been two editions of *I Marry You*.

How Does a Poem Mean?
1959

HOW DOES A POEM MEAN? (decoration) / JOHN CIARDI / *Rutgers University* / *Part Three of* AN INTRODUCTION TO LITERATURE / *by Herbert Barrows, Hubert Heffner, / John Ciardi, and Wallace Douglas* / HOUGHTON MIFFLIN COMPANY / Boston · The Riverside Press Cambridge / (Title covers two pages, with decoration of harp, book, quill and ink, and wreathed head in vertical column on part of left page) xiii, 663-1022 pp. $8\frac{1}{4}$ by $5\frac{3}{8}$ inches. Issued in blue paperback. Lettered on front cover: *How Does a / Poem Mean?* / (decoration in squares similar to title-page) / JOHN CIARDI / (Title and author in white, decoration in black). Lettered on spine, reading downwards: CIARDI *How Does a Poem Mean?* H · M · C · / (Title in white, author in black, publisher's initials in black across spine).

Contains: An Introductory Note, eight essays of various lengths for each chapter, a running commentary on poetry, and more than two hundred poems by English and American authors, selected and edited by Mr. Ciardi.

Note: This paperback edition is from the cloth-bound edition of *An Introduction to Literature* (Boston: Houghton Mifflin Company, 1939, 1331 pp.), in four parts, under the general editorship of Gordon N. Ray. The other parts are ' Reading the Short Story,' ' The Nature of Drama,' and ' The Character of Prose.'

In the Year of the Longest Cadillac
1959

[To be published by Rutgers University Press.]

The Reason for the Pelican
1959

[To be published by J. B. Lippincott Company.]

Material by John Ciardi in Books

New Poets. Prairie City, Illinois: The Press of James A. Decker, 1941. [Contains 13 poems by John Ciardi, pp. 19-31: 'George Washington Bridge,' 'Time Is The Late Train Into Albany,' 'Song,' 'Boy Or Girl,' 'I Warn You, Father Smith,' 'VIII. *from* Elegy For The First America,' 'Joe Hill, the Swede,' 'Elegy: For You, Father,' 'Spring In Statue Square,' 'Cryptogram For My Pupils,' 'The Sound Track Jumps,' 'Elegy For The Face At Your Elbow,' 'Museum.']

Compass: A Quarterly Anthology of Modern Poetry. Edited by Tom Boggs. Prairie City, Illinois: The Press of James A. Decker, 1941. [No. 7, April 1941, contains 2 poems by John Ciardi, pp. 25-26: 'Song for the Face at Your Elbow,' 'Awakening' *from* 'Elegy: For You, Father.' 'Song' is a misprint for 'Elegy.' On p. 50, among 'Credos: What Some of the Poets Believe About Poetry,' is a statement of two long paragraphs by John Ciardi: 'I Believe in God, the Father Almighty, Mr. Boggs.']

Witches Three. 'Conjure Wife,' by Fritz Lieber; 'There Shall Be No Darkness,' by James Bush; and 'The Blue Star,' by Fletcher Pratt. Introduction by John Ciardi. New York: Twayne Publishers, 1952.

La Cucina: The Complete Italian Cookbook. By Rose L. Sorce. New York: Twayne Publishers, 1953. [Contains an introduction by John Ciardi.]

An Introduction to Literature. In Four Parts: ' Reading the Short Story,' by Herbert Barrows; ' The Nature of Drama,' by Hubert Heffner; ' How Does a Poem Mean,' by John Ciardi; and ' The Character of Prose,' by Wallace Douglas. Boston: Houghton Mifflin Company, 1959. [The section of the anthology edited, with commentary, by Mr. Ciardi appears on pp. 663-1022. This was also issued separately in paperback with the title, *How Does a Poem Mean?*]

Poems by John Ciardi in Periodicals

'Letter for Those Who Grew Up Together,' *Poetry*, LV (November 1939), 69.

'Museum,' *Yale Review, n. s.* XXIX (March 1940), 530-531.

'Letter to Mother,' *Common Ground*, I (No. 1, 1940), 18.

'On a Photograph of a German Soldier Dead in Poland,' *Poetry*, LVI (July 1940), 182-183.

'Boston: North End,' *Common Ground*, I (No. 3, 1941), 13.

'Letter for My Pupils,' *Yale Review*, n. s. XXX (March 1941), 481-482.

'Hometown,' 'Massachusetts Bay,' *Poetry*, LIX (October 1941), 20-21.

'Ode for School Convocation,' *New Republic*, CV (8 December 1941), 802.

'Long Wharf: Boston,' *Common Ground*, II (No. 2, 1942), 7.

'Love in Coal Alley,' *Atlantic*, CLXIX (February 1942), 245.

'Vision for Avenue N,' *New Mexico Quarterly Review*, XII (August 1942), 340.

'Aubade,' 'Poem from a Hired Room,' 'Love Makes No Music,' *Poetry*, LXI (October 1942), 372-374.

'Fourth of July,' *Common Ground*, II (No. 4, 1942), 42.

'Ballad of How Adam Saw It,' 'Suddenly Where Squadrons

Turn,' 'Elegy for Lucasta,' *Yale Review*, n. s. XXXII (December 1942), 237-239.

'Ballad of How Adam Saw It,' 'Night Mail,' 'Record Crowds at Beaches,' 'Poem for a Soldier's Girl,' 'Girls Going to Church,' *Poetry*, LXII (April 1943), 26-31.

'Night Piece for My 27th Birthday,' 'Mission,' 'Night Celestial,' *Poetry*, LXIII (November 1943), 59-63.

'On Sending Home My Civilian Clothes,' *New Yorker*, XX (18 March 1944), 45.

'Song: The Green Girl Going from Surf to Sand,' *New Yorker*, XX (3 June 1944), 20.

'Reveille for My 28th Birthday,' 'Reflections While Oiling a Machine Gun,' 'Mission,' 'Vagary of the Simple Heart,' 'Monday Morning Reveille,' 'First Snow on an Airfield,' 'Summer Evening,' *Poetry*, LXIV (July 1944), 179-187.

'Mechanic,' *Atlantic*, CLXXIV (October 1944), 73.

'On My Nephew's Globe Bank,' *Yale Review*, n. s. XXXIV (December 1944), 225-226.

'Pine Hill,' *Atlantic*, CLXXV (February 1945), 87.

'Reverie During Briefing,' 'Elegy for a Seaman,' 'Goodmorning with Light,' 'P-51,' 'Journal,' *Poetry*, LXVI (May 1945), 85-91.

'Death of a Bomber,' 'Elegy Just in Case,' *Atlantic*, CLXXV (May 1945), 66-67.

'Letter from an Island,' *Atlantic*, CLXXVI (September 1945), 60-61.

'Poem for My 29th Birthday,' *Poetry*, LXVII (January 1946), 192-195.

'Wafflebutt,' *Atlantic*, CLXXVII (March 1946), 104.

'Chelsea Naval Hospital,' *New Yorker*, XXII (2 March 1946), 30.

'Cape Cod,' *New Yorker*, XXII (17 August 1946), 69.

'Hometown After a War,' 'Balancing Act,' 'Ode for the Burial of a Citizen,' 'Serenade in a Drugstore,' 'Poem for My Thirtieth Birthday,' *Poetry*, LXIX (October 1946), 1-9.

'Prosthetic Ward,' *New Yorker*, XXII (16 November 1946), 38.

'House of Many Clocks,' *New Yorker*, XXII (23 November 1946), 34.

'A Christmas Carol,' *New Yorker*, XXII (14 December 1946), 50.

'On a Photo of Sgt. Ciardi, a Year Later,' *New Yorker*, XXII (18 January 1947), 34.

'Winter Solstice,' *New Yorker*, XXIII (22 February 1947), 48.

'Letter to Virginia Johnson,' *Poetry*, LXX (June 1947), 117-123. [See pp. 146-150.]

'To My Students: Last Class, Last Words,' *New Yorker*, XXIII (7 June 1947), 40.

'Summer Night,' *Saturday Review of Literature*, XXX (9 August 1947), 17.

'Homecoming, Massachusetts,' *New Yorker*, XXIII (30 August 1947), 30.

'A Visit to Aunt Francesca,' *Atlantic*, CLXXX (September 1947), 104.

'Chorus,' *New Yorker*, XXIII (30 September 1947), 38.

'Prologue for a Play,'*New Yorker*, XXIII (8 November 1947), 36.

'Christmas Eve,' *New Yorker*, XXIII (27 December 1947), 56.

'New Year's Eve,' *New Yorker*, XXIII (3 January 1948), 24.

'To Judith,' *Poetry*, LXXI (February 1948), 240-243.

'Hawk,' *Harper's*, CXCVI (March 1948), 249.

'Philosophical Poem,' *New Yorker*, XXIV (17 April 1948), 28.

'Business Failure,' *New Yorker*, XXIV (22 May 1948), 32.

'Sunday Near a Naval Air Base,' *Atlantic*, CLXXXII (July 1948), 37.

'Population 302, Speed Limit 20,' *New Yorker*, XXIV (7 August 1948), 28.

'Halloween,' *Yale Review*, n. s. XXXVIII (September 1948), 28.

'Rain Tonight and Tomorrow,' *New Yorker*, XXIV (2 October 1948), 34.

'Fruit Salad,' *Atlantic*, CLXXXII (November 1948), 122-124.

'.22,' *New Yorker*, XXIV (4 December 1948), 32.

'Laing's Goat,' *Harper's,* CXCVIII (February 1949), 52.

'The Turtle,' 'Window Dresser,' 'Epilogue for Any Bedtime Story,' 'Sighs for Helen, Never Mrs. Poe,' *University of Kansas City Review,* XVI (Winter 1949), 126-128.

'Three Eggs Up,' 'Metropolitan Ice Co.,' 'To Judith Asleep,' *Poetry,* LXXIV (April 1949), 16-20.

'Webster's Collegiate,' *New Yorker,* XXV (7 May 1949), 38.

'For My Nephew Going to Bed,' *New Yorker,* XXV (28 May 1949), 32.

'Vale,' *New Yorker,* XXV (25 June 1949), 26.

'Letter to Harry Winner,' *University of Kansas City Review,* XV (Spring 1949), 164-166.

'Letter from a Rubber Raft,' *University of Kansas City Review,* XV (Summer 1949), 304-307.

'Hotel Room,' *New Yorker,* XXV (21 January 1950), 28.

'Mystic River,' *New Yorker,* XXVI (22 April 1950), 30.

'The Lamb,' *University of Kansas City Review,* XVI (Spring 1950), 162-163.

'Memorial Day,' *Atlantic,* CLXXXV (June 1950), 56.

'Home Revisited: Midnight,' *New Yorker,* XXVI (3 June 1950), 32.

'The Cow,' 'Elegy Deferred for F. O. M.,' *Beloit Poetry Journal,* I (Fall 1950), 19.

'Elegy for G. B. Shaw,' *New Yorker,* XXVI (16 December 1950), 110.

'Monday Morning Montage—London,' *Beloit Poetry Journal,* I (Summer 1951), 17-21.

'Dante's "Inferno," Cantos I-V,' *University of Kansas City Review,* XIX (Winter 1952), 75-91.

'Ars Poetica,' *Beloit Poetry Journal,* II (Spring 1952), 3.

'College Library,' *Harper's,* CCIV (April 1952), 101.

'Lines for an Epitaph,' 'Once in the Redwood Forest,' 'Kristoffer Second,' *Colorado Quarterly,* I (no. 2, 1952), 224.

'Carlo Crivelli Muses Before a Madonna,' *Kenyon Review,* XIV (Autumn 1952), 608-612.

'Flowering Quince,' *Poetry,* LXXXI (October 1952), 18-19.

' Crossing," *Atlantic*, CXCI (March 1953) , 96.

' Measurements,' ' Elegy for Jog,' ' Domesticity,' *Poetry*, LXXXII (April 1953) , 12-13.

' Progress of the Soul,' *University of Kansas City Review*, XIX (Summer 1953) , 229-230.

' Temptation,' *Poetry*, LXXXII (June 1953) , 145.

' Old Woman on a Doorstep,' *New Yorker*, XXIX (5 September 1953) , 34.

' Three Views of a Mother,' *Yale Review*, XLIII (December 1953) , 185-187.

' January 2, Morning,' *Harper's*, CCVIII (January 1954) , 69.

' Lines While Walking Home from a Party on Charles Street,' *Antioch Review*, XIV (March 1954) , 34.

' Elegy for Sandro,' ' Sunday Morning,' *Poetry*, LXXXIV (April 1954) , 1-7.

' Thursday,' ' A Variation on Some Lines,' *Beloit Quarterly*, IV (Summer 1954) , 6-13.

' In the Witch-Hunting Season,' *Nation*, CLXXIX (7 August 1954) , 116.

' To Judith,' *Atlantic*, CXCV (January 1955) , 65.

' A Sermon Beginning with the Portrait of a Man,' ' A Thought about Shiek Bedriddin,' *Epoch*, VI (Spring 1955) , 212-213.

' Thoughts on Looking into a Thicket,' ' On Looking East to the Sea with a Sunset Behind Me,' ' Elegy,' *Poetry*, LXXXVI (May 1955) , 63-70.

' SPQR Domus Claudius,' ' Noon: Romagna,' *New Orleans Poetry Journal*, I (July 1955) , 18-19.

' On the Birth of Jeffrey to William and Barbara Harding,' *Ladies Home Journal*, LXXII (August 1955) , 132.

' Naples,' *Nation*, CLXXXI (1 October 1955) , 287.

' The Reason for the Pelican,' *Ladies Home Journal*, LXXII (November 1955) , 208.

' The Principal Part of a Python,' *Ladies Home Journal*, LXXII (December 1955) , 31.

' Lines While Sitting on a Seawall with the Sea Rising to My Waist,' ' Showing a Foreigner Through His Studio,

Leonardo Answers a Question,' 'A Thought of Ladies,' 'For Giordano Bruno's Monument in the Campo Dei Fiori,' 'The Baboon and the State,' 'An Inscription for Richard Eberhart,' *Quarterly Review of Literature*, VIII (No. 4, 1956), 276-282.

'Snowy Heron,' *Ladies Home Journal*, LXXIII (March 1956), 144.

'College for Women," *College English*, XVII (April 1956), 373.

'For Bernard DeVoto,' *Saturday Review*, XXXIX (14 April 1956), 14.

'Washington, D. C.,' *Nation*, CLXXXIII (28 July 1956), 84.

'A Praise of Good Poets in a Bad Age,' *Saturday Review*, XXXIX (11 August 1956), 13.

'Of History, Fiction, Language,' *Nation*, CLXXXIII (1 September 1956), 184.

'Memory of Paris,' *Nation*, CLXXXIII (15 September 1956), 226.

'Bufo Vulgaris,' *Harper's*, CCXIII (October 1956), 38.

'Some Figures for Who I Am,' *Poetry*, LXXXIX (December 1956), 171-175.

'Thousandth Poem to Dylan Thomas,' *Saturday Review*, XXXIX (15 December 1956), 21.

'To Judith,' *Atlantic*, CXCIX (March 1957), 67.

'Requiem for Hungary,' *Nation*, CLXXXIV (27 April 1957), 363.

'For Ezra Pound,' *American Scholar*, XXVI (Fall 1957), 428-429.

'Ulysses,' *Literary Review* (Fairleigh-Dickinson University), I (Autumn 1957), 72-74.

'Conversations at the Zoo,' *New Yorker*, XXXIII (2 November 1957), 164.

'To W. T. Scott,' *Grecourt Review* (Smith College), I (December 1957), 21-22.

'George Gordon of Gight,' *Saturday Review*, XLI (4 January 1958), 15.

'Sermon,' *Ladies Home Journal,* LXXV (February 1958), 154.

'SPQR, a Letter from Rome,' 'To Lucasta, about That War,' *Poetry,* XCI (February 1958), 287-291.

'At Cocktails,' *Antioch Review,* XVIII (Winter 1958), 497.

'The Colossus in Quicksand,' *Calliope* (Western Michigan University), IV (Spring 1958), 26-27. [Typographically mixed up on p. 27.]

'After Sunday Dinner We Uncles Snooze,' *Patterns,* II (Fall 1958), 2.

'Ballad of the Ikendick,' *Nation,* CLXXXVII (13 September 1958), 136.

'Dream,' *Atlantic,* CCII (November 1958), 74-75.

'The One Dull Thing You Did Was to Die, Fletcher,' *Saturday Review,* XLI (22 November 1958), 38.

'For Ezra Pound,' *Yale Literary Magazine,* CXXV (December 1958), 17.

'An Antarctic Hymn,' *Saturday Review,* XLII (17 January 1959), 71.

'To Dudley Fitts,' 'Homage to Jacques Lipchitz,' 'Dialogue,' *Prairie Schooner,* XXXII (Winter 1958-1959), 287-291.

'Rain Sizes,' *Ladies Home Journal,* LXXVI (February 1959), 19.

'In Ego with Us All,' *Grecourt Review,* II (February 1959).

'Canto I of Purgatory' [translation from Dante], *Venture,* III (Nos. 1 & 2, 1959), 56-60.

'Clipper Museum,' *Syracuse 10* (Syracuse University), I (March 1959), 23.

'There Once Was an Owl,' *Ladies Home Journal,* LXXVI (March 1959), 182.

'A Sonnet for Robert Frost But Not About Him,' *Saturday Review,* XLII (21 March 1959), 20.

Articles and Reviews by John Ciardi

'Spokesman of What?,' *Poetry*, LXVIII (September 1946), 349-351. [Review of *Crusade*, by Captain John Waller.]

'Bach, Brazil and Bluejays: A Notion of Poetic Style,' *University of Kansas City Review*, XIII (Spring 1947), 203-207.

'Cid Corman,' *University of Kansas City Review*, XIII (Spring 1947), 208-210.

'E. L. Mayo—A Modern Metaphysical,' *University of Kansas City Review*, XIV (Autumn 1947), 17-22.

'John Frederick Nims and the Modern Idiom,' *University of Kansas City Review*, XIV (Winter 1947), 105-110.

'Letter from John Ciardi,' *Poetry*, LXXII (August 1948), 261-263.

'Letter from Harvard,' *Poetry*, LXXIV (May 1949), 112-113.

'Peter Viereck—The Poet and the Form,' *University of Kansas City Review*, XV (Summer 1949), 297-302.

'What Does It Take to Enjoy a Poem?,' *Saturday Review of Literature*, XXXII (10 December 1949), 7-8, 25-28.

'At Least as Well as Prose,' *Writer*, LXIII (March 1950), 75-78.

'Edna St. Vincent Millay: A Figure of Passionate Living,' *Saturday Review of Literature*, XXXIII (11 November 1950), 8-9, 77.

'Poets and Prizes,' *English Journal,* XXXIX (December 1950),
545-552; *College English,* XII (December 1950), 127-134.

'The Burial of the Dead,' *University of Kansas City Review,*
XVII (Summer 1951), 333-336. [Short story.]

Review of *The Riddle of Emily Dickinson,* by Rebecca Patter-
son, *New England Quarterly,* XXV (March 1952), 93-98.

Review of *Where the Compass Spins,* by Radcliffe Squires,
Western Humanities Review, VI (Spring 1952), 189-191.

Review of *Achievement of American Poetry: 1900-1950,* by
Louise Bogan, and *The Background of Modern Poetry,*
by J. Isaacs, *New England Quarterly,* XXV (September
1952), 425-426.

'Diction of Poetry,' *Writer,* LXVI (March 1953), 74-76.

'The Poetry of Archibald MacLeish,' *Atlantic,* CXCI (May
1953), 67-68.

'The Shock of Recognition,' *Journal of the American Association of University Women,* XLVII (October 1953), 10-14.

'Poets of the Inner Landscape,' *Nation,* CLXXVII (14 Novem-
ber 1953), 410. [Review of *Collected Poems,* by Conrad
Aiken; *The Waking: Poems 1933-1953,* by Theodore
Roethke; and *Poems 1940-1953,* by Karl Shapiro.]

'Art of Making Men,' *Saturday Review,* XXXVI (21 November 1953), 43.

'Heresy and the High Mind,' *Nation,* CLXXVIII (27 March
1954), 251-252.

'"Thing Is the Form,"' *Nation,* CLXXVIII (24 April 1954),
368-369. [Review of *The Desert Music and Other Poems,*
by William Carlos Williams.]

'Two Nuns and a Strolling Player,' *Nation,* CLXXVIII (22
May 1954), 445-446. [Review of *Poems, A Selection,* by
Léonie Adams; *Collected Poems, 1923-53,* by Louise Bogan;
and *Mine the Harvest,* by Edna St. Vincent Millay.]

'Strictness and Faithfulness,' *Nation,* CLXXVIII (19 June
1954), 525. [Review of *The Lysistrata of Aristophanes,*
by Dudley Fitts; and *The Fables of La Fontaine,* tr. by
Marianne Moore.]

38

'Wallace Stevens's "Absolute Music,"' *Nation*, CLXXIX (16 October 1954), 346-347. [Review of *Collected Poems*, by Wallace Stevens.]

'Sensitivity Without Discipline,' *Nation*, CLXXIX (4 December 1954), 490. [Review of *This Rowdy Heart*, by Frances Frost.]

'The Seductiveness of E. E. Cummings,' *Nation*, CLXXX (12 February 1955), 142. [Review of *Poems 1923-1954*, by E. E. Cummings.]

'The Poet's Family Circle,' *New York Times Book Review*, LXI (29 May 1955), 4, 17. [Review of *Emily Dickinson's Home*, by Millicent Todd Bingham.]

'An Ulcer, Gentlemen, Is an Unwritten Poem,' *Canadian Business*, June 1955.

'Selected Verse,' *Nation*, CLXXX (11 June 1955), 508-509. [Brief reviews of nine books of poetry.]

'Over the Edge of Bathos,' *Nation*, CLXXXI (30 July 1955), 100. [Review of *Selected Poems*, by Randall Jarrell.]

'Dante for the Missionaries,' *New Republic*, CXXXIII (22 August 1955), 18-20. [Review of *Introductory Papers on Dante*, by Dorothy L. Sayers.]

'Selected New Books,' *Nation*, CLXXXI (24 September, 17 December 1955), 268, 540. [Brief reviews of ten books of poetry.]

'The Critic in Love,' *Nation*, CLXXXI (8 October 1955), 307. [Review of *Book of Moments*, by Kenneth Burke.]

'Wallace Stevens 1879-1955,' *Nation*, CLXXXI (22 October 1955), 335-336.

'Out of the Top Drawer,' *Nation*, CLXXXI (5 November 1955), 397-398. [Review of *Emily Dickinson: An Interpretive Biography*, by Thomas H. Johnson; and *The Poems of Emily Dickinson*, edited by Thomas H. Johnson.]

'Muscles and Manners,' *Nation*, CLXXXI (10 December 1955), 515-516; CLXXXII (11 February 1956), 128. [Review of *Selected Poems*, by Roy Campbell; and *Collected Poems*,

1955, by Robert Graves. See Henry Regnery, 'On Roy Campbell,' 11 February 1956, p. 128.]

'Auden and the Search for Values,' *Saturday Review*, XXXIX (18 February 1956), 48.

'Everyone Writes (Bad) Poetry,' *Saturday Review*, XXXIX (5 May 1956), 22, 27.

'Freud and Modern Poetry,' *Saturday Review*, XXXIX (5 May 1956), 8.

'Whitman's Principle of Selection,' *Walt Whitman Newsletter*, II (March-June 1956), 10-11.

'Poverty on Parnassus: The Economics of Poetry,' *Saturday Review*, XXXIX (28 July 1956), 7-8, 29-30.

'Our Most Melodic Poet,' *Saturday Review*, XXXIX (18 August 1956), 18-19. [Review of three books by Richard Wilbur.]

'What Every Writer Must Learn,' *Saturday Review*, XXXIX (15 December 1956), 7-8, 37-39.

'Verse to Remember,' *Saturday Review*, XXXIX (22 December 1956), 15.

'A Close Look at the Unicorn,' *Saturday Review*, XL (12 January 1957), 54-57. [See Norman Cousins in Biography and Criticism, below.]

'The Reviewer's Duty to Damn: A Letter to an Avalanche,' *Saturday Review*, XL (16 February 1957), 24-25.

'Researched Mistress,' *Saturday Review*, XL (23 March 1957), 36-37. [Review of *Homage to Mistress Bradstreet*, by John Berryman.]

'Morality of Poetry: Devotion and Discipline vs. the Push-button,' *Saturday Review*, XL (30 March, 4 May, 11 May 1957), 11-14, 34; 29; 25. [See replies by J. Donald Adams, 4 May, p. 29; and Thomas Lask, 11 May, p. 25.]

'What Every Writer Must Learn,' *Writer*, LXX (June 1957), 5-9.

'Shock Reaction to Poetry,' *Saturday Review*, XL (20 July 1957), 9-11, 41.

40

'Parable for Critics,' *Saturday Review*, XL (28 September 1957), 24.

'Merrill Moore: A Goodbye,' *Saturday Review*, XL (12 October 1957), 27.

'Rome,' *Saturday Review*, XL (19 October 1957), 40-42.

'The Poet's Duty to Poetry,' *Saturday Review*, XL (19 October 1957), 15-16, 63.

'Writers as Readers of Poetry,' *Saturday Review*, XL (23 November 1957), 32.

'Learning the Techniques of Poetry,' *Saturday Review*, XL (28 December 1957), 14-15.

'In a Child's Head,' *Saturday Review*, XLI (25 January 1958), 30. [Review of *First Poems*, by Minou Drouet.]

'The Real Thomas,' *Saturday Review*, XLI (1 March 1958), 18, 31. [Review of *Letters to Vernon Watkins*, by Dylan Thomas.]

'The Birth of a Classic,' *Saturday Review*, XLI (8 March 1958), 11-12, 48. [Review of *J. B.*, by Archibald MacLeish.]

'What Is Bread Loaf?,' *Middlebury College Bulletin*, LIII (April 1958), 1-2.

'Robert Frost: The Way to the Poem,' *Saturday Review*, XLI (12 April 1958), 13-15, 65. [See 'Germinal Stuff,' 3 May, p. 23; and 16 readers' letters, 3 May, p. 23, and 10 May, pp. 19-20.]

'Concepts of Literature,' *The Journal* (Wofford College), LXXXI (May 1958), 5, 22. [Note in an article by Tom Wright.]

'Poetry and Student Poetry,' *Anthologist* (Rutgers University), XXIX (May 1958), 7-11.

'Letter to Letter Writers,' *Saturday Review*, XLI (17 May 1958), 15, 48. [See 11 more letters, 31 May, p. 19.]

'This Year's Girls,' *Wells Express* (Wells College), XLIV (June 1958), 8-11. [Commencement address, revised form to be published by *Glamour Magazine*.]

'Poetry,' *Saturday Review*, XLI (21 June 1958), 43-44. [Comments on *I Marry You*, by John Ciardi.]

'The Silences of Poetry,' *Michigan Alumnus Quarterly Review*, LXIV (9 August 1958), 298-307.

'Inside a Poem With the Poet,' *Think* (IBM Corporation), XXIV (September 1958), 20-21. [A poem, 'Bridal Photo, 1906,' and a prose commentary.]

'SR's Quarterly Round-up,' *Saturday Review*, XLI (27 September 1958), 17-19.

'The Epic of a Place,' *Saturday Review*, XLI (11 October 1958), 37-39. [Review of *Paterson*, by William Carlos Williams.]

'Six Hours of Dylan Thomas,' *Saturday Review*, XLI (15 November 1958), 50. [On Thomas's recordings.]

'Dialogue with the Audience,' *Saturday Review*, XLI (22 November 1958), 10-12, 42.

'The Seven Stages of the Soul,' *Saturday Review*, XLI (13 December 1958), 17. [Review of *The Odyssey: A Modern Sequel*, by Nikos Kazantzakis.]

'A Poem Talks to Itself: One Thing Calls Another Into Being,' *Saturday Review*, XLII (24 January 1959), 12-13.

'Literature Undefended,' *Saturd·y Review*, XLII (31 January 1959), 22. [Excerpt from the College English Association presidential address.]

'Robert Frost: Master Conversationalist at Work,' *Saturday Review*, XLII (21 March 1959), 17-20, 54.

Review of *In Sicily*, by Elio Vittorini, *Book Find News*, Issue No. 87.

Review of *The Odyssey: A Modern Sequel*, by Nikos Kazantzakis, *Book Find News*, Issue No. 236. [From the *Saturday Review*.]

Reviews of John Ciardi's Books

Homeward to America

Bogan, Louise. 'Verse,' *New Yorker*, XV (27 January 1940), 52-54.

Lechlitner, Ruth. 'First Generation U. S. A.,' *New York Herald Tribune Books*, XVI (26 May 1940), 13.

Rosenberger, Coleman. 'The Blood's Latitudes,' *New Republic*, CIII (1 July 1940), 36.

Taylor, Frajam. 'A New Adventure,' *Poetry*, LVI (September 1940), 337-340.

Untermeyer, Louis. 'Escape and Acceptance," *Saturday Review of Literature*, XXI (30 March 1940), 13, 18 [see p. 18].

Untermeyer, Louis. 'Look Homeward, America,' *Yale Review*, n. s. XXIX (March 1940), 599-603.

Walton, Eda Lou. 'Poems in a Time of Conflict,' *New York Times Book Review*, XLV (25 February 1940), 5.

A. L. A. Booklist, XXXVI (15 March 1940), 279.

Christian Science Monitor, 4 May 1940, p. 12.

Springfield Republican, 16 June 1940, p. 7e.

Wisconsin Library Bulletin, XXXVI (June 1940), 110.

Other Skies

Bogan, Louise. 'Verse,' *New Yorker*, XXIII (15 November 1947), 130, 133-134.

Meredith, William. 'The Problem of the Second Volume,' *Poetry*, LXXII (May 1948), 99-102.

Meyer, Gerard Previn. 'Accident of Chaos,' *Saturday Review of Literature*, XXX (6 December 1947), 60.

Strachan, Pearl. *Christian Science Monitor*, 20 December 1947, p. 11.

Virginia Kirkus Bookshop Service, XV (15 September 1947), 530.

Live Another Day

Benziger, James. 'New Verse,' *Furioso*, V (Winter 1950), 65-70 [see pp. 68-69].

Bogan, J. W. *Springfield Republican*, 30 October 1949, p. 8c.

Daiches, David. 'Rich, Controlled Imagery,' *New York Herald Tribune Book Review*, XXVI (1 January 1950), 6.

Irvine, Maurice. 'Two Poets in Progress,' *New York Times Book Review*, LIV (23 October 1949), 47.

Lougee, David. 'The Sounding Vision,' *Voices*, No. 143 (Autumn 1950), 37-41 [see pp. 38-39].

McDonald, Gerald. *Library Journal*, LXXIV (15 September 1949), 1326.

Saul, George Brandon. 'From Aridity to Affirmation,' *Western Review*, XV (Autumn 1950), 68-73 [see pp. 70-71].

Mid-Century American Poets

Bogan, Louise. 'Verse,' *New Yorker*, XXVI (4 November 1950), 142-147 [see pp. 146-147].

Fjelde, Rolf. *Poetry New York*, No. 3 (1950), 38.

Humphries, Rolfe. 'Verse Chronicle,' *Nation*, CLXXI (12 August 1950), 152-153.

McDonald, Gerald. *Library Journal*, LXXV (July 1950), 1189.

Meyer, Gerard Previn. 'Presenting 15 Faces,' *Saturday Review of Literature*, XXXIII (22 July 1950), 18-19.

Prahl, Victor. *Springfield Republican*, 14 May 1950, p. 10c.

Rosenthal, M. L. 'Fifteen in Transit—An Interim Anthology,' *New Republic*, CXXIII (21 August 1950), 18-19.

Strobel, Marion. *Chicago Sunday Tribune*, 9 April 1950, p. 8.

Untermeyer, Jean Starr. 'Newer Directions,' *Voices*, No. 142 (Summer 1950), 51-54.

Williams, William Carlos. 'Voices in Verse,' *New York Times Book Review*, LV (16 April 1950), 6, 28.

School and Society, LXXI (25 March 1950), 190.

'Not So Modern Poetry,' *Time*, LV (17 April 1950), 118, 120.

'American Poetry Today,' *Times Literary Supplement*, 19 January 1951, pp. 29-31.

From Time to Time

Crane, Milton. 'Elegies, Rich and Strange,' *New York Times Book Review*, LVII (25 May 1952), 27.

Evans, Oliver. 'Two Poets and a Critic,' *Voices*, No. 148 (May-August 1952), 49-51 [see pp. 49-50].

Ferling, Lawrence. *San Francisco Chronicle*, 3 February 1952, p. 27.

Marsh, Willard L. 'Little Boy Blue and the Beautiful Rose,' *Antioch Review*, XII (December 1952), 486-494 [see pp. 489-491].

McDonald, Gerald. *Library Journal*, LXXVI (15 December 1951), 2114.

Sawyer, Kenneth B. 'Praises and Crutches,' *Hopkins Review*, V (Summer 1952), 126-132 [see pp. 128-129].

Vazakas, Byron. 'Eleven Contemporary Poets,' *New Mexico Quarterly*, XXII (Summer 1952), 213-230 [see pp. 217-218].

Dante's *Inferno*

Fitts, Dudley. 'Translated Into American,' *New York Times Book Review*, LIX (4 July 1954), 4.

Fuller, Edmund. 'Dante and the Modern Idiom,' *American Scholar*, XXIII (Autumn 1954), 482, 484.

Hilborn, Harry W. *Queen's Quarterly*, LXII (Spring 1955), 135-136.

Hutchens, John K. 'On Books and Authors: Translation (Cont'd),' *New York Herald Tribune Book Review*, XXX (20 June 1954), 2.

Kenner, Hugh. 'Problems in Faithfulness and Fashion,' *Poetry*, LXXXV (January 1955), 225-231 [see pp. 228-231].

Lattimore, Richmond. 'The "Inferno" as an English Poem,' *Nation*, CLXXIX (28 August 1954), 175.

MacAllister, Archibald T. 'The Literature of Italy,' *Yale Review*, n. s. XLIV (September 1954), 155-159 [see p. 158].

McDonald, Gerald D. *Library Journal*, LXXIX (15 September 1954), 1592.

Nemerov, Howard. 'A Few Bricks from Babel,' *Sewanee Review*, LXII (October 1954), 655-663.

Pellegrini, Anthony L. *Modern Language Quarterly*, XVII (June 1956), 183-186.

White, Lawrence Grant. 'Dante for Americans,' *Saturday Review*, XXXVII (18 September 1954), 13, 27.

A. L. A. Booklist, L (15 July 1954), 447.

College English, XVI (October 1954), 82.

[Dante's *Inferno* was also reviewed in *The Argonaut*, San Francisco, 9 July 1954; *Binghamton* (New York) *Press*, 19 September 1954; *Books on Trial*, Chicago, January-February 1956; *Catholic Review Service*, St. Mary's College, Kansas; *Episcopal Church News*, Richmond, Virginia, 22 August 1954; *Erie* (Pennsylvania) *Times*, 27 June 1954; *Evansville* (Indiana) *Press*, 13 June 1954; *Fort Worth* (Texas) *Morning Star-Telegram*, 19 September 1954; *The Living Church*, Milwaukee,

1 August 1954; *Louisville Record,* 4 October 1954; *Milwaukee Journal,* 29 August 1954; *New Brunswick Sunday Times,* 27 June 1954, 10 October 1954; *New World,* Chicago, 29 October 1954; *Newark News,* 30 August 1954; *San Antonio Express,* 15 August 1954; *San Diego Union,* 20 June 1954; *Trenton* (New Jersey) *Sunday Times-Advertiser,* 8 August 1954; *Youngstown* (Ohio) *Vindicator,* 13 June 1954.]

As If

Brodsky, Bernard. 'Definition of Wit,' *Chicago Review,* X (Autumn-Winter 1956), 87-90.

Clancy, Joseph P. 'Singers for the Summer Months,' *America,* XCVII (13 July 1957), 408.

Flint, F. Cudworth. 'Ciardi's New Poems,' *Nation,* CLXXXI (19 November 1955), 444.

Frumpkin, Gene. *Coastlines,* No. 4 (Spring 1956), 30-31.

Hall, Donald. *New England Quarterly,* XXIX (June 1956), 247-252 [see pp. 247-248].

Irvine, Maurice. 'No Labels Available,' *New York Times Book Review,* LX (20 November 1955), 16.

Jarrell, Randall. 'Graves and the White Goddess—Part II,' *Yale Review,* n.s. XLV (March 1956), 467-480 [see p. 479].

Jerome, Judson. 'Among the Nightingales,' *Antioch Review,* XVI (Spring 1956), 115-125.

McDonald, Gerald. *Library Journal,* LXXXI (1 April 1956), 839.

Nicholl, Louise Townsend. 'By Three Rewarding Poets,' *New York Herald Tribune Book Review,* XXXII (29 January 1956), 10.

Salomon, I. L. 'Revelation in Rhyme,' *Saturday Review,* XXXIX (28 January 1956), 24.

Sandeen, Ernest. 'The Flung World,' *Poetry,* LXXXVIII (July 1956), 267-273 [see pp. 267-268].

A. L. A. Booklist, LII (1 November 1955), 97.

Bookmark, XV (December 1955), 55.

Essential Books, I (October 1955) , 31.

Tufts Alumni Review, May 1956.

Virginia Quarterly Review, XXII (Spring 1956) , liv.

[*As If* was also reviewed in the *Boston Morning Globe,* 25 September 1955; *Clarksdale* (Mississippi) *Press-Register; Jackson* (Mississippi) *Clarion Ledger-Daily News,* 22 April 1956; *Jackson* (Mississippi) *State-Times,* 22 April 1956; *New Brunswick Sunday Times,* 25 September 1955, 29 January 1956; *Trenton Sunday Times-Advertiser,* 30 September 1955.]

I Marry You

Ciardi, John. ' Poetry,' *Saturday Review,* XL (21 June 1958) , 43-44. [Not a review, but ' a statement of intent.']

Dorn, N. K. *San Francisco Chronicle,* 17 August 1958, p. 30.

Laing, Dilys. ' Some Marrying and Some Burning,' *Nation,* CLXXXVII (13 September 1958) , 137-138.

McDonald, Gerald D. *Library Journal,* LXXXIII (15 October 1958) , 2845.

Rexroth, Kenneth. ' Animals, Stars and People,' *New York Times Book Review,* LXIII (3 August 1958) , 6.

Thompson, John. ' Just a Bit of This and That,' *Hudson Review* (Autumn 1958) , 443-450 [see pp. 445-446].

Wright, James. ' Four New Volumes,' *Poetry,* XCIII (October 1958) , 46-50 [see p. 46-47].

A. L. A. Booklist, LV (1 October 1958) , 68.

Virginia Kirkus Bookshop Service, XXVI (15 April 1958) , 328.

[*I Marry You* was also reviewed in the *Abilene* (Texas) *Reporter-News; Anniston* (Alabama) *Star,* 29 June 1958; *Denver Post,* 14 September 1958; *Eureka Springs* (Arkansas) *Times-Echo,* 27 October 1958; *Fort Wayne News-Sentinel,* 7 June 1958; *Jackson* (Mississippi) *Clarion Leader-Daily News,* 27 July 1958; *Memphis Commercial Appeal,* 15 June 1958; *Newark News,* 27 July 1958; *Pittsfield* (Maine) *Advertiser; San Diego Union,* 15 June 1958; *Sioux Falls* (South Dakota) *Argus-Leader,* 3 August 1958.]

Biography and Criticism

C[ousins], N[orman]. 'John Ciardi and the Readers,' *Saturday Review*, XL (16 February 1957), 22-23. [Following Mr. Ciardi's review of Anne Morrow Lindbergh's *The Unicorn and Other Poems* in the *Saturday Review*, XL (12 January 1957), 54-57, the periodical received the 'biggest storm of reader protest in [its] thirty-three year history.' Of these hundreds of letters, 7 were printed on 2 February, p. 23; 25 were printed on 9 February, pp. 23-24; 14 on 16 February, pp. 23-24; 9 on 23 February, p. 25; 30 on 2 March, pp. 23-25; and James Benét's 'Coterie Leader' on 9 March, p. 24. In the same issue with Mr. Cousins's article, Mr. Ciardi wrote 'The Reviewer's Duty to Damn: A Letter to an Avalanche,' pp. 24-25, 54-55. See also Holzhauer, Roth and *Time* articles below.]

Cowden, R. W. 'A Note on John Ciardi at Michigan,' *The Tuftonian: The Magazine of Tufts College*, IV (Fall 1944), 118-119.

Holmes, John. 'A Note on John Ciardi at Tufts,' *The Tuftonian*, IV (Fall 1944), 122.

Holmes, John. 'John Ciardi: Tufts Poet,' *The Tuftonian*, XII (Fall 1955), 21-24. [Followed by 'Elegy,' 'V-J Day,'

'Landscapes of My Name,' 'On a Photo of Sgt. Ciardi a Year Later,' 'A Box Comes Home.' This article and the Ciardi poems were reprinted as a 12-page pamphlet in paper covers. It also includes the illustrations in the original.]

Hall, Donald. 'The New Poetry: Notes on the Past Fifteen Years in America,' *New World Writing: Seventh Mentor Selection* (New York: The New American Library, 1955), pp. 231-247 [see p. 239].

Holzhauer, Jean. 'Uncritical Critics,' *America*, XCVII (27 July 1957), 444-446.

Kunitz, Stanley. 'Ciardi, John,' *Twentieth Century Authors: First Supplement* (New York: The H. W. Wilson Company, 1955), pp. 200-201.

Peragallo, Olga. 'Ciardi, John,' *Italian-American Authors and Their Contribution to American Literature*, Edited by Anita Peragallo (New York: S. F. Vanni, 1949), pp. 45-47.

Roth, Philip. 'Mrs. Lindbergh, Mr. Ciardi, and the Teeth and Claws of the Civilized World,' *Chicago Review*, XI (Summer 1957), 72-76.

Scott, Winfield Townley. 'Three Books by John Ciardi,' *University of Kansas City Review*, XVI (Winter 1949), 119-125. [The Three books are *Homeward to America*, *Other Skies*, and *Live Another Day*.]

Webster, Harvey Curtis. 'Humanism as the Father Face (A Critical Preview) [of "Letter to Virginia Johnson"],' *Poetry*, LXX (June 1947), 146-150.

'Critic Under Fire,' *Time*, LXIX (18 February 1957), 44, 46.

Song

Apr. '58

I draw the breath I am about,
I tie the shoe I wear, I tell
Truth, as it comes, with parts left out.
With parts left out the truth goes well.

I keep the house I live in let
With what I keep of what I sell.
Love and comes inhabit it.
Some t
I keep some things locked out of it.
Some things locked out, the house goes well.

2

3
All, god knows, goes well in part.
The part left out goes as it goes.
Leaving out is the one art.
Once everything is let in — god knows.

All, god knows, goes well in part.
The part left and goes as it goes.
To leave out is the telling art.
Leaving out in the
The part left and goes as it goes.
Leaving out is the one art,
Once all has been let in — god knows
Once If everything were let in
Once
If everything were let in — god knows.

And when
If ever the whole god in - god knows.

All, god knows, goes well in part.
What's left out goes as it goes.
Leaving out is the one art.
Once everything been let in — god knows.
Let everything in and we're done, god knows.

(the telling art)
And what of all is let in? god knows.
If everything is let in - god knows.
Let all in
And having

Work sheet for John Ciardi's 'Song'
(from the Feinberg Collection)

MSS and Other Material in the Feinberg Collection

'An Afternoon,' 'College Campus,' 'A Motto' (cancelled),
'Dogwood is no,' and 'The names blur on their stones.'
[Autograph MS, the first four poems on a sheet of paper,
the fifth on the back of a letter; the first, second and fourth
rewritten on three 5-by-7 inch cards.]

'Another School Year: Why?.' [A 4-page reprint for distribution by Rutgers University, condensed from an address and
first printed in the Rutgers *Alumni Monthly*, 1957. Title
on page [1]: Another School Year / Why? / (device:
1766) / Presented to the high school students of New
Jersey by their State Univer- / sity with the belief that
those who read and think about the enclosed message /
will find a real inspiration and challenge /. Text on pages
[2]-[4].]

'At a Hospital Window.' [Autograph MS work sheets, 2 pages;
typescript with autograph changes, 3 pages; carbon copy,
3 pages.]

'Breakfast in Bed in the Hospital.' [Autograph MS work sheets,
2 pages.]

51

'Devotions.' [Autograph MS work sheets, 2 pages; typescript, 1 page.]

'Dialogue.' [Autograph MSS, two versions, 2 pages each.]

'Dialogue with the Audience.' [Autograph MS work sheets, 14 pages; typescript with title 'For Whom Should the Poet Write,' 15 pages; carbon copy, typescript, with title 'For Whom Is a Poem Written?: A Dialogue with the Audience,' with autograph changes, 15 pages (misnumbered 14); carbon copy, typescript, letter to Peter Ritner, *Saturday Review*, dated 21 October 1958; two copies, one with autograph presentation, of *Saturday Review*, 22 November 1958, containing the essay.]

'Dylan Thomas.' [Autograph MS, 9 pages; typescripts, original and carbon copy, 24 pages, of essay for *Saturday Review* on Thomas's records; typescripts, original and carbon copy, 1 page each, of letter to *Saturday Review*; also a typed letter, 1 page, from Richard Weddell to Irving Kolodin.]

'An Exhortation by a Druid Sunday School Teacher.' [Autograph MS work sheets, 8 pages; typescript, original and carbon copy, 1 page each, with title 'An Atheist Exhorts Sunday School Teachers'; all except one of these 10 pages cancelled by a vertical stroke with a red pencil.]

'The Fishers.' [Autograph MS work sheets, 8 pages; typescript, original and two carbon copies, 1 page each, with autograph changes on all three.]

'Girls Waggling in Dusk, Boys Prowling.' [Autograph MS with changes, 4 pages.]

'Happiness.' [Autograph MS, 2 pages; typescript with two stanzas cancelled, 2 pages.]

'A Highland Boy Died Fighting on His Mountain.' [Autograph MS with changes, 1 page.]

'Homage to Jacques Lipchitz.' [Autograph MSS, work sheets and fair copy, 4 pages.]

'Home from a Good Evening,' 'Three Thoughts of You,' 'Draught,' 'College Campus,' 'Japanese Imitations,'

'Three Sentiments.' [Autograph MS work sheets, 8 pages plus 1 written on the verso, of various sizes.]

'Manhattan from the Sea: A Hymn Departing.' [Autograph MS work sheets, three versions of the poem, 9 pages plus 1 written on the verso.]

'Margaret Nash Got Wet But I Don't Know How.' [Autograph MS of light verse, with changes, on 4 pages of an examination 'blue book' used at Rutgers University.]

'Mary Died and Went to God.' [Autograph MS with changes, 1 page.]

Notebook of Poems. [Autograph MS notebook, containing notes, trial lines and fair copies on 36 pages; on the last page is 'The Rutgers Plan for Mass Ed. in the Humanities,' the notebook having been turned upside down and started from the back.]

'On Writing an Unfavorable Review.' [Autograph MS with changes, 1 page.]

'Once I Had a Thousand Roses.' [Autograph MS work sheets; 3 pages of small sheets, marked 'I'; 10 pages of larger sheets torn from a notebook, marked 'II'; 10 pages of still larger yellow sheets, marked 'III'; typescript of the poem, with first page missing, 5 pages.]

'One Day, Like a Dream Shifting, the World Married.' [Autograph MS work sheets; 2 pages plus 1 written on the verso; 1 page containing a later version with changes.]

Photographs. [Three photographs of Mr. Ciardi, inscribed, all dated 1955 on the verso; another photograph is of Mr. Ciardi with the Emerson letter to Walt Whitman, also a clipping from the New Brunswick *Sunday Home News*, 16 November 1958, 'Emerson Letter to Whitman / Shown for Day at Rutgers', with the photograph in the newspaper.]

Poems. [Typescripts, carbon copies, of 13 poems, all except one ('The D Minor,' 2 pages) on a single page each, with the first page of another poem ('For the New Men') missing, 14 pages. The poems: 'I Saw My Father,' 'The Pool,'

'Wagon Train,' 'The Uninfected,' 'In the Web,' 'Letter to Karl Shapiro,' 'En Route,' 'Nausea,' 'The D Minor,' 'El Greco,' 'For the New Men,' 'Oracle,' 'Anglo-Saxon.' Autograph note to 'For the New Men': 'Mayo's copy of the whole poem sent to Steinberg.']

'A Praise of Good Poets in a Bad Age.' [Autograph MSS, work sheets, typescripts, originals and carbons, 25 pages; autograph MS fair copy, with changes, 5 pages; typescript, original and two carbons, 2 pages each. The poem, with a sub-title 'to the memory of Wallace Stevens,' is marked for the Stevens issue of the *Saturday Review*.]

'Somerville, Massachusetts.' [Autograph MSS, first version on 2 pages torn from a notebook, second on one 5-by-7 inch card; typescripts, one on a *Saturday Review* letterhead, another of 2 pages on the verso of two such letterheads, the four versions of the poem apparently written in this order.]

'Song.' [Autograph MS, beginning 'I draw the breath I am about / I tie the shoe I wear,' work sheets, 2 pages.]

'Suddenly,' 'A Look of Understanding.' [Autograph MSS, fair copies with changes, on 5 pages torn from a notebook.]

'To Dudley Fitts.' [Typescript with autograph changes (1 page entirely autograph), 6 pages of carbons, 12 pages in all.]

'To Men of My Country on Memorial Day.' [Autograph MS work sheets, two versions, 5 pages.]

'To W. T. Scott.' [A 4-page reprint from *The Grecourt Review* (Smith College) in blank paper covers, with the poem on pages [1]-[2], and pages [3]-[4] blank. Two copies, both inscribed and with autograph corrections.]

Translation of Dante's *Divine Comedy*. [Autograph MS of work sheets of 'Purg. III,' lines 1-146, with annotations, 8 pages; typescript, carbon copy, of these lines, with autograph changes, 7 pages (two copies); typescript, carbon copy, of 'Purg. II,' lines 1-131, with autograph changes, 6 pages.]

'An Ulcer, Gentlemen, Is an Unwritten Poem.' [A 4-page reprint of an article from *Canadian Business*, October 1955.]

Printer's copy: typescript of the complete text, with autograph changes, 305 pages. [With a typed letter about the book from the *Atlantic Monthly*.]

Editor's plan for the book: 'What Is Modern Poetry?,' typescript, carbon copy, of the editor's introduction, 12 pages; preliminary pages of the book, typescript, carbon copy, 6 pages; questionnaire for the poets in the book, autograph MS, typescript, hectograph, 3 pages; poets' addresses, autograph MS, 1 page.

Permissions and royalties: autograph letters, typescripts, originals and carbon copies, telegrams, contract forms with autograph and typed notations, all dealing with publication matters, 51 pieces in all.

Bishop, Elizabeth: 6 autograph letters, 1 typed letter, 1 typed answer to suggestion sheet; 1 autograph note from Richard Eberhart; 6 typed letters, carbon copies, from John Ciardi.

Eberhart, Richard: 2 autograph letters, 4 typed letters, 1 typed note, 20 typed poems, 1 typed answer to suggestion sheet, 1 clipping from magazine, loose pages from *Burr Oaks* (New York: Oxford University Press, 1947).

Holmes, John: 1 typed letter, typed prose comments (12 pages), 10 typed poems (16 pages).

Jarrell, Randall: 6 autograph letters, 1 autograph note, typed prose comments, 2 copies (7 pages each), 13 typed poems (24 pages); 5 typed letters, carbon copies, from John Ciardi.

Lowell, Robert: 1 autograph letter; typed MS, 'Robert Lowell's Poetry,' by Randall Jarrell (12 pages); 1 autograph note from John Ciardi, 3 typed letters, carbon copies, from John Ciardi.

Mayo, Edw. L.: 5 autograph letters, 1 autograph Christmas card, 1 autograph note, typed prose comments, 2 copies (19 and 15 pages), 12 typed poems, 2 copies (14 and 15 pages); 1 typed letter, carbon copy, from John Ciardi.

Nims, John F.: 1 autograph note, 4 typed letters, typed prose comments (9 pages), 10 typed poems (19 pages); 2 typed letters, carbon copies, from John Ciardi.

Roethke, Theodore: 10 autograph letters (26 pages), including 4 typed poems; 2 autograph notes; typed prose comments, 2 copies (7 and 6 pages); 8 typed poems (17 pages, with extra copies of 6 of them); 1 autograph letter, carbon copy, from John Ciardi; 2 typed letters, carbon copies, from John Ciardi.

Rukeyser, Muriel: 4 autograph letters, 3 typed letters, typed prose comments, 2 copies (7 and 6 pages, with a poem in the first copy); 8 typed poems (17 pages); 4 typed letters, carbon copies, from John Ciardi.

Schwartz, Delmore: 6 autograph letters, 2 autograph notes, typed prose comments, 2 copies (8 pages each), 7 typed poems (21 pages), with clippings, 2 autograph letters, carbon copies, from John Ciardi; 5 typed letters, carbon copies, from John Ciardi.

Scott, Winfield Townley: 5 typed letters; typed prose comments, 3 copies (4 pages each); 10 typed poems, 3 copies (16 pages each).

Shapiro, Karl: 14 autographed and typed letters, 1 telegram; typed prose comments, 2 copies (5 pages each); 10 typed poems (22 pages); autograph notations in a copy of *Poetry*, LXXI (January 1948), containing ' Farewell to Criticism,' by Karl Shapiro; 6 typed letters, carbon copies, from John Ciardi.

Viereck, Peter: 17 typed letters, 11 typed notes; typed prose comments, 2 copies (19 and 16 pages); 11 typed poems (24 pages, with 1 clipping on 1 page); 3 typed poems, several copies (22 pages); 9 galley proofs, 2 clippings, 2 photostats of prose by Peter Viereck; 7 typed letters, carbon copies, from John Ciardi.

Wilbur, Richard: 1 typed letter, typed prose comments (9 pages), 10 typed poems (10 pages).

Addenda

⌇

Poems by John Ciardi in Periodicals

' Ode to My Bomber and Other War Poems ' (*Contains*: ' Port of Embarkation,' ' Death of a Bomber,' ' Sunday Pass,' ' Sidewalk Ballad on a Twelve Hour Pass,' ' Reverie During Briefing,' ' Ode to My Bomber,' ' Reflections While Oiling a Machine Gun '), *The Tuftonian: The Magazine of Tufts College*, IV (Fall 1944), 120-122.

' Bell Buoy,' ' Cézanne,' *Quixote*, Spring 1947, pp. 14-15.

' Over the Sea Wall, Looking Down,' ' Pin-Up,' ' Saipan,' ' Elegy for Kurt Porjescz,' ' Cycle,' ' Poem for My God-Child,' *Epoch*, I (Fall 1947), 45-53.

' Snapshot,' *Lyric*, XXXIII (Summer 1953), 199.

' Theories of Flight,' ' I Thanked the Lunatic for a Particular View,' *Volusia Review*, I (No. 1, 1954), 25.

' Day,' *Patterns*, I (October 1954), 15.

' Doctor Faustus,' ' Lines for Woodlawn,' ' To Judith (V),' ' To My Father,' *Pennsylvania Literary Review*, V (No. 3, 1955), 9-14.

' Mecánico,' *Revista Mexicana de Literatura*, No. 5 (Mayo-Junio 1956), 447-448. [Tr. by Jose V. Amaral of ' Mechanic.']

'Dante Alighieri: *Purgatorio*, V' [translation], *Italian Quarterly*, I (Summer 1957), 3-7.

'Faces,' 'An Island Galaxy,' *Coastlines*, III (Winter 1957-58), 28-29.

Articles and Reviews by John Ciardi

'The Middle Muddle (Notes of a " Confused Progressive "),' *Harvard Advocate*, CXXXII (28 February 1949), 10-11, 13.

'Open Letter to Mr. Ober,' *Harvard Alumni Bulletin*, LI (25 June 1949), 706, 708. [Concerning the suggestion that Harlow Shapley and John Ciardi be fired for subversion.]

'The Hypnoglyph,' *The Magazine of Science-Fantasy Fiction*, V (July 1953), 25-32. [Science-fantasy fiction, published under the name of John Anthony.]

'Again The Anthologist,' *Anthologist* (Rutgers University), XXV (May 1954), 3.

'On the Impossibility of Translating Poetry,' *New York Times*, 18 July 1954; *Bulletin de l'Association Tecknologique de Langue Française d'Ottawa*, IV (Novembre 1954), 2-4. [Appeared under ' Speaking of Books,' *New York Times Book Review*, p. 2.]

'Another School Year—Why?,' *Rutgers Alumni Monthly*, XXXIV (November 1954), 2-3.

'L'ipnoglifo,' *Fantascienza* (Edizione italiana di The Magazine of Fantasy and Science Fiction), No. 2 (Dicembre 1954), 66-74. [Tr. of ' The Hypnoglyph ' by John Anthony.]

'Poetry and the Practical Man,' *Management Review*, XLIV (October 1955), 700-702.

'Dickinson's " I Heard a Fly Buzz When I Died," ' *Explicator*, XIV (January 1956), Item 22.

'Why Read Modern Poetry?,' *Think* (IBM Corporation), XXII (March 1956), 28.

'The Idea of a Writers' Conference,' *Middlebury College Bulletin*, LI (April 1956), 1-2.

'Director's Foreword,' *Middlebury College Bulletin*, LII (April 1957), 1-2.

Index of Titles

Titles of books by John Ciardi are in capitals; titles of books containing contributions by him are in capitals and small capitals; titles of poems are in upper-and-lower case type; and titles of articles and reviews are in italics.

59

63

Designed by Richard Kinney

Set in Baskerville and Bulmer Type faces
Printed on Warren's Olde Style Antique paper
Bound in Linweave Text Laid Antique paper
Manufactured in the United States of America

HANNAH, DIVIDED

Distributed by
The Drop In Learning Center
a United Way Agency
442-4466

HANNAH, DIVIDED

DIVIDED

ADELE GRIFFIN

HYPERION PAPERBACKS FOR CHILDREN

NEW YORK

Text copyright © 2002 by Adele Griffin
All rights reserved. No part of this book may be reproduced
or transmitted in any form or by any means, electronic or
mechanical, including photocopying, recording, or by any
information storage and retrieval system, without written
permission from the publisher. For information address
Hyperion Books for Children, 114 Fifth Avenue,
New York, New York 10011-5690.
Printed in the United States of America
First Hyperion Paperback edition, 2004
1 3 5 7 9 10 8 6 4 2

This book is set in Horley Oldstyle.
Library of Congress Cataloging-in-Publication Data on file.
ISBN 0-7868-0879-9 (tr.)
ISBN 0-7868-1727-5 (pbk.)

Visit www.hyperionbooksforchildren.com

For my aunt, Elizabeth Sands

CONTENTS

PART THREE

PART ONE

THE CITY VISITOR

NEVER HAD Brintons Bridge School looked so presentable. Its floor had been swept, its windows and chalkboard washed, its standing globe dusted, and a jam jar of marigolds placed on the windowsill. Never had its students appeared so scrubbed, either. Miss Cascade had asked them to pay close attention to fingernails, necks, and ears. Even Elgin Winnicker's cowlick was spit-flattened neat to the back of his head.

All this fuss in preparation for Mr. Sweet, who, according to Miss Cascade, "just might be the most influential gentleman, ever, to step through our door."

Hannah Bennett turned the words over in her head. *Most influential gentleman, ever.* She pictured Mr. Sweet as a combination of Moses and Charles Darwin. Only, Mr. Sweet was not traveling from Egypt or the Galápagos, but from Philadelphia, and he was coming to give their school money. Perhaps. Miss Cascade had read his letter out loud, the one he had written in response to Miss Cascade's request for aid from the Wexler Foundation, the charitable trust for which Mr. Sweet worked. Mr. Sweet's answer had been not quite yes but not quite no. *Perhaps,* he had written.

That was why their schoolhouse looked sharp as a needle today. To help push Mr. Sweet's answer away from *perhaps* and closer to *yes.*

Miss Cascade looked up from her desk to waggle a finger at her students. "Class, we must remember politeness," she said. "Everyone knows that our school needs a new roof and modern textbooks. Politeness counts." Her eyes darted to Hannah, who often forgot about politeness.

Hannah lifted her chin and straightened. She had been helping the fifth graders with their long-division problems. She had been good all day and would continue to be so. She would not vex and disappoint.

Peggy Stone pulled at Hannah's sleeve. "Hannah, my answer turned out to be not enough numbers."

"Because you forgot the decimal point, Peggy." Hannah picked up the pencil and dotted it in. "Five point one and point five one are different amounts when you—"

Her concentration broke with the faint sound of a car's engine, gurgling and chugging down Brintons Bridge Road. Was that a motorcar? But nobody arrived at school by car! She leaped out of her seat and ran to the window.

"He's here! It's Mr. Sweet from Philadelphia!"

"Hannah! Sit down!"

"Lookatit, lookit his automobile! Brand

spanking new! That's a swell lot of money, I'll say!"

Books banged to the floor as students jumped from benches to cram into the schoolhouse's open doorway. The polite, pent-up waiting of the afternoon was broken.

"A Super Eight Packard Touring," breathed Elgin, who was nuts for automobiles and could name every model. "Musta just rolled out of big Bay City!"

"Could be quite a chunk of money sunk in that Wexler fund, if Mr. Sweet can arrive in such style," said Betsy Seal.

"Girls, boys!" implored Miss Cascade. "Hannah!"

But once on her feet, Hannah could hardly bring herself to sit down again. The banana-yellow Packard veered off the road, stirring up a riot of dust, and charged the narrower graveled footpath to the school's front door, where it hiccuped to a stop. Its engine gurgled and cut, and the driver's-side door jerked open on oiled hinges. Hannah stared as one two-toned shoe, then another, planted itself to the ground. How peculiar—Mr. Sweet wore ladies' shoes! Then the rest of a strong, stout woman emerged.

"Miss Cascade?" The woman's voice was a bellow.

"Yes! Yes, I am! And you—?"

"Mrs. Theodora Ann Sweet!" the woman announced. "From the Wexler Foundation of Philadelphia! My friends call me Teddy. So may you!" She offered the favor grandly.

"*Mrs.!*—Teddy—Sweet!" Miss Cascade disguised her surprise with a friendly smile. "Please, madam, won't you come in? By your name, I mistakenly thought . . ."

Mrs. Sweet was not listening. She palmed shut the car door as if she were closing a vault. Then she used her handkerchief to spit and rub at a smudge on the side window. "Mitts off my baby!" she ordered as she faced them. "She's only three months old!"

Ignoring Miss Cascade's offered hand, she

barreled up the short flight of stone steps to the schoolhouse. Students parted at the door to give her way. A fearsome woman, Hannah thought, but so smartly dressed, in a gray suit cut thick as a slipcover, and matching tipped beret over her dark, bronze-rinsed hair. A silk sprig of lilac drooped sideways from her lapel, and an envelope bag fell slantwise from one broad shoulder.

Hannah counted seven suit buttons, eleven footsteps, and five syllables in her name. From bag to beret, Theodora Sweet seemed to be an odd-numbered, slant-sided sort of person.

Miss Cascade shooed boys and girls back to their seats while Mrs. Sweet's gaze skipped across the room for a chair. Finding none, she scooted herself up onto the dunce stool, which caused a surge of giggling. Miss Cascade frowned the room into quiet.

Unconcerned, Mrs. Sweet pulled a clipboard and pen from her envelope bag. "Even for back-woods Chadds Ford farmland, this school is teensy-weensy! How many are you?"

"I teach fifty-six students." Miss Cascade stood in front of her desk, her politeness smile now stretched into place. "Some of our older boys have left to work their family farms for the harvest. We'll get them in school again before the first frost."

"What bad form, to interrupt schooling with farming." Mrs. Sweet scribbled on her clipboard. Left-handed, with her legs crossed and head inclined, she looked slightly skewed. Hannah tilted her own head to observe the woman better. "Let's see." Mrs. Sweet used her pen as a pointer. "Stove in back, organ in front. . . . Is that the door to the W.C.?"

"To the cellar, where we store wood and coal," answered Miss Cascade. "We have a separate facility out back for our . . . ablutions."

"Well, hold my hat! An outdoor can, in this day and age!" Mrs. Sweet spoke in such a boom that another wave of laughter swept the schoolhouse and again was calmed by Miss Cascade's strict eye.

Hannah peered down her row at the line of folded hands and upturned faces, each boy and girl hoping to win Miss Cascade's approval and Mrs. Sweet's charity. Didn't anyone care that Mrs. Sweet was rude and bossy? Calling their school "backwoods" and "teensy-weensy"! Making fun of their outhouse!

"Give us our money, and good riddance," Hannah murmured.

Betsy turned and pushed a finger to her lips. "Hannah, gracious! Hush!"

"Each row is grade-divided. First to eighth. After graduating, most will continue on to the Consolidated School." Miss Cascade's smile now seemed pulled against its will. "Here, the older ones tutor the younger. We enjoy reading and ciphering and history and music. We put on a pageant every spring. All of my students partic- ipate, and we invite most everyone in Chester County to come see it."

"Lovely." Mrs. Sweet made no attempt to hide her yawn. But Miss Cascade's pageants were wonderful! Certainly nothing to yawn about! Was nobody going to speak up for them?

"Miss Cascade! Tell how last spring, we did a tribute to Benjamin Franklin!" Hannah called out on impulse. "Tell how my big brother Roy was Mr. Franklin himself, and he was so good! How he wore a pigtail and flew a kite and signed the Declaration of—"

"Hannah!" Miss Cascade interrupted. "What do I say about talking out of turn?"

"Oh, pageants are fine sport." Mrs. Sweet flicked her fingers. "But they're no education. Nor is having older children teach the babies." Her eyebrow lifted. "Isn't that so?"

Nobody answered. Nobody laughed, either. Mrs. Sweet's words were mean. They sliced open the school and dismissed it as if it were bruised fruit. Hannah bit her lips to stop from shouting that she *loved* teaching math to the younger students. In fact, math was the only subject where she felt clever. Enough with this visitor, this snooty Mrs. Sweet! They didn't need her goodwill. Their old school roof would do—it only leaked in back, and Miss Cascade caught the water easily enough using bread pans.

Hannah looked to her teacher to see what she might say next. Miss Cascade smoothed her white bib. Hot spots of color had appeared on her cheeks.

"These are the times we're living in, er, Teddy," explained Miss Cascade. "In our schoolhouse, the most important lesson we learn is to help one another. It's true there isn't much extra to go around. But nothing gets wasted, either."

Mrs. Sweet waved off Miss Cascade's words. "And nothing gets accomplished!"

The shifts and whispers among the others agreed that now Mrs. Sweet didn't seem half as nice as her name or her car. She was far from Hannah's image of "the most influential gentleman, ever."

"What a snob," Hannah murmured. "That's the last time I pick marigolds for Mrs. *Sour*."

This time, nobody shushed her.

"HARK! AH, THE NIGHTINGALE—"

WHEN MISS CASCADE dismissed the class for the day, her finger pinned Hannah back to her seat.

"Hannah," she said. "Don't go yet. I want Mrs. Sweet to have a word with you."

Boys and girls were bouncing toward the door.

"Mitts off my baby!" warned Mrs. Sweet.

Betsy and Tru looked at Hannah pityingly as they collected their lunch pails and stuffed their books into their satchels.

"Remember, be *polite*, Hannah," said Frank Dilworth. "It'd be nice to have new books and such."

"But don't let that city slicker bother you about your reading," whispered Betsy.

"I will. I won't. See you tomorrow." Hannah could feel her face reddening under the sympathetic eyes of the departing students. Everyone knew why Hannah was being kept inside.

Boys and girls jostled out the door as Hannah dragged herself to the first-row bench at the front of the room. Miss Cascade waved good-bye and called last-minute reminders. Mrs. Sweet stood by the window and kept an eye on her Packard. Now it was only the three of them as the others swarmed, free as bees, down the road.

"Mrs. Sweet, this is Hannah Bennett," said Miss Cascade, perching next to Hannah. "I had mentioned her in my letter to you."

She had? How shameful! Hannah set her chin and stared unblinking at the chalkboard.

"Yes. The illiterate." Mrs. Sweet dropped

14

heavily on the bench at Hannah's other side. Her voice, loud and tired, was like that of a deaf doctor who has made too many house calls in one day.

Hannah's eyes did not move from the board. It's not so awful that I can't read, she thought miserably, as it is to be singled out and scolded for it. Though Miss Cascade's voice was gentle as she spoke. "During my three years here, I have done everything in my power to teach Hannah to read. Sadly, I haven't made progress. Hannah cannot see the structure of a sentence. She confuses word order. Is this something you've come across in your visits to other schools?"

"Certainly!" Mrs. Sweet snapped. "And I'd bet that sloth is at the root of it. Sloth is our undoing!"

Already she was rummaging through Hannah's book sack. She tugged from it Hannah's most dreaded schoolbook, *My Poem and Verse Companion*, and flipped its soft pages.

"Ah, 'Philomela'! Miss Bennett, what do you see when you look at 'Philomela'?" She held the open book aloft, cracking its spine.

Hannah stared. "Letters."

"Don't be fresh about Matthew Arnold, miss! We *all* see letters! When arranged into groups, they are called words!"

"I didn't mean—I meant . . ." Hannah took a breath. Politeness first, she reminded herself. She would not disappoint Frank and Betsy and the others. "The letters make a pattern. The *t*s and the *l*s and the *r*s." She leaned forward to examine them.

"These words are simple and lovely," needled Mrs. Sweet. "Read them, don't fear them!"

Fear them? Was Mrs. Sweet trying to provoke her? Hannah stared, hard-eyed, at the words, each packed in like a boxcar of letters, willing her to unload it, to count and stack its contents into a proper grouping.

She tapped the page corners with her finger and stared across the first line.

H a r k ! a h , t h e n i g h t i n g a l e—

Hark!ahthenightingale

Hhh aaa r k tt ee nn ii gg l

"Three *h*s, three *a*s, r, k, double *t*, two *e*s, two *n*s, two *i*s, double *g*, *l*," she said. She scanned down the page, collecting *e*s. "The *e*s will likely win in the end."

Miss Cascade made a clucking sound. "Hannah is quite good in math," she asserted. "Multiplication tables and fractions and her long division."

"Well, that's nothing to sneeze at," said Mrs. Sweet. "What's nine times seven?"

"Nine times seven," Hannah repeated. By now, though, 'Philomela' had spiraled itself like a kaleidoscope into her eye, burying the answer to nine times seven beneath it. She filled the air with a whisper of other numbers: "One point two eight five seven—" before it washed to surface. "Sixty-three!" She pressed a hand to her heart. "How could I forget? Sixty-three!"

"Hannah, softer, please," whispered Miss Cascade. "We're right here."

"I do know my times tables, truly," Hannah assured Mrs. Sweet. "And my ma said that if I

17

was no better at reading this year, she'd teach me next summer. We'll use the Bible. The Bible ought to have every word I'd ever use! So don't trouble yourself over me, ma'am."

She was not speaking politely enough. Mrs. Sweet looked from Hannah to Miss Cascade to Hannah again.

"One point two eight . . . " she murmured. "And how many *t*s in 'Philomela'?"

Hannah glanced at the page and the number flew across her mind like a blackbird. "Seventy-four."

"Hannah, dear," reproved Miss Cascade. "Don't answer as if you *know*."

"Hmm." Mrs. Sweet flipped the page. "Oh, gorgeous! William Wordsworth, 'Strange Fits of Passion Have I Known.' Count the *a*s, please?"

In the pause of the next moment, Hannah sensed a crackle of attention on either side of her. Ma had long warned her not to show off her counting trick. It was peculiar, Ma said, and put people on edge, like speaking backward.

Counting off numbers—if it must be done—ought to be similar to reciting bedtime prayers. A private comfort, said Ma, though Granddad McNaughton saw it differently. Proud of her math, he liked Hannah to show it off a bit.

"The *a*s," Mrs. Sweet repeated. So vexing! Egging Hannah on.

And the answer was irresistible. "Forty-three."

Miss Cascade laughed. "Oh, that couldn't . . . it's not true." She snatched the book from Mrs. Sweet. Her lips moved silently as her finger popped along the page. "Forty-two. A very good guess, though, Hannah."

"You missed one," Hannah said. "Your finger skipped the second *a* in *wayward*."

Mrs. Sweet snatched the book and cut to another place. "Aha. Christina Rossetti, 'The Goblin Market.' Four pages! Count the *p*s. All of them!" Her tone dared Hannah to try.

Hannah took the book onto her lap. The pattern was beautiful, big and small *p*s flicking their tails like fish. Her mind dropped over them like a net, caught and counted them into their proper school. "Two hundred twenty-eight."

"The *r*s!"

The small *r*s were curved canes; their upper cases walked on two legs under fat stomachs. "Nine hundred thirty-one."

"And the *e*s?"

Ah, wonderful *e*s, the lower *e*s in clusters like tiny mushrooms to be picked, with a single uppercase *E* standing alone as a broken ladder. Hannah gathered them all up. "One thousand, seven hundred eleven."

Mrs. Sweet's snort startled Hannah from her counting trance. "Now, this is poetry, Miss Cascade!" she cried. "Strange poetry, but nonetheless! The girl can read numbers into eternity! How could you not have known?" She laughed in a pleased but startled way.

Miss Cascade was not laughing. "Goodness, Hannah, you never made use of this . . . *game* during math class." She shut the book and held it on her lap as if it were Pandora's box. She seemed stumped as to what to say next.

"I don't take math, Miss Cascade," Hannah reminded. "I tutor it. You told me in the beginning of last year that I'd learned all the math skills I'd ever need. You wanted me to concentrate on my reading." *And that math was more practical for boys.* Hannah kept that part to herself, as well as the fact that Granddad McNaughton had been tutoring her privately for years. Poor Miss Cascade looked upset enough.

"Miss Cascade is correct. Reading *is* essential, for a full and productive life." Mrs. Sweet peered at Hannah with something like hunger in her eyes. It made Hannah feel uncomfortable, but a tiny thrill of pride swelled through her, too. If nothing else, she had impressed both Mrs. Sweet and Miss Cascade with her counting.

She returned Mrs. Sweet's gaze directly. "I don't much care about being illiterate, Mrs. Sweet, especially when there's so many others—my best friends, Tru and Betsy, plus Ma and my brother Roy—to read aloud to me. Ma says there's bigger problems in our country than not understanding when the *e* is silent." She drew a breath. "And if you must know, I don't care for poetry, either. Thankfully, it's our first class, so I don't have to dread—"

"All right, Hannah." Miss Cascade lifted and dropped her hands. "I think we're finished here. Get along home. Your family will be wondering."

Mrs. Sweet nodded in agreement. Hannah leaped from her seat and nearly knocked over the dunce stool on her way out the door.

"Take heed, Hannah," warned Miss Cascade. To Mrs. Sweet, she said, "You must understand, her difficulties are greater than you perceive. I can't see how you might think . . ."

Hannah was not listening. She did not much care what Mrs. Sweet might think. She ducked outside, floating into the warm welcome of a September afternoon. Free.

3

RUNNING, COUNTING, STACKING

HANNAH DECIDED to run home.

She had to. The counting had given her energy. It was like performing a circus entertainment, like spinning plates or eating fire. Counting was a bolt of hot, bright lightning in her brain. It was a habit and a comfort, yes, but it also opened her mind to a vastness of numbers that overwhelmed her.

No matter how fast Hannah ran, she could always count faster.

She was counting, even now. She had started with the poems and she could not stop.

She counted her steps, the draw and release of her breath. She counted fence posts, birds, Holsteins, rocks strewn along her path.

She counted inside things, too. Rounded up this afternoon to four o' clock and from there, she counted off the hours until the dawn of her birthday, April fourteenth. Then she counted the hours she had lived since her last taste of chocolate ice cream, the minutes her seventy-nine-year-old self would be on this earth at eight in the morning of the first day of the year 2001 (factoring in the 1,440 minutes per extra day times 20 leap years).

Finally, she took this year, 1934, and divided it by two. Over and over, skipping the decimal point like a checkers piece until it stood at the front of the line.

Granddad McNaughton encouraged her mathematics. Sunday afternoons, they passed gleeful hours inventing games with figures and sums, making up riddles and puzzles to solve. Until recently, Granddad himself was always up and running, too, either to clear branches or chop wood or weed his vegetable garden. Mental tasks must be balanced by the physical, Granddad liked to say. He'd been feeling poorly of late, but he never said no to a walk in the outdoors. And he still loved math.

Hannah's shoes were thick with dust by the time she turned off Brintons Bridge Road and onto Orchard Way. The same sprint, an equal length of distance, every step. She rounded the Applebee farm and the Roe farm and Indian Rock. Objects whizzed by, and she gathered them mentally, easy as *ps* and *rs* and *ts*.

It was not until she reached her front gate that she stopped and stood, panting, triumphant. She closed her eyes to set the final sums in a row.

Steps: 1, 657

Paired breaths: 520

Fence posts: 192

Birds: 29

Holsteins: 44

Rocks: 170 (gray: 111; black: 53; mixed: 6)

Hours left until April 14: 5,041

Hours since last taste of chocolate ice cream: 3,212

Minutes lived on planet Earth at eight o'clock A.M. of 1/1/2001: 41,927,680

1934 divided: 967, 483.5, 241.75, 120.875, 60.4375, 30.1875, 15.09375, 7.546875, 3.7734375, 1.8867188, .9433594

4

LATE

MA WAS TAKING down the bedsheets in the side yard and listening to the kitchen radio tuned to *The Betty Crocker Hour*. Hannah saw her undergarments flapping on the line. Not again—as if she hadn't asked Ma a thousand times to please let her dry her delicates in the privacy of her bedroom!

But Ma, always busy and never modest about such things, often forgot.

Hannah dashed across the yard, shouting a flapping, strutting Homer out of her way, then jumped for a pair of waving underpants. She jiggled the line hard. Roy's spare coveralls and one of Pa's kerchiefs dropped to the dirt.

"Careful, Hannah! Look before you leap."

Hannah had heard that warning too many times to pay attention to it. She yanked down an undershirt and folded it over her arm. "Ma, I've wished a hundred times you would allow me care of my own underclothes."

"If wishes were horses . . ." Ma answered. "Hurry now. You're late to milking."

"Ladies, you may also use honey or Karo syrup in place of white sugar," assured the gentleman announcer.

Ha! Karo syrup was a special-occasions treat. In fact, most sweet food was a special-occasions treat. The announcer ought to stick to explaining Bisquick and red cabbage. But *The Betty Crocker Hour* was Ma's favorite show, and Hannah knew better than to talk over it.

She hurried into the house and upstairs to her bedroom. Her underwear was dried stiff enough to put away. She took care to fold each article just so before placing it in her clothes cupboard, though Ma wearied of Hannah's insistence on ruler-straight edges and right angles, on stacking every pair of stockings and underwear neat as saucers.

"Your habits have more hold on you than you do on them," Ma often chided.

Hannah shut the cupboard and stood at the window an extra moment, feeling the house all around her as she looked out over the view. She stared across the field to the barn's red roof, half-hidden in a green canopy of maples. Here in her bedroom, across the hall from the room where she'd been born, and staring out over the low hills at a spread of family-owned property—here was safety. She tapped a pattern on the paint-thickened windowpane. She loved her home, with its swept corners and known secrets, its worn, dark furniture, its every scent and view familiar to her.

And now it was September. Soon the leaves

would change color, and there would be much to reap for the autumn harvest. In addition to the dairy, the farm had a small oat piece, a potato piece, a garden piece, as well as three acres of orchard. Come winter, sacks of feed would be put away for the livestock, as well as potatoes stacked next to cans of pickled cucumbers, stewed tomatoes, and jar upon jar of Hannah's favorite preserves, plum and peach, which she and Ma likely would be pitting until late October.

Late! Quickly, Hannah shed her school clothes for milking slacks and a sweater. Then she tied on her white floursack apron, knotting it twice around her middle. The apron was an old one of Ma's, and though Hannah was taller, she didn't have quite Ma's girth yet.

On the way out to the barn, she checked her reflection in the tarnished kitchen mirror. It stopped her. She batted her eyes and gave her best movie-star smile. Then she peered harder at herself. Her face, swamped in a quantity of pale, flyaway hair, looked soft and indistinct. She wished she were a more precise-looking person, with Joan Crawford's hurt, liquid eyes or with the sly smirk of Claudette Colbert. But the face in the mirror might belong to any girl.

"Hannah!" Her mother's voice broke Hannah from her thoughts. She turned. Ma stood in the doorway, the laundry basket at her hip, Hannah's milk buckets held out in her opposite hand. "There's a sight. Gazing at yourself when you're needed in the milk house. Where is your sense?"

"I'm going, I'm going." Hannah collected the buckets and ducked out the door.

Down at the milk house, Roy, Pa, and Ben were finishing up. The cows were back in the barn, fed and content, and Ben was washing down the floor to its center drain. When he saw Hannah, he nodded acknowledgment and looked away.

The year before, when Ben had come to work for the family, Hannah had decided he was a terrible grouch. Now she knew better: that Ben was a private man, given to long fits of low spirits, pining for his wife and son in Ohio. He almost never spoke of them, but he sent his pay home every month, riding with Pa in the pickup into town and handing the envelope to the postmaster as if it contained a living thing.

Pa said that Ben was lucky to have work when most men didn't, though *lucky* was not the word that came to Hannah's mind. *Lonely* fit Ben better.

Roy and Pa were huddled in the corner, gingerly lowering the last milk cans into the new electric cooler. They'd only had it for two months, every spare nickel of last year and most of this one sunk into its purchase. But the dairy had been bedeviled by the need for the cooler (Pa's words), and since the farm almost never earned out in plain cash money, the cooler had been a long time in the waiting. It was here now, and better than any Christmas gift, Hannah reasoned, as this winter she and Roy would not have to pry up ice from the pond to keep the milk chilled overnight.

"Hannah, where've you been to?" asked Pa. "We could have used your touch roundabout a half hour ago. Dosey was acting persnickety."

"I was held back after school. They had a special lady come in from some charity in Philadelphia. I suppose Miss Cascade thought she'd have the right answer to my reading problem."

"And did she?" Pa took off his cap and wiped his forehead with it. He looked upset. School and reading had been a struggle for him, as well. "Think she might tighten some screws in your noggin?"

"They'll tighten themselves, Pa," Hannah assured him. She refrained from saying more. Pa would not want to hear about the other part of the visit, about her counting letters and the surprise that washed over Mrs. Sweet's and Miss Cascade's faces. No, that was a show-off story; a tale for Granddad's ears alone.

"C'mon, cover these, lollygagger!" called Roy. He disliked it when he had to pull Hannah's share.

She got to work. All that was left to do was to fasten the straining cloths over the two remaining milk cans and to secure the fabric in place with wooden clothespins, a final step before the cans were stored in the cooler until tomorrow morning's delivery.

She was good at fastening. The cloth spread evenly, no puckering, smooth as a painter's canvas.

"Radio ought to wipe out most recreational reading altogether," said Pa after a few moments, speaking to Hannah in a burst as if he'd been stewing on it. "Folks hear faster than they can read, and it's no strain to the eyes neither."

Hannah nodded. She liked that idea.

5

EVENING SURPRISE

HEPP'S LETTER, unopened in the middle of the table, would be more sumptuous than dessert. Ma planned to read it out loud after dinner. Roy, who could mow through a plate of food in two minutes, kicked Hannah under the table to hurry her. She paid no mind and ate her usual way—clockwise, after arranging the food around her plate from least to greatest. Biscuit, rice, bacon lardons, sliced tomato.

Pa stirred all the food on his plate into a puddle and sank a pool of gravy in the middle, as did Ben, but a look from Ma made Roy decide against it. Ma didn't hold Hannah and Roy to much proper behavior, but she'd been a doctor's daughter before she became a farmer, and she kept an entire set of rules like a chest of antique silver tucked in a corner of her head.

As he did every night directly after supper, Ben stood and nodded his good-night, taking leave to smoke his pipe under the stars. Once Hannah had cleared the table and soaked the dishes, Ma reached for the letter.

"Shall we?"

"Yes!" chorused Hannah and Roy, while Pa stayed silent but took out his pipe.

Ma tickled her finger beneath the envelope flap, unable to wait another minute. It had been two years since Hepp left home, and everyone missed him sorely. Hepp was a full-grown twenty years old now and still footloose, "crisscrossing the states like a common tramp," in Pa's words.

Hepp's had not been a peaceful departure, either. Hannah could still recall the shouting in the living room, Hepp insisting that he'd never been a farmer and never would be one, and so he might as well take a look at the world and find the right spot to plant roots. Hepp was no good with the dairy, and he had as much feel for the land as the man in the moon. No, her oldest brother preferred wandering to any other activity, and he had spent most waking hours with his head lost in a book of travel or adventure.

But it was not until he'd left home that Hannah fully understood. Hepp out in the world also meant her world without Hepp. It grieved her. She kept one of his impossibly long socks in her dresser, along with the thick pamphlet Hepp had sent her from last year's World's Fair in Chicago. Only nothing was as nice as the sound of his voice, blending through Ma's as she read out loud.

Dear Family,
   Except for the red chili peppers growing
plentiful as crab apples, Santa Fe was a
dead bust. Two weeks of picking and then

*no work, and now I'm twiddling my thumbs
in Macon. We'd had word there was hiring
out for cotton crops, seems we were wrong
and there's a hundred men for every job—
the usual story.*

*I got here by rail with my usual boys—
Fat Mike and Billy, and it took us three
days. We traded turns sleeping to keep an
eye skinned against the law. Okie Slims
and Texas Slims are quick to shoot you off
a train—only to scare, Ma, not to harm.
You'd laugh to see me, I swapped most of
what was in my bindle for food during a
stopover in Austin, so I use one map spread
over me for a blanket and the other folded
up for a pillow. We're hungry some, and
disappointed, but Mike's got a hunch to
head for Alabama. We hear there's pine
mills might need men for sawing—*

Ma broke off, startled at the noise. Pa
stopped knocking his pipe against the wall.

Hannah recognized the sound of that automobile. Mrs. Sweet! What was she doing here? Whether to discuss Hannah's poor reading or show-off counting, this unexpected visit would not likely please either Ma or Pa. Apprehension bunched in Hannah's chest as Roy leaped down the hall to throw open the door. There was a dog's belief in Roy that his brother might be coming home any day now.

Ma and Pa both scraped back their chairs and stood as Mrs. Sweet entered the kitchen in a bustle, introducing herself and pumping hands mightily all around.

"I'll sit, but I can't stay long!" she began when Pa indicated the vacant chair. "I have come to offer Hannah a once-in-a-lifetime opportunity, made possible by Wexler's generous auspices!"

"Wexler? I never heard of any Mister Wexler," said Pa, reseating himself when Mrs. Sweet settled into her chair. "He's not from these parts, anyhow."

"Because Wexler is a place, Pa, not a body,"

said Ma, moving to the kettle to prepare Mrs. Sweet a mug of hot tea.

"No, it's a thing," said Roy. "It's money, I bet."

For once, Hannah stayed as mute as if she'd been set on the dunce stool.

"It's a person, place, and thing!" Mrs. Sweet harrumphed. "It's a charitable trust, and I am its executive director, appointed by Philadelphia's own Mayor Moore. Part of our good work is to award scholarships to children who otherwise might not be receiving the usual advantages. So that he—or she—can prepare for a university education." She nodded thanks as she accepted the mug. "I did not travel out to these parts looking for a diamond in the rough, but it seems Hannah has a gift for numbers."

A gift for numbers. Hannah liked that, even if praise came from such a bossy-boots as Mrs. Sweet. And a scholarship! Well, wouldn't Granddad McNaughton be pleased to hear that!

Though one glance at her parents showed that they were not. "Oh, Hannah's got a *knack*," agreed Pa warily. "She does all the family invoicing. Puts the bills in the bottles at the end of the month. She's kept track of every cent for years. Course, farms don't get paid out always in money, so precision's not the upmost."

"Rest assured, Hannah would be taught more than invoicing!" retorted Mrs. Sweet. "She would be taught advanced concepts, algebra, geometry, proofs, theorems—"

"Madam, I ought to tell you now, it's a mighty far-fetched conversation we're having here," interrupted Ma. "It's not as if we have the money to send Hannah to a fancy university once you've taken all the effort to prepare her! And, it's not as if Hannah could qualify to study other subjects, what with all her reading troubles."

Pa nodded. He picked up Hepp's letter and began to fold it into small and smaller squares. Hannah knew that if Pa started to fold, things were knotting up inside his mind. "My wife speaks for us both," he said. "It's Hannah's reading where we'd like to see improvements. And truth be told," Pa added, "I don't myself see much point to girls learning fancy math."

"At Ottley Friends, in Philadelphia, Hannah will be reading quicker than you can say boo," said Mrs. Sweet. "As for girls and math, why, Mr. Bennett, we have lived to see Marie Curie twice win the Nobel Prize, once for Physics and once for Chemistry. Lord rest her soul."

Pa shook his head. "Cities are no use to children. Young ones are wild cockalorum and grown best out of doors." He set down Hepp's letter. His fidgeting fingers found and drew a long match from his breast pocket to strike against the table leg, and he turned his head from Mrs. Sweet to relight his pipe with slow, labored puffs.

"When did Miss Curie pass on?" asked Roy.

"This summer," answered Hannah. "And she was a doctor, not a miss, and it's pronounced cure-eee, not curry, dummy."

"Who's a dummy? It's not like *you* could've *read* it in the newspaper!" Roy scoffed.

"*Children*," Ma scolded.

Mrs. Sweet turned to Hannah. "This is a wonderful chance, dear. Toward the end of December, state qualification exams are given to determine scholarship candidates. While Hannah prepares for them, she could lodge for the semester with me—or another sponsor family, if she prefers." Her voice began to frog into speechmaking tones as she addressed the room in general. "As a patron of Mayor Moore's education reform movement, I am an advocate of progress and learning experiments."

Hannah flinched. *Experiment* was the wrong word to use. The last experiment of Pa's had been to trade his best Holstein, Ruby, for two scrawny, deer-faced Jerseys, though Ruby gave more milk than the pair of them, and had a better temper besides. The last experiment of Ma's had been to repair the worn places in the kitchen tablecloth by patching it over in a cartwheel quilt pattern, but she hadn't had enough lemon-checked gingham to complete the design, and the tea-dyed woolsy she'd finished with gave the cloth a stained appearance.

"Roy, Hannah, go to your rooms," said Ma. "We'll move to the front room. This is grown-up talk now."

"I was going anyhow," said Roy in a low monotone as they both stood and shuffled from the kitchen. "Most boring conversation of my life."

Yet he looked upset, and he pushed past Hannah when he overtook her on the second-floor landing. "If you get to see the Liberty Bell before me, you're toasted and roasted," he said. "It's not fair, I'm almost fifteen, I read great—I was even Benjamin Franklin!—and I never saw Philadelphia. Not one blamed time. All I saw is New York City the way it looked in *King Kong*, which hardly counts a bean."

He slammed himself into his room, opened his door, and slammed it again.

There was no reasoning with Roy when he flared up that way.

Hannah crept to her own bedroom and looked out her window into the night. Treetops floated in a bath of fog, but the sky above was star-studded and clear. She breathed on the glass and drew circles with her finger. She spun her favorite number, thirty-two, through its cat's cradle of tricks. Thirty-two, the fifth power of two. Thirty-two pieces stood on a chessboard, and thirty-two were the numbers of teeth in a mouth—if none had been pulled.

Thirty-two would not stop Hannah's heart from pounding, though. She had to know what was being said below. At the very least, she should be allowed to hear enough to form her own opinion! She was owed that much, wasn't she?

After a few more minutes, she could not bear the suspense. On silent feet, she tiptoed back down the stairs. Mrs. Sweet was voicing her good-byes in the front hall. Too late! Before she could quite think it through, Hannah slipped around the corner, through the pantry, and out the kitchen door.

Mrs. Sweet had already swung through the gate to her Packard, which was parked at the edge of the lawn, looking as out of place as a sleeping yellow lion.

"Mrs. Sweet, ma'am?"

Mrs. Sweet turned. Hannah dropped to a walk, then stopped and held her ground, shifting her weight as she scratched a nagging itch of spider bite on her elbow. Now that she had Mrs. Sweet's attention, she was not sure what she wanted to say.

"Ah, Hannah." Mrs. Sweet shook her head. "Seems your parents are more country hardheads than I'd have figured. I'm sorry to fail you, but I'd easier talk a pair of parrots into reason."

Hannah frowned but stepped closer, resting each hand on a round-end picket post. "They're not hardheads, they're cautious, is all. And Ma's always said that counting numbers is no more than an odd trick."

"But you can do better than count, can't you, Hannah?" Mrs. Sweet leaned over the gate to speak in a hushed voice. She smelled like Pepsodent and sweet lilacs, as well as the more costly things of a world Hannah could not place.

"Nine times seven," prompted Mrs. Sweet. "I'm no fool! When I asked you what nine times seven was this afternoon, you divided it first, didn't you? Nine divided by seven is . . ."

Divided it? Hannah had not realized. "One point two . . . eight five seven one . . . one four—"

"That's not counting, see," interrupted Mrs. Sweet. "That's *calculating*."

"Calculating," Hannah echoed. It seemed too strong a word for what she'd done, slipping seven through the sieve of nine and sifting out the leftovers. "My granddad McNaughton . . ." she began, but her voice lost its way. *Speak up!* she commanded herself silently. She cleared her throat. "I was curious, ma'am. What's to d-do in Philadelphia?" she stammered.

"What's to do?" Mrs. Sweet looked

indignant. "Why, everything's to do! On a given Saturday, ladies and gentlemen attend the matinee and then stroll to the Bellevue-Stratford hotel for tea. There are ice sculptures and fountains there, and a woman in the tearoom who plays the harp like an angel. You can't find that here, can you?"

"My granddad McNaughton . . ." Hannah coughed again. She was floundering and she could see that Mrs. Sweet was losing patience with her. "Has been to Philadelphia," she finished.

"Lovely. And perhaps you'll see it one day, too. Or perhaps not. Look me up if you do," said Mrs. Sweet. Her voice was quick, false, done with talking. "*Au revoir*, Hannah. You're too young and ignorant to know the shame of this chance slipping you by, but remember one thing. It was Theodora Sweet who first spoke up for your math."

"That's not true!" Hannah exclaimed. "My granddad McNaughton has been speaking up for my math since I was little! He even sent away for a pamphlet about a special math school up in Boston, Massachusetts. He was thinking to take me to visit it this summer, but he hasn't been feeling himself lately. But it's Granddad who has the last word, see. Our farm is part McNaughton property." She stopped, horrified at what she had let slip out of her mouth. She clamped her hands together to stop from scratching her spider bite raw.

Silence held the air for a long moment before Mrs. Sweet spoke again. "Is that so?" she asked, her voice turned to honey, a coppery hook of eyebrow lifted. "Would it be helpful, then, Hannah, if I paid your grandfather a visit? McNaughton, is that his name?"

"Yes, ma'am." Hannah was glad the dark hid the flush in her face. Oh, she was in for it! Ma and Pa would fume with her for telling! But what was she supposed to do? She stepped back. "See him if you like, he lives just up the road—good night!"

"And good night to you, Hannah," said Mrs. Sweet as she wrenched open the car door. "Perhaps not all is lost."

Hannah allowed herself to scratch as soon as Mrs. Sweet ducked into her car and bumped down the road. Watched and scratched, until there was nothing to see but the smear of headlights aimed at the night ahead. The weight in her chest had become difficult to breathe through.

She consoled herself knowing that Granddad would have been furious with her if she hadn't spoken up. No gossip ever escaped Granddad's ears, and eventually he would have learned all about Mrs. Sweet. Hannah had grown used to the narrow seesaw she walked between pleasing Granddad and pleasing Ma and Pa. To suit her folks always meant putting Granddad's nose out of joint, and vice versa.

"I had to do it," Hannah said out loud, to reassure herself that it was so.

6

COFFEE OR TOBACCO

T HE NEXT MORNING, Hannah woke earlier than usual. She bathed and dressed in her milking clothes—sweater, slacks, apron, boots— then crept downstairs to the kitchen to throw a pinecone and a few sticks of dry birch in the stove's hungry underbelly, stirring up the embers for breakfast.

Outdoors was chilly, the darkness like cool black silk thrown over the morning. She lit the gooseneck and collected her pail, placing both lamp and pail in the wheelbarrow, along with a first haul of glass bottles Ma had sterilized the afternoon before. The others would bring the rest. As she set off for the barn, lamplight cut out her shadow as it glided on the ground.

Ben, up and about first no matter how early anyone else rose, already had led a group of cows to the milk house, where Mouser was mewing for a first taste of the day. Hannah pulled up her stool in front of Dosey, then squirted the cat's face to appease and shoo him. Ben sat opposite.

"Bags washed, or do I need to?" she asked.

"Done," Ben replied.

Hannah made a loose loop in Dosey's tail and hung it on a tack so she wouldn't twitch—tail-twitching was Dosey's specialty—then got to work. The sound of milk, its swish and beat sure as a drum, was a morning rhythm as familiar as the hot breakfast that would follow. Mouser watched from the windowsill, licking his paws.

Soon, Pa and Roy stomped in. Roy began to lead the milked cows back to the barn and to collect another lowing, udder-heavy group to be relieved. Pa milked the Jerseys himself. Hannah knew her father well enough to hear impatience in the puff of his breath. He was still regretful about trading good old Ruby. But *No talking* was an unspoken rule of morning chores. Better to get the jobs finished and everyone's stomach filled—both animal and human—as soon as possible.

After the milking, Ben washed down the floor while Pa fed the cows. Roy and Hannah took care of the new supply; Roy pouring the translucent milk from the large cans into delivery quarts, which Hannah then fastened with cardboard lids and collars and hoisted into the wheelbarrow for Pa to cart to the truck. The air was cold enough that the cream was already separating to the top. On a winter morning, the milk would push the cream up over the cardboard, but temperatures would not drop to frost for another month at least.

"Your ma and I was up late," Pa said, slowing his gait to let Ben and Roy step ahead a pace as they all walked up to the house. "Talked about you, some."

"Me and Philadelphia?"

Pa's chin cut a quick yes and he cleared his throat. "We're set against it, Hannah. You've always been clever with your sums, nobody's arguing it, but there's too many cautions for us to rest easy. You've never traveled off the farm alone, and you're too young to be planked down in the middle of a big city. Neither your ma nor me reckon on Mrs. Sweet being careful guardian to you, either."

Hannah could feel her mouth thin into a stubborn line. "Granddad McNaughton always wanted me to advance in math," she reminded. "He even sent away for information about that special school in Boston, remember."

Pa stopped and turned to look at her. "On account of Granddad McNaughton's health," he said, his words falling as if driven by a mallet, "he'll not be consulted by us about any of this business."

Hannah said nothing, but her scalp prickled in dread anticipation, remembering what she had told Mrs. Sweet.

They reached the gate just as the sun broke, and Homer tossed his crooked comb and preened his feathers and crowed the new day. Oh, it was all so far-fetched, anyway, she thought. The farm was all she knew. Math was a joy, but nothing to leave home for.

Inside the kitchen was filled with sweet warmth.

"Doughnuts!" exclaimed Hannah.

Ma smiled. "Thank Miss Crocker. It was yesterday's recipe. I made them with part wild clover honey and part Karo. Thought we all could use a treat this morning."

She did not want to mention Philadelphia. Ma tended to close the door on topics that unsettled her.

They sat for grace and a breakfast of boiled ham and doughnuts.

On the outside, thought Hannah as she

looked around the kitchen, this morning was the same as every morning. There was bleary-eyed Roy—likely he'd been up late, reading Krazy Kat funny papers by moonlight—and Ma moving from table to stove, stiff on her arches that troubled her during cold snaps. There was Pa and Ben sipping from their mugs of nicotine tea, home brewed from hot water and crumbled tobacco, with fresh spearmint added for taste. Coffee was scarce this year. Last year it had been opposite—enough coffee, no tobacco.

"You can never get your hands on one without bemoaning the loss of the other," Pa had said. "What you get is what you get."

But sometimes isn't there a choice? Hannah wondered uneasily.

She'd pay a visit to Granddad McNaughton, she decided, after afternoon milking. Granddad would tell her the things that she needed to hear.

7

JUMPING, JUMPING

"WHY, YOU CAN hardly bumble through the *Stepping Stone* primer, Hannah. How will you get by at a city school? Scholarship!" Betsy flicked the jump rope for emphasis. "What do your folks say?"

"They say no."

"'Course they do! *I've* been to see Philadelphia, remember," said Betsy. "Trust me, you won't fit in. And what kind of people is Mrs. Sweet, anyhow? At first, she reminded me of Mrs. Roosevelt, but then I decided no—it was only her clothes that did. I bet in person, Mrs. Roosevelt is far gentler."

Tru, who was turning the opposite end, pounced to Hannah's innermost fear. "Besides, you'd be terrible with homesickness. Wouldn't you, Hannah?"

Just then, Margaret tangled in the rope. "Oh, please, let me try . . ." she began, but was overruled in a shriek of *nos* to the end of the line.

"My turn!" Hannah shouted. She jumped into the rope and began to sing.

How many mules from here to Mile-a-bry?
Threescore and ten!
Can I get there by candlelight?
Yes, if your legs are long, you might.
Watch out! Mighty bad witches on the road tonight!
Count one, count two, count three, count four . . .

Usually, Hannah loved this rhyme, but today

it seemed to shout a warning. A warning that echoed what Pa had said. She had never traveled off the farm alone. Only occasional trips into town for back-to-school supplies at Nutley's and a few times to the movies, once to see *Babes in Toyland* with Laurel and Hardy, once to see *Little Women* with gorgeous Katharine Hepburn starring as Jo March. And last month—after begging her folks, who gave in only because it was Melinda Snow's thirteenth birthday and because everyone else was going and because the Snows were Methodist, after all—to watch *The Gay Divorcee* with Ginger Rogers and Fred Astaire.

Movies were Hannah's favorite entertainment in the entire world. She speculated how far city folk lived from the cinemas. Walking distance, hadn't Mrs. Sweet mentioned? Her own curiosity surprised her, like swallowing snow, a mild slip-sliding shock. She shut her eyes and let the counting take over. "Thirty-two, thirty-two, thirty-two!" She always counted thirty-two a few extra skips, for luck.

"Boy, oh, boy, I'd give my eyeteeth to spend a month in Philadelphia with all those swells and bon tons," said Tru.

"My folks'd never let me," snapped Betsy. "It's fine and all to visit—like I did—but cities is full of none but thieves and thieving!"

Then other girls in the line chimed in, each voice lifting to deliver its story.

"You'll have to be on watch for falling bodies. One bad day in the stock market, and business-men start jumping out of windows—"

"I heard society ladies wear dresses made out of thousand-dollar bills and dance on top of—"

"My pa says crooks park their yachts near South Street seaport and sell black-market meat to anyone who—"

"Forty-four, forty-five, forty-six, forty-seven!" Hannah listened only to the rope. She jumped and counted and her heart pumped its blood-beat, faster and faster in her chest.

"Hannah, you can't leave Chadds Ford!" Betsy cried finally. "No place is better than here.

Besides, you and Tru and me already planned to be June brides and live down the road from one another. In white houses with wisteria and morning glory climbing up the lattice. My house will have green shutters and Tru's will have red shutters and yours will have blue shutters! Like we planned, Hannah!"

"She's not listening," said Tru. "She'll make it be her turn forever. Show-off!"

Hannah kept jumping. Perhaps she was a show-off, but jumping was delightful, like running and counting, and she felt as though she could stay in motion forever. Even after the other girls got tired and raised the rope and sped the rope and complained that their wrists ached, even then Hannah bet she could keep up with it, and outlast them all.

8

CHEESE, SARDINES, AND GRANDDAD MCNAUGHTON

HANNAH SPIED Granddad outside on his front-porch rocker, chewing a plug of tobacco while he watched the last gold of sun slip off the fields. His hair was combed to cottony floss, and he was impeccably dressed in green twill pants, a waistcoat over his starched white shirt and a shine on his boots. Buttoned and pressed as usual, though the new tremble in his fingers made knotting knots and looping loops a time-eating hindrance.

But that was typical of Granddad McNaughton. He was set in his ways. Stingy with his affection, too. Certainly there was precious little of it for Ma, Pa, Hepp, or Roy, which made Granddad's fondness for Hannah seem as indulgent and quirky as a plumed hat on a monk's head.

"He loves you best because you're just like him," Roy groused to her once. "For Granddad, seeing you is the same as looking in a pond, like old Narcissus."

When Granddad spied her, he leaned down to the split of watermelon at his feet, scooped up a chunk, and winged it for Hannah's catch.

"You missed her by minutes, that dratted Mrs. Sweet," he said. "She wants to take you away in her monstrous car. Didn't like the look of her, no indeed, and so I didn't offer her one twist of my chew."

Hannah scrutinized her grandfather as she bit into the sweet end-of-season fruit. Delicious. She sat on the porch step. "Then you think I ought to stay here, Granddad? Is that what you're saying?"

"Stay here? Not on my will! Why, you're as natural to math as sparks fly upward, Hannah Bennett. I've been shouting it for years." Granddad's smile turned to a cackle, and then to the rasping cough that had plagued him all summer. Hannah waited for it to subside. "How can you ask me such a foolish question?"

"Because Ma and Pa want me home. They worry for my reading problem. And for my safety in a city."

Granddad's thistly brows knit. "That so? And do they worry for your life wasted, boiling and baking and milking and pickling away all your days here simply because you can't comprehend the sports page?"

Hannah laughed. "You make it sound too simple, Granddad. But you know we can't afford to lose one more body off the farm, not with Hepp gone. Hiring Ben's been an expense enough." She cast an eye on her grandfather, who kept his own face expressionless. "I know an opportunity like this has been a dream of yours. But I can't figure out if it's a dream of mine."

Granddad McNaughton spat over his shoulder. "Doubt on every color of the rainbow if you like, but we also both know what's what. That's why you steered Mrs. Sweet in my direction. I got stuck in Chadds Ford because nobody pushed me forward." When he opened his eyes, their pale blue light had become twin embers of anger. "A country doctor. What I could have been! No, you need to learn to speak math with people who are fluent in it. You'll rust out here, Hannah. You're rusting already."

Hannah listened, though she had heard this speech a hundred times before. "I want to go and I don't. I'm curious, but confused," she admitted.

"Bah!" Granddad retorted. "Curiosity expands us. And the way Mrs. Sweet explained it to me, if you get that scholarship, it sets you on a road that might even lead to a university education. Think of it, Hannah!"

She nodded as her fingers tapped a pattern on the porch step. To Granddad, curiosity and knowledge were all that mattered.

"Wipe that frown off your face a minute. I've got a riddle for you!" Granddad grinned. "If Hannah May Bennett opens her math book and finds that the sum of the facing pages was two hundred forty-one, what pages did she open to?"

"Pages one twenty and one twenty-one," Hannah answered promptly. She spit a watermelon seed in a perfect arc. "That's too easy. Here's one for you. Of fifty people at a picnic, forty-one like sardine sandwiches, thirty-five like cheese sandwiches, and thirty like both. How many like neither cheese nor sardines?"

"That would be . . . four. Four remaining." Granddad answered. Then he slapped his knee. "Aha, four. Your ma, your pa, Hepp, and Roy. I don't know how it is those four can't get a taste for either of our favorite sandwiches. And everyone knows that cheese and sardines are delicious together, too. Now scat, Hannah. Tell your folks they need to pay me a visit. Tell them I want a word."

"Yes, sir." She tossed the watermelon rind into the box hedge, then stood and pecked Granddad's cheek. Yet it seemed to her that she left holding the same bag of troubles she'd arrived with. All that Granddad had made clear was his own opinion, as usual.

Ma was waiting for her at the crossroads. "Mrs. Sweet paid us another visit," she said. "Seems she found a backer in your grandfather."

"I'm sorry, Ma," said Hannah. "I really, truly am. I've been wild and sleepless with sorry. But it seemed only fair that this be Granddad's business, too. I couldn't stay quiet."

Ma shook her head. "What sort of nature do you have, Hannah, to go behind-hand against your parents?"

Hannah swallowed hard. The right answer did not rise easily. "This is what Granddad's always wanted for me. How could I keep it from him, especially with him feeling so low these days?"

"Your grandfather . . ." Ma began, and Hannah was sure that Ma was on the verge of recollecting a story about her own youth, and Granddad's remote parenting, the solitary hours he'd spent in his study, more preoccupied with work than family.

But she didn't. "Thirteen years old," she said instead. "And here I thought Hepp was young to leave home at eighteen." Her voice sounded small, defeated. Family meant everything to Ma, and for a moment Hannah wanted to throw her arms around her mother and tell her it was all just a lark, because of course she would never leave, of course she wouldn't run away to Philadelphia simply on account of math. Math! Why, there was plenty of math right here in Chadds Ford. No, she did not have to go all the way to the city to get a proper math education.

But even as Hannah thought it out, she knew it was not true. There was scant more math that Miss Cascade, or even Granddad, could teach her anymore.

"I can always come back home," Hannah said, "if things don't work out. But at the very least, I owe Granddad a try."

Ma nodded, and they walked home in silence, uprooting bunches of watercress along the stream that marked their way. Boiled watercress was not as tasty as it was filling, but a quantity of salt and black pepper and butter made it bearable.

When Ma spoke again, she was all business. "In Philadelphia, you'll need to find a church to restore your faith come Sundays," she said. "And promise you won't listen to radio muck like *Amos 'n Andy*. Nor any of those haunted-house programs, either, that you and Tru love." She stopped to tug free a bunch of watercress, shaking rocks and soil from its roots. "I can't conjecture how you'll take to that city. You had better know, Hannah, even if you have Granddad's support, your pa's and my blessing is mixed."

"Yes, ma'am."

"First Hepp, now you," said Ma. "I keep faith it's not for permanent, not with either of you. McNaughtons and Bennetts have lived in Chadds Ford since always."

"Of course I'll come back, Ma," protested Hannah. "I belong here."

But Ma was finished talking. Her eyes slid past Hannah to another patch of watercress and she picked her way toward it, leaving Hannah to trail behind.

9

THE VIEW FROM BLOOM

WITH THE EXCEPTION of Grand-
dad's, Hannah had nobody's full blessing. Not
even Miss Cascade's, as Mrs. Sweet had written
a letter to her stating that all of the Wexler funding that might have gone to Brintons Bridge
School now would be used toward Hannah's
semester of board and tuition.

Miss Cascade had read the letter out loud to
the class while Hannah sat hunched, her shoulders up near her ears and blood tingling in her
face. Her teacher's disappointment was worse

than the students' baffled grumbling, and Hannah felt like a crook, robbing her schoolhouse of its treasures almost by accident.

Home was hardly a relief. Roy had grown unbearable. He baited and goaded, then mocked her when she complained. "Ooh, stop it, stop it! I'm a *scholarship* girl now!" he would squeak while pressing the back of his hand to his forehead. But Hannah knew that behind it, he was hurt and sad. Roy hadn't even finished missing Hepp, and here she was, two years younger than Roy and setting off on her own. Not to mention that she was leaving him to pick up the weight of her chores. Worst for Roy, she knew, was that here was another example of Granddad singling her out, aligning Hannah to his own ambitions.

It would take some time to set things right with Roy.

The evening before her departure, Hannah paid a final visit to the Applebee farm.

"Mrs. Sweet called our telephone. She said don't pack galoshes," Tru reported. "When are

your folks getting a telephone? It's awfully convenient."

"Pa says it's foofaraw." Hannah looked down
at her fringed-tongue oxfords, bought just last
month for one dollar and seventy-eight cents at
Nutley's. "No galoshes? Boy, she's discouraged
me from bringing much of anything."

"I'd put dibs Mrs. Sweet wants to buy you
minks and diamonds and trick you over into a
real city girl. By Christmas, you might be the
worst kind of snob." Tru's laugh had an edge to
it. Then she reached out and squeezed Hannah's
hand. "Come into the front room and see what
the Philco man brought us today!"

In spite of all their financial strains, Tru confided to Hannah that her pa had taken another
bank loan in order to purchase their brand-
new, brass-and-walnut Philco-Transitone plus
Inclined Sounding Board. The Applebees were
fancy like that, always wanting the latest, newest
things. It was almost a sickness with some people, Pa said.

"The only radio scientifically designed as a musical instrument." Hannah mimicked the advertising announcer's voice as she tripped a finger across each beveled knob. One, two, three. Three, two, one. One, two three.

"Stop your tapping. *The Witches' Tale* comes on in five minutes," Tru said. "Let's listen, but this time, Hannah, you can't act all scaredy-cat and foolish."

"I won't, I swear."

Mrs. Applebee had prepared cherry Jell-O in glass dishes, and she let the girls take their dessert out to the side-porch swing. Tru turned up the volume so that they could hear the program through the open window.

The fuzz of static soon was replaced by music, heavy and thunderous, followed by the crash of a rainstorm. Hannah shivered in anticipation. *"Skelly Oil now presents* The Witches' Tale. *Written and produced by Alonzo Dean Cole,"* intoned the announcer in his deep, spooky voice. *"Let us now join Witch Magda and her black cat, Satan."*

"Ooh, I see her! I see Witch Magda!" Hannah yelled.

"Shh, don't wreck it!" hissed Tru.

Hannah shivered and tried to keep from wriggling as she listened to old Witch Magda cooking up her usual diabolical elixirs. Horrifying! She sneaked a peek across the Applebees' dark pasture. The longer she listened, the easier she could see those hunch-backed witches. There, in the shadows, now swooping slap over the split rail!

"I've got here a potion to melt the flesh of my worst enemies!" Witch Magda cawed as Hannah listened, delirious with dread. Oh, yes, she saw those witches perfectly! Black-robed, the warts on their chins as fat as gooseberries.

She gave up. "Turn it off, oh, turn it off!" She set down her dish and jumped from the swing. Hands clapped to her ears, she sprinted off the porch, vaulting the stairs in a bound. "Let's climb Bloom!"

Bloom was Hannah and Tru's pet name for

the giant maple that grew in the Applebees' front lawn. The girls had agreed long ago that it was the most magnificent climbing tree in the world. When she reached Bloom's base, Hannah tore off her shoes and stockings, then jumped and caught the lowest branch, and swung herself up.

Tru watched a moment, before she ducked into the house to snap off the radio. When she reappeared, she was wrenching off her shoes and running to Bloom.

"It's a sorry day when all it takes is a tin-pan rainstorm and a radio actress to put you up here!" Tru clucked her tongue as she wedged herself sidesaddle into one of the branches' sturdy forks.

"I'm safe in a tree." Hannah looked up at the stars. "I like an autumn sky better than spring-time, don't you, Tru?" She pointed. "Look, there's Cassiopeia."

"And Orion, there."

"And Sirius."

"And the Big Dipper."

"I wish I knew the math of stars," said Hannah wistfully. "What energy they're made of. What makes them burn."

"The view is enough for me." Tru dropped her gaze from the sky. "Betsy and I bet you won't last a month in the city, Hannah," she said. "Who would understand you? My granny says it's only when folks have known each other since birth that we make allowances for peculiarities."

"I'm not peculiar," Hannah retorted.

"'Course you are! What with your fingers always tapping how they do, and the way you shout out whatever's in your head, whenever the mood hits!" exclaimed Tru. "There's no *polish* to you, Hannah! Oh, don't glare at me. Maybe I ought not have spoken so truthful. But, listen, I've got some luck to pass along about your precious thirty-two." She grinned. "My uncle Frank told me that you can get thirty-two pounds of starch from a bushel of corn."

"That's a good one, Tru!"

Tru smiled. "See, Hannah? It's when you've

been friends as long as us that you can find the perfect gift." She hugged herself tighter against the tree and sighed. "I do hope you meet a new friend," she added after a thoughtful moment. "Temporarily, while you're there, I mean. All it takes is one chum to make the world shrink to a comfortable size. Wouldn't you say?"

"I'd say!" Hannah agreed, though she had never given the idea much thought.

PART TWO

10

MUDTOWN

SHE HAD GROWN up hearing the whistle of this train, used by the larger dairies to transport milk from Chadds Ford to Media Junction and then on to Philadelphia. Never, though, had Hannah boarded one of the three attached passenger cars. From her seat at the window, she watched the countryside pass by. The train took its journey slow, chugging steadily to stop an interminable time, then chuffing onward again. The stations changed, but the landscape stayed the same, fields and hills dulled to dishwater colors by the overcast sky. She pressed her fore-head to the glass and kept count of the trucks and tractors, horses and cows, barns and silos, and the odd automobile.

In the last few minutes, the flow and curve of the country gave way to the city outskirts of storefronts and paved roads. Red brick and gray stone walls appeared solid before Hannah's eyes. That's when she stopped counting. Looked away. Now it that was grinding and whistling to a halt, the journey seemed all at once too quick.

Filth-adelphia, Hannah heard a man com-plain as the train pulled to the wide, barren con-course that was Suburban Station. She kept her eyes on her shoes as the train stopped. Head bowed, she stood and collected her bag, and hur-ried down the stairs.

Don't look up, she warned herself. Not yet.

Inside the echoing station, Hannah followed her feet to the nearest empty bench, where she opened her bag and reclaimed her pungent cheese-and-sardine sandwich. When she first had unpacked it to eat in the train, a young woman sitting opposite had wrinkled her nose and whispered something to the man next to her. Embarrassed, Hannah had hastily dropped the smelly sandwich into the bag's side compartment alongside her thermos of milk, jam crackers, kerchief, hand towel, bottle of Listerine, cake of soap, and three Q-tips that Ma had deemed necessary for an all-day trip.

Now Hannah closed her eyes and chewed hungrily. She recalled that morning's good-byes, which had been strained and brief.

"If I could spare myself, or even Roy for a day off the dairy, I'd do it," Ma had fretted. "To settle you in."

"I'll settle myself, Ma," Hannah had reassured.

From Pa: "Keep safe, be good." Pa was inclined to go gruff when he felt a loss.

And Roy had put in: "Don't get yourself hit by a runaway truck."

The memory of Hepp's departure weighed

on all of them, Hannah knew. The mood was not helped when Granddad surprised them with a visit. Short of breath and leaning hard on his mottled sycamore cane, he had presented Hannah with a brass-and-rosewood ruler. "'Hide not your talents, they for use were made. What's a sundial in the shade?'" he had quoted with a wink. "So says Poor Richard's Almanac."

"Well, *I* knew that," Roy had grumbled. "I was the one who got to be Ben Franklin."

"Make me proud, Hannah," was the last thing Granddad told her. His hand had dropped heavy as a paperweight on her head. "You're taking the chance we've both been waiting for." His tone so smug that Pa had plucked his cap from its hook and stomped outside to wait in the truck.

Now Hannah realized she was gripping the bag's handle so hard that she could feel the beginning of a welt across her gloved palm. She released her hold, unbuckled the bag, and fumbled for the ruler. She tapped it, back and forth, end to end.

"You, there. Yes, you. Are you the milkmaid I'm sent to fetch?"

Hannah looked up. A boy who looked to be somewhere between her age and Roy's was planted, arms crossed, in the space in front of her. He was shabbily dressed in a woolen jacket and an oversized cap that shaded his dark-skinned face. Italian, Hannah guessed. Or Black Irish, or something else. She stopped tapping, straightened, wiped her mouth with her fingers. Nodded yes, although she didn't like this boy's tone or being called *milkmaid*.

"Christmas!" The boy pointed. "What's that, a doctor's bag?"

"It belonged to my grandfather," Hannah said.

"And in it's all you got?" The boy reached over and hefted its weight.

"Mrs. Sweet said not to bring much." Hannah stood and gave her hand for him to shake. "I am Hannah Bennett. Are you . . . hired by Mrs. Sweet?" she ventured.

"Hired." The boy scowled. "That's called a

presumption, you dumb bunny. My name's Joe Elway."

"I didn't mean to presume," Hannah snapped back. "Just as I'm sure you didn't mean to be nasty about it."

"Well, 'scuse me, country mouse." Joe thrust the bag back into her hand. "This way to the hack stand. C'mon."

Hannah dropped her eyes to the ground. Her oxfords, fresh-polished last night by Pa, smacked the wet sidewalk, and she wished she'd worn her galoshes. Rain had flooded the gutters and laid a thin skin of mud the color of chocolate milk on the pavement. She did not look up. On a glance, the city's patterns were complex and unnatural. They confounded her.

Instead, she counted her footsteps, the cracks in the sidewalk, the gurgle of horns, how many times Granddad McNaughton's bag slapped her shin. She listened to the rain rapping the roof of her beret and she tapped a matching beat on the side of her leg.

Joe whistled through his teeth, and Hannah looked up long enough see a yellow taxicab roaring toward them. In the next moment, it splashed water all over her shoes and skirt. She shrieked and jumped back. "You did that on purpose!"

"Did not!" But Joe laughed delightedly. "A city stinks and shakes water everywhere when it gets wet. Same as a dog. Nothing you can do." He opened the passenger door.

Hannah slid into the automobile with some misgiving. She had been in her father's truck on many occasions, and gone along on plenty of jaunts in the Applebees' Ford, but never had she shared a ride with not one but *two* strangers. She steeled her eyes to her lap and wished Mrs. Sweet had come to collect her in person.

"If you'd pick your beams off the ground a minute, I can point you out some sights along the way," Joe said. He leaned up to speak to the driver. "We're going to Delancey Place, but cut us up Market Street first, wouldja, pal?" He settled back and stretched his hands behind his head. "I'm more a bus-and-trolley man myself, but Mrs. Sweet told me to show you around. Even dropped me half a buck for traveling costs, so I got to honor her squandering. She'll try to make us pals, only the truth is, milkmaid, I'm your public enemy number one. But I'll fill you in on that later."

Hannah stared ahead and said nothing. This Joe Elway was worse than any boy in Miss Cascade's class. Even worse than Elgin Winnicker, who liked to pick slugs from his mother's lettuce patch and drop them down girls' blouses.

"Here we're coming up on City Hall," Joe continued. "Look, look out the window, wouldja? See the statue on top of that building? That's Billy Penn, and no building is allowed to rise higher than his head. It's the law. Cross the street and you've got your John Wanamaker's, the department store, you must've heard of it, huh? Piece of the Renaissance in your own backyard—though

I'm more of a skyscraper fella myself. Take this one, just went up. Look, wouldja look at it!" Joe rapped the window glass. "One Penn East. Twenty-seven stories high, polychrome, designed compliments of Ritter and Shay, the best architects this city's known since Frank Furness. And if you're keen on that, you should see the Packard Building! Well, all right, then, milkmaid, if you won't give anything the up-and-down, we might as well stop wasting my time. Delancey Place, cabby. You can turn on Eighteenth."

Eighteen. Nine times two, or nine plus nine, or three times three times two, or three times six, or thirty-six divided by two. Eighteen was how many men survived the Magellan expedition. Eighteenth of April, 1906, was the day that a terrible earthquake shook San Francisco. Eighteen was powerful, and not necessarily lucky.

After a few more minutes, Joe said, exasperated, "What are ya, homesick? You're a real wet blanket, huh? Well, it's not like I'm jumping out of my socks for you, either."

Hannah bristled. Wet blanket! Joe Elway talked as if he were one of Roy's favorite Dick Tracy thugs. She smiled thinly and said nothing, but she made up her mind that she did not like him.

DOLL FACE

MRS. SWEET LIVED at 5 Delancey Place, in a three-story townhouse. She seemed to attract odd numbers like a magnet. Her home was grand, with a large first-floor bay window and a brass doorknocker in the shape of a sharp-eyed fox. Hannah lifted her eyes long enough to appreciate the snug street of houses peppered with lacquered black shutters and fronted with fanlights and dormers and iron-railed stoops. As she faced the front door, her fingers reached out to tap the fox's eyes. One, two. Two, one. One, two.

Joe pushed her hand away and knocked, then stepped back and shouted, "Bev-er-leee!"

From inside came a thud and a scurry and then the door was yanked open by a girl wearing a formal maid's uniform that did not quite suit her mouse-nest hair and the coltish dangle of her arms and legs.

"You know I hate it when you yell, Joe," the girl scolded. "Come in from the rain. What'd I say about an umbrella?" She nodded at Hannah. "Let me take your coat and things. Oh, not *your* coat, Joe." She yawned as she held out a hand for Hannah's wet gloves, jacket, and beret.

"Sleeping on the job, Miss Lingle?" Joe asked, tossing his jacket and cap for Beverly to catch. He winked at Hannah. "When she's not pretending to dust around here, Beverly studies piano at the Academy. She's another Sweet discovery. We're hoping for great things, ain't that right, chippy?"

"Quit it, Joe. Lucky Mrs. Sweet is up in Boston, or she'd slap you sideways for talking to me that way," said Beverly. "Cook's off, and I'm chopping carrots for a beef stew, so you'll have to play host. Take Hannah up to her room and settle her in, how about?" To Hannah, she said, "We'll make better acquaintance over supper. When I'm not so rushed and rattled."

Before Hannah could answer, Beverly bounded off. Now Hannah caught a faint smell of simmering beef. Delectable. Beef stew must be a special Sunday treat.

"C'mon," said Joe. "You bunk down the hall from me, only I got a view and you don't, but that's how the cookie crumbles, doll face. This way."

Doll face! Not even Elgin or Roy was this irritating. Hannah gritted her teeth as she followed Joe across the foyer and up the two flights of polished pine stairs. Thirty-one steps in all, another odd number. Joe's rapid-fire speech could not distract from Hannah's astonishment at the details of Mrs. Sweet's fine house; its parquet floors and papered walls and swaths of cranberry velvet window drapes that pulled back to reveal the wet world of granite and pavement below.

But Joe demanded attention. His voice was loud, and he kept pivoting to catch Hannah's eye as he spoke.

"Most scholarship huckleberries settle in with ordinary families who live outside the city. But ole Sweet likes to keep an eye on her own investments," he told her. "That's not to say we're a team. No sirree, it's me against you, and us against all the other country rubes. We test for the Wexler cabbage before the end of December.

"If you score big, you'll ride free to some fancy school, which helps the universities sit up and take notice. If you turn out to be a dope, well, that's another story. Back to the cow patch you go. Beverly's seventeen, and she's still a dope at everything but piano. She's been Sweet's pet this year, even though she flunked the last set of exams back in June. It's no secret Sweet won't board a kid longer than one semester, but

Beverly's hanging on for one more try. Full-time student in exchange for part-time scrubbing. Without Sweet, Beverly would have got the boot back to York last year. Ever been to York, Pennsylvania? No? Well, you wouldn't want to return. Here you go, end of the hall. We'll be sharing the crapper. It doesn't got a lock, so you better learn to knock." He did a short tap dance with this last sentence.

Joe was not only rude, but also vulgar, Hannah decided. She turned her back and said nothing as she pushed open the door open on a room built plain as her bedroom at home. There was an iron bed, a desk and swivel chair, a narrow wooden bureau and matching wardrobe, and a window that looked out onto a wall of bricks. The softening touches—net drapes, the water-color that hung from a tack on the wall, a fringed-shade lamp set crooked on the sunless sill—seemed to try too hard for pleasantness.

"Sharp digs, eh?" Joe's voice boomed in her ear. "Beverly's on the ground floor, in the cook's old room, since the cook is a five-day daily, but which five days depends on her whim. Beverly likes it 'cause it's easy to sneak out with her regular beau, Charlie. That's from my mouth to your ears. Say, don't you want to know how much dough there is versus kids for the Wexler fund?"

"Not really."

"Half as much."

"All right, then."

"It's you against me. Like I said." Joe lingered, whistling. He watched as Hannah took her ruler from her bag to measure and readjust the lamp so that it was centered on the windowsill.

"That'll be all, Joe, thank you," Hannah said finally.

Joe scowled, then grinned wolfishly and held out his hand, palm up. "Christmas! If you're gonna treat me like a bellhop, you might as well tip me," he said. "Make it worth my while. That is, unless you caught on how to handle your public enemy number one, milkmaid." When she didn't answer, Joe frowned, made a shallow bow, and shut the door. He was still whistling as he walked down the hall.

Alone, Hannah felt all the fear she'd been holding back come to rest in an ache behind her eyes. She walked the edges of the room, tapping each corner. No view. A watermark on the ceiling and a scent of ammonia in the air. A cheeky boy across the hall instead of Roy—who could also be taxing, but was family, at least.

On the bureau, she found a pen and pad of paper. There was a note from Mrs. Sweet on the top page, written in a wind-bent slant. She did her best to read it.

Dear Hannah,

I (something) not to be here. Joe will (something a something something) as host. My (something) for the (something). Becca will keep you (something). I'll be home (something)! Teddy Sweet

Becca will keep you . . . Mrs. Sweet must be

referring to the little wooden doll wedged between the bed's bolster pillows.

Hannah went to the doll and picked it up. Becca was dressed in button-up shoes and a heavy gingham smock, and her yarn hair was tied in two plaits.

Was it mockery? A country doll companion for a huckleberry farm girl? Or was Becca truly meant to be a comfort?

Hannah tapped the corners of Becca's artfully sewn patch pocket, then placed her in the bottom drawer of her bureau and shut it. Whatever Mrs. Sweet's intention, she ought to realize that thirteen-year-old girls did not play with dolls.

12

NO X, BUT PLENTY LEFT OVER

NOBODY KNEW where the milk came from.

"Germantown, I s'pose," said Beverly when Hannah asked that evening. The three of them were gathered at the kitchen table for their beef stew supper. "The butter-and-egg man's from Germantown. It's top-notch, although they bring more than we need."

Hannah did not doubt it. There was too much to eat tonight. The stew contained chunks of beef, carrot, onion, and potato generous enough to cut with a fork and knife, and there was whipped syllabub for dessert. Hannah started on the beef, eating from least to greatest, and was only up to onions before she thought her stomach would pop, and yet she could not finish what was on her plate. Beverly, who seemed to be in a permanent state of hurried distraction, was also unable to finish her portion. Only Joe made everything disappear.

Afterward, watching Beverly scrape the leftovers straight into the garbage bin, Hannah was appalled to see the amount of food wasted. At the farm, anything not eaten was saved in the ice chest for the next night, or fed to the animals, or put aside for the occasional wandering tramp who knew that the X marked on the Bennetts' back door meant he could find hospitality and a warm supper inside.

There was no X on Mrs. Sweet's kitchen door. Hannah had checked. Was that because there were no hungry people in Philadelphia? She could not imagine a band of tramps ringing the bell at fashionable Delancey Place.

"Mrs. Sweet asked me to deliver you to Ottley Friends tomorrow morning," Beverly mentioned as they tidied the kitchen together, Joe having shot off as soon as he finished eating. "The school uniform—the gray jumper and middy—are hanging in your closet. We'll walk, but we ought to leave by seven o' clock prompt, and no oversleeping, please. I have a piano lesson at seven-thirty."

No oversleeping! Hannah had to roll her lips together to resist laughing. At her house, if she or Roy slept past five, they were called lazybones and got last breakfast dibs—bread heels and pan-burnt potato.

She followed Beverly as she turned off the downstairs lights and locked the doors. "It's quiet here most days," Beverly explained. "There's the radio in the pantry, but Mrs. Sweet discourages school-night listening. We each get to pick one show a week. Joe prefers *The Lone*

Ranger, of course, and I skip between *The Romance of Helen Trent* and *Lights Out,* depending if I want tears or chills."

"Is there a Mr. Sweet?"

"Died in the war. Best not to mention it. All right, we're finished here. I'm going to the parlor to practice. I'll try to play quiet so as not to disturb you, but it's Bach, so I might get carried away. Good night."

"Good night."

As Hannah reached the third floor landing, Joe's bedroom door opened, and he poked his head out. "G'night, milkmaid," he chimed, singsong. Then he made a mooing noise, stuck out his tongue, and snapped back into his room, turning the lock.

Don't provoke and you won't be provoked. That's what Ma would have said.

Politeness counts. That's what Miss Cascade would have said.

Joe Elway needed to be taught a little lesson. That's what Hannah decided. She went swiftly to her room and from her bag unearthed the tin of Miss du Fleur's Elderberry Essence hair pomade that Betsy had given her for her last birthday. She used her handkerchief to rub a dollop of it onto Joe's doorknob until it was slippery as a leg of mutton.

Serves you right, she thought.

Back in her room, Hannah unpacked and refolded and stacked or hung the few articles of clothing and personal items she had brought. She used her ruler to space her hairbrush, comb, and mirror, as well as to center the watercolor and throw rug.

Finally, she paced the length of the room thirty-two times, touching each corner for luck.

After she changed into her nightgown, brushed her teeth, and said her prayers, she slid into the too-soft bed that was not hers, and she closed her eyes against this strange new moonless space. She tapped a pattern up and down her ribs and listened to the rise and fall of her breath.

Here I am, she thought. Right where

Granddad wanted. She tried to be happy about that, but then her mind made a picture of home: of Ma reading the Robertson's seed catalog while Pa fumbled with his pipe, Roy stretched out on the hearthrug between them. The last thing Hannah heard before she fell asleep was the forlorn *plink* of Beverly at the piano, the same piece played and broken off and taken up again. It made Hannah feel more homesick than she wanted.

13

MEETING MR. BARNABY

WHEN HANNAH opened her eyes into the soft shadows before daybreak, she needed a moment to remember. No milking, no chores. She rose and bathed quickly anyway, then struggled into the unfamiliar gray uniform. It was loose and long, with a slide fastener up the back, and its sewn-in tags read *Friendly Frocks*. Was that a shop? A catalog? The fabric was not quite flannel and not quite wool and almost itched.

Dressed, she crept downstairs to the kitchen window with her tablet and pen and waited for sunrise.

It was not a farmer, however, who appeared with the dawn, slowing his cart and dobbin to the street corner, but a young man in a gleaming white truck. MILK MEANS HEALTH! proclaimed the script along its side. The man was outfitted in a formal uniform; white suit, black-and-white-striped tie, and white gloves. He greeted Hannah at the kitchen door with a small crate of four milk bottles and a tip of his cap.

"Up early, miss."

"Good morning, sir. I was curious to know where the milk comes from."

"Why, it comes from a bottling plant, owned by the American Dairy Industry."

Hannah thought. "But surely there is a single dairy for our milk?"

"Ouch, you might have caught me, miss." The milkman raised his eyebrows. "I'm not familiar with the process from cow to doorstep. I just drive the truck. Thing is, I've only had this job three weeks." He offered his hand. "Name's Barnaby. I was in lithographs, see, before the last round of layoffs."

Hannah shook the gloved hand. "I'm Hannah Bennett, pleased to meet you. My parents run the Bennett Dairy? In Chester County? In Chadds Ford?"

"Not familiar, sorry." Mr. Barnaby's smile stayed friendly nevertheless. "Well, Hannah Bennett, I have nine streets on my route. Nine before eight, elsewise you're late. It's the rule."

After he left, his truck clattering down the cobblestones, Hannah placed the milk bottles in the electric refrigerator. She marveled at the treasury of food packed inside. Meats, hard and soft cheeses, bottles of juice, paper packets of thin-sliced smoked fish, Hellmann's real mayonnaise, a tub of fresh horseradish, another of champagne mustard. Where did it all come from? Who made it? How much did it cost?

Apparently, none of that seemed to matter to Philadelphians. As long as it arrived on time, as long as it was fresh for the taking.

14

TOO LONG AND WRONG

FROM HER FIRST step inside the school, Hannah saw that Tru had been right. Ottley Friends girls *were* different. Graceful and glint-eyed, they called to Hannah's mind a throng of Siamese cats. In their sleek company, Hannah felt as scraggly as Mouser. As soon as she had walked through the door, she wanted to turn around and run.

For one thing, not one single girl wore a shoulder-length hairstyle. Blunt bobs and flips and pageboys were all Hannah saw as Beverly guided her up the broad stairs to Miss Jordan's office. A few of the older girls even wore finger-wave marcels. Movie-star styles, all of them! Hannah thought. She herself might as well have arrived in grosgrain-ribboned plaits, like poor Becca, for all she felt her difference.

If that weren't bad enough, her *Friendly Frocks* hemline dropped a good three inches lower than everyone else's. Between the extra length of hair and extra length of dress, Hannah felt over-burdened, a sensation similar to last night's when she had gone to bed on a too-full stomach.

"Welcome, welcome," greeted Miss Jordan, the school headmistress, in whose care Beverly had dropped her before dashing to her piano lesson. Miss Jordan was a cheerful, energetic package of a woman whose office window was filled with jeweled glass lamps and fern sprays in glazed pots. "This must seem odd to you—a townhouse school. But it's really very simple. There are five floors, with our dining hall on the fourth floor, and our overnight boarders on the top. The girls take elocution and calisthenics in the ground floor theater.

"Mrs. Sweet has told me both of your abilities in math and of your struggle with reading. We want you to make great strides in both subjects here. Mr. Cole is an excellent math teacher, and I'll be supervising your reading lessons myself. Don't you worry, Hannah. We'll get you spit-and-polished for the scholarship!"

Hannah returned Miss Jordan's informal smile, but was privately vexed. She had been half-hoping that the Ottley girls did not know about her scholarship, and that she might slip into the school day posing as an exotic niece or cousin of Mrs. Sweet's.

But Helene Lyon, the snub-nosed, swan-necked girl Miss Jordan had entrusted to guide Hannah through her first week, quickly set her straight.

"My parents generally believe in education reform to help others less fortunate," Helene said right off. "We hope you find that Ottley Friends is a honey of a school. And let me say, we're all charmed to bits that you have this opportunity."

Hannah scowled and averted her eyes. It was one thing to have Mrs. Sweet talk about Hannah's opportunity, but it was quite another to hear about it from a girl her own age. And how exactly was she "less fortunate" than Helene? Perhaps Helene was tactless to everyone. She certainly seemed like a fool, from the way she carried on.

"Ooh, what a nifty little bag, Bethany!" Helene cried as she and Hannah progressed down the hall. Or, "Say, Ruth Ann, I saw you on Pearl Street yesterday in that positively chic fox-collar coat. Is it from Strawbridge's?" Or, "Lillian Shay! I want the latest on your lunchtime tête-à-tête with you-know-who!" Helene was so interested in what the other girls had seen or done or purchased over the weekend that she often forgot to introduce Hannah.

"Oh, boy! Silly me!" she would exclaim,

touching her fingertips to Hannah's shoulder. "Ruth Ann, Bethany, Lillian. This is Hannah Bendel. Don't you remember? Miss Jordan gave us a lecture about her last week?"

"Bennett," Hannah corrected, as the girls smiled and looked at her in the charitable way that one might regard a child's painting.

"Pleased to meet you, Hannah," they would chorus, then return to whatever they were doing. Pleased to meet her and pleased to leave her utterly alone.

By lunchtime, Hannah felt her smile start to hurt, as if she had borrowed it from somebody else and it did not fit.

"Miss Jordan told us you live on a dairy farm," said chubby, blond Lillian Shay, when the girls had gathered at the long table for a lunch of cold chicken and fruit.

"That's right," Hannah answered.

"Do you have to touch smelly cows?" asked Helene. She wrinkled her nose as if a terrible smell had been placed under it.

"How else are they going to be milked?" Hannah scoffed.

"Eww," squealed Lillian with a shiver. "I could never!"

"You seem to enjoy the butter and cream," said Hannah. She made a show of looking Lillian up and down. "Maybe a cow wouldn't want to touch you, either!"

"Oh, so rude!" sniffed Lillian, a blush blotting her cheeks. "Manners must be in short supply on your farm."

"Hannah, why do you keep tapping your fingers under the table?" Helene's friend Ruth Ann pointed accusingly. "You were tapping this morning, during Chapel. It's really quite distracting."

"Don't sit next to me, then," Hannah snapped. She did not mean to say it. Her mouth was going its own way, blurting things in a terrible fashion.

"Why, I wouldn't sit next to you on a dare." Bethany shook her pageboy flip so that a lock of hair fell over her eye. "You rude thing."

"Stop it, girls," said Helene. "It's not Hannah's fault who she is, rough and uneducated." She smiled frostily at Hannah. "Some ladies are bred, other need to be taught."

Hannah clenched her fists and willed herself to silence as she finished her lunch. Tru had warned her well enough that these girls wouldn't know what to think of her. It was up to Hannah to fix her peculiarities.

Starting with a new hemline and a haircut, before the end of the week.

15

PROOFS OF OLD CODGERS

MR. COLE DID not arrive at Ottley
Friends until late afternoon, when Miss Jordan
had despaired that he would appear at all.
According to Miss Jordan, he was punctual only
when the mood took him. By then, she and
Hannah had settled into Miss Jordan's office to
read *Nursery Rhymes for Boys and Girls*. A baby
book, Hannah fumed.

Miss Cascade had tried a similar tactic last
year, but the tales of Jack Horner and Georgie
Porgy hardly seemed worth reading once, let

alone mucking through for hours. Also, Hannah was terrified that Helene Lyon might flounce in. Wouldn't Helene throw a giggle fit if she saw what Hannah was reading!

When the door finally did fling open, Hannah sprang from her chair like a rabbit from a trap. The nursery book thudded to the floor.

"My goodness, Hannah!" exclaimed Miss Jordan as she bent to retrieve it. Hannah forgot to apologize as she turned her attention to her new math teacher.

On a first glance, Mr. Cole reminded Hannah of the scarecrow in Ma's backyard garden patch. His graying hair poked up from his head like Homer's raggedy feathers, and his clothes seemed not to be dressing a body so much as shaping a collection of chicken-wire joints and straw parts beneath. His bushy mustache, skewed bow tie, and the blob of coffee stain down the front of his vest gave him a look of someone who had decided on an academic appearance, but then forgot to maintain it.

"Pythagorean theorem?" he asked, swiveling to stare oddly at Hannah. His right eye darted like a silvery green fish, while the left one seemed to fix onto a nonplace just past her. "Glass," he said matter-of-factly. "Sometime I'll pop it out and show you. We begin with Pythagoras. Have you got to him yet?"

When Hannah shook her head, puzzled, a smile lifted Mr. Cole's mustache. "Oh, beautiful. Proofs, proofs, proofs are beautiful! I'll show you. Come along, come along."

Miss Jordan waved an encouraging good-bye as Hannah stumbled after Mr. Cole, who was walking at a clip.

"Coffee?" he asked over his shoulder. Students jumped out of his way, giggling, though Mr. Cole himself never broke stride.

"Um, no, thank you."

"Coming through, coming through!" sang Mr. Cole. "Keep up with me, Hannah! Mathematics is changing all the time."

He led Hannah up three flights of stairs, down

a narrow corridor, and into a tiny classroom that seemed to be all his—judging from the clutter on the desk and in the bookshelves. He motioned for her to sit at a front desk, then he spun on his heel twice before he located a piece of chalk, which he used to draw a square on the board.

Inside the square he drew a triangle.

Beneath the triangle, he wrote the equation $a^2 + b^2 = c^2$.

"I don't care if you ever learn how to spell Pythagoras or Bhaskara or Chang Tshang, Miss Bennett," said Mr. Cole. Aligned, both his real and glass eye regarded Hannah with equal seriousness. "And if any of those old codgers were alive today, I'd bet they wouldn't give a hoot, either. They'd rather have you master their proofs. You'll have questions, but try to follow along. We'll take coffee in forty minutes. I can't go too long without it. We'll start with our friend Mr. P. From this single theorem, one can devise an infinite number of algebraic proofs. For example. Let *a* equal six point two five."

6.25. The numbers appeared in Hannah's head as if inked there. She drew the first easy breath of her day. Mr. Cole's face was a study in enchantment as he prepared to dive headlong into the Pythagorean theorem, and soon Hannah could see nothing but numbers as she slipped through the door of her mind and lost herself inside.

16

SATURDAY WITH MAE

JOE SAID NOTHING about his pomade-greased doorknob, but when Hannah came home from Ottley Friends that afternoon, she found that every ruler-ordered object in her room had been set askew.

What a nuisance Joe Elway was turning out to be!

But he was not a tattletale. When Mrs. Sweet returned from Boston at the end of the week, Joe pretended that he and Hannah had made cordial introductions.

"I showed her around town, just as you asked, ma'am," Hannah overheard him say. "I think she's settled in fine."

Mrs. Sweet, after checking in on Hannah and asking her some questions about how she had settled into her school, left promptly for a night at the opera.

"You'll find Sweet hardly takes a blind bit of notice to us," Beverly explained to Hannah during dinner. "If you haven't figured out already, all she wants is for us to win scholarships so that her photograph will appear in the *Inquirer* alongside the city bigwigs, and Mayor Moore'll grant her a goodwill ambassadorship or something. What she doesn't want is for us to be pesky."

"Her sons are grown and scat, one to England and the other to California," added Joe. "I'da moved across the country, too, to get away from all that bossing."

Hannah soon determined, however, that Mrs. Sweet's presence was not so bossy as akin to a mild haunting. She was a patter of footsteps, a rattle of the tea tray, a faint burst of laughter through the air ducts of her bedroom down into the kitchen. Mostly, however, Mrs. Sweet was out. Out at ladies' lunches, or out to meet friends at the Wanamaker's eagle for a day of shopping. She often returned with purchases for Joe, Beverly, or Hannah, dropping the packages of galoshes or gloves on the table in the foyer.

"Though she never troubles to ask beforehand what any of us might need," said Beverly as she handed out new toothbrushes and socks, the spoils of one of Mrs. Sweet's excursions. "With Mrs. Sweet, you get what you get."

"Like coffee or tobacco," said Hannah.

Beverly laughed. "I guess so."

On the first Saturday after her return, Mrs. Sweet did supervise Hannah's haircut, telephoning the appointment herself and walking Hannah to her own personal beauty parlor.

"Very up-to-the-minute, Hannah," Mrs. Sweet said as she jotted the check to the hairdresser. "And here's fifty cents for lunch and a matinee. The cinema's just 'round the corner. I'm meeting some of my friends for bridge in Willow Grove. Ta!"

"Oh." Hannah had hoped this Saturday Mrs. Sweet might show her some of the city's sights— maybe even the Bellevue-Stratford Hotel with its harp-playing angel. But it seemed that Beverly was right; Mrs. Sweet was not prepared to take a blind bit of notice.

Disappointed, Hannah watched Mrs. Sweet's jaunty beret dissolve among the throng of caps and cloches. All around her, the city bustled, moving swiftly on its various joints and hinges. If only Granddad were here, she thought. He would know the right way to spend the afternoon. He would know where to take her.

Hannah stared at the quarters in her palm. Fifty cents was a stupendous amount of money. All she ought to be was grateful. She clutched the coins as she made her way dutifully to the cinema, where she lined up for her ticket among the sweetheart couples and family clusters. The fingers of her one hand tapped up and down the newly exposed nape of her neck while the other gripped her two quarters.

The new W.C. Fields film, *It's a Gift*, was playing. But on a last-minute impulse, Hannah bought a ticket to see *I'm No Angel*, starring Mae West. With thirty-eight cents left over, she decided to spend another nickel on a packet of jelly babies.

It was at the counter that she heard the voices.

"See her there? Up in front. Her hair's changed."

"Where? Oh, I see."

Helene Lyon and Lillian Shay! And they were talking about her! Hannah stopped tapping her neck and plunged her hands into her pockets, forcing herself not to turn around while her ears pricked up to eavesdrop on their prattle.

"How odd for Miss Tippity-tap to attend the cinema by her lonesome," remarked Helene.

Lillian sniggered. "Well, it's not as if she can

spend the afternoon browsing in a bookshop or library!"

"Poor thing," said Helene lightly. "I suppose I could lend her some of my baby brother Dixie's picture books. He's got no need for them since he started kindergarten."

"Oh, reading's only one of Miss Bennett's afflictions," said Lillian. "If she gets that scholarship, it'll be nothing short of robbery."

Then they *did* know! And Hannah had thought she had kept her reading a secret. Blushing hotly, she made her request to the candy-counter girl, and squared her back against Lillian and Helene as she hurried into the theater. She chose a seat in the last row and wriggled all the way down in it so that the girls would not see her when they trotted past. Miss Tippity-tap—what a mean nickname! If only she had a couple of Elgin Winnicker's garden slugs on hand!

The lights darkened, and she tried to shake the girls, and their insults, from her mind.

Luckily, the newsreel was brief and was followed by two childish but funny Donald Duck shorts. And Mae West was divine, like a glittery, friendly witch. It was only after the magic was over and the lights were brought back up again that Hannah remembered about Helene and Lillian.

She watched as the pair swept out through the front exit. Good riddance, she thought as she crept out the back, although she couldn't help but wonder where the girls were off to.

No, I'd rather be alone than with them, she thought. Even if alone means lonely.

As it was, the rest of Saturday afternoon loomed. No chores, no afternoon milking, no helping Ma with pitting peaches or ironing sheets or waxing floors and furniture. Hannah followed her feet to the vendor's cart on Front Street, where she bought a soft pretzel with an extra spatula swipe of mustard. From another peddler, she bought a pickled egg. She ate with her chin tucked rather than witness the city speed along too fast. She could never find order in its patterns. If she counted a blockful of cars or people, by the next minute, the number had changed.

It was past dinnertime when Hannah arrived at 5 Delancey Place. The house was dark. In the pantry she found a covered plate of baked apples and lamb chops. Nobody was waiting up to reprimand her, or to hear of her adventures, or to express relief that she had found her way home at all. From the parlor came the *plink-plink* of Beverly practicing scales. From everywhere else, silence.

17

DINNER AT DELANCEY PLACE

"Command performance!" Mrs. Sweet bellowed as she pushed through the kitchen door the following Friday morning, startling everyone because traditionally she took breakfast on a tray in her room. "I've got a dinner party tonight, and I expect you *all* here. Very important people will be in attendance. First, Hannah will do her numbers tricks; then Joe will recite, with Beverly's music in the parlor to close. Yes, you, Joe!"

Joe stared glumly into his bran mash, but he did not protest.

"Settled? Splendid. You'll eat in here as usual, and I'll summon you during cheeses."

After Mrs. Sweet left, Joe stuck his tongue at the door. "No better than an organ grinder's monkey," he said. "I'm gonna ask her if I can get paid for this stint."

"Are you really?" asked Hannah.

"Sure I'm really!"

Hannah could not tell if Joe Elway was joking. Day to day, she did not see or speak to him much. His school was on Girard Avenue, north of the city and a long bus ride from Delancey Place, and he was crabby most mornings, besides. In the afternoons, he stayed in his room, and when he wasn't there, he kept the door locked and wore the key on a frayed bootstrap looped around his neck, a reminder that he treasured his privacy.

In truth, Hannah had not worked hard for Joe's friendship, either. After he'd played the trick of rearranging her room, she had hidden two chunks of broiled cod in each of his galoshes that he'd left to dry at the kitchen stove. The next day, she'd seen him scrubbing his boots out in the washtub, using bleach to kill the stink.

He never said a word, but he never tattled on her, either.

Joe Elway would have fit in at Brintons Bridge School, thought Hannah. He understood the code of pranks.

She was reminded of this later that morning at school during morning assembly, when she opened her hymnal to find a drawing of a girl sitting astride a cow. Out of the girl's mouth was a bubble that read: *A B C and 1 2 3. Looky here, Maw, I kan reed 'n cownt togethar!*

From all around her, Hannah heard the twittering laughter of Lillian and Ruth Ann and, of course, Helene. Her fingers gripped the edge of her hymnbook so as not to start tapping. That would only make the girls giggle more. She flipped the hymnal to the correct page, stuck up her chin, and sang "In Your Glory, O God, I Take Refuge" extra loud. Instead of tapping, she blinked her eyes along with the hymn's meter.

That picture wasn't funny, Hannah thought unhappily. It was *mean*. There was a difference.

At lunch, Ruth Ann passed out her Halloween party invitations. Hannah pretended indifference when she did not receive one. No matter how hard she tried not to notice, she spent the rest of the afternoon spying the creamy-white envelopes. Some of the girls made it a point to keep a corner peeking out of their uniform pockets for all to see.

Mean.

Hannah wondered if back home, Frank Dilworth might be planning his own annual Halloween pumpkin-carving party. Frank Dilworth, who gave out his invitations simply by standing upon a chair and announcing it to the entire class.

By the time school let out, Hannah had forgotten all about Mrs. Sweet's dinner party. It was a surprise to return to 5 Delancey Place and find the house scented with silver polish and lemon wax and the papery freshness of cut roses, and to see Mrs. Sweet herself standing in the hall, gossiping on the telephone. "Oh, my, yes . . . and it didn't help that he smashed up two flivvers in a month . . . Imagine, a man of his age, stepping out with that Strickland girl. . . . Darling, it's unspeakable!"

Mrs. Sweet could hold a line forever. Hannah had never known anyone to use a telephone in such a way. Pure frippery, Pa would say.

Without breaking the flow of her chatter, Mrs. Sweet handed Hannah a letter postmarked from home. A quick glance at the handwriting and Hannah knew it was from Betsy. Hannah grinned and raced upstairs to her bedroom to enjoy it in private. Even in Betsy's round, easy print, the words came slow.

Last Saturday, all bodies keen and able arrived at school and fixed that roof. 'Bout time! Miss Cascade is getting hitched to

Wendel Nutley, but she won't come out and say. Frank's Halloween party is this Saturday next and Tru's got a dear new twinset in a cherry print—lucky child! I'm wearing my same navy.

Tru had printed in the postscript.

P.S. 'lo, Hannah! A new one for you: Thirty-two is the F° at which water freezes. We miss you dearly! Tru.

Hannah folded the letter and placed it in her top drawer with her various other notes, most from Ma and Pa and Granddad and Roy, and even a bulletin from Hepp that Ma had forwarded on. *You'll be home in a month*, Tru had predicted. And now a month had passed, and it seemed to Hannah that home was the only place in the world where she wanted to be.

18

THE VOICE OF ULYSSES

SOON HANNAH heard cab doors slam and shouts of greeting as guests began to arrive for Mrs. Sweet's dinner party. By the time she had readied herself and joined Beverly and Joe in the kitchen for supper, the parlor was alive with conversation.

Like Hannah, Beverly wore her Sunday best, but Joe was defiantly dressed in his regular school clothes, his precious key dangling like a charm around his neck.

"Mrs. Sweet has invited a heap of people," said Beverly. "I'm sure they'll gum it up all night." She stifled a yawn. "And tomorrow the house'll need a tips-to-tails cleaning, with cigar ash and wine spills everywhere! There goes my morning practice!"

As guests trickled into the dining room, Hannah heard Mrs. Sweet's bellow as she rearranged place settings. Millicent and Roseanne, two sisters who were friends of Beverly's from the Academy, had been hired for the evening. They stepped quickly back and forth from kitchen to dining room, carrying out the heavy serving plates. Voices became more boisterous as the night wore on.

"I haven't much experience with crowds," Hannah said. She took a last bite of roast beef and moved clockwise to her sweet potato, swallowing hard past the fear that stuck in her throat.

"There's nothing to experience here except hungry academics and boring chumps who come for the filet." Joe slurped his milk and banged down the empty glass. "Most people with their heads stuck on straight think Teddy Sweet is the dopiest dame in a dope pack."

Beverly grinned. "That's not true. Maybe we're the dopes."

"Naw. Tonight, Bev, we're the organ grinder's monkeys," said Joe. "I ought to have dressed as a clown or a doorman."

Millicent and Roseanne, slouched in tipped-back chairs by the stove, were using their between-courses break to smoke cigarettes and drink Pepsi-Cola mixed with a splash of kitchen sherry. "Give us a jingle, Joe," prompted Millicent. "If you're in a mood to entertain."

Immediately and in a creaky voice Joe jumped up and sang, "'Leprosy! You've got leprosy! Was that your eyeball that fell into my highball?'" Even Hannah joined in the laughter as Joe scratched his head and sides and hopped around the kitchen. The sound of the buzzer stopped him. "You're up to bat, milkmaid," he announced. "I'll go out with you."

The dining room was layered blue with smoke and was thick with the scent of steak as Hannah entered, Joe at her side. She blinked.

There were the Baltzells, the Austins, and the Klines, all friends of Mrs. Sweet's whom Hannah had met before, as well as a few people she'd never seen. One guest struck her eye immediately. He was a young colored man, smooth-cheeked as a girl, with toffee-colored eyes so wide-set it seemed that he could look around and at her at the same time.

"*This* is my little math ward, Dr. Claytor," said Mrs. Sweet, addressing the man. She was enthroned at the head of the table, wearing enough diamonds, Hannah figured, to start her own pawnshop. To Hannah, she said, "Dr. Claytor has just earned his Ph.D. in mathematics from the University of Pennsylvania. He is publishing his thesis on . . . oh, darling, help me! I can't even pronounce half the words!"

Dr. Claytor smiled. "'Topological Immersion of Peanian Continua in a Spherical Surface,'" he answered.

There was some laughter. "Twenty-six years old, and a future as bright as the sun," remarked gruff Mr. Kline. "Nothing to stop you, William."

Dr. Claytor inclined his head in acceptance of the remark. "Perhaps nothing, Donald," he countered, "and then again, perhaps our good friend, Dr. Robert Lee Moore."

"Now, but we mustn't ruin our party with talk of such hostile things!" retorted Mrs. Sweet. She clapped her hands together. "Not when Hannah has this wondrous trick. Now, dear, count some letters in the first five pages of *Light in August*. It's on the butler's table. Awful novel, *I* thought. Vulgar Southerner! Dolores, you pick the letter, so you know it's not been fixed beforehand."

"The *b*s," said Mrs. Kline.

Guests turned their attention to Hannah. Alarm swept her in a wave from head to toe. She did not feel confident under the attention. She wished she could be more like Roy, who had given such swagger to Benjamin Franklin. Quickly, she tapped the book's hardcover corners. Then flipped the first five pages and scanned the *b*s. "Ninety-seven."

"No, no! Impossible!" Mrs. Kline held out her hand for the book. "How could you see them all so fast?"

While Mrs. Kline took the book and re-counted, Hannah answered some simple word problems that Mr. Kline made up about apples and grasshoppers.

Then Mrs. Kline held up the book and exclaimed, "Ninety-seven, exactly!"

There was some scattershot clapping, and Hannah was finished. She stepped back from the table. When no one was looking, she crossed her eyes and stuck out her tongue at Joe. Ha—let's see you top ninety-seven *b*s, she thought.

Mrs. Sweet called on Joe to recite. "Anything! As long as it's an important person!"

"Tennyson's 'Ulysses'?" asked Joe. "There's two important people. I'll skip the beginning and cut straight to my favorite part."

Mrs. Sweet nodded and swooped a conductor's finger for him to start.

"'I cannot rest from travel,'" Joe began. His voice was clear and calm. "'I will drink life to the lees. All times I have enjoyed greatly, have suffered greatly, both with those that loved me, and alone.'" Without pause or falter, Joe stepped into the role, becoming the old hero, Ulysses. No mugging, no hamming, as Joe made Ulysses' troubles come alive, transporting Hannah to a world even more vivid than Miss Cascade had ever brought to her schoolroom.

After he finished, the table sat silent, spellbound, until Mrs. Sweet broke the mood with a ping of her spoon on her wineglass.

"Thank you, Hannah and Joe," she said. "You may go now."

"Hold up, Joe. Do you know any Eliot?" asked Mr. Baltzell. "'Prufrock', perhaps?"

"Sure do," Joe answered, holding out his palm. "You got a penny for it? I *am* a professional, after all. Need to earn my keep."

Now that, Hannah thought, was most certainly rude. Her fingers began to tap the cover of *Light in August* as the room went silent. Mrs. Sweet's eyes widened, and her jaw dropped. She looked to Hannah rather like a lace-wrapped trout. Mrs. Kline touched a nervous hand to her tarnished-silver curls. Then Dr. Claytor threw back his head and roared. His laughter was followed by Mrs. Baltzell's, and it wasn't long before everyone at the table was convulsed in mirth. Joe was laughing hardest of all.

Mr. Baltzell pulled out a chair and offered him the platter of cheese, which pleased Joe—although, Hannah noticed, it annoyed Mrs. Sweet.

"Yes," said Mrs. Sweet, her smile set as carefully as her centerpiece. "Both you children, sit. And when we're ready to move to the parlor, I'll get Beverly to come play a teensy sonata for us. What sharp kiddos!"

"Here, here," cried Mrs. Baltzell, raising her glass.

19

BLOWN BACK

As THE DINNER party began to break up, Beverly, Joe, and Hannah helped the guests with their coats. Hannah made sure she got hold of Dr. Claytor's. She held his hat and gloves for him as he buttoned his overcoat.

"Why are you looking at me that way, my friend?" he asked.

"I wanted to know, sir, who is Dr. Robert Lee Moore?"

"Ah, Robert Lee Moore." Without changing expression, Dr. Claytor's features seemed to harden as if glazed by an invisible frost. "The good professor is favored to become the president of the American Mathematical Society next year, and last I heard, women were discouraged from attending his lectures, and coloreds were prevented." He fell silent, giving the words their space. Then he winked at Hannah and his expression turned to flesh and blood again. "You will learn in time that while some doors are open, others are stuck and need pushing. A good strong push from one is a push for us all."

He set his hat on his head, raised it to Hannah, and replaced it. "Good night."

"Good night," she answered.

She watched as Dr. Claytor departed, leaving her to her thoughts.

While Pa and Ma had expressed a few doubts, Granddad McNaughton hardly ever mentioned the limitations of becoming a woman mathematician. Certainly at Ottley Friends, Miss Jordan and Mr. Cole did not treat Hannah as if doors were closed to her.

But of course some doors would be, Hannah contemplated. In spite of her best efforts. Dr. Curie probably had had to push against a lot of doors. She had likely seen her share of knuckleheads such as Robert Moore. If she could do it, then so can I, Hannah decided. That's what Granddad would say. Real learning was harder work than pushing against homesickness, or pretending not to care about a Halloween invitation snub or a cruel cartoon drawing.

Now Hannah envisioned Dr. Moore as another, fiercer caricature, like a storybook painting of the North Wind. Eyebrows like lightning bolts and cheeks rounded, blowing her and Dr. Claytor like seeds in the opposite direction of wherever the fields of math might lie.

It made her shiver, as if some of that wind already had puffed through her. She went to the front hall window and pulled aside the velvet drapes and watched Dr. Claytor as he strode alone down the street, past the last lamppost and into the darkness.

When she rounded the stairs to her bedroom, Hannah found Joe waiting for her, sitting at her desk as if it were his own.

"Counting letters." He snapped his fingers. "Not a bad trick!"

"Knock it off!" she said, surprising herself because this was not an expression she used. It was Mae West's, she realized. "My math teacher, Mr. Cole, says it's better than a trick," she bragged shyly. "He says some people read numbers naturally in sequences. I'm not bad at breaking codes, either."

"Christmas, a human cipher!" Joe exclaimed in a voice of genuine envy. "I'da counted you for a lost cause, but you might grab a scholarship out of my hands after all." His voice dropped, as if he were letting Hannah in on a secret. "There's fancy boarding schools that admit Wexler-funded kids, you know. That's where I aim to go. Breathe clean air again, up in New Hampshire or Rhode Island." He used his palms to launch a full swivel before facing Hannah again. "Would you head north? If you took my scholarship money, that is?" His face turned serious.

"Joe, I'm not fixing to take *your* scholarship."

"But if you did."

"I can't imagine going anywhere except close to home," Hannah confessed. "I miss home." In a blurt, she added, "I've got no friends here, see. Not that I care," she ended weakly.

"Well, who'd be your friend, bunny?" Joe's frown disappeared. "You're nobody's idea of fun. You've got no spirit. You're a wet-blankety, sulky, boring girl."

"I am not!"

"Plus, you're a snob." Joe's smile crinkled the corners of his eyes.

"A snob? I'm a snob?" Hannah blinked. "I'm not a snob!"

"Shows what *you* know." Now Joe seemed to relax. He propped his boots on the desktop, leaned back, crossed his eyes, and stuck out his tongue at her. "Not a real, born-and-bred Ottley snob. But in your own right, you're as bad as

Sweet. Wearing her clothes, eating her hash, spending her lettuce."

"I'm only trying to make the best of things." Hannah opened her door wider and stomped her foot to make Joe leave. "Shows what *you* know."

Joe didn't move, except to point a finger at her. "The best of things! Huh. Name one best thing you've done since you got to this city, milk-maid, or one thing that interests you. Besides playing the odd prank on me."

One best thing. The challenge stopped her. She thought of movies she'd seen and candies she'd eaten. She thought of the small steps she'd taken in her reading. She thought of her morning chats with Mr. Barnaby. She thought of the new music program, *Fifteen Minutes with Bing Crosby*, that she and Beverly tuned into on nights when Mrs. Sweet was out. She thought of riding on the subway, the weight of the city above her head and the shake of the tracks beneath her feet.

Yet she knew that none of these things would be best enough for Joe Elway.

"What have you done so swell yourself, Mister Elway? Have you been to see the Liberty Bell? Have you drunk tea at the Bellevue-Stratford?"

"I'd say not." Joe looked indignant. "The bell's broke, and there's no fun in a bunch of tea-drinking dames. I get to places where a fella can breathe and stretch. If you don't do it regular, you go flabby. Tell you what. I don't know how you've been wasting your time—napping at the cinema and gnawing bonbons, probably. But if you're around tomorrow, I'll show you the town. You got to promise not to be a snob or a bug, though. 'Cause this'd be a favor from me to you, milkmaid. From the goodness of one guy's heart." He thumped his chest, slid up from her chair, and, whistling, walked past her. "'Night, then."

She said good night and shut the door, puzzled. Was Joe serious?

And was she really all of those things Joe said—sulky, snobby, boring? Could it be that some of her difficulties did not lie inside this house or school, or even in Philadelphia, but inside herself?

The thoughts chased through her mind as she prepared for bed, only to find that Joe had short-sheeted it.

20

ALUMINUM CITY

THE NEXT MORNING, Hannah had finished breakfast and was staring out the bay window. Waiting for Joe, though she might have denied it if asked.

Suddenly, she spied him outside walking toward Eighteenth Street. His cap was pulled low and his hands dipped deep in his coat pockets. He must have seen her and decided to sneak out the back door! Well, he wouldn't get off that easy.

"Wait up!" Hannah called, rapping on the window. She dashed for her coat on the way out the door and caught up, breathless, at the end of Delancey. "Where are you going? You said you'd show me the town today! I want to stretch my legs!"

"Aw, quit yawping." Joe looked her up and down. "If you're serious, you better know my day runs different from yours, milkmaid. From stem to stern."

"That's fine. I still want to come along." She shadowed Joe he strode around the back alley. From behind a horse trough, he kicked forward a skato.

"My escape vehicle," he told her.

Hannah had not known Joe owned a skato, though she had seen lots of boys riding them since she'd arrived in Philadelphia. Even back in Chadds Ford they were the fashion. Roy had built a skato for himself, using a pair of wheels pried off his outgrown roller skates, a piece of board, and an orange crate. But it hadn't worked on the dirt roads, and had collapsed into pieces when Roy tried to jump it off a homemade ramp he'd built from a stack of stripped truck tires.

Joe's skato looked nicer than Roy's, Hannah had to admit. It was sleek and narrow instead of box-sided, and was painted blue, with rubber-padded T-shaped handlebars.

"I built it with scrap-yard parts and added an extra set of wheels," Joe said proudly. "That's why it's strong enough to carry extra junk. Or an extra person." He straightened the wheels and stepped on. "Hold me around the side and push off with your right foot when I say go."

Hannah faltered. "You want me to ride with you on that?"

"Look, like I was saying, you better not be a snob or a bug about—"

"I won't!" She stepped onto the skato and held Joe's waist firmly. "I'm ready."

On Joe's "One-two-three—go!" and a strong push, they shot down the alley.

"Lean into my turns and keep your eyes up, not down watching your toes grow," Joe said. "I've seen the way you walk, milkmaid. We're hooking a left on Sansom."

Hannah squinted, enjoying the sun and the numbing breeze on her face. Buildings slipped past at a clip as the paving bumped beneath her shoes.

"'Scuse me! Coming through!" called Joe.

A car honked for them to move to the side. "Gee, buddy, there's room for us all!" Joe scowled, raised and shook his fist. "Curse it, but automobiles think they own these roads!"

"Where are we going?"

"On a mission."

"For what?"

"For aluminum."

"Aluminum?" Hannah laughed. "Why?"

"'Cause once we get enough, we'll sell it to Mr. Lee, the rag and junk man. He buys everyone's old scrap iron and aluminum, even newspapers. Twelve cents a pound is what he'll pay for metal. You can sweep in an easy couple of dimes, good clean money, if you know how to look."

Hannah leaned with Joe as they made a right

onto Sansom Street. Almost immediately, and with a triumphant "Aha!" Joe braked. He hopped off the skato, nearly upsetting it, ran halfway down the street, then leaned over and picked something off the road. He jogged back holding a twist of aluminum between his fingers, which he crushed into a ball and tossed for Hannah's catch. "Keep the goods in your coat pocket. I got a sack for when we start hauling. Just you watch how this adds up."

She dug her fingers into Joe's overcoat pockets as they continued up Sansom, Joe whistling passersby out of their path. A glint caught Hannah's eye.

"Stop! I see something!" she cried. Once Joe set his foot on the pavement, she jumped off the skato and ran to where an empty box of cigarettes was lying inches from the gutter. She bent to retrieve it, then unpeeled the sheet of foil from the thin paper and held it high for him to see.

Joe pointed. "And there's two more packs in that trash can there. Get 'em."

It only took a moment's deliberation before Hannah nodded, rucked up the sleeve of her wool coat, leaned over, and dug through the garbage bin until she had grasped hold of both empty cigarette packs. She unstuck the aluminum foil and mashed it with the other pieces into a silver ball the size of a plum. They would need to find lots more aluminum to weigh in a pound, she figured.

The adventure was what counted, though, and Philadelphia seemed almost friendly with Joe in it. He talked Hannah through its sights just as he had that first rainy afternoon. Which didn't seem quite so terrifying today, perhaps because not only did Joe know places, he knew people. Tony the ice man. Mrs. Oppenheimer, who made and sold boxed Japanese gardens on the corner of Sansom and Fourth. The skato gang: Si and Marshal and Francis, who were lingering in the doorway of the butcher shop, hoping for pocket money by delivering meat to houses and restaurants.

"Hullo, Joe!" said Francis, steering his yellow-striped skato in a slow circle around them. "Whaddaya know? Gonna introduce us to your sweetheart?"

"She's no sweetheart. This is only Hannah," said Joe. "You know I got a girl already. Ole Hannah's helping me collect aluminum."

"Saw some lucky bird haul a whole radiator to Mr. Lee this Thursday last," Marshal told them. "Got nine dollars for it, special patriot's rate, what with Armistice Day 'round the corner. She'll be eating caviar and blinis for a month."

Joe scoffed. "We'll earn double that, the rate we're going. See ya later, boys."

It wasn't until they were on their way again, the boys gone from sight, that Hannah had to ask, "Who is your girl, Joe? I never met her."

"'Cause I don't really have one is why. But a fella's gotta say what he's gotta say, and your lips aren't smoochable enough to be any million-dollar doll face of mine."

"Joe Elway, you don't even know from smoochable!" Hannah retorted.

"Takes one to smooch one," he called over his shoulder.

They combed the city all morning, peeling their treasures from discarded cigarette packs and wheeling into some better luck with an empty tin of Bon Ami and two Campbell's soup cans that had been dropped in plain sight off the South Street wharf. Toward noon, it was Joe who spied their best prize, a muffin pan abandoned in an alleyway on Panama Street.

"That gives us five pounds, easy," said Joe, parking the skato and then dropping to sit on the curb. "We'll go around to see Lee after lunch." He pulled a squashed, waxed-paper package from his jacket and unwrapped it to reveal a lumpy sandwich. "I'll split. Cheese and mustard."

Hannah dropped down next to him. She was tired and surprised to hear her stomach gurgle. Back home, she'd always been hungry before every meal, but at Delancey Place, the food arrived before the appetite. She took the offered half of sandwich gladly.

"Say, Joe, are those boys, Francis and those fellows, are they friends of yours from school?"

Joe snorted. "I only wish! They go to Our Lady of Lourdes, where I'd wanna be, too, but it doesn't give out scholarships. My school's full of fellows so lousy with money they can't even tell what it's worth. Meantime, back home, my brothers sleep head to foot, two to a cot, and live underground fifteen hours a day."

"Underground? How's that?"

"I mean coal mines. Elways are coal men. How we all live and die, till me."

"Then how did Mrs. Sweet find you, if you were underground?" Hannah asked.

Joe rolled his eyes. "My sister Sally's to blame. She said it wasn't natural to remember things like I do, word for word, like church sermons from years ago. She thought I might have a blessing or a curse on me. I was like a joke that she couldn't decide was funny or not. This past April, Sally blew her last nickel to send me to Pittsburgh to be looked at by Monsignor Carroll. I met him all right. Recited the entire Advent, from First Kings, 'The Miraculous Rain,' Chapter Eighteen, verses one through forty, through 'The Birth of John the Baptist,' Luke One, fifty-six through eighty. And all the psalms in between."

He smiled. "Monsignor said the only thing unnatural was to allow my mind to go to waste. He fixed me up with some academic big shots. Which is how I came to meet Sweet. Sally's got different plans for me now. Wants me to invent something useful, like a flying car. A get-rich-quick-scheme, so she can drive a Ford coupe and serve oxtail consommé out of a gold tureen."

"Is that what you want?"

Joe pondered it. "Sure I'd like to help out my family, after all this educating. But I'm no money-grubber. And so far as I see, the only people who should have boatloads of cash are bank robbers. Those're the ones risking their necks. Betting on their lives. Of course, Hoover and all his men zotzed the bravest ones. Bonnie and Clyde both took their hits this past spring. John Dillinger got picked off in July, standing right outside the cinema. Heard they sold scraps of his bloody shirt as souvenirs. And Pretty Boy Floyd!" Joe sliced his hands together, brushing off bread crumbs. "He got the lead pump only last Monday, while he was holed up in Wellsville. Wellsville! Poor guy died under an apple tree. Guess you didn't read about it. And so now," Joe concluded unhappily, "all there is left is Baby Face Nelson. But Mr. Special Agent Hoover's never gonna put his cubs on *him*."

"Baby who? I never heard about a crook named Baby Face." Hannah had not heard of some of those others, either. She wondered if Joe was only teasing.

Joe turned on her, indignant. "Whaddaya talkin' about, you never heard of Baby Face Nelson? Don't you read the papers? Don't you hear the song? 'Baby Face! You got the cutest little Baby Face.' I've cut out all his clippings for my scrapbook. Coppers and gumshoes need eyes in the back of their heads to catch Baby Face."

"I heard the song, but I don't read the papers," Hannah admitted. "Can't, that is."

"Can't what?"

"Can't read. I mean, I can a little. But not a lot. Not a newspaper's amount."

"Can't read? Ha!" Joe laughed. "For Pete's sake, if that's not the dopiest thing I ever heard."

"It hardly bothered me back home," Hannah confessed. "But the Ottley Friends girls aren't as . . . *charitable* as my real friends in Chadds Ford. Most days I'm more concerned that Helene Lyon is spying at me through the keyhole while I'm having my tutorials in Miss Jordan's office."

"I guess Ottley Friends isn't so friendly to milkmaids," said Joe. "Anyhow, you'll never get my scholarship if you can't *read*!" He laughed, slapping his knees. "Here I've been in a horse sweat over the competition! Aw, get a look at that sourpuss face on you. Cripes, I'm mostly ribbing. I *know* I'll get a scholarship. I'm so sure on that, I'll teach you to read myself. First you gotta figure what you want to read. Then it's easy as fish stew." He snapped his fingers.

Hannah shrugged as if it didn't matter to her. She could never tell if Joe was being earnest. He seemed awfully confident about being able to teach her. If it was only in jest, though, she did not want to appear eager.

"Boy, oh, boy, I'd like to see you try," she said in a Mae West–ish, careless way, but she tapped a hopeful pattern on each knee before she could stop herself.

21

RITTENHOUSE WILLOW

SHADOWS HAD grown longer than their objects by the time they wheeled all the way to Forty-sixth and King Street, where Mr. Lee kept his cart parked out front of the Coal, Coke & Wood Warehouse. In exchange for their scrap metal, Mr. Lee gave Hannah and Joe twenty-three cents apiece. Hannah held the two silver dimes and three copper pennies tight in her palm.

"This is the first cash money I ever earned," she admitted. She didn't know why she was so happy about it. After all, Mrs. Sweet had tossed her fifty cents' allowance just last week! Yet Mrs. Sweet's money had made her feel guilty, and she'd spent it in a hurry. This money was different, Hannah decided. It was more important. It was *hers*.

She buttoned the coins into the inside breast pocket of her coat.

"We ought to get home." She lifted her face to the darkening skyline. "Chestnut would be quickest." It had not taken long for the grid of the city to unfold smooth as a map in her mind's eye. Its patterns were clear, even math-minded, now that she'd spent the whole day navigating. She was glad Joe had followed her suggestions when she told him the quickest way to get from here to there. Joe was not one to pretend he knew more than he did.

"Chestnut," Joe agreed. "Only first lemme show you something. Hold on."

Hannah held on and pushed off with a leg that was aching sore from the strain of use. Joe sped them downtown on Chestnut Street. When they turned onto Walnut Street, Hannah saw they were on their way to Rittenhouse Park.

The park was a wide square of ground, inlaid with flower beds and footpaths and belted on four sides by wrought iron gating that resembled asparagus. The recent cold snap had stripped its trees of their leaves and discolored its grass, but it was still impressive. The dinner hour had reduced its usual hubbub of fashionable people to only a uniformed nanny pushing a baby carriage and an elderly couple who sat on a bench surrounded by bobbing pigeons.

"Watch me!" said Joe, as he parked the skato by the open front gate. He peeled off his shoes and socks and tore across the lawn. "Don't be a chicken! C'mon!"

Hannah glanced around. Nobody seemed to care what Joe was doing. Nor was anyone watching to see if Hannah would copy him. Discreetly, she unlaced and pulled off a shoe and stocking. Then their mates. It had been over a month, she realized, since she had been barefoot outdoors. She shrieked to feel the cold grass scratch the bottoms of her feet.

Joe shot the length of the park and was steering toward one of its largest willow trees. She saw him grip its lowest branch expertly, twisting himself up the trunk, then hauling his body still higher. Up and up. Was he allowed? She doubted it.

"Betcha can't climb a tree anymore, milkmaid!" Joe shouted.

She was already to the willow's base. "Betcha you're wrong!"

This tree was not as thick as Bloom, but its branches were lower and more plentiful. Hannah gripped and pulled herself until she was a full head higher than Joe. No, she had not forgotten a thing about trees.

Settled, she swung her feet, enjoying the bite of October cold on her toetips.

"Go careful," Joe warned, looking up at her. "This tree is trickier that it looks. I fell out of it a few months back. Bruise on my keister looked like I'd skid across a patch of motor oil."

"I'm safe," she assured him.

They stared across the cityscape. At the edge of the park's gate, the lamplighter propped his ladder, and soon the first light of a city evening sparked to a glow.

Hannah leaned back and threw her arms wide and up so that they brushed the feathery fringed tips of what few leaves remained. "This was a best day," she declared. "Thanks, Joe."

"Yeah, yeah, it was nothing."

"It was better than nothing."

"One thing about a city, there's always enough to do to push you out of a sulk," said Joe. "Even without me to show the way. And don't forget, when it comes to the competition, it's still you against me."

"You against me!" Hannah agreed.

22

BABY FACE NELSON

SUNDAY, JOE ignored Hannah. He galloped upstairs after she came home from church in the morning. He sneaked out of the house without her in the afternoon.

Perhaps he hadn't had any fun yesterday? Hannah slumped in the parlor's front window seat. Perhaps he preferred to be left alone?

A noise in the doorway startled her. She turned. Joe must have come inside through the kitchen. A worn brown notebook was tucked under his arm.

"Here's the thing," he said. "If you don't

know all there is to know about Baby Face Nelson, I don't see how we're gonna be buddies. You might say I'm off my head, but I feel like he's a personal acquaintance of mine. You got anyone like that?"

"Madame Curie and Pythagoras and Mae West," Hannah answered.

"There you have it! And look here. Francis's ma bakes on Sundays. Reading and eating, see, they go together." Joe jumped up onto the window seat beside her, removed his cap, and pulled a handkerchief-wrapped slice of butter cake from his pocket. "We'll split."

Hannah broke the cake in half as Joe opened his scrapbook across their laps. She stared at the newsprint, a sly jumble of words set alongside grainy photographs of storefronts or automobiles or a close-up image of a man whose boneless face appeared to have taken a few punches. "Mushy Face Nelson, they ought to call him," she pronounced. "Oh, boy, the newsprint is too small!"

"Don't sulk. Reading's a cinch if you're on to

the right story," Joe answered. In one crocodile bite, he dropped a piece of cake into his mouth. Crumbs flew everywhere. "We'll begin at the beginning, how 'bout? First, I'll take you through the history on the official FBI report. You watch my finger hit the words." He brushed the crumbs off the page, cleared his throat, and began to speak in his "Ulysses" voice. "'Baby Face Nelson was born Lester M. Gillis in December 1908, in Chicago. He spent his youth roaming the city streets with his gang of juvenile hoodlums, committing petty crimes. By the age of fourteen, Baby Face was an accomplished car thief.'"

Hannah watched the words under Joe's finger as she listened to a story that was as good—if not better—than any radio program she'd ever heard. Baby Face was just a few years older than Hepp, and what a life he'd led! All that shoplifting, car stealing, street fighting, liquor smuggling, and bank robbing!

Joe had arranged the articles in sequence so that Baby Face's records read like a mystery thriller. He broke apart the harder words into chewable pieces.

Tom-my-gun. Fed-er-al in-ves-ti-ga-tion. Plain-clothes-men.

The light thinned as they wound their way through Baby Face's grisly history.

"Gosh, Joe," Hannah said, closing the book with a contented sigh after they had finished. "I do believe that is the best story I ever read."

"Toldja!" Joe grinned. Then he explained that with John Dillinger dead, Baby Face was now the FBI's Most Wanted. "Armed and dangerous!" Joe wriggled his eyebrows.

"How do you know Baby Face won't come to Philadelphia next?" squeaked Hannah.

"Uh-uh, he won't come here. Too many men in blue."

"But what about the banks?" Hannah insisted. "There's loads of banks in Philadelphia."

"Naw, see, you don't understand Baby Face. He's best in the heartland, where he can lay low from prying—"

"Aha! Joe and Hannah!" Neither of them had heard Mrs. Sweet enter the house. Startled, Hannah looked up to see her leaning slantways into the room. Her features were unpleasantly bunched, as if tied and held to the middle of her face by invisible string. "I'm looking for Beverly. Where is she?" She glanced at the empty piano bench as if Beverly ought to be there.

"She's out," said Joe. That Beverly spent her Sunday evenings with her regular beau, Charlie, was a secret from Mrs. Sweet.

"When she gets in, tell her that I want a word," said Mrs. Sweet. "No matter the time. Hear me? Tell her to knock on my door."

Hannah and Joe nodded. Mrs. Sweet turned and huffed upstairs.

"She didn't even say good night. D'you think something's wrong?" Hannah asked nervously.

"I don't know from wrong, but something's on the cooker," Joe answered.

23

ABANDONED

"**Y**OU'RE GETTING the boot?" Joe's voice was incredulous.

Beverly nodded. "I've got two weeks' notice. Sweet tells me the new crop of students entering the Academy is too young and talented for me to compete. Classically trained," she whispered. She dabbed at her eyes. "Even if I passed the exams, I might not be guaranteed placement, and she doesn't want to chance it."

Hannah counted the chimes as the grandfather clock in the foyer struck midnight. An hour earlier, on Beverly's knock, both she and Joe had sneaked downstairs, where Beverly had heated a pan of milk and poured it into mugs sweetened with sugar. Now Beverly raised her mug as if in a toast. "Truth is, Sweet wants a real, sensible maid." She took a long sip. "Someone who actually remembers to dust."

"Christmas!" Joe sputtered. "It was never about the dust! Who ever heard of a maid with fingers too soft to scrub a floor or press a sheet? You're the worst dratted maid in all of Philadelphia, Bev. But you're a fine musician."

Under the table, Hannah's fingers tapped an anxious rhythm. Her stomach felt pulled as taffy. What else could Beverly do, if she couldn't play music?

"Sweet told me a house of young people had been amusing at first, but we were starting to crowd her," said Beverly. "'It's true I've been lonely now that both my boys have left me,' she says. 'But what if I want to see in Paris in the springtime?' she says. 'Why's it left to me to mind you three, to serve your every need? I've bit off more than I chew.'" Beverly shook her head in disbelief. "Boarding us kids—it's been nothing but a rich folks' fad, if you ask me. Same as those puffy goose-down jackets ladies took to wearing last year."

"I'll wager there's plenty other families who'd take you in." Joe thudded a fist into his palm. "A beezillion people living a stone's throw from the Academy who are nuts for music, and who've got a spare room, and who aren't blasted dopes." He didn't sound convinced.

"There's no such number as beezillion," said Hannah. She knew it was the wrong thing to blurt out, but no one remarked on it.

"My luck's burnt down to the wire," said Beverly tiredly. "Charlie teaches piano, so he's always in the big fancy houses, and he says the newest trend is to bring poor students over from Europe to teach arts on the cheap."

"If Charlie teaches piano, maybe you could, too," Hannah suggested.

"Oh, sure I could, but that's no way to make a living." Beverly sighed. "Charlie's real paycheck comes from working down at the wharf. Piano's his hobby. Hannah, please quit drumming your fingers under the table. It's driving me bats." Beverly stood and pushed in her chair. "I don't have money to live on my own *and* work *and* study. I'll be eighteen next month. Too old for dreams."

"It's not fair," said Hannah. "It's not fair for Mrs. Sweet to close a door on you all of a sudden like that!"

Beverly shrugged, but her smile was sad. "Perhaps things'll look smoother by morning. I'll go to sleep and see. Good night, you two." She leaned over and dropped a kiss on each of their heads before slipping off through the kitchen door to her bedroom.

"Poor Bev," Hannah murmured. "Poor us, too. What if Mrs. Sweet wants to chuck us all out? What if it's true, Joe, that we're nothing but a fad?"

"Time will tell. But without Beverly around pretending to take care of things, this joint is gonna get pretty empty." Joe's voice was matter-of-fact to disguise the hurt in his face. More than once Joe had mentioned to Hannah that Beverly was the same age as his sister, Sally. In the short time they'd lived here, Beverly had become a big sister to them both. The house wouldn't be the same without Beverly and her music, thought Hannah miserably.

Apparently, however, Mrs. Sweet did not hear it that way.

PART THREE

24

A PHONE CALL

BEVERLY HAD packed and left by the end of the following week. Her "jiffy" plan, as she called it, was to lodge with Charlie's sisters until she got her bearings. After that, Beverly said, the future might land her anywhere.

"Anywhere there's a piano, you mean?" Hannah asked that last afternoon as she flopped herself upon the stripped mattress in Beverly's empty room. She felt as if she had asked the same question a hundred times before, but she could not bear to think of Beverly existing anyplace without a piano.

"Stop fretting about me." Beverly already sounded more adult than she had a week ago. "Oh, and I've got a farewell gift for you, Hannah. I've been meaning to pass it along." She straightened and clasped her hands behind her back, professor-style. "It's on my authority that during his life, Ludwig van Beethoven wrote a total of thirty-two sonatas. Not only that, but Johannes Bach's thirty-two Goldberg Variations are among the best known of his works. How about that for your lucky number, thirty-two?"

"Gosh, sometimes thirty-two seems more than lucky," said Hannah wonderingly, "and closer to magical. Thanks, Bev."

"Oh, but that's not my gift," said Beverly. "This is—I stole some sheet music from the Academy. If you help me push my trunk out to the front hall for Charlie to pick up, I'll play you Bach's Aria and his first two Variations. What do you say?"

Hannah was already dragging the trunk by its

handles. "I'd say I'm all ears! This'll be the first concert you've ever played for me, Beverly."

"Guess I never had the time to spare, before."

Once the luggage was stacked at the front door, Hannah ran into the parlor and sat cross-legged on the ottoman. Beverly took her usual place behind the piano.

"Good-bye, Steinway, dear," she said softly, rubbing the piano's polished ebony surface. Then she spread her fingers over the keyboard and began.

Hannah closed her eyes as the short elegant stacks of sound marched and melted through her head. Beverly's mind must be full of counting patterns, too, Hannah thought. Except that Beverly's patterns made a tune instead of a proof or equation.

When Beverly finished, Hannah clapped and whistled through her teeth the way Joe had taught her. "Oh, Bev, I'm sure going to miss you. Who'll sing along to Bing Crosby with me now?"

"Joe might, for a nickel." The corner of Beverly's mouth tucked up, the first smile Hannah had seen from her all day.

Even after Charlie rang the doorbell and Beverly was gone, Hannah could hear the echo of her music. Once the sound of the piano playing had given Hannah pangs of homesickness. Now, in the silence, Hannah missed Beverly instead.

Before she left, Beverly had roasted a chicken and boiled some potatoes and parsnips for Hannah and Joe's supper, but the next evening, with the kitchen dark and Mrs. Sweet nowhere in sight, there was another downside to Beverly's absence. Hannah prepared no-fuss horseradish-and-ham sandwiches while Joe chopped a tomato salad.

Midway through their meal, Joe lifted his head. "Sweet's back."

Hannah strained to listen. "She sneaks in so quiet, you'd need the ears of a bat to hear her."

"She doesn't want us to hear, otherwise she'd hafta stop in for a chat." Joe rolled his eyes.

"Even if we both the pass the exam, we'll need another house to hang our hats come June," he warned. "Mark my words."

Now Hannah could detect a ghostlike footstep in the upstairs hall.

"Say, it's Thanksgiving next week," Joe remarked. "Are you spending it with friends?"

"Oh, no. I've got too much work."

"Me, either," said Joe with a wink. "Snobs."

"Snobs," she agreed.

From the hall, the telephone jangled. Neither of them looked in its direction. The telephone was always for Mrs. Sweet, and so it was all the more surprising when her voice resounded through the air vent.

"Haaa-naaah," she called. "You're wanted on the telephone!"

Joe raised his eyebrows.

Hannah's heart jounced. She jumped up and ran out of the kitchen to the hall phone and she picked up the heavy receiver. "Yes? Who is there?"

"Hannah!" Ma's voice sounded small but close, almost as if she were in the next room.

"Ma! Is something wrong? Why are you at the Applebees'?"

"No, I'm right here in the kitchen. Pa and I decided to install a telephone."

"Oh!" Hannah tried to picture her mother speaking into a telephone mouthpiece. It seemed too movie star-ish for Ma.

"Folks change their milk orders last minute," Ma explained, "and with you and Hepp gone, we ought to be in touch. You simply tell the operator to connect you to Chadds Ford, Bennett, number seventy-two."

"Seventy-two," Hannah repeated. The number of inches in six feet. The number of days it took Nellie Bly to travel the world. Now, the telephone number. The future had poked in its nose and turned into the present.

Over the line, Ma was skittering on in a breathless manner about how the telephone man had come to install the line and had run the cord wrong, before she abruptly interrupted herself. "But that's not what I rang you up for, Hannah. I'm not sure how to say this without being able to see you, but I suppose there's no other way." Ma's breath on the line was as loud as radio static.

"What is it, Ma?"

"The reason I called was to say that. To say that. That Pa and I hoped you might be able to free yourself to come home for a spell. Tomorrow."

"Is something the matter, Ma? Is the family well? Is there word from Hepp?"

"Mrs. Bennett, Miss Bennett," interrupted the switchboard operator. "You'll have to get off the line. There's a few callers wanting to get hold of Mrs. Sweet."

"Another moment, thank you," said Ma. "Hannah, it's your grandfather."

"What's news of Granddad?" asked Hannah. Her fingers twisted the phone cord to keep herself from tapping. "Is he in trouble? Is he hurt?"

"Hannah, Granddad McNaughton passed

away last night. In his sleep, peacefully." Now Ma was speaking quickly, as if she were in a train moving faster and faster away from Hannah. "You'll need to hurry home for the funeral this Sunday. There's a train that leaves the city tomorrow morning at eight sharp. Pa will pick you up at the station. Please ask Mrs. Sweet if we might borrow expenses for the ticket and send the reimbursement back with you. I'm sorry to give you this news. Hurry home, Hannah!"

The line clicked as Ma hung up. Hannah was left staring into the receiver. Her mind whirled, though her feet seemed to be made of clay. No, no, it couldn't be, she thought wildly. Impossible. Last night, when? Last night, when she was studying Mr. Cole's worksheet about capacity in customary units? Or when she had been brushing her teeth, or arguing with Joe about who was the better baseball player, Dizzy Dean or his brother Daffy?

Surely some part of her ought to have felt it—a confused, drowning rush of grief that she could mark in her head as the same moment her grandfather had departed.

But last night had been so ordinary!

The nagging voice of the operator finally pushed Hannah from her trance, reminding her that Mrs. Sweet's call was being connected, and that she had better run and fetch her.

25

HOME AGAIN

PA KEPT HIS eyes on the road as the truck rattled and looped along the familiar route. He had been the first person whom Hannah had spied when the train pulled in. Standing alone in his denim coveralls and brown field coat, he was instantly recognizable, and yet it seemed an eternity since Hannah had seen him last.

She had been scared that Pa would look older, or different, but he did not. In fact, it was she who seemed to take him aback.

"Sakes, you're a sight, Hannah," he said,

reaching out to tug the snipped ends of her hair, then stepping back to look her up and down. "Nothing but sunk eyes and bony legs. Don't they feed you in Philadelphia?"

She shook her head. "There's too much on the table, if anything."

Pa's forehead wrinkled, but he did not respond.

They climbed into the truck and fell into silence. Hannah could not pluck up the nerve to ask any questions about Granddad. Pa and Granddad had shared a cantankerous relationship, further strained by the fact that Pa worked a property Granddad had partly and stubbornly owned. In her parents' hearts, Hannah realized, Granddad's passing must have come qualified with slight relief.

"Will Hepp show for the funeral?" she asked instead.

"Dunno. We sent word by telegram to Kansas City day before last, but heard nothing back. He must have cleared out beforehand."

Hannah caught the note of Pa's irritation.

It had never made sense to Pa that Hepp could drift in and out of touch with the family so easily.

She stared out the window. Chadds Ford was dressed for winter. Cooled of color, stripped of blossom, with the sinking sun pulling the last bit of haze from the sky, it was not the prettiest time of season. Yet the familiarity of it set a lump in her throat.

A midday dinner was ready when she and Pa walked through the kitchen door. Over the steaming pot roast, Ma appeared tired, but Roy whooped and squeezed Hannah, jumping her up and down until she thought she'd crack a lung. These months as an only child must have been lonesome for Roy, she figured.

"Jeepers-creepers! You went and chopped your best feature into a haystack." Roy tousled her hair once he released her. "And you look worn through."

"Hannah, you've been studying too hard," reprimanded Ma.

"No, I haven't." Her family's concern baffled her. Pleased her, too. It was nice to be fussed over.

During the meal, Ma heaped Hannah's plate and kept an eye that she ate everything on it, and Roy even leaped up to fetch a glass of milk, while Pa made remarks about the dangerous effects of polluted city air. With all the attention foisted on her, it was not until the end of the meal that Hannah noticed.

"But where's Ben?"

"He left a week ago. Day after he collected his paycheck," said Pa.

"Nobody even saw him leave," Roy added. "He must have hopped a midnight train back to Ohio. Caught us all by surprise. Suppose he'd had enough of being away, and needed to get back home." Roy hesitated, then said, "We kept thinking you'd do the same, Han."

"Me?" It had never crossed her mind to leave the city as long as Granddad kept watch over her progress there. After all, it was to him that she had sent her graded math tests and Mr. Cole's weekly evaluation reports.

Granddad was the reason I left Chadds Ford, thought Hannah as she helped Ma tidy the kitchen afterward. Now Granddad has left Chadds Ford, too. Where does that put me? The question circled, searching for an answer that lay outside her reach.

Entering her bedroom later that evening was like reuniting with a childhood friend. Hannah tapped its corners and straightened and reordered her personal items; her faded, half-forgotten collection of Rudy Vallee press clippings, her stuffed calico horse. Though the night was too cold for it, she cracked open her window so that she could listen to the round echo of owl song.

She changed into her nightgown and climbed into bed, relishing its familiar softness. She imagined Granddad sitting on his porch, impeccably dressed, alone but never lonely. Her eyes would not close as she whispered problems for him to solve.

"If Granddad McNaughton smokes eight cigarettes and eats three fifteen-ounce servings of watermelon at four pennies an ounce . . . "

She fell asleep with images of Granddad in her head and an ache in her heart.

The next morning, Ma had to knock twice on Hannah's door to rouse her for chores. She felt as if she were moving through glue. Throughout the milking and breakfast, she tried to smother her sadness, but more than once she caught Roy peering intently at her.

As they walked together ahead of Ma and Pa the half mile to the church, Roy threw an arm around her shoulders. "Lean in, if you'd like," he said. "Poor sis. You're a walking advertisement for why I'd never live in a city."

The church was airless and crowded with familiar faces. Tru and Betsy burst from their pews to hug her, whispering promises to visit as soon as they could get away. It seemed as if the whole of Chadds Ford had come to pay respects to Granddad. As many people as could fill a

Saturday matinee in Philadelphia, Hannah realized. The main difference being that she could recite every name in this entire congregation.

So many kind smiles, so much concern as folks stopped by the Bennett pew to pass along a consoling word about Dr. McNaughton. The Arnolds, the Applebees, the Dilworths, the Winnickers, the Seals. Even Miss Cascade was present, wearing a new pair of spectacles, Wendell Nutley at her elbow. The closeness of Chadds Ford struck Hannah solemn and real as a church bell, holding her to all she had left behind.

As Mrs. Lind struck up the organ, Hannah inclined slightly into Ma's side. In other days, when she and Granddad had found themselves in the midst of crowds, they had invented percentage problems. Now Hannah tried to pick up the thread of the game. What percentage of people wore stripes, how many had mustaches, how many carried hymnals in their left hands versus right? Questions washed in and answers washed out.

Reverend Kenyon's voice rumbled from the pulpit as he spoke of Granddad, building up his smarts to make up for his general grouchiness. The memory of summertime on Granddad's porch spread upward from Hannah's feet, and her eyelids grew heavy as she imagined herself and Granddad sitting together, making wishes on watermelon seeds.

"Hannah!" Ma hissed. "Hannah, wake up!"

Hannah's eyes snapped open as she caught her breath. Faces were turned toward her. What had she done?

Reverend Kenyon was not speaking. He frowned down at Hannah and roughly cleared his throat.

Roy leaned forward past Ma. "Sis! You were snoring!" he whispered.

No! So disrespectful! How could she have done such a thing? Now Hannah sensed the amusement in the room, the collective smile that Hannah Bennett might have gone off to Philadelphia to fill her mind with math, but she was the same unpolished, unfinished Hannah as ever.

Blushing, Hannah folded her hands and looked down at her lap, but she pinched the tops of her legs so that she would stay awake for the rest of the service. At least there were no Ottley girls present to poke fun.

Reverend Kenyon cleared his throat once more and resumed.

26

HEPP

HANNAH MATCHED her mother's long strides as they made their way home. Pa and Roy had stayed behind with some of the other men to help with the burial, and most of the congregation would be stopping by the house later for refreshments.

"Well, it's done, then," said Ma. "Your granddad's in heaven now, pestering the angels. Oh, I'll miss him, though. He'd been failing a while, but naturally he refused to see a specialist. Doctors make terrible patients." She shook her head, rueful. "He wouldn't give up his smoking nor his chew, even with that cough. Said the tobacco refreshed his lungs, though I'm sure the effect was directly opposite."

Hannah agreed with a nod.

"There's things at the house Granddad wanted you to have. Books and such," said Ma. "You'll need to sort through."

Hannah nodded again. She listened to the crunch of their boots on the frost-hardened earth.

When Ma spoke once more, it was as if the words had been mulling inside her. "You ought to know, Hannah, we've sold Granddad's property to the Winnickers."

This time, Hannah could not be silent. "Why, how awful!" she blurted. "Elgin Winnicker living in Granddad's house? But Elgin's such a blasted chump, he can hardly tell the difference between a numerator and a denominator!"

"Such language, Hannah!—and it can't be helped. We need the cash money," said Ma.

"We're going to use some of it to build on to the dairy. Pa is hiring extra labor, and we want to buy a pasteurizer. Keep ourselves a step ahead." She paused, then hurried on. "Which means to say that a lot is happening here. And you might want to think about returning home to help Pa and Roy and me. Home for keeps." Ma's voice softened. "Where you belong, where you'll be healthy and watched over and lonely no more."

"I haven't been lonely," Hannah said stiffly. It was a struggle to lie to her mother. She had not mentioned her loneliness in any of her letters home. She did not want to confess to it now.

"Oh, Hannah, it's not hard to see that—"

"Ahoy, there! Ma! Hannah!"

At the sound of the voice, they both looked toward their house, which loomed on the horizon. Hannah could just make out the outline of a familiar figure standing on the front porch. At the same instant, they recognized him.

"Why, you!" exclaimed Ma under her breath. "You!"

Bunching their skirts, they sprinted the remaining distance. Ma, in a spurt of coltish energy, beat Hannah by a pace.

Hepp, at last! Hannah hugged him hard once Ma let him go. Immediately, she saw the changes in her oldest brother. He was thinner, the bones of his cheeks and shoulders and collarbone whittled sharp, his hands felt callused in her own, and he sported a fibrous mustache redder than the auburn of his hair.

"Just arrived. I had to walk from the station," he told them. His smile turned solemn. "There's not a body on the road. The whole town must be eulogizing. I'll pay my private respects to Granddad tomorrow."

"Some of the congregation will be by here later," said Ma. "So you can have a proper reunion with everyone in town."

There was a knock at the back door. "But that's awfully early for the guests," said Ma, startled. She went to answer it, and returned a moment later looking preoccupied. "A tramp outside wants dinner and shelter. I'll give him food, some milk, and he can stay overnight in the barn with a quilt and pillow."

As Hepp and Hannah watched, Ma shook some coins from her crockery pot on the windowsill. "And seven cents to see him on his way," she said, counting it out. "That'll have to do. I spent nearly every penny on a Thanksgiving turkey from Brandywine River Farm. Oh, it's a shame. Two days' time and there'd be meat to give him, along with pie and chestnut stuffing. He looks so gaunt, I'd like to send him off with more."

"But I have money!" Hannah cried as she ran to her coat that hung from the hall peg. She dug out her aluminum-collecting money, her two dimes and three pennies, and added it to the pile in her mother's hand. "Thirty cents," she pronounced. "That's a better number."

"Better," said Ma, and she hurried out to tend to the stranger.

27

THE HEART OF IT

HEPP HAD matured, everyone agreed. Although he had developed no more passion for the dairy, he was reliable with chores, and his storytelling kept the mealtime hour filled with intrigue. The return of Hepp's easy, lighthearted presence pulled everyone into a joyful mood.

Without quite intending to, Hannah swept thoughts of Mrs. Sweet and the Wexler Scholarship and Ottley Friends into a corner of her mind and left them there. She never shared stories of Philadelphia. Not that anyone pressed her. Nobody inquired of her studies. Nobody asked whether or not she would pass next month's exams.

Hannah reasoned that, with Hepp home, she would stay through Thanksgiving, but that day came and left without any talk of her returning to the city. By then, her hands had reacquainted themselves with her old chores so easily, it was as if she had never left them off. She was concerned, though, about the pending telephone call from Mrs. Sweet, and her mind tumbled with different excuses.

Only, Mrs. Sweet did not telephone.

Home Is Where the Heart Is promised the faded cross-stitch on a pillow Ma kept on the horsehair sofa in the front room. Hannah had aired out, plumped up, and propped her feet on that pillow countless times without pondering its meaning. Now the words pulled at her with new insistence.

Yet every night, opening her Level Seven math book, she seemed to turn into another self.

By lamplight, she reviewed her worksheets and drafted new ones. She even labeled them with Mr. Cole's whimsical headlines—*Geometry Chums! Keen Scalenes!* She could almost feel Mr. Cole's glass eye hovering over the house, brilliant and coolly watchful as the moon.

I must get back to Ottley Friends, Hannah insisted to herself. No matter how much I detest it there. I'm three math levels higher than any other girl in my grade. I can't be blown back, even if my heart is here at home. Granddad would have hated for me to quit.

And yet her convictions seemed to fade with each sunrise.

Saturday dawned. After that morning's milking, Pa, Hepp, Roy, and Hannah trooped into the kitchen to find coffee on the boil, eggs in the poacher, and sections of *The Chronicle* scattered on the table.

"You have the weekend paper delivered?" Hannah asked as she reached for it.

"It's Will Emery's new job," Ma told her.

"He's trying to make some money delivering *The Chronicle* and *The Little Bee* to the area."

"Rolls up here in his daddy's half-broke Hudson quarter past six on the dot," Pa added. "Noise to wake the dead."

"Oh, we're already awake, and it hardly costs," Ma said. "The neighbors are chipping in. The Emery farm is in danger of foreclosure this spring."

"Look at you, Hannah Bennett! Pretending to read the National news section with more airs than Mrs. Vanderbilt." Hepp reached across the table and batted the paper at its crease. Hannah shook it out indignantly.

"I can read *some* words," she retorted.

Roy grinned and watched from where he stood at the door, a biscuit in one hand as he used the other to button his overcoat. He was teaching himself to drive by taking over the morning milk deliveries. Bit by bit, Roy was learning how to manage the entire farm and dairy. He would be the one to run it one day. Hannah saw that now.

Hepp tweaked her ear. "What are these *some* words telling you?"

"For your information, I'm following an item on Baby Face Nelson," she said. "He's on the lam. Stole a car in Nevada and he's heading north toward the Corn Belt. But he'll never get caught. He's got coppers so spun around they'll need eyes in the back of their head to catch his tail."

"Listen to you!" Hepp snorted.

"How can you read about such horrors in the world?" asked Ma. "Hardened criminals like Mr. Nelson are who keep me up nights!"

"Ma, it takes nothing to keep you up nights." Hepp laughed. "Two years ago, you were locking our bedroom windows against baby kidnappers, and all of us full grown!"

"World is full of troubled and troublesome people, and it's your ma's right to lock a window against 'em," said Pa, raising a hand against Hepp's laughter and closing the subject.

Hepp went quiet but his glare trapped Pa's a moment too long. Last evening, Pa and Hepp had argued over the best way to repair some fencing out in the south pasture. It was the same tired back-and-forth, the same old struggle between them. Hannah suspected that it would not be long before Hepp itched to leave home and travel again.

The way life used to be was not the way it was meant to last.

28

PLEASE YOURSELF

LATER THAT DAY, Hannah pulled on her coat and walked to the cemetery in search of a solitary moment of prayer for Granddad.

Instead, she found Hepp sprawled flat on his stomach on a barn blanket. He was reading a book.

"Gee, it seems chilly for picnics, don't you think?"

Hepp looked up. "Last winter, I lived in a Hooverville outside Chicago. Since then, I learned I can read just about anywhere. Plus Granddad McNaughton feels close to me here. Wish there'd been time for one last visit—not that I was special to him, grumpy old man that he was." He shut the book. "But he would have liked this. John Muir, *Travels in Alaska*." He rolled up to sit, leaning back on his elbows, as Hannah dropped down onto the blanket beside him. She touched Granddad's simple headstone that stood next to the marker for Grandma McNaughton, who had died before Hannah was born. Granddad's dates were 1866–1934.

"Thirty-four years in each century," she noted. "An even divide, just the way Granddad would have wanted." Then she leaned back against the slab and tried to grasp the cold, real fact of it. Her eyes filled.

"Say, when are ya heading back to Philly, city slicker?" Hepp's coaxing cowboy drawl made Hannah laugh even as she rubbed at her eyes.

"I'm no slicker." She nudged Hepp in the ribs with the toe of her boot.

"Ah, but the city's changed you," Hepp contended. "Question is, for the better?"

"Our folks don't think so. All I'm hearing is how pale and tired I look. But if I don't get back by next week, I ought not to return at all," said Hannah. "I'll be too far behind in my studies."

Hepp stretched out his legs, crossing his feet in their funny shoes that were made of a thin, clownish rubber that Hannah had never seen before. "Then why are you still knocking around?"

"Suppose I'm confused," Hannah answered honestly. The interest in Hepp's face encouraged her to continue. "It's likely I won't pass that blamed exam, and I'd been dreading my defeat in Granddad's eyes. He was so sure I'd be his legacy. Now he won't have to witness my failure."

Hepp ran a thoughtful finger over his new mustache. "Pass or fail, you'd disappoint Granddad's memory if you copped out altogether," he said. "To quit now might not sit easy with you, either."

Hannah nodded. She knew it was true, but it was still hard to hear. "How do you do it, Hepp?" she asked. "With all your traveling.

How do you step into a new place and make it yours?"

"It's not against the rules to slip a bit of your old home into the new. You're only as much a stranger as you want to be. Simple, really." Hepp stood. "I'll leave you to your time alone. Gotta keep moving, anyhow, so Pa can't catch me reading." Briefly, he rested a hand on the crown of Hannah's head. "Granddad's passing must be hard on you. But I suppose it was burdensome, too. He was tough to please. Now you're free to please yourself. Remember to bring in that blanket."

Hepp set off down the hill. He had lost his childlike lope, Hannah noticed, but he had gained a stance that would not tip over easy.

"He *was* hard to please," she said softly to herself. "But when he was pleased, there was nobody happier." And she knew that some part of her would continue trying to please Granddad. Even if he was no longer here in the space of his body, she would always feel connected to the space of his soul.

29

NOBODY'S SWEETHEART

TRU AND BETSY came to visit late that afternoon. Tru had brought half a mince pie and Betsy, her ridge-grip jump rope.

Three were not enough jumpers for a real team, and it was too cold and getting dark, besides, but Hannah shooed Homer and the hens out of the way so that the girls could set up a game in the side yard. Tru had invented a count from a new radio song.

Who's that little chatter-box?
The one with curl-ee auburn locks?
Who do you see?

It's Lit-tle Or-phan An-nee!
Count all the orphans,
How many do you see?
One, two, three, four, five, six, seven . . .

Hannah counted to only fourteen orphans before she tangled and tripped. Then she and Tru turned the rope and watched as Betsy, braids flopping, jumped and jumped until Hannah's hand began to hurt.

"You've gotten expert!" Hannah exclaimed.

"And you're out of practice!" Betsy retorted. "Don't you have any good jump-rope partners in the city?"

Hannah shrugged and let the question go unanswered.

Afterward, the threesome gathered in the kitchen for Tru's pie along with hot cider spiked with cinnamon sticks. The girls told Hannah all of the gossip about school and sweethearts. Elgin was sweet on Melinda and had given her a sandalwood jewelry box that opened to play

"The Great Crooner"—which by now they were all sick to death of hearing. Tru still preferred Hollywood men to Chadds Ford boys, and was sweeter on Clark Gable than Lane Chandler these days. Betsy was sweet on Roy—but a hawkish look from Betsy stopped that piece of news midway out of Tru's mouth.

And did Hannah have a sweetheart? Their eyes were shiny, waiting.

Hannah pressed her mug to her lips and held back her answer, though she was thinking of Joe. He was different from her sweetheart, she realized. Joe Elway just might be her best friend, same as Tru and Betsy were each other's best friends. But how could she explain to them that a boy was her best friend? How would they hear it without twisting her arm for another meaning?

"No," Hannah answered after a lingering moment. "My school is only girls. Fact is, I hardly know any boys these days."

"How wretched!" exclaimed Betsy. "Poor you. That sure takes the fun out. And the girls?"

"Hateful," said Hannah. "Full of airs and snubs."

"Why, I could have told you that, silly!" said Tru, a lilt of satisfaction in her voice. "What did you expect? Oh, Hannah, stay here next week for the church tea dance! Everyone'll be there, and you could use some real fun."

"Besides, if you're not meeting any fellas, how'll we all become June brides?" demanded Betsy. "And live down the street from each other in our own dear little white houses? Mine with green shutters and Tru's with red shutters and yours with blue shutters!"

Hannah had forgotten about her white house with its blue shutters. She missed chatting with the girls, too, and jumping rope, and hearing the school gossip. She missed all of it dearly. But her mind's eye could not seem to picture herself in that white and blue house. Perhaps it was because she did not have a sweetheart.

Later that evening, up in her room, Hannah sat at her desk and picked up her math book. She fanned its pages. She had finished the workbook exercises the night before, and her Level Seven book was complete. If she wanted a challenge, she would have to get hold of Level Eight, which was propped on Mr. Cole's crowded shelf. If Mr. Cole sent the book to Chadds Ford by post, she could teach herself. But Level Nine was an introduction to calculus, a fresh learning expedition that demanded the expert guidance of Mr. Cole.

If she stayed in Chadds Ford, the mysteries of Level Nine and every level thereafter would remain unanswered.

Abruptly, Hannah stood and paced her room thirty-two times. She stopped and looked out her window at the moon. It wasn't fair. She itched to know. She craved to know, or Levels Nine and Ten and onward and upward would tempt and haunt her forever.

Perhaps there was no one correct place to be. Whatever she decided, she would be acting on instinct. And that would have to be reason enough.

30

WOODEN KIMONO

BY EARLY NEXT morning, Hannah was packed and ready to go.

"My mind's made up," she stated during breakfast after the milking. "I thought Roy might drop me off for the early train while he made his delivery rounds."

She knew from their faces that Ma and Pa were unhappy to receive this news. Roy went stubbornly mute. Hannah could feel her mouth fix in a determined line. She looked to her older brother for help.

"Good girl," said Hepp, firmly on Hannah's side. "About time."

There was a silence. Then Pa set down his fork. "No Bennetts are quitters, anyhow," he said. "Take that dollar from my wallet. It's in my jacket hanging on the peg. Ought to pay your way, plus you owe some to Mrs. Sweet." He looked at Ma.

"Suppose you owe Mrs. Sweet the effort, as well," agreed Ma slowly, adding, "and completing that exam would have been your grandfather's wish. Let me make you a lunch. I believe there's a tin of sardines in the pantry, and some Thanksgiving turkey to take along."

It was decided. No one would hold her back, neither by guilt nor doubts nor reason. Hannah held tight to her emotions as she made her good-byes. Luckily, Hepp would be staying on in Chadds Ford through the week, which softened the blow, for Ma especially.

Hepp's hug ended in a slight push of Hannah's shoulders toward the door.

Silent, Roy carried Hannah's bags and flung them into the cab. He drove the truck too fast, too, with gripped fists and a marksman's concentration on the road. "But will you continue on, Hannah, even if you do make the grade?" he asked finally, breaking his own silence as the Chadds Ford train station came into sight. "How would you expect to spend *years* away from home?" His voice cracked on its edge.

Years was hard for Hannah to think about, too. She felt dizzy, but she tried to attribute it to Roy's perilous driving.

"I'd rather you wish me luck than leave me worries," she said. "Pass or fail, I'll be home for Christmas."

"Good luck, then," said Roy, "for what it's worth. I'll double back here when I'm done my deliveries, to see that the train got you. Or if you changed your mind."

As Hannah watched the truck drive away, old fears gripped her. She imagined herself calling Roy back, skipping and chasing behind the truck like a tumbleweed. What a peaceful morning it would be if she could share it with her brother, delivering milk to their neighbors.

Even the engine's whistle sounded lonely when the train eventually pulled in.

The force of her step hid the quaver of her spirit as Hannah boarded. She found a seat on the aisle so that she did not have to watch the countryside pass by. Instead, she flipped back through her Level Seven book. "Level Eight will be in my hands by tomorrow," she reminded herself in a whisper. She ate her cheese-and-sardine sandwich without looking to see whose nose she offended.

Entering Suburban Station, Hannah ran into the headline everywhere, both in bold black newspaper type as well as in the urgent echoing chants of the newsboys.

BABY FACE NELSON SHOT DEAD!

BODY FOUND IN CEMETERY DITCH!

She fished a discarded *Philadelphia Inquirer* from one of the dustbins and stood frozen in place, trying to make sense of the news.

Poor Joe!

She picked through the words. Baby Face had not stood a chance. Special Agent Hoover wasn't as thick as Joe had said. But Hoover's right-hand men, Cowley and Hollis, both had been killed in the line of duty. It was a terrible shame. Two good lives dashed out in the name of one scoundrel. Hannah had never warmed to Baby Face. She was frankly relieved that he had met his bloody end.

She rolled the paper under her arm to finish the article on the subway, where she became so engrossed that she missed her stop and had to haul her bags down five city blocks in the freezing cold. Strangers grumbled and stepped around her.

"'Scuse me! Coming through!" She whistled in her best imitation of Joe.

It was not raining, but the afternoon was dark and soggy, nearly the same weather as that first day Hannah had arrived, only now with a winter bite. The sky was lumpy as a bowl of mush. As she walked past Rittenhouse Square Park, Hannah saluted her willow. A familiar tree was better than no familiar living thing at all.

She arrived at 5 Delancey Place to find it quiet. She spied Joe through the open door of his bedroom, his boots on and facedown on his bed. When she crept closer and spoke his name, he turned his head, and she saw that his eyes were red-rimmed.

She perched on the edge of the bed. "Gosh, Joe, I'm real sorry about Baby Face. I know he meant a lot to you. A terrible end."

"Did you read he took seventeen bullets?" Joe turned his baleful eyes on her. "I never thought that fella'd get the wooden kimono. Nope, I never thought it for a minute, milkmaid."

Milkmaid. Joe had not used that nickname in a while.

"Perhaps it was his time," she said.

"Christmas! The good guys never win," Joe lamented. "Ever!"

It did not seem to Hannah that Baby Face

Nelson could have so much as breathed the same air as the good guys. Some people's heroes were beyond comprehension.

"Are you hungry? My ma packed me some leftovers." Hannah jumped up. "I'll warm them on the stovetop for us, and we'll have a feast."

"Sounds fine. Thought I'd seen the last of you," Joe admitted. "The headmistress of Ottley Friends, that Miss Jordan, has been ringing up here every second. I musta took down a gadzillion messages on the phone pad. If Sweet weren't up in Boston, she'd likely boot you for missing more school than you said. Crumple up the notes, and she'll never be the wiser. And don't tell me there's no such number as gadzillion."

"All right, I won't," said Hannah, "even if there isn't."

In the kitchen, Hannah found the red wax pencil Beverly had used to make grocery lists. She opened the back door and on it drew a perfect X. Maybe tramps did not come to 5

Delancey Place, but there was plenty of food in this house. Now any passerby could see it plainly. It was one piece of Hepp's advice she could put into effect. She would add some of her old home into the new. Starting with hospitality.

31

FUTURE PERFECT

UPON HER RETURN from Boston, Mrs. Sweet summoned Hannah and Joe to the parlor, where she give them the news they had been waiting for. "The Wexler scholarship exams will be held at Thomas Jefferson High School in North Philadelphia on December eighteenth," she announced. "It's rumored that nearly one hundred students have registered.

"My bridge partner, Rose DeVrees, has a boarder, a scrap of a thing from Providence, Rhode Island, who received full academic aid on a Carnegie Scholarship. But I told Rose that our Hannah could count numbers from here to Timbuktu." The hungry smile Hannah knew well by now appeared in Mrs. Sweet's face. "Oh, I can pick a clever child from the herd. I wasn't appointed to the Mayor's Education Reform Board for nothing. Run along, now. I expect you've both got plenty of studying to do."

The test was twenty days away, Hannah noted when she was back in her bedroom. Twenty. She tried to get a feel for the number. Twenty was where calcium appeared in the Periodic Chart. 20/20 was perfect vision. Yes, Hannah reassured herself. Twenty meant strong bones and sharp eyes and good luck.

"Miss Jordan says I deserve a scholarship," Hannah told Joe the next night after supper. "But, Joe, if each teacher says that to each student, then which ones of us don't deserve it?"

"*I* deserve it," said Joe. "I'm smart and I'm ready." He knotted a length of butcher's twine tight around the remains of a beef brisket while

Hannah held the paper in place. They had taken to packing their leftovers into a hamper for Mr. Barnaby, who had come to Hannah's aid when she had inquired about local soup kitchens. Mr. Barnaby's fiancée, Eleanor, said she could use anything for the Goodwill with much appreciation.

Hannah wished she had thought of it beforehand. Sometimes the simplest learning came so slow.

"Do you think I deserve it?" she asked. "Honest, Joe. Do you think I'm ready?"

"Who knows? You against me, remember? But it's a crying shame to give out a taste of learning and then egg-candle us, looking for our dark spots. Picking out the best, sending home the rest." Joe began to jump around the kitchen, tossing the wrapped brisket and catching it like a football.

Joe was a piece of India rubber these days, Hannah decided. With the exams approaching, he bounced harder and higher. He was reaching to grab the scholarship with both hands.

I'm reaching high, too, Hannah thought. I deserve it as much as Joe, don't I?

She could not imagine working any harder, and yet at the same time she could feel herself sinking deeper into the usual obstructions. Patterns and sequences began to crowd in thickly from their safe edges to the center of her day. Thirty-two absorbed more time than usual. Sixteen wipes of each side of her face with her washcloth, sixteen raps upon each side of a plate before eating from it, sixteen chews on either side of her mouth before swallowing. She even paced thirty-two times around her room every time she entered or left. It made her comings and goings cumbersome.

Thirty-two did not stop at the door of Ottley Friends, either. Hannah found herself tapping any doorknob thirty-two taps before using it. Thirty-two was how many times the point of her pencil had to touch the upper right-hand corner of her paper before she got to work.

The girls noticed. They giggled or made fun, but one of them must have complained to Miss

Jordan. When Miss Jordan summoned Hannah to her office, she was sympathetic.

"I'll tell you a secret, Hannah. I always triple-check the locks on my front door before I go to sleep." Miss Jordan leaned forward. "Not once, not twice, but three times!" She laughed gently. Her face was open, inviting Hannah's confidence. "To me, triple-checking is a safeguard against danger. Is that what you believe your tapping and counting might be? A safeguard against dangers?"

"It was Helene Lyon who ratted me out, wasn't it?"

"Hannah, what an expression! And that's not the point. The point is that you must try to stop these impulses."

"I'll try to hide them better, Miss Jordan," Hannah answered truthfully, "but I don't think I can stop." Even as she spoke, her fingers itched to tap a pattern on her knees. Her heart was beating fast and frustration prickled at her skin.

"Dear, there's no need to shout." Miss Jordan held out her empty hands, palms up. "I wish

I comprehended your affliction, Hannah. It couldn't be easy for you. But you've come so far. It would a shame if you stumbled on account of this distress."

Hannah nodded and blinked first one eye then the other.

Onetwothreefour. Onetwothreefour.

And again. And again.

"You are driving yourself into a state," observed Miss Jordan. "You need to relax and take deep breaths. Also remember to chew your food slowly, and get plenty of sleep."

Hannah could feel her cheeks and temper flame. As if she didn't know that! As if she wanted patterns of thirty-two galloping around and around her brain like tireless horses on a racetrack! Miss Jordan talked as if tapping might be cured with the right trick, like having someone scare you to stop your hiccups!

Thank goodness for Joe, the one chum who had made the world shrink to a comfortable size. During their evenings of supper and study at the kitchen table, Joe's good-natured conversation provided freedom from the grip of her day.

"These word problems are dopey," Joe declared one night, looking up from a set of drills that Hannah had created just for him. "Christmas! Who cares how many cakes of soap Mr. Hooper sells, or how many miles Milo walks in five point three hours? I say, take the bus, Milo!"

"Math always means something. It always has an answer. I'll tell you what's dopey—grammar." Hannah scowled at her primer. "These tenses—ugh! The past progressive. The future perfect. 'I will have been gone.' 'We will have been finished.' Why is it called the future perfect? It's neither."

"The future perfect," said Joe patiently, "is easy as fish stew."

"You're cracked!" Hannah threw her arms open wide. "The future perfect is like saying that what *had* happened and what *will* happen have crashed into each other, like trains on the same rail out of different stations!"

"Well, all right." Joe laughed. "Read something good, instead. Look here, I've saved you a clipping on our boy Dutch Schultz. He's out on parole for tax fraud in New York, but if I know the Dutchman, he'll get himself off scot-free."

Joe drew a square of folded newspaper from his trouser pocket and flipped it across the table. "Go on, read it. Schultz is Hoover's plus Mayor LaGuardia's new Public Enemy Number One. I'm starting a new scrapbook on him. All right, don't read it, then. Gee, you're so het up, lately, Hannah."

"I am not!"

"You are, too."

"Am not!"

"Are, too, and you should see your face!" Joe looked around, then pushed up from his chair and crossed the kitchen, where he detached the silver metal teakettle from its hook above the sink. He brought it back and held it in front of Hannah as if it were a mirror. "Look!"

Hannah stared at her dented, lopsided image.

She was no Joan Crawford, no Claudette Colbert, either, but her fierce eyes and the passion of feeling that ignited her face startled her so much that she burst out laughing.

"Well, if I'm het up, then so are you," she retorted. "Only you bounce, while I boil."

"I won't argue with that," Joe admitted. "And I won't argue with you. But you ought to find some enjoyment in your day. You can borrow my skato anytime I'm not using it. I wouldn't charge you more than a penny an hour."

Which was kind of Joe, especially since he loved his skato, but Hannah knew that math itself was her one pure enjoyment. With sharpened focus and speed, egged on by Mr. Cole's enthusiasm, she redoubled her efforts. She constructed bases, built areas, balanced equations, and memorized the laws of right angles and the hypotenuse. The answer was there, its question a lock to be picked and pried. Natural, integer, rational, real. The answer was always waiting and perfect and standing alone.

In some ways, Hannah thought, studying was like milking. If you weren't concentrating on the task in hand, the twitch of a cow tail or buzz of a fly or jump of a cat could shock and tip you smack off your stool.

Don't tip, she scolded herself, and then she tapped under her desk eight times, for luck, and then another eight, and then another, and another, until she had to jump up from her desk with her hands squeezed together to make herself stop.

32

A GLASS WISH

"**I** LOST IT IN THE war," said Mr. Cole abruptly on the afternoon of their final lesson.

Hannah looked up from her paper. "Lost what?"

"My eye," said Mr. Cole. "Grazed by a German Maxim MG. It fires six hundred rounds of bullets per minute, but it only took one bullet to cancel my vision."

She put down her pencil. Mr. Cole had never spoken of anything so personal before. He spoke of math, and sometimes of his other passion, coffee—Mr. Cole's favorite coffee was a roasted bean from the Yakima Valley in Washington, almost impossible to get hold of. But he never spoke of the Great War.

"Would you like to see it?" he asked. On her surprised look, he offered, "I'll hold my hand over the socket, so as not to scare you. Because," he explained, "it's my superstition that if a scholarship candidate holds my eye and makes a wish, it might come true. Well, frankly," he added, now looking slightly embarrassed, "I've never taught a scholarship candidate."

Hannah nodded agreement. "I can see how you might consider your glass eye to be a lucky charm, sir," she said. "Like my thirty-two."

Mr. Cole looked pleased to hear it. He set down his chalk, turned his back, and in the next moment had pivoted around to face her again. He dropped the eye into Hannah's open palm as his other hand patched tight over his eyeless socket.

Hannah cupped Mr. Cole's eye. Warm and marbled blueish-green, it was heavier than she would have imagined. She stared hard into the oblong eye that had watched her so unflinchingly all these weeks. An eye that had checked her homework and looked for her mistakes and remembered to find the places to praise her, too.

It might be an object through which to see the future. Or, yes, even something to make a wish on.

"You must have been in shocking pain, sir," she said. "A horrible thing, to lose an eye."

"I would have given more," Mr. Cole answered quickly. "It's not much to sacrifice, one eye, if it brings hope that the futures of our children are safe from war. I hope never to bear witness to another."

Hannah placed the eyeball in Mr. Cole's palm and he turned away. When he faced her again, he was his regular, two-eyed self. "Good luck tomorrow, Hannah," said Mr. Cole. "It's been difficult for you, these past few weeks. But whatever the result, it is always important to test your mettle."

The shock of his words made her flinch. Why, he believes that I will fail, she realized in a pulse of fresh unease. "Mr. Cole, if I don't get that scholarship, am I finished forever?" she blurted. "It happened to my friend Beverly. She never got a second chance. Who's to say where I go next?"

It seemed to her that Mr. Cole's answer came rushed, as if he had given thought to the matter. "Well now, Hannah, second chances are not impossible," he said. "There are other schools and other scholarships, if you know how and where to look. Just last week, I read of plans to initiate a Marie Curie Fellowship, that will be particularly encouraging of young female scientists and mathematicians."

Hannah bit her lip. "Before he got sick, my granddad McNaughton knew of a school up in Boston. Perhaps I could look into that." Speaking Granddad's name set an immediate lump in her throat, and she twisted her fingers together, trying to resist the urge to tap.

Then she could not help herself and she tapped the sides of her chair.

Mr. Cole did not reprimand her. "Boston, exactly. Follow up on your tips and leads, as the newsmen say. Now." The gaze of Mr. Cole's sighted and glass eye bore into her. "Did you make a wish?"

Hannah nodded yes, although she had forgotten.

33

AN OTTLEY FRIEND

"I HAVE ONE FINAL announcement," said Miss Jordan toward the end of that afternoon's school assembly.

Soft grumbling and squeaks of shoes on the bare floor sounded in impatient protest. It was the last hour before Ottley Friends let out for the holiday break, and the assembly had been interminable, with assorted recitations, hymns, and concertos.

Plenty of style, thought Hannah, but with little of the intimacy of a Miss Cascade production.

Miss Jordan squinted from her podium and spied Hannah in a shadowy corner of the theater. Dread sent a twinge down her spine. *Don't,* her mind whispered fervently. *Don't point me out.*

Unfortunately, Miss Jordan was no mind reader. "Hannah Bennett, will you stand up a moment, please?"

Reluctant, mortified, Hannah rose to her feet while the speculating eyes of the other girls met hers as they turned to stare. Whatever this was about, she wished she had been warned! Personal appearance had not been first in her thoughts these past weeks. After two months' growth, her bobbed hair exactly resembled the haystack Roy had called it. Besides which, she was wearing her same wrinkled middy from yesterday. She probably looked as if she had been receiving fashion tips straight from Mr. Cole.

Beaming and oblivious, Miss Jordan lifted her voice. "Everyone knows that Hannah Bennett has been our guest here at Ottley Friends as she prepares for the very difficult

Wexler scholarship exam that is taking place tomorrow. Mr. Cole has declared that Hannah's achievement in mathematics is equal to a college student's. I, too, can vouch that her progress in other subjects has won my confidence." Miss Jordan's smile raised Hannah's own hopes. "Girls, join me in wishing Hannah good luck tomorrow."

"Good luck tomorrow, Hannah," sang the uninspired chorus. Yet some of the girls' gazes lingered, even after Hannah mumbled her thanks and ducked deep into her seat. Well, college-level mathematics was no small potatoes, as Joe would say, thought Hannah with some pride. More importantly, Miss Jordan spoke with real faith in her abilities. Perhaps the scholarship was within her reach, after all.

After the Ottley Friend's alma mater was sung and the assembly dismissed for the year, Hannah darted from the theater to avoid the gaggles of socializing and holiday plans. Halfway down the corridor, a voice stopped her.

"Hannah! Wait a minute!"

She turned.

Lillian Shay's plump cheeks were pink as she hurried to catch up. "I don't know when you're going back to . . . um . . . your country home," she started, her soft hands twisting the straps of her beaded purse, which was the Ottley fashion fad of the moment. "But some of us girls are gathering at my house tomorrow evening. It's my family's annual Christmas tree-trimming party. I'd be keen for you to come, too. That is, if you're not tired out from test taking."

Before Hannah could answer, Lillian reached into her purse and pulled from it a small green envelope. On it, the name *Miss Hannah Bennett* was neatly scripted in gold ink. As if Hannah, too, were one of Lillian's friends. For a moment, a sparkle of excitement lit inside her. She'd never been to a tree-trimming party—what fun! What a thing to tell the girls back home!

Then reason caught the better of her.

"I appreciate your charity, Lillian, but I'm

afraid I must decline," she said. "You've spelled my name wrong besides. It's Miss Tippity-tap to you girls, isn't it?"

The pink in Lillian's cheeks deepened. "I'm not offering charity. And I didn't mean to tease about your funny tapping habits, queer as they are. At least, I didn't mean for you to overhear. Oh, Hannah, do you truly think I don't know how perfectly hateful it is to wear an affliction on the outside?" she exclaimed in a burst of feeling. "Gosh, I'm forever being teased about my weight—no matter how much I'd love to be slim, it's an impossible task. Everyone's terribly hard on me for it. No one seems to understand that it's not for lack of work or will." Lillian's face was puckered with sincerity. "Hannah, if it's not too late, I'd like to make amends."

She extended her hand that held the envelope. Hannah's gold-scripted name glinted temptingly. "Please. Would you consider it?"

With careful fingers, Hannah reached out and took the invitation. Then she slipped it deep into her pocket. She swallowed; her throat had become dry with unexpected and overwhelming shyness. "Thank you, Lillian," she said. "I'm not leaving for Chadds Ford until Monday. Of course I'll consider it. And," she added honestly, "I think it's awfully nice of you to consider me, too."

| |

ON THE MORNING of the eighteenth, Mrs. Sweet appeared in the kitchen, all dressed up with a fresh metallic rinse in her coppery-brown hair and crimson paint on her pointed fingernails.

"A valet from the garage is bringing around the Packard," she bellowed. "We'll all drive to Thomas Jefferson High School together. It's an important day to be spot on the dot! Hurry and finish your breakfasts. I'll be waiting outside."

Joe rolled his eyes, but did not say anything

as he and Hannah cleared their dishes, collected their coats, and joined Mrs. Sweet outside on the front stoop.

"I've got terrible butterflies," whispered Hannah low enough so that Mrs. Sweet, plucking dry leaves from her window box, did not hear her.

"Naw, it's a banner day for test taking," Joe answered cheerfully as he tugged his cap lower on his head. He inhaled and pounded his chest. "The air's so clean, it even smells like pencil shavings. And there's the car!" he announced as it swung rakishly around the curb.

Hannah had to suppress a smile when she noticed that Mrs. Sweet's precious automobile was being driven around by none other than Joe's friend Francis, who took Mrs. Sweet's ten-cent tip with a wink in Joe's direction, before touching his cap and dashing off.

"It's a super job, I hear. Tips galore," Joe whispered. "But if Sweet saw Fran steer a skato, she'd never let him inside fifty feet of her precious Packard." Joe smirked as he and Hannah climbed into the backseat.

"Try not to muss the leather," warned Mrs. Sweet. "Hands on your laps."

"Truth be told, I never rode in this boat before today," said Joe.

"Me, either," Hannah whispered back.

Mrs. Sweet was a careful driver, and her automobile was so padded and upholstered that the city streets and sounds reeled past like a silent movie or a dream. Hannah stared out at the landmark and lesser buildings that she had come to recognize. She bet that she could find her way through most of Philadelphia. The thought gave her quiet pleasure.

Suddenly, Mrs. Sweet's face appeared slantways in the rearview mirror.

"Whatever happens, children," she said, "it was I who spoke up for you both. I was your first sponsor. Everyone is aware of my charitable causes. It's been rumored that the mayor might appoint me Special Educational

Advisor to the City. And I'm not even a lawyer or a man. But my good works will not go unnoticed!"

"My sister, Sally, was my first real sponsor," mumbled Joe.

"Granddad McNaughton was my first real sponsor," Hannah answered. They shared a private smile as the car rolled up to Thomas Jefferson High School's brick walls and slate painted doors.

"Aw, but nobody's standing outside to see our Hollywood entrance!" Joe lamented as they climbed out.

"It's been my experience that most schools have too many children lurking around for my auto to be safe," said Mrs. Sweet. "Therefore, I'm off. Good luck, both of you. The school has arranged for a bus to take you home at the end of the day."

They both waved good-bye as Mrs. Sweet and her Packard drove off.

"By this time next year, ole Sweet won't

remember our names," said Joe. "Suppose she's a good egg, anyhow. She sees a problem and works to fix it."

"Guess that's better than most people. Well, Joe, if nothing else goes right today," said Hannah, "it was a beautiful ride."

"Don't be such a wet blanket. You gotta pass this thing, Hannah. You can't leave me stuck at 5 Delancey all by myself till June! Everything'll go swell," Joe assured.

He was wrong, though.

Problems began to shake loose and rattle Hannah right from the registration table, crowded with students of all ages. Half as many scholarships, Hannah recalled. No, it wasn't fair. Not when she looked at all of these serious, hopeful faces. It wasn't right to give out a taste of learning, as Joe said. A taste was just enough to know the strength of your appetite.

"Bennett, Bennett. Yes, here you are," said the registration proctor, a balding man squeezed too tight into a loud checkerboard suit. He crossed off

Hannah's name with his fountain pen and handed her a placard marked with the number 11.

Hannah stared at the two dark lines, straight and hard as prison bars.

"Eleven?" She took the placard and blinked. It couldn't be.

"Eee-lev-en." The proctor drew out the sound as if he were an auctioneer.

Eleven! It was the worst numbers luck she had ever faced. Not in her wildest imagination had Hannah figured that numbers would fail her.

Not today of all days.

"I'm sorry, sir," Hannah said. She held the placard from its strings so that it would not touch her. "I can't quite manage this number. I'll have to be another number."

"You can't be another number because you are Bennett, Eleven," countered the proctor. "Right after Barrington, Ten. Right before Boote, Twelve."

"Please, let me be ten or twelve," she volunteered.

"That is not the way it works, miss."

"C'mon, will ya!" The boy standing behind her butted Hannah's heel with the toe of his shoe.

"See, because a prime number can't be reduced," Hannah argued. "It's divisible only by one and itself. Eleven is an odd, upsetting sort of number for me, sir. Though perhaps somebody else might not mind it?" She did not expect the proctor to soften his position. Not with law of the alphabet on his side.

"Go on, Bennett, Eleven." The proctor pointed a finger on her.

"C'mon, Hannah." Suddenly Joe appeared next to her. He grabbed her hand and pulled her away. She could not believe her eyes.

Joe was wearing a placard marked with the number 32.

"Thirty-two! I'll trade you," she exclaimed. "Quick, before anyone sees!"

"I would, but we'd be found out in a minute, because we're alphabetized. Christmas, Hannah, you could turn all the milk in Philadelphia sour with that face."

"You don't understand! Thirty-two is *my number*. My magic number." She reached out and tapped the corners of Joe's placard. She tapped again. Then she couldn't stop.

Joe caught her fingers and held them. "There's no such thing as a magic number, Hannah. Fact is, there's no such thing as a number! You can't get bit or punched or shot or scratched by eleven, 'cause eleven is not even really here! So cut it out. Thirty-two, thirty-three, thirty-four—it doesn't make a jot of difference." He released her fingers, his face softening. "C'mon. Keep your head up. I'm only one classroom down from you. Remember, it's you against me, right?"

Hannah was speechless. She wanted to touch thirty-two again and to have some of its numbers luck rub off on her. Her fingers tapped a scrambled minuet along the sides of her legs. Her mind seemed to be made of soup, and she felt the support in her legs begin to crumble.

"Eighteen days was too few," she said.

"Stop that talk." Joe snapped his fingers in her face. "I've got a bright idea. When all this is over, don't take the bus. It's hardly two miles to Rittenhouse Park. It's cold, but it's clear. Tree weather. You just hafta get to the end of the test. Think of Baby Face! Even when he knew his gig was up, he kept right on driving. Drove himself all the way into that ditch, and all on his own will. Right?"

"Sure." Hannah frowned. Was taking this exam as bad as driving into a ditch?

A loud crowd of boys moved past them. Joe turned.

"I know that fella. Hey, there, sport! You, in the yellow shirt!" And Joe was gone, whistling, as he ran down the hall to catch up. Ready for anything.

Hannah was left alone with eleven. Her mind worked to sweeten it.

Her great-great-great-great grandfather Bennett had distinguished himself in the Battle of Brandywine with the 11th Pennsylvania Regiment.

Backward, eleven spelled *nevele*. That was pretty, although it meant nothing.

Another proctor, a woman with springy hair and plunking footstep, appeared in the crowded hall. She clapped her hands and asked that Numbers One through Twenty follow her. On a wave of other students, Hannah allowed herself to be swept along, as the woman led them to a large plain classroom at the end of the hall.

I could have been Number One, she thought. Or Twenty-one. Or any other number. Easily.

She slumped to her assigned desk. Desk Eleven. She blocked off the noises of the other students as they scuffled to their seats, or sharpened pencils at the sharpener, or loitered by the room's one sun-flooded window that gave a view of playing fields and bright blue sky. Everyone seemed a bit nervous, or lost, or out of place.

At the front of the room, the springy-haired proctor explained the rules, and then she passed out brand-new Blue Jay notebooks, one for each student. Hannah rolled her pencil in her hands, back and forth, in four sequences of eight. She tapped the corners of the book's mottled black-and-white pasteboard cover. Then she flipped through its endless blank, blue-lined pages, closed it, and tapped thirty-two again.

The morning passed in a fog of squeaking pencils and smothered coughing. Immediately, Hannah sensed that her reading would drag her down. Other students' workbook pages turned too quickly. She would not be able to keep up with them.

Worse, she could not make eleven leave. Her brain was plunging off into odd directions no matter how she tried to make it drop anchor. Pascal's Triangle could be computed in powers of eleven. 11, 121, 1331 . . .

Giving into the impulse, she tapped the corners of her placard. Eight, eight, eight, eight. Eight, eight, eight, eight. Eight, eight, eight, eight. Eight, eight, eight, eight.

Time was slipping away.

The slithery sounds of essay-writing filled her ears while she struggled through the multiple-choice section. Occasionally she cast sidelong looks at her fellow test takers. All of these girls and boys had spent the past few months living in variations of luck and upheaval, and all of them knew it would come to this day, and some of them even knew they would fail.

The pale-lashed boy sitting next to her fidgeted in his chair. Barrington, she recalled. Number Ten. The number Hannah might have been if Barrington had not existed.

At the front of the room, the proctor clanked a small cowbell. "Fifteen-minute break," she said. "Close your books. Apples and rolls are being served in the registration hall. We will resume with more reading comprehension, and then math."

Hannah shut her book and sat in her chair through the break. She bet by now Joe had made half a dozen friends.

"Psst. Hey, girl," Barrington said when he returned to his chair. "You, Bennett. Cut it out with that clicking on your card. It's distracting."

"I'll trade you my eleven for your ten," Hannah offered.

"No chance. Ten's lucky."

Hannah's stomach lurched. Even Barrington knew.

The bell rang, and the test resumed. In the next room, Hannah sensed that Joe was moving deftly through this exam, easy as fish stew. Elway, Number 32, and the Voice of Ulysses besides. He would pass this exam and the next, and the next, and on and on. Reciting, filling in the blanks, inching himself smoothly forward. He was smart and he was ready.

But she was not quite ready. She would not get this scholarship.

Not this time, but maybe next time.

The thought surprised her. Next time, yes. She would try again, and she would find her second chance. That's what Mr. Cole had been telling her. Next year, when she knew more things. When she could read better. When she could manage her tapping easier.

If a taste was just enough to know the strength of your appetite, perhaps that was not such a bad thing, after all.

At the final clank of the bell, Hannah passed up her notebook. She apologized to Barrington for her disruptions.

He nodded, his pale eyes flickering cautiously. "Think ya did all right?"

"Better than I expected," she answered, "but I didn't pass."

"Sorry." Barrington tried to blank his face over his obvious relief.

Outside the classroom, she saw Joe, his shoulder to the wall, thick in a conversation with a group of boys. She did not want to interrupt, but she was too impatient to wait for him. She would start and he could catch up later.

Hannah buttoned her coat, pulled her beret over her ears, and pocketed a roll from the basket at the registration table. Then she stepped through Thomas Jefferson's doors and into an ordinary beautiful winter afternoon. Piercing blue sky and needle thin air. It was almost three o'clock, and it would grow dark soon, but now there was some light and time.

Her feet carried her swiftly to Rittenhouse Park. Along the way, she counted off all of the beautiful objects in the city. The iron gates, the fire hydrants, the cars and carts and horses and street signs and storefront awnings. The city ticked and clacked and hummed and made a different pattern every day. It was always changing, there was no fixed and final answer, and, actually, she had come to appreciate it, because she was the same way.

I'll find the right doors and I'll push them as hard as I can, she thought. Math is everywhere, and it has always belonged to me if I wanted it. And now I know that I do, more than anything. I'll go anywhere for it.

At the gate's entrance, Hannah kicked off her

shoes and rolled her socks into a ball. Her bare feet sang with cold as she walked across the grass to her willow tree. She tested a hand to its base and caught hold of one branch. Pulled herself up and caught another.

Up and up.

Climbing a tree was the silliest thing in the world. It didn't really get a person to anywhere in particular, and once up, you were immediately presented with the puzzle of how to get down.

That hardly mattered, though. What did matter was that she had found a perfect place to enjoy a perfect hour. She pressed her nose against the bark, inhaling the scent of the tree and the faint woods of where it came from. Then she swung her legs free, back and forth, delighting in the fresh air on her skin and the wide-open view of the city, as she waited for Joe to join her.

AUTHOR'S NOTE

For their tremendous assistance with the particular details of this story, I thank my editor, Donna Bray, as well as Brian Carey, Allison Heiny, Erich Mauff, Monica Mayper, Adele Sands, James Sands, Bill Stedman, Thorin Tritter, Kathy Wandersee, and Robert Watson. These books also were especially useful: *Since Yesterday: The 1930s in America*, by Frederick Lewis Allen; *Philadelphia Boyhood: Growing Up in the 1930s*, by Paul Hogan; *An Architectural Guidebook to Philadelphia*, by Francis Morrone with James Iska; and *Hard Times, An Oral History of the Great Depression*, by Studs Terkel. Additional guidance was provided by the following Web pages: "American Life Histories: Manuscripts from the Federal Writers' Project" (memory.loc.gov/ammem/wpaintro/wpahome.html), "The Hollywood Thirties: The Daring Films of 1930–1934" (www.geocities.com/hollywood/lot/4344/stage7.html), "The Original Old Time Radio" (www.old-time.com), and "The Chadds Ford Historical Society"(www.chaddsfordhistory.org).

HANNAH, DIVIDED
A READER'S COMPANION

IN 1930s PENNSYLVANIA, it's unusual to find a country kid going to high school. Hannah has her chance to stretch her mind in a private Philadelphia school, thanks to a strange benefactor. Her extraordinary mathematical skills are at first only seen as a parlor trick. And her homesickness for her family and the farm make it hard for her to adjust to life in the city. Will she ever fit in? Will she forget her home? Will she be able to decide what's really important to her, Hannah?

1. Hannah finds comfort in numbers. On page 8, we read, "Hannah counted seven suit buttons, eleven footsteps, and five syllables in her name. From bag to beret, Theodora Sweet seemed to be an odd-numbered, slant-sided sort of person." On page 25, we see a list of Hannah's counting on her way home from school: "Steps: 1,657; Paired breaths: 520 . . . Rocks: 170 (gray: 111; black: 53; mixed: 6). . . ." Sometimes Hannah's numbers help her. How do they get in her way?

2. Throughout the book, Hannah collects interesting facts and trivia about her favorite number, 32. What are some of the facts she discovers? Why is 32 her favorite number?

3. On page 16, we get a view of how Hannah sees letters on a page of text. Can you see letters this way? How would you describe some of the other letters on the page?

4. On page 34, Pa predicts that radio will take the place of reading. Has this happened? What did people say when television became popular at home? What are some people saying about e-books?

5. Tru, one of Hannah's two best friends in Chadds Ford, wishes Hannah well in the city: "I do hope you meet one new friend," she added after a thoughtful moment. "Temporarily, while you're there, I mean. All it takes is one chum to make the world shrink to a comfortable size. Wouldn't you say?" (p. 78). How do Hannah's experiences in the city and with Joe remind us of Tru's wish?

6. One of the contrasts we see in the story is between Hannah's busy working life at home on the farm and her luxurious life in Philadelphia. Is Hannah

happier living in luxury? What appeal does life on the farm hold?

7. When Hannah first went to the city to study, it was in large part to fulfill Granddad's dream. After his death, Hannah gains new self-knowledge. How has his death changed things on the farm? What should Hannah do now?

8. At Mrs. Sweet's party, Hannah notices "a young colored man" who is introduced as Dr. Claytor. Dr. Claytor tells her about Dr. Robert Lee Moore, who will not accept "coloreds and women" at his lectures. This is the first indication Hannah has had that there might be other obstacles in her path to learning. Does this discourage Hannah? Dr. Claytor says, "A good strong push from one is a push for us all" (p. 143). How could this relate to today's opportunities and challenges for women and minorities?

9. In the end, Hannah comes to a realization about herself and her goals in life. Although she feels she will not get the scholarship this time, she decides, "Next year, when she knew more things. . . . When she could read better . . ." (p. 261). Does this seem satisfying and realistic?

10. Hannah is spelled the same backward and forward. Hannah would have found that very interesting. The literary name for this is a "palindrome," and there are quite a few words that are palindromes. There are even whole sentences that are palindromes. http://www.palindromes.org/ is one Web page that has compiled lists of palindromes, including palindromic poetry. It can be fun to discover new palindromes!

AN INTERVIEW WITH
ADELE GRIFFIN

Q: When did you know you wanted to be a writer?

A: I wrote my first book when I was seven years old, after my mother sent me to my room for refusing to turn off the television. Once I finished my temper tantrum, I found a school notebook and, in felt-tip pen, wrote a sulky and defiant version of the experience in a short story that I titled "One Poor Girl Called Linda." Linda, like myself, had been unjustly banished to her room by her cruel mother. Unlike me, Linda escaped out the window to live with her grandmother.

The story was so validating that, even after I was forgiven and reunited with the TV, I kept going, adding illustrations and chapters, and adjusting the title. Then I got my mom to mail the complete "Aventures" (*sic*) of Linda to my grandmother, who called me a few days later and gave it a rave. Every year thereafter, until I reached high school, I wrote a notebook novel for my grandmother. She always believed that I'd pursue a writing career, and she has kept the notebooks, including the debut "Aventures," in a locked drawer in her desk. Locked, I think, so that nobody else in my family can read the notebooks and issue less favorable reviews.

Q: What authors have you read that you really loved? Who would you consider an influence?

A: Some writers whose work I admire are: David Almond, Melissa Bank, Francesca Lia Block, Melvin Burgess, Michael Chabon, Michael Cunningham, Louise Erdrich, Daniel Handler, Lillian Hellman, Kazuo Ishiguro, Ha Jin, Julius Lester, Jonathan Lethem, Joyce Carol Oates, Michael Ondaatje, Cynthia Ozick, Carole Maso, Robin McKinley, Lorrie Moore, Francine Prose, Zadie Smith, and Jacqueline Woodson. It's hard for me to pinpoint influences, and I consider myself to be a better reader than a writer. Reading is my first delight, and a hugely important part of my day.

Q: Do you have a writing routine? A special time, a special place?

A: My desk is as long and wide as a single bed, and I love that it can accommodate the whole mess of my notes and pens and Post-its. I'm at my desk all day, but on the rare occasion that I'm elsewhere, I carry a notebook in case a particular thought that had been hiding from me decides to pop up at the bank or in the drugstore.

After I shut down the computer, I enjoy listening to music or going out to noisy public places and meeting friends because the morning and afternoon have been so thoroughly silent.

Q: An important theme in all your books is family— good family, bad family, peculiar family. Does this tie in to your own family at all?

A: It is hard for me to see a unifying theme that connects all of my books, but family is often an inspiration. My own family is large and close and odd, and their personalities spur the creation of many of my book characters. I feel most in touch with protagonists who are creeping toward the edge of decisions that can't be easily predicted (and I guess it could be argued that this, too, is a family trait). I also like to write about crucial, rite-of-passage experiences, a marked characteristic of books for young people.

Q: How did Hannah's reading and math ability come to you? They're so unusual!

A: In *Hannah, Divided,* I wanted to underline Hannah's difficulties by putting emphasis on her aptitudes. So she can't read, but is brilliant in math. Her math-mind works in patterns and sequences, both a skill and a problem because she isn't able to stop the patterns when they become oppressive. And while Hannah has a safe and pleasant home life, she is averse to experiencing unfamiliar places and meeting new people. In Hannah, I always looked to destabilize a benefit with a predicament, so that she is continuously testing her limits as she faces her challenges.

Q: Some authors say that characters start them writing; others have a story to tell. What gets you started on a novel?

A: Page one of any book gives me little more than a vague idea. I don't use outlines, and usually I've worked on between two and five "false start" manuscripts before the right one takes hold. I used to agonize (more) about these false starts, and my colossal, ever-growing "Unfinished" file of failed material sometimes unnerves me. It is extremely unlikely after I complete a novel that the subsequent project will take off into a smooth, resolved story. But I keep plugging along, even after the idea has flopped, while I wait for something better. I figure there's no harm in practicing. Future projects are always exciting because I'm never too sure what they might be.

Q: Do you have any advice for young people who are interested in writing?

A: My advice for young writers is: aim for The End. I know firsthand that this is easier advised than achieved, but once a short story or novel or poem or play or screenplay is done, then you can really take a look at it and see what you've got. In my opinion, a completed work is also easier to share with other people, critique and support-wise. And whatever the outcome, nothing can diminish the private, personal sense of achievement in reaching your last page. That feels great.

BIOGRAPHICAL SKETCH

ADELE GRIFFIN often uses family as a metaphor for our relationships with ourselves, others, and society. Some of the pictures she presents are dark, but she always shines a light of hope in a disturbed world. Her characters are unusual and memorable, and frequently it is the vision of the narrator that forms the world in her works. She presents us with vignettes from life, and though we may be left wanting to know more about Hannah, Delia, Rock, etc., we have also seen them reach a resolution of their problems and demonstrate the strength to go on.

Adele Griffin was born on July 29, 1970, in Philadelphia. She graduated from the University of Pennsylvania and then went to work in the publishing industry in New York City. Her work as an assistant editor in children's books brought her back to reading books for children and young adults and encouraged her to write her own. In the relatively short time she has been writing professionally, she has produced several works of literature that have garnered much acclaim.